MAJESTY AND HUMILITY

The Rabbi Soloveitchik Library

Series Editor: Rabbi Jacob J. Schacter

The Rabbi Soloveitchik Library
Series Editor: Rabbi Dr. Jacob J. Schacter

Volume 1
MEMORIES OF A GIANT:
EULOGIES IN MEMORY OF RABBI DR. JOSEPH B. SOLOVEITCHIK
edited by Michael A. Bierman

Volume 2
RABBI JOSEPH B. SOLOVEITCHIK ON PESACH, *SEFIRAT HA-OMER*
AND SHAVU'OT
by David Shapiro

Volume 3
MAJESTY AND HUMILITY: THE THOUGHT OF RABBI JOSEPH B.
SOLOVEITCHIK
by Reuven Ziegler

Majesty and Humility

The Thought of Rabbi Joseph B. Soloveitchik

Reuven Ziegler

רמב"ם Maimonides School

OUPRESS

URIM PUBLICATIONS
Jerusalem • New York

Majesty and Humility: The Thought of Rabbi Joseph B. Soloveitchik
by Reuven Ziegler
The Rabbi Soloveitchik Library – Volume 3
Series Editor: Rabbi Dr. Jacob J. Schacter

Book design by Ariel Walden

Printed in Israel

First Edition
ISBN 978-965-524-076-4

Maimonides School
34 Philbrick Road
Brookline, MA 02445

OU Press – an imprint of the Orthodox Union
11 Broadway, New York
NY 10004
www.ou.org

Urim Publications   Lambda Publishers, Inc.
P.O.Box 52287   527 Empire Blvd.
Jerusalem 91521 Israel   Brooklyn, NY 11225 U.S.A.
                           Tel: 718-972-5449
                           Fax: 718-972-6307

www.UrimPublications.com

To my parents

Rabbi Zvi and Sandra Ziegler

שלי שלהם

Contents

Preface

Rabbi Reuven Ziegler's *Majesty and Humility: The Thought of Rabbi Joseph B. Soloveitchik* constitutes a meaningful contribution to our corpus of Jewish religious thought. Studies of the Rav's persona and intellectual harvest have, of course, been undertaken previously, from different perspectives and with various degrees of accuracy, lucidity and scope. However, Rabbi Ziegler's opus is singular in several key respects. First, as a *talmid* of the Rav in the areas of both Halakhah and *mahshavah*, who has labored for over a decade within the context of the Toras Horav Foundation on seeking, deciphering, arranging, editing and publishing hitherto unavailable material, he has benefitted from a degree of comprehensiveness not fully available to predecessors. Secondly, precisely due to his background, proclivities and commitments, he utilizes his fundamental intellectual candor to present the Rav rather than to represent him – and, a fortiori, rather than to exploit him as an axe to grind.

Hence, readers familiar with both the Rav's persona and his writing will be favorably impressed by the sensitivity manifested in the book – both that of its author and that of his subject.

Ultimately, however, such a study must be judged by the quality of its content, by the incisiveness of its insight, by the depth of its probes, by its innovative clarity, by its service to the existing corpus of knowledge, and by its correspondence to any addenda to that corpus. And, from both an intellectual and an ethical standpoint, it must be judged by the underpinnings of its motivation.

Although I write as a friend and colleague of the author, this introduction itself must stand by the bar of quality and be tested by its canons. I trust that my vote of confidence in this opus is fully justified, as it is indeed deserving of high regard with respect to the foregoing criteria.

This volume's contribution to the corpus of Jewish religious thought is threefold. At one plane, it enhances our limning of the parameters of the central issue highlighted in its title: the interactive encounter, both integrative and conflictual, of these moral and theological aspects immanent in the relation of man and the *Ribbono shel Olam*, on the one hand, and the nuanced nature of the historical exposition of the universal treatment of the phenomenon, on the other. At a second plane, we benefit from the analysis of the problem, as developed by the architects of classic religious expression and experience – foremost, by the Rambam. Finally, as was to have been expected, the most significant contribution – deriving from the book's primary focus – is the presentation, elucidation and analysis of the thought of the most prominent modern exemplar of the twin pursuit of, and innovator in, the cognate areas of Halakhah and *mahshavah*.

Two specific, and related, points are worth particular notice – the narrow epicenter of the volume, on the one hand, and its more general context, on the other. The Rav's concern with the specific theme of majesty and humility is, of course, well-known. Equally familiar, as profoundly grounded in *Hazal*, is its relevance to both man's relation to his Creator, at the purely religious plane, and to his fellow and to himself, at the ethical and psychological plane. Equally familiar, as rooted in both his Brisker training and in his neo-Kantian roots, is his orientation, at both the methodological and the substantive level, and his penchant – I might almost have said, his passion – for dialectical thought. Rabbi Ziegler goes a step further, however, in expounding and developing the role of the specific issue of majesty and humility as a lever and fulcrum to be wielded in dealing with a range of issues. And I believe that he does so without presenting the Rav as capitulating to his perception. One cannot imagine the Rav as echoing John Donne's observation to the effect that if David Ha-melekh had been fully humble, he would have said that he was a man and not a worm, as the former is inferior to the latter.

At issue is much which lies beyond the bounds of pure ethical and religious theory. On the scales are aspects of the good life proper – from its infrastructure to its parameters. Majesty and humility contribute to each other's enrichment of human existence and experience. Humility rescues the individual – as, in a sense, it rescues the Rambam and the Rav – from the crest of elitism, as majesty lifts one above the pitfall of lassitude. Theirs is a tension and a fusion well worth studying and attaining.

Rabbi Dr. Aharon Lichtenstein
Rosh Ha-Yeshivah, Yeshivat Har Etzion

Foreword

It is with great pleasure that I introduce this most important book on the teachings of Rabbi Joseph B. Soloveitchik, *zt"l*, by Rabbi Reuven Ziegler.

Commenting on the phrase, "and there was evening" (Genesis 1:5), the Midrash (Gen. Rabbah 3:7) states:

> R. Judah b. R. Simon said: "Let there be evening (*yehi erev*)" is not written here, but "*and* there was evening (*va-yehi erev*)." Hence we know that a time order existed before this. R. Abbahu said: This proves that the Holy One, blessed be He, went on creating worlds and destroying them until He created this one and declared, "This one pleases Me; those did not please Me."

The apparently extra *vav* in *va-yehi* leads the Midrash to conclude that this first day of creation was following other acts of creation that preceded it and which *Ha-Kadosh Barukh Hu* did not find to his liking. But the question is obvious. Why was all this necessary? Why did *Ha-Kadosh Barukh Hu* need to create so many worlds until He found the one He wanted, until He got it right? *Ha-Kadosh Barukh Hu* needed practice! He was unable to create the world of His choice the first time!

Taught Rabbi Joseph B. Soloveitchik: Of course *Ha-Kadosh Barukh Hu* did not need practice. Of course He could get it right the first time. But He deliberately "failed" – and "failed" again – to teach us, human beings, a powerful lesson. Do we not also attempt to build worlds in our personal lives and then they sometimes get destroyed? We put time and energy into relationships, we work to create worlds, and sometimes they get destroyed. We invest time and energy in a business, we work to create a world, and sometimes it gets destroyed. Often we find it hard to pick up the pieces, to muster the energy necessary to go on and to create again. Says *Ha-Kadosh Barukh Hu*, in the teaching of Rabbi Soloveitchik: "Don't despair. Don't get frustrated. Follow in the footsteps of the divine. I did it. You too can do it. I started again. You too can start again. You too can be successful in creating for yourself a world that will be a strong and lasting one."

Great people are born, and great people die. Worlds are created, and then worlds come to an end. When a great person passes away, a world is destroyed. To borrow a talmudic teaching (*Rosh Hashanah* 18b), "The death of the righteous is equivalent to the burning of the House of our Lord." And those who remain behind wonder how they will survive absent the presence and direct influence of the departed leader and teacher. But here too the lesson of this Midrash rings true. Don't despair. Don't get frustrated. There will be a new generation of leaders and teachers who will assume responsibility for inspiring and instructing the next generation. A world was destroyed, but new worlds will be created.

But while this is true, it is only possible if the new world is predicated upon a deep knowledge of and familiarity with the Torah and teachings of the old. New leaders need to become a link in the chain of the *mesorah*, receiving the Torah of the past and transmitting it to those who live in the present and will live in the future.

One such leader and teacher was Rabbi Joseph B. Soloveitchik, the Rav. In his lifetime, Rabbi Soloveitchik was well-known and highly respected for his original mind and charismatic personality, his intimate knowledge of and appreciation for the totality of Jewish tradition while enjoying mastery over the philosophical contributions of Western culture, his intense fealty to the *mesorah* combined with a real openness to the best in the world around him, his spellbinding oratorical skills and charming sense of humor, his radical intellectual honesty and demanding search for truth, his dazzling intellect and total lack of pretense, his extraordinary power of self-revelation and deep-seated sense of privacy, the courage of his convictions to blaze his own trail, to do what he felt was right even when it was not easy, and his amazing ability to present our tradition, unadulterated and uncompromised, in a way that profoundly resonated with the modern American mind. He was an extraordinary teacher, a master pedagogue, who challenged and excited young and old alike.

But Rabbi Soloveitchik is no longer with us. His physical presence has passed on and the world that he was is gone. But new worlds remain to be created; new generations, including our own, need to be nurtured and educated. And, for us to be successful at this task, to face the challenges of our times, to inspire the members of our generation and those yet unborn to thrive in the joy of Jewish living and learning, we need to understand his teachings and appreciate their relevance to us. What needs to endure for the future is the substance of his ideas, the compelling nature of his teachings, and the content of his Torah.

And for this we express deep and profound gratitude to Rabbi Reuven Ziegler. Rabbi Ziegler has devoted many years to studying the works of the Rav and we are the beneficiaries of his wisdom and his efforts. Because Rabbi Soloveitchik's writings can be challenging to the uninitiated, as many can attest, I asked Rabbi Ziegler to present his ideas in a way that could be grasped by the broader public. He has done a masterful job in formulating the teachings and world-view of the Rav in a clear, organized, thoughtful and comprehensive way. Through a careful analysis of the many works of the Rav, Rabbi Ziegler has succeeded in explicating his complex ideas and complicated language in a comprehensible manner and making them accessible to a wide audience interested in more fully understanding and appreciating the world of this spiritual and intellectual giant of Torah. Moving from theme to theme and through essay after essay in the Rav's multi-faceted oeuvre, and with complete mastery of the growing secondary literature on his subject, Rabbi Ziegler's careful and sensitive analysis is extraordinarily insightful, highly compelling and exceptionally well-done. The world of Rabbi Soloveitchik the person has been lost, but the world of Rabbi Soloveitchik the thinker, author and teacher has been gracefully and magnificently preserved.

I also want to express our special thanks to the members of the family of Abraham Levovitz, *z"l*, for sponsoring this volume *le-iluy nishmato*. Abe was a deeply devoted disciple of the Rav who sought every opportunity to spend time with him and to learn from him, and who devoted much of his creativity and talents to insure the success of the Maimonides School, an institution that was founded by the Rav and his wife and remained very close to his heart. Abe was a larger-than-life personality, a giant in his selfless devotion to school, shul and community. This book, about the person he deeply respected and even loved, is a most appropriate and fitting tribute to his memory. *Yehi zikhro barukh.*

Rabbi Dr. Jacob J. Schacter
Series Editor

Dedication

לעילוי נשמת אברהם בן הרב ראובן הלוי

One cannot form a friendship unless he finds in it the realization of a value
long cherished by him . . . I must discover the thou, recognize him as real and
approve of him as good, as a person worthy of my love and friendship (*Family
Redeemed*, 28).

This book is dedicated to the memory of Mr. Abraham Levovitz, *z"l*. Mr.
Levovitz was the recognized leader of both the Maimonides School and
the Maimonides Synagogue in Brookline, Massachusetts, for over forty
years. Abe was a student, a close friend and a confidant of Rabbi Joseph B.
Soloveitchik, *zt"l*, the Rav.

Abe, an observant Orthodox Jew, was an outgoing, ambitious, driven and
incisive businessman who was focused on deal-making, investment opportunities and financial markets. Abe was at ease dealing with government and
business leaders alike. The consummate gentleman, he was tall and stately
and always a meticulous dresser. In a word, Abe was dignified.

The Rav, scion of an illustrious rabbinic family whose life was focused on
Torah, education and teaching, was the "halakhic man" par excellence and, as
he often confessed, a very "lonely man of faith." Why did the Rav consider
Abe to be one of his very select close friends? What did Abe have in common
with the Rav? I believe their friendship was based on three pillars: mutual
respect, a unique *rebbi-talmid* relationship, and shared objectives.

In *The Lonely Man of Faith*, the Rav describes Elisha prior to his
transformational encounter with the Prophet Elijah. "Elisha was a typical representative of the majestic community . . . a man of property whose interests
were centered around worldly, material goods such as crops, livestock and
market prices. His objective was economic success, his aspiration – material

wealth. The Bible portrays him as efficient, capable and practical, remindful of a modern business executive" (109–10). Prior to his evolution into a disciple and prophet, Elisha was a prime example of a majestic personality. I believe the Rav considered Abe to be in this same mold and respected him for it.

In that work, the Rav also regarded the majestic personality to be in total harmony with the "man of faith." He wrote, "Many a time I have the distinct impression that the Halakhah considered the steady oscillation of the man of faith between majesty and covenant not a dialectical but rather a complementary movement" (83). Abe, too, was not majestic man alone. Every weekend, the assertive businessman and prosperous entrepreneur was himself transformed via harmonious oscillation into the Rav's private attendant, driver, student and devoted participant in the Rav's weekly Bible and Talmud classes at Maimonides School. And the Rav respected him for it.

The Mishnah in *Pirkei Avot* (1:6) states, "Acquire for yourself a friend." In his commentary, Maimonides mentions the three different levels of friendship based on Aristotle's description in his *Nicomachean Ethics*: a friend for benefit, a friend for pleasantness, and a friend for virtue (*haver le-to'elet, haver le-de'agah, haver le-de'ah*).

In the Rav's description of a friend of virtue, he states, "Not in everybody does one confide; not with everybody may we share our grief or excitement. For this purpose alone, one must have a *haver le-de'ah*, a friend in whom he or she has absolute trust and faith, a person about whom one has no fear that he is an insincere and false friend" (*Family Redeemed*, 28).

Maimonides provides a surprising example of a friend for virtue, *haver le-de'ah*, "Friends of virtue are two friends who share a common desire and goal, namely the good. And each wants to seek his fellow's help in the attainment of this good for the two of them. That is the friend the Mishnah instructs us to acquire. An instance of this sort of friendship is that of the teacher for his student and the student for his teacher."

Professor Berel Septimus of Harvard University points out that Aristotle maintains that the perfect friendship can only exist between equals and could never apply to a teacher and his disciple. Maimonides, however, highlights precisely such a relationship as an example of ultimate friendship. Professor Septimus explains that while the highest form of Aristotelian friendship occurs when friends are attracted to each other by the shared goodness they have acquired, Maimonides describes that the highest form of friendship is based on a shared quest for the good.

While Abe was a devoted student and friend of the Rav, their relationship was indelibly bound by their shared quest to ensure the future of Orthodox

Judaism through Jewish education and particularly by their shared love for the Maimonides School. They were true *haverim le-de'ah*.

In Abe's description of his friendship with the Rav he writes, "Some of the most meaningful memories, however, were these intimate moments, when after *shul* on *motza'ei Shabbos*, while the Rav waited the extra *zeman* to be able to ride home, you could catch him and ask him anything. He was relaxed, the Shabbat was over, and the burden of the week ahead was not yet hovering over him. During those wonderful, cherished moments, he would often open up, express his innermost thoughts, desires, yearnings, wishes, failures, disappointments, and you had the feeling that he was letting you into his *sanctum sanctorum*, the innermost reaches of his being, a place reserved for the select few. It was a special place where he was very exposed, tender, and vulnerable. At these times, we came to love him as one would a friend . . ." ("The Rav's Human Qualities Invoke Indelible Memories," in *Memories of a Giant*, ed. Michael A. Bierman [Jerusalem and New York, 2003], 233).

For allowing me to witness these tender moments, I am eternally grateful to Abe, my mentor and friend. May this book be a fitting memorial for this remarkable man and may his memory continue to be a blessing for his family and for all those who were privileged to have known him.

Itzhak D. Goldberg, MD, FACR

Introduction

Among the ranks of modern Jewish thinkers, Rabbi Joseph B. Soloveitchik holds a special place. A talmudist of the first rank and a profound expositor of the Bible, Midrash and other Jewish texts, he also brings to his writings an academic training in philosophy and broad erudition in Western culture. His highly distinctive and creative works explore the meaning and depth of Jewish religiosity, while at the same time speaking to the general human condition.

Perhaps his primary concern is the role that Halakhah (Jewish law) plays in the Jew's life – both as a system of thought and as a way of living. Halakhah provides the Jew's central mode of relating to God, a medium for his or her religious experience, a guide to self-development and community building, and a means of understanding the world and engaging it. Yet, out of its commandments and insights there emerges a view of human nature and its potential that has universal application. The individual is majestic and humble, natural and spiritual, burdened by incompleteness, vulnerability and distress but capable of creation, self-transcendence and greatness.

Drawing on his understanding of Jewish tradition, Western thought and human nature, Rabbi Soloveitchik also focuses his attention on another crucial issue: the confrontation of religion with modernity. He addresses not only the ideas and events of modernity, but also, perhaps most importantly, its temper, mindset and attitudes. His works, which evince both an acute analytic mind and a deeply feeling soul, convey to moderns the conceptual and emotional depth, drama and power of religious existence, and specifically of halakhic life.

*

Encountering the Rav's[1] writings is an exciting and fascinating endeavor, but not always an easy one. He demands effort from his readers, effort that is richly rewarded. This book attempts to facilitate the reading of Rabbi Soloveitchik's works by providing explication and analysis of his thought. Ideally, I would like the volume to encourage and accompany the reading of Rabbi Soloveitchik's works, not substitute for it. Nevertheless, recognizing that not everyone will read the primary sources, I have striven to make this book self-contained.

I have structured the book like a course, treating the more accessible essays and topics first before turning to the more difficult ones. For this reason, the Rav's earliest essays – which are also the most challenging of his writings – are discussed in a concentrated fashion at the end of the book, though I cite from them extensively throughout. Also, as in a course, the later parts often build on earlier ones. However, to facilitate research of individual subjects, I have tried to cross-reference the various discussions in the book. I have also provided "For Further Reference" sections at the end of each chapter for those who wish to pursue topics beyond the scope of this work. The book concludes with two chapters that summarize its contents and synthesize its major themes.

My treatment of Rabbi Soloveitchik's major works is dictated by the subject matter and structure of each book. In the case of *The Lonely Man of Faith*, I provide a detailed, chapter-by-chapter reading – essentially a reader's companion – because this is the most tightly argued of his major works and the one most relevant to a broad audience. *Halakhic Man*, however, does not develop an argument so much as examine facets of the title character – his personality, consciousness and worldview. Hence, instead of examining the book chapter-by-chapter, I have explained its background and purpose, delineated the contours of the title character and his approach, and analyzed a number of issues necessary to understand this work. *U-Vikkashtem mi-Sham* presents a sequential development of man's religious odyssey, but this progression is very complex. Therefore, I have devoted my efforts to clarifying the structure of the book's argument, highlighting its major ideas, and discussing its place in Rabbi Soloveitchik's oeuvre. *The Halakhic Mind* is the most arcane of Rabbi Soloveitchik's works, written in a heavily technical philosophical style and, for most of the book's length, focusing not on Halakhah but on the philosophy of religion in general. I address its specific relevance to Judaism

---

1 Rabbi Soloveitchik's students often referred to him respectfully as "the Rav," the master, the teacher *par excellence*. We will adopt this usage, as well as the use of the honorifics "Rav" or "R." before his name.

in Chapter 31 and treat various aspects of the work in other chapters as the need arises.

Rabbi Soloveitchik wrote much more than he published, and since his passing a large number of volumes drawn from his manuscripts have been published by the Toras HoRav Foundation – a project in which I have been fortunate to participate. I have incorporated discussions of these posthumous volumes into this book, thereby fleshing out the portrait of his thought. Although I do not cite from manuscripts that still remain unpublished, reading them has certainly informed my understanding of the Rav's approach. Rabbi Soloveitchik spent far more time teaching Talmud than teaching philosophy. This should be kept in mind when reading a book that focuses on his thought and not on his talmudic scholarship. It should be noted, however, that his contribution in the field of Talmud lies not only in his electrifying *shiurim* and his many novel interpretations and ideas. It also resides in the fact that his philosophy and his personal example reinforced the central position of Talmud study within Jewish religiosity – a subject that will be addressed at length in this book.

Rabbi Soloveitchik believed that life is always a work in progress, requiring perpetual creativity and growth. This leads to two concluding thoughts.

First, all works can be improved through feedback, and I would be delighted if readers would share their questions and comments with me at ziegler@etzion.org.il.

Second, while I have worked hard to make this book accessible, engaging and enlightening, the most important work remains to be done by you, the reader: applying to your own life those insights of Rabbi Soloveitchik that you find most personally resonant and meaningful.

Section I

ENTERING THE RAV'S WORLD

Chapter 1

Introduction to Rav Soloveitchik's Life and Thought

Students of philosophy in general, and students of Jewish philosophy in particular, often study a thinker's ideas without reference to his biography. Neglect of the biographical element is in general ill-advised, but especially so in the case of Rabbi Joseph B. Soloveitchik. I say this for several reasons.

First, as in the case of many religious thinkers from the nineteenth century and onward, Rav Soloveitchik's philosophy revolves around human experience. He characterizes Judaism as being "theo-centric *but anthropo-oriented*,"[1] and this is an apt description of his own thought: while placing God at the center of human existence, it nevertheless focuses its attention on man[2] and his problems. For example, unlike medieval philosophers who assert that the existence of evil in the world is merely an illusion, that evil does not really exist from God's perspective, Rav Soloveitchik treats evil as an undeniable human experience. Accordingly, he does not try to explain the existence of evil, but rather focuses on how it does and should impact on man. Similarly, he is not interested in describing the attributes of God, but rather man's relationship with God; not the effects of Torah study on the metaphysical realm, but rather its influence on the human personality. Given his focus on human experience, and the fact that, naturally, the human experience with which Rav Soloveitchik is most familiar is his own, it is not surprising that he incorporates that experience into his philosophizing. In a sense, his thought

---

1 This appears in an oral discourse from the 1950s on the Jewish doctrine of man. See also *Out of the Whirlwind* (Jersey City, 2003), 94.

2 Following the conventions of his time, the Rav used the term "man" when referring to humankind.

begins with himself. Hence, an understanding of his life is pertinent to an investigation of his thought.

Indeed, many passages in Rav Soloveitchik's writings are explicitly autobiographical; he frequently veers from philosophic or halakhic analysis to intimate and touching personal confessions. Such passages are quite rare among the writings of other *gedolei Torah* (giants of Torah), especially when they appear in published articles. The subjectivity of many of the Rav's writings does not detract from their relevance, brilliance or originality. On the contrary, it charges his works with a power they would have lacked had they been more detached and objective.

A second reason to preface our study of Rav Soloveitchik's thought with an examination of his biography is that, as a communal leader, he addressed current events and the contemporary social and religious scene. His philosophical works are relevant and applicable to these concrete, real-life challenges, many of which remain with us now, a few decades later. Works like *The Lonely Man of Faith* amply demonstrate that he was an astute observer of societal trends and a sharp critic of contemporary religiosity. For example, though it is widely noted that the Rav provided intellectual and spiritual legitimacy to the ideology of Modern Orthodoxy, it is less often noted that he frequently critiqued the way it was practiced. He also expressed discontent with contemporary religiosity in general.

A third reason to incorporate the Rav's biography into the study of his thought is that understanding his family tree and his educational background can help us better appreciate his intellectual and emotional makeup. This is especially important regarding his Brisker heritage, which was central to his self-perception.[3]

Fourth, it has been claimed that insight into the Rav's life can help us understand the seemingly different tones of his early and late essays, and may help us understand why he addressed certain issues and not others.

Finally, it is important for us to know about the Rav's life because, beyond his masterful and creative halakhic scholarship and philosophic thought, it is the image of the Rav himself, heroic and yet human, which is so captivating.

---

3 As we shall see, within his life he also experienced the transition from a traditional, Old World society to a modern, New World society, and this dual exposure left its imprints on his thought.

Family

Rav Joseph Baer (Yosef Dov) Halevi Soloveitchik (1903–1993) was born in Pruzhan, Poland. Named after his great-grandfather, the "Beit Halevi" (1820–1892), who had headed the Volozhin Yeshivah (the "mother of *yeshivot*") and served as rabbi of Slutsk and Brisk, he counted among his forebears almost all of the most prominent scholars of Lithuania, such as Rav Hayyim of Volozhin and Rav Naftali Zvi Yehudah Berlin (the Netziv). His father, Rav Moshe (1879–1941), was the son of the illustrious Rav Hayyim Soloveitchik of Brisk (1853–1918), founder of the "Brisker" method of Talmud study. His mother, Rebbitzen Pesia (1880–1967), was the daughter of Rav Eliyahu Feinstein of Pruzhan (1842–1928), a prominent scholar and disputant of Rav Hayyim on many matters of public policy.[4] Heir to a distinguished heritage, he grew up surrounded by outstanding scholars and religious exemplars.

In many ways, the Soloveitchiks and the Feinsteins were a study in contrasts. Although the Soloveitchiks were renowned for their extreme acts of kindness, they were known primarily for their rigorous intellectualism, self-discipline and ideological extremism.[5] These expressed themselves in an almost single-minded devotion to Torah study, unyielding opposition to secular studies and to Zionism, and refusal to compromise on these matters. The Feinsteins, on the other hand, although no less committed to Torah study, were known for their warmth, openness and tolerance. Their home was host to Jews of all kinds and their children were encouraged to study languages, literature and science.[6]

The Rav was thus exposed to two very different influences within his home. Although in his writings the Rav repeatedly stresses his Soloveitchik heritage, we must bear in mind that he was a Feinstein as well. While cognizant of the different temperaments and backgrounds of his parents, he did not attribute these differences to their upbringings so much as to a general difference between what Proverbs (1:8) labels *musar avikha* and *torat imekha*, "the instruction (or discipline) of your father" and "the teaching of your mother":

---

4 The great halakhic decisor Rav Moshe Feinstein was the Rav's first cousin once removed. Although the Rav's grandfather (Rav Eliyahu Feinstein) and Rav Moshe Feinstein's father shared the same last name, they were not related to each other; rather, they were married to two sisters. In fact, Rav Eliyahu Feinstein was a *Levi* and Rav Moshe Feinstein was a *Yisrael*.

5 Rav Soloveitchik takes pains to modify or to round out this portrait in some of his writings, such as *Halakhic Man* and "*Be-Seter u-ve-Galui*" (printed in *Divrei Hagut ve-Ha'arakhah* [Jerusalem, 1982], 163–86).

6 For biographical sources on Rav Soloveitchik and his family, see For Further Reference, #1.

We have two *massorot*, two traditions . . .

Father teaches the son the discipline of thought as well as the discipline of action. Father's tradition is an intellectual-moral one . . .

What kind of a Torah does the mother pass on? . . . Most of all I learned [from my mother] that Judaism expresses itself not only in formal compliance with the law but also in a living experience. She taught me that there is a flavor, a scent and warmth to the *mitzvot*. I learned from her the most important thing in life – to feel the presence of the Almighty and the gentle pressure of His hand resting upon my frail shoulders. Without her teachings, which quite often were transmitted to me in silence, I would have grown up a soulless being, dry and insensitive.[7]

As this passage reveals, the Rav placed great emphasis on both the intellectual and experiential aspects of Judaism; we shall see this duality emerge as a leitmotif in his writings. In fact, it is the fusion of thought, action and emotion in his philosophy that endows it with much of its considerable potency.

Brisk

The Rav's most formative childhood years were spent in Khoslavitch, Belorussia, where his father served as rabbi from 1913 until 1920. Though the town was populated primarily by Chabad (Lubavitch) *hasidim*, it had a tradition of employing *mitnaggedim* as rabbis. When his mother detected that in *heder* he was being taught far more of the foundational Chabad work *Tanya* than Talmud,[8] she complained about this to her husband and later to her father-in-law, who recommended that Rav Moshe assume personal responsibility for his son's education.[9] The following formative period in the Rav's development is described by Rav Aharon Lichtenstein, Rav Soloveitchik's disciple and son-in-law:

During the next twelve years, young Soloveitchik dedicated himself almost exclusively to the study of Jewish law. Under Rav Moshe's tutelage he was trained in the "Brisker" method, with its insistence on incisive analysis, exact definition, precise classification and critical independence. Gradually, the

---

7 "A Tribute to the Rebbitzen of Talne," *Tradition* 17:2 (Spring 1978), 76–77.

8 The Rav maintained a lifelong fondness for the writings of Chabad, based on this early exposure.

9 Some of the fruits of these years of joint study were published under the title *Hiddushei ha-Gram ve-ha-Grid al Inyanei Kodashim* (New York, 5753). In addition, the Rav's later correspondence with his father on matters of *lomdus* has been published under the title *Iggerot ha-Grid Halevi* (Jerusalem, 5761).

acute dialectic of halakhic logic – so rigorous and yet so subtle; so flexible and still so firm – became second nature, and Soloveitchik emerged from this period thoroughly imbued with the religious and intellectual discipline of the Halakhah.[10]

It is worth noting the characteristics of the Brisker method pinpointed by Rav Lichtenstein above.[11] The Brisker method innovated by Rav Hayyim Soloveitchik quickly conquered most of the *mitnagged* yeshivah world. Although it had intellectual precursors (such as the eighteenth-century *Ketzot ha-Hoshen* and the nineteenth-century *Minhat Hinukh*) and often presented itself as merely uncovering the logic of the *Rishonim* (medieval commentators), it was widely viewed as having wrought a revolution in Talmud study, which the Rav himself compared to the Newtonian revolution in physics. The method's denigrators referred to it as "chemistry," due to its penchant for breaking down concepts into their component parts and its transformation of Halakhah from a series of dicta into an abstract and quasi-scientific system of interlocking concepts.

At the heart of the Brisker enterprise is the attempt to understand all the possible conceptual approaches to a talmudic issue, rather than adopting one position and trying to defend it against attack. In "*lomdish*" parlance, this can be described as "trying to answer a difficult Rambam without making the Ra'avad look like an *am ha-aretz* (ignoramus)." Classic Brisker learning usually identifies two basic approaches to an issue,[12] both of which are necessary to understand an issue in its entirety. The distinction between these two approaches is referred to as a *hakirah* (lit., investigation). Rabbi Jonathan Sacks nicely describes the power of this analytic methodology:

> [By] drawing out the conceptual presuppositions of the Halakhah, apparently unrelated arguments could be seen as instances of an overall pattern of disagreement. As a hermeneutic tool, it was a powerful method of extracting universal themes from a literature which had hitherto seemed utterly concrete and case-specific.[13]

While this pluralistic approach may not be very conducive to reaching practical conclusions, it does sensitize one to the complexity of issues, the

---

10 "R. Joseph Soloveitchik," in *Great Jewish Thinkers of the Twentieth Century*, ed. Simon Noveck (New York, 1963), 283.

11 The Rav's fullest treatment of the Brisker method appears in his eulogy for his uncle Rav Yitzhak Zev (Velvel) Soloveitchik (1888–1959), entitled "*Mah Dodekh mi-Dod*," in *Divrei Hagut ve-Ha'arakhah*, 57–97.

12 Of course, numerous hybrid or median opinions may also exist.

13 *Tradition in an Untraditional Age* (London, 1990), 39.

legitimacy of different approaches, and the frequent need to maintain opposing concepts in dialectical tension or balance.

The Rav's early immersion in "Brisker *lomdus*" affected not only his Talmud study, but his entire method of thought.[14] All of his philosophical essays revolve around dialectical pairs of ideas: cognitive man vs. religious man, Adam I vs. Adam II, majesty vs. humility, the natural religious consciousness vs. the revelatory religious consciousness, etc.[15] These dialectical pairs can be viewed as the two sides of a *hakirah*, both of which are legitimate and necessary, and both of which are required for a proper understanding of an issue in its entirety. The Rav extended this method even into the reading of biblical texts, most notably in his reading of the two accounts of the creation of man. He was not afraid of a contradiction and, in fact, believed that the whole truth can be attained only through the dialectical interplay between conflicting approaches. Among the hallmarks of his thought are its complexity and honesty, and its eschewing of simplistic solutions to complicated problems.

The Rav's employment of the method of philosophical typology might also be influenced by his Brisker background. The Brisker method constructs abstract, ideal halakhic categories that account for the functioning of complex halakhic phenomena. The typological method constructs a number of different ideal personality types in order to understand the functioning of complex human beings; in an actual human being two or more of these types may interact. This method is evident in the Rav's depictions of the "pure ideal type"[16] of halakhic man, the lonely man of faith, etc.

In his halakhic scholarship, the Rav followed Brisk in transforming halakhic dicta into an abstract system of legal concepts; but in his philosophy, the Rav took this approach a step further and derived philosophic concepts from the halakhic sources. Finally, the critical independence of the Brisker approach played no small role in fostering the Rav's independence of thought.

This early period was crucial to the Rav's life not only because it was when he mastered the Brisker method along with large sections of the Talmud, but also because it cemented his bond with his father, giving rise to his conception of the ideal *rebbe-talmid* (teacher-student) relationship. The Rav's relationship with his father was one of the two most central relationships in his life, the other being that with his wife; three of his major philosophical

---

14 To be sure, the Rav also engages and draws from the thought of numerous Western philosophers, especially those with dialectical or phenomenological approaches. Yet I would argue that their ideas resonated with him precisely because of his Brisker orientation.

15 These dialectical pairs appear in the following works, respectively: *Halakhic Man, The Lonely Man of Faith*, "Majesty and Humility," and *U-Vikkashtem mi-Sham*.

16 *Halakhic Man*, 139, n. 1.

works carry dedications, one to his father and two to his wife. He keeps referring back to these relationships in many of his essays.[17]

Surprising as it may seem to some today, the Rav never attended a yeshivah and his only *rebbi* was his father. The identification of father with teacher was crucial for the Rav; not only is a father supposed to be a teacher, but a teacher must be a father as well. Just as his father inducted him into the chain of Brisk, so must every teacher induct his student into the chain of the *masorah* (tradition). Teaching, for the Rav, is not just a meeting of minds, but a merging of minds and of experiences, an act of identification on the part of the student with his teacher. This holds true of the Rav and his father to such an extent that almost all the Torah of Rav Moshe we possess today has come to us through his son.

Berlin

The Rav's father considered Talmud study so self-sufficient that not only did he disapprove of secular studies, but it is said that he never even opened the Rambam's philosophic masterpiece, *The Guide of the Perplexed*. This is especially striking when we consider the centrality of the Rambam's halakhic code, the *Mishneh Torah*, to the Brisker mode of study. The Rav, by contrast, maintained an active interest in Jewish thought. Furthermore, he acquired from his mother a taste for literature and poetry, reflected in the literary flair and poetic bent of many of his own writings.

Recognizing his son's genius early on, Rav Moshe intensively and somewhat mercilessly groomed him to be the next leader of Orthodox Jewry. For many years Rav Moshe believed that mastery of halakhic literature would suffice to attain this goal. Eventually he came to believe that, due to changing times, familiarity with secular knowledge was also necessary. Thus, in his late teens, the Rav received the equivalent of a high school education from a series of tutors. In his early twenties, after having "filled his belly with the bread and meat"[18] of halakhic study, he set out to attend university in order to encounter the best that the outside world had to offer.[19]

After three semesters studying at the Free Polish University in Warsaw, the Rav entered the University of Berlin, where he was to remain for much of

---

17 In fact, the essays mentioned in n. 5 above can both be read as eulogies for his father. Regarding the Rav's views on parenthood and marriage, see Chap. 19 below.

18 Rambam, *Hilkhot Yesodei ha-Torah* 4:13.

19 As will become apparent, his positive attitude towards secular studies differed from his father's instrumentalist approach.

the next six years, earning his Ph.D. in 1932. Berlin was one of the intellectual and cultural centers of Europe, and the 1920s were a time of tremendous intellectual ferment there. Great breakthroughs were being made in the sciences, especially physics, and in the humanities too there was palpable excitement regarding new ideas and approaches being formulated.

The Rav arrived upon this scene, curious, confident, ready to master new systems of thought and to face the challenges they might present. He studied mathematics and physics, but concentrated primarily upon philosophy, and maintained a lifelong interest in all these subjects. Attracted to ideas of the Marburg School of Neo-Kantian philosophy, he wrote his thesis on the epistemology (theory of knowledge) of Hermann Cohen (1842–1918), a leader of the Marburg school, when he could not find an advisor for a thesis on the Rambam.[20]

Anyone opening *Halakhic Man* or *The Halakhic Mind* will immediately be struck by the extent to which the Rav mastered the entire tradition of Western thought.[21] Penetrating secular knowledge to its very depths, he understood it intimately, as an insider – its power and beauty as well as its danger to the religious spirit. In fact, Rav Soloveitchik is virtually alone among modern *gedolim* in the serious philosophical training he received and in the high value he attached to this knowledge.[22] On occasion, the Rav's education lends his writings a dated quality (now that the "modern" philosophy of the 1920s is not as modern). Generally, though, it facilitates his shedding new light on familiar topics and adds depth to his understanding of the confrontation between religion and the modern world.

In Berlin the Rav also encountered a new type of rabbi, one who mastered traditional modes of text study but was also trained in critical academic methods. He befriended two brilliant and fascinating Orthodox scholars: Rav Yehiel Yaakov Weinberg (1885–1966), author of *Seridei Esh* and head of the

---

20 We can hear echoes of some of Cohen's ideas in Rav Soloveitchik's essays *Halakhic Man* and "*Mah Dodekh mi-Dod*," where the Rav finds parallels between the Neo-Kantian view of scientific knowledge and his own view of *talmud Torah*. See Lawrence Kaplan, "Rabbi Joseph B. Soloveitchik's Philosophy of Halakhah," *The Jewish Law Annual* 7 (1988), 139–97.

21 In *Halakhic Man*, in the space of n. 4 alone, he cites Kierkegaard, Hegel, Barth, Otto, Rousseau, Bergson, Nietzsche, Klages, Spengler and Heidegger.

22 See, for example, the comparison to Rav Kook in Chap. 22. Interestingly, although the Rav did write essays justifying his support for Zionism, he never wrote essays – like those of R. Samson Raphael Hirsch or R. Aharon Lichtenstein, for example – justifying his engagement with general wisdom. See R. Yitzhak Twersky, "The Rov," in *Rabbi Joseph B. Soloveitchik: Man of Halacha, Man of Faith*, ed. R. Menachem Genack (Hoboken, 1998), 23–34, and David Shatz, "The Rav and *Torah u-Madda*," in *Mentor of Generations: Reflections on Rabbi Joseph B. Soloveitchik*, ed. Zev Eleff (Jersey City, 2008), 210–17.

Hildesheimer Rabbinical Seminary, and Rav Hayyim Heller (1878–1960), head of the *Beit ha-Midrash ha-Elyon*, who became a father figure to him. Armed with the conceptual Brisker method, the Rav found that academic critical-historical text study did not hold much interest for him. But he did maintain a close lifelong relationship with Rav Heller, who later moved to New York. His masterful eulogy for Rav Heller is not only a moving tribute to the man, but an important presentation of some of the central ideas of the Rav's thought.[23]

Marriage

The Rav's most important and fateful encounter in Berlin was that with his future wife, Dr. Tonya (Lewit) Soloveitchik (1904–1967). A student at the University of Jena, where she obtained a doctorate in education, she was introduced to Rav Soloveitchik by her brother, a fellow student at the University of Berlin. Although a scion of the illustrious Soloveitchik family was expected to conclude a match with the daughter of a prominent rabbi or at least a successful businessman, Rav Soloveitchik fell in love with Tonya Lewit and married her in 1931, heedless of her family's less distinguished lineage and lack of means.

As mentioned above, the Rav's relationship with his wife was one of the two most significant relationships in his life. He had unlimited esteem for her; the dedication of *The Lonely Man of Faith* reads: "To Tonya: A woman of great courage, sublime dignity, total commitment, and uncompromising truthfulness." He respected her opinion and heeded her advice, both in practical and in intellectual matters. It was on her advice that he changed the topics of his annual *yahrzeit* (memorial) lectures for his father, which attracted thousands of listeners, to matters to which non-scholars could relate (such as prayer, Torah reading and holidays).[24] In a poignant passage from a *teshuvah* lecture delivered a year and a half after his wife's death in 1967, following a long struggle with cancer, he recounted how he used to consult with her before speaking:

> The longing for one who has died and is gone forever is worse than death. The soul is overcome and shattered with fierce longing . . . Several days ago, I once again sat down to prepare my annual discourse on the subject of repentance.

---

23 This eulogy, *"Peleitat Sofreihem,"* appears in *Divrei Hagut ve-Ha'arakhah*, 137–62, and is translated into English in *Shiurei Harav* (Hoboken, 1994), 46–65.

24 The halakhic portions of some of these lectures are collected in the two volumes of *Shiurim le-Zekher Abba Mari z"l* (Jerusalem, 5743 and 5745; rev. ed., 5763).

I always used to discuss it with my wife and she would help me define and crystallize my thoughts. This year, too, I prepared the discourse while consulting her: "Could you please advise me? Should I expand this idea or cut down on that idea? Should I emphasize this point or that one?" I asked, but heard no reply. Perhaps there was a whispered response to my question, but it was swallowed up by the wind whistling through the trees and did not reach me.[25]

In *The Lonely Man of Faith*, Rav Soloveitchik distinguishes between "loneliness" and "aloneness."[26] His natural proclivity towards loneliness was heightened in his philosophy to an ideal, which expresses itself in an invigorating sense of one's own uniqueness. One can be "lonely" even, or perhaps especially, when surrounded by friends, colleagues and family. This is a constructive force that propels a person toward his individual destiny, while also motivating him to seek a depth-connection with God and with his fellow man. "Aloneness," by contrast, is a disjunctive emotion – it is a sense of lacking companionship, of being abandoned and forlorn. The passage above highlights the Rav's almost unbearable sense of aloneness following his wife's death. He is reported to have said, "After my father's death, I felt like a wall of my house had fallen down. After my wife's death, I felt like the entire house had collapsed."

The year 1967 was extraordinarily trying for the Rav; within months, his wife, mother and brother all passed away. Although he did manage to return to a productive career of teaching after this period of crisis (and in fact said that the study and teaching of Torah had helped him overcome it), echoes of it reverberate throughout his later writing.

Many attribute to this period (early- to mid-1960s) a significant change in the Rav's temperament. In an address at Yeshiva University at the conclusion of the Rav's *sheloshim* (thirty-day mourning period), his son Prof. Haym Soloveitchik related his different experiences in the Rav's Talmud *shiur*. In the 1940s and 50s, the Rav had been "a volcano, a storming lion in the classroom . . . he could crouch like a tiger and leap at the slightest error that a student would make." However, when he entered his father's *shiur* in 1969, he was shocked to find him "gentle, forbearing; very little upset him." Why the change?

According to Prof. Soloveitchik, the Rav's father had trained him with the assumption that everything was superable through effort. Indeed, contrary to most people's impression of a meteoric career, the first forty years of the Rav's life had been an endless overcoming of obstacles – war, poverty, antisemitism,

---

25 *On Repentance* (Jerusalem, 1980), 280.

26 See also *Family Redeemed* (New York, 2000), 15–16.

politics, etc. Thus, both Rav Moshe and the Rav believed that, generally, intellectual error was tantamount to a moral failure – a failure of will and effort. Rav Soloveitchik responded to error with fury because he believed it to be a mark of laziness and self-indulgence: if his students would try harder, if they would care more, then they would reach a better grasp of the material they were studying. (Of course, he held himself to the same high standard, devoting long hours of intense preparation for his classes.) However, in the 1960s Rav Soloveitchik had to cope with his own, ultimately successful, bout with cancer, and his wife's, ultimately unsuccessful, struggle with the disease. At this point, he discovered a sense of helplessness; not everything could be accomplished by sheer force of will. This caused a shift in his attitude to his students. He came to terms with human limitations and vulnerability.

This change in temperament may also reflect a shift in emphasis in the Rav's writings. In the writings of the 1960s and 1970s the themes of surrender, humility, the heroism of defeat, and childlike dependence on God assume heightened prominence. Although these themes may be present in his earlier writings, they are certainly not as central.

U.S.A. – Teacher and Spiritual Leader

Soon after his arrival in the United States in 1932, Rav Soloveitchik was appointed Chief Rabbi of the Orthodox community of Boston. Even after succeeding his father in 1941 at the Rabbi Isaac Elchanan Theological Seminary of Yeshiva University in New York, he retained his position in Boston, shuttling back and forth every week for over forty years. Rav Aharon Lichtenstein depicts the Rav's approach to the rabbinate as follows:

> Bred in a tradition that emphasized the intellectual, rather than the pastoral function of the rabbinate, it was Rav Soloveitchik's conception that the rabbi is above all a student, scholar and teacher. Soloveitchik, therefore, dedicated himself to the task of disseminating a deeper knowledge of Torah Judaism. He set out to encourage a general awareness of the values of traditional Judaism and their relevance to modern life. Thus, periodic *derashot* – lengthy public discourses combining halakhic, homiletic and philosophical material – his weekly halakhic *shiurim* (lectures) on the lay level, and his own, richly philosophic understanding of human nature, won for him an ever-growing reputation for wisdom and scholarship.[27]

---

27 "R. Joseph Soloveitchik," *op. cit.*, 285.

This is not to say that he neglected the common functions of the rabbinate – deciding halakhic questions, counseling, performing weddings and funerals; he just did not see these as his focus. Each aspect of his varied career – teacher, scholar, synagogue rabbi and communal leader – gave added depth and breadth to every other aspect.

Rav Soloveitchik's greatest impact was as teacher of Talmud (in Hebrew, a *rebbi* or *rosh yeshivah*) at Yeshiva University, where he taught from 1941 until 1985. In this capacity, he trained thousands of advanced students. His reputation for creativity, clarity and insight brought people from around the world to hear him. His students, many of whom went on to hold rabbinic and teaching positions throughout America and Israel, continued to regard him as their mentor long after they had left yeshivah, thus spreading his influence even farther.

The Rav's Talmud *shiur* was not only the focal point of all his activities – it was the prism through which he viewed everything else. He frequently defined himself as "a *melammed*," a teacher, noting that this is also a description of God ("*ha-melamed Torah le-ammo Yisrael*"). To a large extent, his philosophy flows from this engagement with Halakhah. Although his thought has universal dimensions, it is based squarely within Halakhah and explores Halakhah's role in mediating man's relationship with God, with the world, and with himself. In fact, much of Rav Soloveitchik's thought constitutes an attempt to draw out the philosophy implicit within the sources of Halakhah, as opposed to imposing externally-conceived ideas upon Halakhah. This attempt can be made only after rigorous study of Halakhah, using its own autonomous methods of analysis – and this study is what the Rav devoted himself to in his *shiur*. A staunch advocate of "Torah study for its own sake" (*Torah lishmah*), he did not believe that the value of Torah study depended on its contribution toward the attainment of any other goal, such as formulating a Jewish worldview. Nevertheless, Rav Soloveitchik viewed Torah study as far more than just one of the 613 commandments: it is our main source of insight into the will of God; it gives us knowledge about ourselves and our world; it inducts us into the chain of Jewish tradition, which the Rav calls "the *masorah* community"; and it allows us to encounter God at the experiential level.

The Rav also taught Jewish philosophy for many years at Yeshiva University's Bernard Revel Graduate School. Quite technical in nature, these lectures often revolved around the philosophy of the Rambam. In these and other lectures, the Rav attempted one of his boldest but most overlooked moves: saving the Rambam's philosophy from obsolescence. Although it might seem that the Aristotelian framework in which the Rambam's philosophy is conceived would render it irrelevant to modern Jewish thought, Rav

Soloveitchik set out to reinterpret certain doctrines of the Rambam so as to preserve their contemporary relevance.[28]

Directing his prodigious talent and energy not just to training scholars, the Rav devoted great efforts to educating laymen as well. He taught classes in Bible and Talmud to broad audiences every week in Boston and New York, and his annual *yahrzeit* lectures (memorial lectures for his father and later for his wife) and *teshuvah* discourses attracted both the learned and unlearned alike. In both English and his native Yiddish, he was a dramatic and engaging speaker who could hold an audience spellbound for hours. He also had the rare ability to address a wide variety of audiences (adults and children, scholars and laymen, Orthodox and non-Orthodox, Jews and Gentiles), each at its own level. This resulted from his exposure to a wide variety of people and their problems, his sharp psychological insight, and his innate pedagogical and rhetorical ability.[29]

Rav Soloveitchik also devoted considerable attention to childhood education, seeing education as the key to Jewish survival and meaningful Jewish living. Soon after his arrival in Boston, he founded Maimonides School, the first Jewish day school in New England. He and his wife applied themselves wholeheartedly to ensuring the school's success, both in terms of raising funds and providing educational guidance. The Maimonides School has been quite influential as a model for the day school movement, particularly in the importance it assigned to girls' Torah education.

Although initially a member of the non-Zionist – even anti-Zionist – political-religious organization Agudath Israel, the Rav changed his mind on this issue and became honorary president of the Religious Zionist organization Mizrachi.[30] His only visit to Israel was in 1935, when he ran unsuccessfully for the elected position of Ashkenazi Chief Rabbi of Tel Aviv.[31] In 1960, the Rav was offered the position of Ashkenazi Chief Rabbi of the State of Israel, but he turned it down, citing the position's lack of independence from political influence, and his reluctance to serve in a position that was primarily

---

28 This attempt is especially evident in *U-Vikkashtem mi-Sham*. See Chap. 34 below.

29 What makes this skill more striking is the fact that he learned English as an adult, as his fifth or sixth language.

30 His views on Zionism are set forth in his essay *"Kol Dodi Dofek,"* translated as *Fate and Destiny* (Hoboken, 2000), and in his addresses to Mizrachi, some of which are collected in *Five Addresses* (*The Rav Speaks*) (Jerusalem, 1983). See Chaps. 25–27 below.

31 On that occasion, he met Rav Avraham Yitzhak Hacohen Kook, the other seminal thinker of the Modern Orthodox or *Dati Leumi* community. For more on Rav Kook and Rav Soloveitchik, see Chaps. 22 and 27 below.

bureaucratic and not educational.[32] Certainly, the Rav's concern for the community he would have to leave behind in America served as an additional factor in his decision.

The Rav also exerted great influence in the public arena as chairman of the Halakhah Commission of the Rabbinical Council of America. He was responsible for the formulation of several guiding policies of the Modern Orthodox rabbinate, such as the staunch opposition to mixed seating in synagogues and to interfaith dialogue on matters of creed, as opposed to matters of social justice.[33] However, his primary influence derived not from any official position he held, but rather from his outstanding scholarship, piety and charisma.

Conclusion

Some have suggested that the Rav's works as a whole constitute a spiritual and intellectual autobiography. Thus, in setting out to explore the Rav's thought, we are embarking on a journey as exciting and dramatic as the Rav's own turbulent soul. It is therefore appropriate to conclude with a quote from Rav Lichtenstein that beautifully portrays a major aspect of the Rav's legacy:

W.B. Yeats once commented that a person writes rhetoric about his struggles with others and poetry about his struggles with himself. As an orator, the Rav had no peer in the Torah world. But it is the poet in him which has so touched and enthralled us. He has opened for us new vistas of spiritual experience, vistas within which the drama of human existence, in the form of confrontation with oneself, the cosmos, and above all, the *Ribbono Shel Olam* – all within the context of halakhic existence in its most rigorous Brisker formulation – is charged with hitherto unperceived force and meaning. It is not as if we had engaged in the quest of *"U-Vikkashtem mi-Sham"* and had faltered. We had simply never thought in those categories. It is not as if we had felt tremulous anxiety as lonely men and women of faith mired in the pursuit of mundane daily concerns of faith – but in a minor chord. Most of us had simply never confronted that reality. The Rav did. What we have missed, he experienced – in terms of the dichotomy so cherished by him – at both ends of the scale: *gadlut ha-mohin*, the depth and force of a powerful mind mastering its environment and impacting upon it, and that of *katnut ha-mohin*, the simplicity of the child – not as the epitome of intuited holistic existence idealized by the

32 See R. Soloveitchik's *Community, Covenant and Commitment* (Jersey City, 2005), 173–194; R. Jeffrey Saks, "Rabbi Joseph B. Soloveitchik and the Israeli Chief Rabbinate: Biographical Notes (1959–60)," *BDD* 17 (2006), 45–67; and pp. 280–81 below.

33 Regarding these positions and others, see Chap. 18 below.

Romantics, but as the archetype of a helpless humble spirit groping towards his Father and seeking solace in Him and through Him.

Something of that experience he, through various channels, communicated to us; and, in so doing, he has sensitized us to the need for a fuller dimension of our own *avodat Hashem*. Flashes of what he saw and showed both engage and haunt us; chords of what he heard and said resonate in our ears; strains of what he felt palpitate in our hearts. Beyond detail, however, we have been gripped by *demut diyukano shel Rabbenu* – magisterial but sensitive, winsome and yet, ultimately, inscrutable – and his spiritual odyssey. At home, we have hanging one picture of the Rav with an engaging smile on his face; another, of him bent over pensively, with a somber, almost brooding expression. In looking at the latter, I am frequently reminded of Wordsworth's portrayal "Of Newton, with his prism and silent face, the marble index of a mind forever / Voyaging through strange seas of thought, alone." Only not just a mind, but a soul, not just thought but experience, and above all, not marble, but a passionate human spirit.[34]

---

34 "The Rav at Jubilee: An Appreciation," *Tradition* 30:4 (Summer 1996), 50–51; reprinted in Rav Lichtenstein's *Leaves of Faith, Vol. 1: The World of Jewish Learning* (Jersey City, 2003), 195–96.

For Further Reference

1. **Biography:** A full-length biography of the Rav has yet to be written. In the meantime, see the following: R. Aharon Lichtenstein, "R. Joseph Soloveitchik," in *Great Jewish Thinkers of the Twentieth Century*, ed. Simon Noveck (New York, 1963), 281–97; R. Aaron Rakeffet-Rothkoff, *The Rav: The World of Rabbi Joseph B. Soloveitchik*, 2 vols. (Hoboken, 1999); Shulamith Soloveitchik Meiselman, *The Soloveitchik Heritage: A Daughter's Memoir* (Hoboken, 1995); R. Seth Farber, *An American Orthodox Dreamer: Rabbi Joseph B. Soloveitchik and Boston's Maimonides School* (Hanover, 2004). There is also a documentary film about the Rav entitled, *Lonely Man of Faith: The Life and Legacy of Rabbi Joseph B. Soloveitchik*, directed by Ethan Isenberg (2006).

   For the impression the Rav made on others, see the eulogies and portraits in the following works: R. Aharon Lichtenstein, "The Rav *zt"l* in Retrospect: *Divrei Hesped*," in *Leaves of Faith, vol. 1: The World of Jewish Learning* (Jersey City, 2003), 207–46; R. Hershel Schachter, *Nefesh Ha-Rav* (Jerusalem, 1994), especially 5–33; R. Menachem Genack, ed., *Rabbi Joseph B. Soloveitchik: Man of Halacha, Man of Faith* (Hoboken, 1998); Michael Bierman, ed., *Memories of a Giant: Eulogies in Memory of Rabbi Dr. Joseph B. Soloveitchik zt"l* (Jerusalem, 2003); Zev Eleff, ed., *Mentor of Generations: Reflections on Rabbi Joseph B. Soloveitchik* (Jersey City, 2008).

   For a timeline of events in Rav Soloveitchik's life, see p. 417 below.

2. **Bibliography:** See pp. 418–20 below.

Chapter 2

"The Community":
Individual and Society

In my opinion, an excellent entrée into Rav Soloveitchik's difficult (but rewarding!) major treatises is studying three shorter and more accessible essays
published in the journal of the Rabbinical Council of America, *Tradition*,
vol. 17:2 (Spring 1978).[1] These essays – "The Community," "Majesty and
Humility" and "Catharsis" – were written at different times (1976, 1973 and
1962, respectively), but the arrangement of the essays in *Tradition* is intentional, and they are meant to be read together.[2] Over the next few chapters,
I will utilize these essays to introduce Rav Soloveitchik's religious thought.[3]

Individual and Community

Even a glance at the titles of Rav Soloveitchik's works – *Halakhic Man*, *The
Man of God* (the original title of *U-Vikkashtem mi-Sham*), *The Lonely Man
of Faith*, etc. – suffices to reveal that the Rav focuses primarily on the individual, his struggles and his redemption.[4] The Rav is less concerned with
grand movements of history, or with questions of nationalism and collective
groupings. Rather, he deals mainly with the lonely man or woman, searching
for meaning and self-transcendence, seeking an anchor in a seemingly cold
and indifferent world.

However, this should not lead one to think that the Rav ignores the

---

1 This issue, long a collector's item, is now available for free at the *Tradition* website: http://
www.traditiononline.org/archives. The articles have not been reprinted anywhere else.

2 I heard this from R. Shalom Carmy, who helped the Rav prepare these essays for publication.

3 Ideally, these chapters, like the rest of the book, should *accompany* the reading of the Rav's
essays, rather than *substitute* for it.

4 For the Rav's specific understanding of the term "redemption," see pp. 135 and 204–05.

communal side of human existence.[5] Such a perspective would be almost impossible for someone as rooted in Halakhah as was Rav Soloveitchik. One cannot understand man by considering him only as a lone being; he must also be seen as part of a community. Existence in community is a basic human need, and therefore, if one wants to understand a type of person, one must also examine the type of community he forms. Indeed, this is what the Rav repeatedly does in his writings. For example, in *The Lonely Man of Faith*, after describing the two types of man (Adam I and Adam II) delineated by the Bible's two accounts of creation, the Rav proceeds to explore the communities each of these personalities forms.

A word about the Rav's methodology is in order here. Much of Rav Soloveitchik's philosophy can be described as "philosophic anthropology," the description of different ideal types of personalities. (They are "ideal" in the sense of being pure abstract types, not in the sense of being the best types.) Any specific real person can contain within him a conglomeration of various types. But the point of separating an individual into his component parts is to demonstrate the internal coherence of each personality's orientation, and thus to understand better the complex hybrid produced by their coexistence. For example, every person is expected to embody the positions of both Adam I and Adam II, but in order to negotiate this dialectic successfully, he must understand each component independently. We will discuss this methodology more extensively in the chapters on *The Lonely Man of Faith* and *Halakhic Man*.

Formulating the Question

The Rav begins "The Community" by addressing the philosophical and political debate between collectivism and individualism, represented in his day by the conflict between the communist East and the liberal West. He then posits that:

> Judaism rejects both alternatives . . . Both experiences, that of aloneness, as well as that of togetherness, are inseparable basic elements of the I-awareness (p. 7).

However, as he himself indicates later, this answer does not exactly respond to the question of which political system is preferable. The Rav does not wish to deal with a political or socio-economic question, but rather with an "existential-metaphysical" one:

---

5 Regarding the Jewish People in the Rav's thought, see For Further Reference, #1.

In retreat or in togetherness – where does man find his true self? (p. 9).

This formulation of the essay's central question reveals Rav Soloveitchik's true orientation. He is treating the entire question of community vs. individual from the *individual's* point of view – where does the *individual* find his fulfillment, by himself or as part of a group? Thus, true collectivism, an ideology which regards the individual as subservient to the whole and deriving his rights and identity from the collective, is not even an option for the Rav.[6]

Creation of Man

As the Rav so often does when seeking to determine the fundamental nature of mankind, he turns for an answer to the biblical account of the creation of man.[7] Bear in mind, of course, that the creation story is of universal import; Adam and Eve are the progenitors of all mankind, not just of the Jewish People. Thus, what the Rav has to say here, as well as in his other essays about Eden, is of significance not only for Jews, but for all human beings. However, as a rabbi, his primary interest is in spelling out the implications of this narrative for the Jewish People and in finding expressions of these universal themes within Jewish Law. On the one hand, the Bible describes God creating man as a solitary individual ("Then the Lord God formed man," Gen. 2:7). On the other hand, God declares, "It is not good that the man should be alone" (ibid. 2:18), and therefore He creates the woman and brings the two together. Since God creates man and woman as solitary beings, but also unites them into a community, it follows that Judaism affirms the need for both the community-related individual and the lonely individual.

> The answer to the problem is rather a dialectical one, namely, man is both . . . In fact, the greatness of man manifests itself in his inner contradiction, in his dialectical nature, in his being single and unrelated to anyone, as well as in his being thou-related and belonging to a community structure (8).

The Rav's choice of biblical verses to support the two positions is an interesting one. He makes reference to two verses from Genesis chapter 2, one

---

6 While Rav Soloveitchik does not believe that the individual derives his importance solely from his membership in a community, he also does not believe that the community derives its significance solely by virtue of its contribution to the individual's fulfillment. The individual has significance apart from the community, as we shall see here, and the community has significance apart from the individual, as we shall see in the discussion of *Knesset Yisrael* below (pp. 43–44) and in the chapters on *Kol Dodi Dofek*.

7 For other examples, see Chap. 12, For Further Reference, #1.

describing man's creation and the other his "marriage." It would seem that a more likely source for the doctrines of aloneness and togetherness would be to contrast chapter 1 of Genesis with chapter 2. In chapter 1, man and woman are created together (". . . male and female He created them," 1:27), while in chapter 2 man is created alone (2:7) and woman appears only later (2:22).

However, I believe the Rav's choice of verses is deliberate. In *The Lonely Man of Faith*, Rav Soloveitchik describes the community formed by man of chapter 1 as a functional-utilitarian one, where people merely work together for their own mutual benefit. Man of chapter 2, on the other hand, feels incomplete without companionship; existentially, it is not good for him to be alone (2:18). A simple working relationship with someone else is insufficient for him – he must form a depth connection, a "community of commitment." This community is not merely a pragmatic device, but rather part of his definition as a person.

"The Community" which the Rav discusses in this essay is clearly of the latter kind; as a "prayerful, charitable, teaching community" (24), it is obviously far more than a functional collective. Therefore, it is eminently sensible for the Rav to examine chapter 2 here, not chapter 1. His point is that, within the depth dimension of human existence, we must realize the value of both aloneness and togetherness.[8]

Thus, rather than being a national-political grouping, the community here is a series of interconnecting personal relationships.[9] Although the Rav extols the value of community, he takes care to emphasize that it should not come at the expense of one's individuality; no one should submerge his identity into that of the collective. In fact, ultimately, the community which Rav Soloveitchik values so highly is itself based on the individuality of each member. Each person adds something unique to the community; each therefore complements the rest of the community and, hence, is irreplaceable. In this

---

8 A methodological aside: The Rav would frequently draw different conclusions from the same story each time he studied it, just as he would examine a talmudic passage afresh and explain it differently each time he would encounter it. Therefore, we do not always have to read his essays in light of each other. In this case, however, I believe it is clear that we should correlate the two essays. "The Community" of our title is, in the terms of *The Lonely Man of Faith*, an Adam II community, a "covenantal faith community."

9 The Rav does not ignore the national-political side of Jewish identity; we shall explore his concept of the two dimensions of Jewish nationhood when we study *Kol Dodi Dofek* in Chaps. 25–27 below. It is particularly interesting to contrast the Rav's view to that of Rav Avraham Yitzhak Hacohen Kook. As we will see, their differences lead to different assessments of the past, present, and future of the Jewish People. But since we are just beginning our study of Rav Soloveitchik, we will leave comparisons aside until we are more familiar with his philosophy.

sense, the larger community – in our case *Knesset Yisrael* (the Congregation of Israel) – resembles the smaller marriage community:

> Woman and man complement each other existentially; together they form, not a partnership, but an individuality, a persona. The marriage community is like the general community; its strength lies, not in that which is common to the participants, but in their singularity and singleness (11).

The Unity of *Knesset Yisrael*

As indicated in the above passage, the conglomerate of unique individuals unites somewhat paradoxically to form a single entity. In contemporary secular law, a corporation constitutes an autonomous legal personality; a company's assets are owned not by its executive nor even by its shareholders, but by the "corporation" itself. Similarly, *Knesset Yisrael* is a legal personality which, for example, lays claim to the Land of Israel and is invested with the power to control the Jewish calendar.

However, *Knesset Yisrael* is more than just the subject of legal rights. It is a timeless metaphysical entity that has entered into a covenant with God and that, to an extent, mediates each Jew's relationship with God. For example, on Yom Kippur every Jew must strive to attain atonement both on an individual level and as part of the People of Israel. This is reflected, among other places, in the dual recitation of *viddui* (confession) – first as individuals, during the silent *Amidah*, and then as a congregation, during the repetition of the *Amidah*.

In the first *viddui*, man is judged purely on his individual merits. Therefore, without prologue, he immediately launches into a recitation of his sins, and ends by begging for forgiveness. As an individual, one has no right to demand that God grant atonement, and therefore, as the Rav puts it, the mood of this confession is one of insecurity.

However, communal *viddui* is of an entirely different nature. Because God has made an eternal covenant with *Knesset Yisrael*, the Jews are guaranteed forgiveness as a people.[10] God will never entirely destroy us, nor will He exchange us for another nation. We preface the *viddui* by reminding God of the covenant (through reciting the Thirteen Attributes) and of the love between

---

10 This covenant is expressed in the "Thirteen Attributes of Mercy" (see Ex. 33:12–34:26). Many rabbinic statements attest to the superior merit of the congregation over that of the individual, e.g., "The Holy One does not despise the prayer of the congregation" (*Berakhot* 8a); "The merits of a congregation are greater [than those of the individual]" (*Avodah Zarah* 4b).

Him and His people (as expressed in such *piyyutim* as "*Ki Anu Amekha*" – "We are Your people and You are our God, we are Your children and You are our father . . . We are Your faithful and You are our beloved"). After confessing our sins, we request and even demand atonement for *Knesset Yisrael*, to whom forgiveness has been promised. The entire mood of this confession is one of security and even joy.[11]

Aloneness and Togetherness

After deriving the necessity of both aloneness and togetherness from biblical and halakhic sources, the Rav establishes loneliness as an inescapable human reality. He paints poignant pictures of the inevitability of loneliness even within the closest human relationships, such as the alienation of the terminally ill spouse, and the solitude of the young mother overwhelmed in the middle of the night by a crying child and a sleeping husband. He then proceeds to explain why it was necessary to create man as both a solitary and a social being. There are two reasons why lonely man had to be created:

> 1. The originality and creativity in man are rooted in his loneliness-experi-ence, not in his social awareness . . . Social man is superficial: he imitates, he emulates. Lonely man is profound: he creates, he is original.
> 2. Lonely man is free; social man is bound by many rules and ordinances. God willed man to be free. Man is required, from time to time, to defy the world . . . Only lonely man is capable of casting off the harness of bondage to society . . . The *levado*-awareness[12] is the root of heroic defiance. Heroism is the central category in practical Judaism. The Torah wanted the Jew to live he-roically, to rebuke, reproach, condemn, whenever society is wrong and unfair. The *levado* gives the Jew the heroic arrogance which makes it possible for him to be different . . . Lonely man is a courageous man; he is a protester; he fears nobody; whereas social man is a compromiser, a peacemaker, and at times a coward. At first man had to be created *levado*, alone; for otherwise he would have lacked the courage or the heroic quality to stand up and to protest, to act like Abraham, who took the axe and shattered the idols which his own father had manufactured (13–14).

---

11 This analysis of the two forms of *viddui* appears in *On Repentance*, 127–32. The Rav also discusses the theme of individual vs. communal atonement in the context of the ancient ritual of the scapegoat, the prayers of Rosh Hashanah and Yom Kippur, and the laws of *shofar* blowing. See For Further Reference, #2.

12 I.e., the awareness of standing alone, derived from verses describing Jacob (Gen. 32:24) and Elijah (I Kings 19:10).

However, God also willed that man become a social being. Why?

> Man is not only a protester; he is an affirmer too. He is not only an iconoclast, but a builder, as well. If man always felt remote from everybody and everything, then the very purpose of creation could not be achieved (14).

In "The Community," the Rav presents Moses as one who epitomized both aspects of human identity.[13] On the one hand, he was "the greatest loner, who pitched his tent 'far outside the camp' (Ex. 33:7)." On the other hand, he was "the great leader, father and teacher to whom the community clung."

This example is problematic. Moses lived alone, outside the camp, separated from his wife, and with a veil covering his face! He was *involved* with the community as their leader, but was he really *part* of the community?

At the same time, recall that Moses was the "faithful shepherd" who identified with the members of the community to such an extent that he wished to be destroyed along with them if God would not forgive their sin (Ex. 32:32). We will once again encounter this paradox of being part of the community while being outside it in *The Lonely Man of Faith*, where the Rav describes God Himself as being a member of the "covenantal faith community," albeit, as it were, the senior member.[14]

If we look to history, it would seem that the Rambam, for example, viewed himself somewhat along the lines of the biblical Moses, communing solitarily with God and at the same time guiding the community as a teacher and leader. Perhaps we can speculate that the Rav also saw himself in this light, identifying strongly with the community while also feeling separate from it in his singularity and uniqueness.

Forming a Community: Recognition of the Other

Having established the necessity of both solitude and community, the Rav focuses on how a community is formed. The first step is the recognition of the other, the "thou." By realizing that he is not the only significant being in the universe, solitary man – to use Kabbalistic terminology – "contracts" his "infinite" existence and makes room for the other. In this, man emulates God's primordial act of *tzimtzum* (contraction), whereby He "made room" for an existence other than His own, i.e., the universe.[15] Thus, Rav Soloveitchik

---

13 For a nuanced portrait of Abraham as both a lonely iconoclast and as a social being, see "A Wandering Aramean" in *Abraham's Journey* (Jersey City, 2008), 73–89.

14 See pp. 142–43 below.

15 We shall explore the concept of *tzimtzum* in the next chapter. At this point, note merely

arrives at the equation: "creation [of a community or of the world] = recognition = withdrawal = an act of sacrifice" (p. 15).

Many aspects of Halakhah reflect this insight. For example, the Halakhah assigns great significance to greetings exchanged between people, because recognition implies affirmation of the other person's value, and draws the two people together into a community. Thus, we are commanded to return greetings, and sometimes to extend them, even when reciting the *Shema*. Recognition of one's fellow, relieving him of his loneliness, does not contradict the act of *kabbalat ol malkhut Shamayim* (acceptance of the yoke of Heaven) entailed in the *Shema*. Similarly, the Halakhah is exceedingly strict in prohibiting one from causing even the slightest distress to a widow or orphan, since these individuals are extremely sensitive and prone to losing their sense of dignity and worth.[16] Although it is not always clear whether the Rav is deriving his philosophical ideas from the Halakhah or whether he is explaining the Halakhah by means of his independently formed philosophical ideas, such insights are common in his writings, giving his thought firm grounding in Jewish sources.

Mutual Commitment

By recognizing the "thou" and forming a community with him, one automatically assumes responsibility for him: "Recognition is identical with commitment" (p. 18). This, again, is emulation of God, who not only created the world but also continually provides for it. On a human level, this leads to the formation of the prayer community, which the Rav explains thus:

> It means a community of common pain, of common suffering. The Halakhah has taught the individual to include his fellow man in his prayer . . . Halakhah has [thus] formulated prayer in the plural . . .
> The individual prayer usually revolves about physical pain, mental anguish, or suffering which man cannot bear anymore. At the level of individual prayer, prayer does not represent the singularly human need. Even the mute creature in the field reacts to physical pain with a shriek or outcry . . . However, prayer in the plural is a unique human performance . . . I am aware, not only of my pain, but of the pain of the many, because I share in the suffering of the

---

that the Rav raises the issue of *imitatio Dei*, emulation of God, which, as we shall see, is central to his thought.

16 Note the striking aggadic passage (*Semahot* 8:4) quoted by the Rav, which attributes Rav Shimon ben Gamliel's death to inadvertently causing slight distress to a poor widow.

many. Again, it is not psychological; it is rather existential awareness of pain (19, 21).

Due to this awareness, the prayer community must also be a charity community. And indeed, over the generations the Jews have developed a trait of sensitivity to pain and almost compulsive kindness (*rahmanut*), as well as a remarkable tradition of charity.

The Teaching Community

However, according to the Rav, the highest form of interpersonal communion is attained through the teaching community. The true teacher must merge his total experience with that of the student, and they thereby attain a closeness which exceeds the sympathy and mutual aid of the prayer/charity community. A teacher not only trains the mind, but fashions the personality of the student. He shares not only information, but experiences, visions, dreams – in short, his very essence. As the Rav explains in *U-Vikkashtem mi-Sham* (141–42),[17] the personality of the master teacher, like that of the prophet, spontaneously overflows toward the student in an act of self-revelation. This leaves an indelible impression upon the student's soul and binds the two together intimately.

In fact, the entire enterprise of the *masorah* (passing on the tradition) is based on the unity of teacher and disciple:

> Within this fundamental principle [i.e., unity of teacher and student] is hidden the secret of the Oral Torah, a Torah which by its nature and application can never be objectified, even after it has been written down. "Oral Torah" means a Torah that blends with the individual's personal uniqueness and becomes an inseparable part of man. When the person then transmits it to someone else, his personal essence is transmitted along with it (*U-Vikkashtem mi-Sham*, 142).

A word of explanation about the previous quote: Unlike the Written Torah, which is crystallized in a clearly defined text, the Oral Torah is by its very nature amorphous. It is borne not by parchment, but by the human being, who both shapes it with his own unique contribution and understanding, and who in turn is shaped by it. The Rav elaborated on this theme on several occasions, among them a memorial lecture for his wife in 1971:

---

17 Throughout the book, I will refer to *U-Vikkashtem mi-Sham* by its more familiar Hebrew title, but page references will be to the English translation by Naomi Goldblum, entitled *And from There You Shall Seek* (Jersey City, 2008).

Can the Oral Torah pass on *kedushah* (holiness) . . . in the sense that the Written Torah sanctifies *tefillin, mezuzah,* the Torah parchment, etc.? . . . It would be folly to conclude that the Oral Torah is inferior in this respect. The answer is that the Oral Torah operates in a more subtle manner, transmitting sanctity through study and its relation to the mind of the student . . . The parchment of *talmud Torah* is the human mind, the human heart and personality . . . The old halakhic equation that every Jew is a *sefer Torah* (Torah scroll) is, in this light, fully understandable. The living Jew is the *sefer Torah* of the *Torah she-be-al peh*.[18]

By bringing the student into the living chain of tradition, the teacher inducts him into a community which transcends the bounds of uni-directional time, uniting both the glorious past and the eschatological future with the present into one great experience. Events from the past, far from being dead, are constantly re-experienced (e.g., the Exodus, the revelation at Sinai, the destruction of the Temple); teachers and heroes of the past are living presences who address their words to us and whom we even can engage in dialogue (through Torah study). At the other extreme, we eagerly anticipate the future redemption of the world and actively attempt to bring some of its perfection into the present. Our experience transcends chronological time, giving us a sense of eternity within the temporal, and sensitizing us to the opportunities and challenges of the present.

In this essay, the Rav portrays the community in both horizontal and vertical terms: horizontal communion with one's contemporaries via prayer and charity, and, superior even to this, vertical communion with generations past and future via the medium of *talmud Torah*. The same progression can be found in the Rav's discussions of community in *U-Vikkashtem mi-Sham* and *On Repentance*. In the latter, Rav Soloveitchik details the need to link up to *Knesset Yisrael* in order to participate in the atonement granted on a communal level. (This does not detract from the need to attain personal atonement for one's individual sins.) How does one connect to *Knesset Yisrael*? By having faith in it.[19] This faith is expressed in the twofold manner we have just discussed:

---

18 "Torah and Humility," http://www.vbm-torah.org /archive/rav/rav11.htm and rav11b.htm.

19 In a celebrated observation, the Rav links our belief in the coming of the messiah to our faith in *Knesset Yisrael* (*On Repentance*, 135), for the Rambam (*Hilkhot Teshuvah* 7:5) ruled in accordance with R. Eliezer that "If Israel repents, they will be redeemed, and if not, they will not be redeemed" (*Sanhedrin* 97b). Since we believe in the coming of the messiah, and the messiah will not come without repentance, it follows that Israel will repent. Therefore the Rambam continues, "The Torah already offered the assurance that Israel will, in the closing period of the exile, finally repent, and thereupon be immediately redeemed" (ibid.).

The Jew who believes in *Knesset Israel* is the Jew who lives as part of it wherever it is and is willing to give his life for it, feels its pain, rejoices with it, fights in its wars, groans at its defeats and celebrates its victories. The Jew who believes in *Knesset Israel* is a Jew who binds himself with inseverable bonds not only to the People of Israel of his own generation, but to the community of Israel throughout the ages. How so? Through the Torah, which embodies the spirit and the destiny of Israel from generation to generation unto eternity (*On Repentance*, 137).

What is implicit in the above quote from *On Repentance* is explicit in "The Community": the highest form of community is that which unites one with the community of all generations, not just with that of one's own generation. In a sense, connection to one's source and destiny has greater inherent value (what the Rav called "axiological" status) than connection to one's fellow. This is not to minimize the importance of bonding with one's contemporaries – the Rav repeatedly emphasizes throughout his writings the necessity of both dimensions of community. In *Kol Dodi Dofek*, he has very harsh words for those who adhere only to the "covenant of destiny" (which promotes the spiritual goal of becoming "a kingdom of priests and a holy nation") while forsaking the "covenant of fate" (which unites fellow Jews in suffering and sympathy). Both aspects are crucial, and a person's Judaism is deficient if he or she maintains only one aspect.

What the Rav means to say is that, in terms of ultimate values, the eternal is of greater significance than the temporal. Spiritual goals, coming closer to God and spreading His word, have greater value than sympathy between finite individuals. Surely, we must surely be compassionate. Yet our mission, perhaps the very reason we were created, is to bring holiness into the world, a piece of the infinite into finite being, a sense of the eternal into temporal existence. In order to realize this goal, which means maximizing ourselves as individuals, we must join a covenantal community, as described in this essay. Thus, the Rav concludes on a note stressing the timeless:

It is a privilege and a pleasure to belong to such a prayerful, charitable, teaching community, which feels *the breath of eternity* (24).

For Further Reference

1. **Jewish nationhood:** For a composite portrait of the Rav's writings on Jewish nationhood, see Gerald Blidstein, "On the Jewish People in the Writings of Rabbi Joseph B. Soloveitchik," *Tradition* 24:3 (Spring 1989), 21–43; reprinted in *Exploring the Thought of Rabbi Joseph B. Soloveitchik*, ed. R. Marc Angel (Hoboken, 1997), 293–322.

2. *Knesset Yisrael* **in Halakhah** –
   (a) *Kiddush ha-hodesh* (sanctification of the month): *Kovetz Hiddushei Torah*, "Kevi'at Mo'adim al Pi ha-Re'iyah ve-al Pi ha-Heshbon," 47–65.
   (b) Ownership of the Land of Israel: *On Repentance*, 115–16.
   (c) Yom Kippur and the scapegoat: *On Repentance*, "The Individual and the Community," 107–37; R. Aharon Lichtenstein and R. Yair Kahn, *Shiurei ha-Grid: Kuntras Avodat Yom ha-Kippurim*, 2nd ed. (Jerusalem, 2005), 87–88; R. Michel Shurkin, *Harerei Kedem*, vol. 1 (Jerusalem, 2000), 141–42.
   (d) *Shofar*: *Mesorah*, vol. 1 (Nisan 5749), 9–11; vol. 7 (Elul 5752), 10–11; and B. David Schreiber, *Nora'ot Ha-Rav*, vol. 1 (New York, 1996).

3. **The prayer community:** See Chapters 20 and 21 below for a fuller discussion of the Rav's views on prayer.

4. **The *hesed* community:** See Chapter 24 below, pp. 265–66, for more regarding the Rav's views on *hesed* and the connection between *hesed* and teaching.

5. **The *masorah* community:** See *Family Redeemed*, 156–57, as well as the discussion in Chapter 35 below, pp. 381–83, of this topic as it appears in *U-Vikkashtem mi-Sham*.

6. **The unity of teacher and student:** See chapter 19 of *U-Vikkashtem mi-Sham*, 139–48.

7. **The merging of past, present and future:** See "Sacred and Profane," reprinted in *Shiurei Harav*, ed. Joseph Epstein (Hoboken, 1994), 4–32; *Out of the Whirlwind*, 14–17; *Halakhic Man*, 113–23; and throughout *On Repentance*. See also Chapter 22 below.

Chapter 3

"Majesty and Humility":
The Centrality of Dialectic

The essay "Majesty and Humility," despite its brevity, presents some of the most important ideas in Rav Soloveitchik's philosophy. It can serve as a key to understanding many of his more complex works, notably *The Lonely Man of Faith*. When read in conjunction with "Catharsis," the third essay we will be using as an introduction to Rav Soloveitchik's thought, it constitutes a powerful statement of some of the most basic principles of Judaism, yet formulated in a fresh and surprising way.

This essay's very title indicates two critical points that the Rav wishes to emphasize:

(1) It refers to characteristics of both God and man. Human morality must imitate God's qualities or actions; hence, since God displays majesty and humility (as the Rav will explain), so too must man.

(2) The nature of human morality, like the nature of man himself, is dialectical – it is composed of two opposing movements which must both be maintained in a tense balance. In other words, the title teaches us that *both* majesty *and* humility are necessary.

Before examining the essay itself, let us discuss these two concepts, imitation of God and dialectic, which are two of the pillars upon which the Rav's philosophy rests.

Imitatio Dei

The principle of imitating God is known in philosophic parlance by the Latin term *imitatio Dei*, and in halakhic terms by the phrase "*Ve-halakhta bi-dera-khav*" ("And you shall walk in His ways"). This concept appears explicitly in the Bible, is expanded upon by *Hazal* (the talmudic sages), and receives its fullest treatment in the works of the Rambam. The phrase *"Ve-halakhta bi-derakhav"* is taken from the verse, "The Lord will establish you as His holy people, as He swore to you, if you shall keep the commandments of the Lord your God and if you shall walk in His ways" (Deut. 28:9).[1]

There are several problems with interpreting this verse as a command-ment to emulate God:

(1) it is phrased as a conditional statement, not a command;

(2) the phrase "to walk in His ways" is open to several interpretations; and

(3) it seems like a general guideline and not a specific commandment.

The Rambam's son, R. Abraham, addresses these problems in a respon-sum.[2] In order not to go too far afield, we will leave his answers aside; but let us just note that the Bible commands emulation of God in a more unequivocal fashion in several other places:

> You shall be holy, for I, the Lord your God, am holy (Lev. 19:2).

> For the Lord your God . . . loves the stranger, providing him with food and clothing; and you too must love the stranger, for you yourselves were strangers in the land of Egypt (Deut. 10:17–19).

> . . . I am the Lord who exercises loving-kindness, judgment and righteousness in the earth; for these things I desire, says the Lord (Jer. 9:23).[3]

The Sages develop *imitatio Dei* into a more general principle. At times, they interpret it as a mandate to emulate certain characteristics attributed to God:

> Just as He is called "merciful," so should you be merciful; just as He is called "gracious," so should you be gracious . . . just as He is called "righteous," so should you be righteous . . . just as He is called "pious," so should you be pi-ous (*Sifrei*, Deut. 11:22).[4]

As we shall see, Rav Soloveitchik (in *Halakhic Man* and elsewhere) expands

---

1 Similar formulations are found in Deut. 8:6, 10:12, 11:22, 13:5, 26:17, and 30:16.

2 *Teshuvot Rabbenu Avraham ben ha-Rambam*, eds. A. Freimann and S. Goitein (Jerusalem, 1937), # 63. It is also printed at the end of many editions of the *Mishneh Torah, Sefer ha-Madda*.

3 At the very conclusion of his *Guide of the Perplexed* (III:54), Rambam explains that "for these things I desire" is a charge to human beings to exercise "loving-kindness, judgment and righteousness."

4 Note that God is only *called* "merciful," for we cannot really attribute to Him character traits or emotions, but man should *be* merciful. See also *Shabbat* 133b.

the list of divine qualities that man should emulate to include, above all, creativity.[5]

At other times, *Hazal* interpret *imitatio Dei* in terms of actions, not character traits:

> Rabbi Hama the son of Rabbi Hanina said: What does it mean, "After the Lord your God you shall walk" (Deut. 13:5)? Can a person indeed walk after the Divine Presence? Does it not say, "For the Lord your God is a consuming fire" (Deut. 4:24)? Rather, walk after [i.e., emulate] His qualities. Just as He clothes the naked . . . visits the sick . . . comforts the mourners . . . and buries the dead . . . so should you (*Sotah* 14a).[6]

The Rambam was the first to formulate *"Ve-halakhta bi-derakhav"* as a specific biblical commandment to develop a virtuous personality.[7] In fact, the Rambam bases his entire system of ethics on this principle. According to his reading, the "way" in which we are supposed to walk is the middle path:

> The right way is the mean in each disposition . . . namely, that disposition which is equally distant from the two extremes . . . This is the way of the wise . . . We are bidden to walk in the middle paths, which are the right and proper ways, as it is written, "And you shall walk in His ways" . . . and this path is called "the way of God" (*Hilkhot De'ot* 1:4–7).

Rav Soloveitchik is reported to have added an interesting twist to the Rambam's approach.[8] Is the middle path a tepid, middling position, a "pareve"

---

5 Of course, there are some characteristics ascribed to God in the Bible which we presumably should not imitate, e.g., "a jealous and vengeful God" (Nahum 1:2). There are several answers to the question of which characteristics we should try to emulate. See, for example, Rambam's *Guide of the Perplexed* I:54.

6 Some of the actions that *Hazal* recommend are, at first glance, surprising: "Rabbi Yehudah the son of Rabbi Simon said: 'After the Lord your God you shall walk' (Deut. 13:5) . . . At the beginning of the world's creation, the Holy One occupied Himself first with planting, as it says, 'And the Lord God planted a garden in Eden' (Gen. 2:8); so too, when you enter the Land [of Israel], occupy yourselves first with planting – and thus it says, 'When you enter the land and plant all fruit-bearing trees . . .' (Lev. 19:23)" (Lev. Rabbah 25:3).

7 The author of the Geonic work *Halakhot Gedolot* (known as "Bahag," generally assumed to be the 9th-century sage R. Shimon Kayyara) preceded Rambam in counting *imitatio Dei* as one of the 613 biblical *mitzvot*, but the *Halakhot Gedolot* seems to interpret it in terms of performing specific altruistic actions, not in terms of striving for the ideal of ethical perfection. See the Makhon Yerushalayim edition of *Halakhot Gedolot* (Jerusalem, 5752), 15, as well as Ramban's comments on Rambam's *Sefer ha-Mitzvot, shoresh* 1, s.v. *"Ve-ha-teshuvah ha-shelishit"* (22 in the standard printing, 24–25 in R. Chavel's edition).

8 This interpretation, proposed by Rav Soloveitchik in a 1954 lecture, is recorded by R. Walter Wurzburger in his article, "Alienation and Exile," *Tradition* 6:2 (Spring–Summer 1964),

form of mediocrity? If we are to draw an analogy to God, the Rav claimed, what emerges is a dynamic middle. Just as God presents a constant dialectic between immanence and transcendence, or between mercy and strict justice, so must man walk down a dialectical median path, oscillating between two poles and incorporating both. Although it seems to me that this is meant more as a creative midrashic use of the Rambam rather than a literal exposition of his position, it leads us to another important motif in the Rav's philosophy.

Two Types of Dialectic

The pair of opposing concepts comprising a dialectic are known in philosophic terminology as the "thesis" and "antithesis" (i.e., the anti-thesis). When the tension between the two eventually leads to the emergence of a third hybrid position, it is labeled the "synthesis." A dialectic consisting of only two sides, which never reaches a harmonious resolution, is known as a Kierkegaardian dialectic (after the nineteenth-century Danish theologian Søren Kierkegaard). If it consists of three positions, ending in synthesis (which in turn can become the thesis of a new dialectic), it is termed a Hegelian dialectic (after the nineteenth-century German philosopher Georg W. F. Hegel).

The Rav takes a firmly Kierkegaardian stance in "Majesty and Humility":

> Judaic dialectic, unlike the Hegelian, is irreconcilable and hence interminable ... To Hegel, man and his history were just abstract ideas; in the world of abstractions, synthesis is conceivable. To Judaism, man has always been and still is a living reality ... In the world of realities, the harmony of opposites is an impossibility (25).

This kind of approach is rare in Jewish philosophy, which often tends to be more harmonistic. It has roots, however, not just in modern philosophy, but in the Rav's methodology of Talmud study. A *hakirah*, as we have pointed out, is also an irreconcilable dialectic.

The Rav's staunchly Kierkegaardian approach here raises the question of whether he maintains it as a motif in all of his philosophical writings. While "Majesty and Humility" and *The Lonely Man of Faith* present irreconcilable dialectics, some of the Rav's other writings, such as *Halakhic*

42–52, reprinted in *A Treasury of Tradition*, eds. N. Lamm and W. Wurzburger (New York, 1967), 93–103, and in his *Covenantal Imperatives* (Jerusalem, 2008), 229–38. This idea can be found as well in R. Wurzburger's book, *Ethics of Responsibility* (Philadelphia, 1994), 100–01. See also For Further Reference, #1.

Man[9] and *U-Vikkashtem mi-Sham*, seem to present more harmonious portraits of personalities who have found a synthesis. I would say that, overall, the Rav's writings are characterized by a dialectic between the different kinds of dialectic. Is this "meta-dialectic" itself Kierkegaardian or Hegelian? Does he display a general preference for one type of dialectic, with only a few exceptions? Bear these questions in mind as we continue to examine the Rav's works.

Man as a Dialectical Being

In the very first paragraph of "Majesty and Humility," Rav Soloveitchik establishes the centrality of dialectic in understanding man and his place in the world:

> Man is a dialectical being; an inner schism runs through his personality at every level . . . [T]he schism is willed by God as the source of man's greatness and his election as a singular charismatic being. Man is a great and creative being because he is torn by conflict and is always in a state of ontological tenseness and perplexity. The fact that the creative gesture is associated with agony is a result of this contradiction, which pervades the whole personality of man (25).

In this opening statement, the Rav does not yet tell us what the dialectic is, nor does he begin by stating that it is a reflection of a divine dialectic. Logically, it might have made more sense to begin by stating, "God is manifested as a dialectical being, and so too must man be a dialectical being," or, "God relates to man dialectically, because man is dialectical." However, as always, the Rav proceeds from the *human* perspective, not the *divine* perspective; he begins all his investigations with what is known to man through his own experience.

Furthermore, the Rav is not yet interested in presenting to us the specific dialectic upon which the essay will focus. He first wishes to establish the fundamental fact that human nature is not tidy and harmonious, but rather is conflicted at its very core.[10] Although often perplexing and discomfiting, this characteristic is the source of man's greatness – his creative power. The harmonious person stagnates; the restless and conflicted person innovates.

---

9 It is true that halakhic man is first described as the product of a dialectic between cognitive man and religious man. However, the personality of the emergent halakhic man is an entirely harmonious and tranquil one. See the detailed discussion in Chap. 28 below.

10 This is the major theme of *The Lonely Man of Faith*.

Of course, some people may not be able to handle the tension successfully. They will either abdicate responsibility by abandoning their commitment to one of the two sides of the dialectic, or their personality may disintegrate altogether under the pressure of the unavoidable tension. One of the roles of Halakhah, then, is to aid man in negotiating the dialectic by providing him with practical guidelines for action. It is to this idea that we now turn our attention.

Halakhah as a Response

If the human personality is indeed dialectical, then it wishes to pursue two different, perhaps incompatible, goals. Sensitive to this conflict, the Halakhah has thus formulated "a dialectical morality," an ethic of majesty and an ethic of humility. Halakhah "did not discover the synthesis, since the latter does not exist. It did, however, find a way to enable man to respond to both calls" (26). This response is developed in the last pages of this essay, and is the focus of the essay "Catharsis."

The Rav's characterization here of Halakhah carries through many of his writings. For example, in *Kol Dodi Dofek*, Rav Soloveitchik states that philosophical solutions to the problem of evil and suffering are inadequate at both an intellectual level (because of man's finite intellect) and at an emotional level (because they deny the legitimacy of man's experience of suffering). The Halakhah, on the other hand, provides a practical response to this insoluble intellectual and experiential question through the mandate of repentance as a reaction to suffering.

Repentance enables man to take cathartic, therapeutic action in response to adversity, thereby turning a potentially destructive experience into a redemptive one. By responding in a constructive manner, one maintains one's dignity in the face of absurdity; instead of being buffeted by blind forces, one "takes control" of the situation by means of creating (i.e., self-creation, which is the essence of repentance).[11]

Just as Halakhah provides a practical response to suffering without "solving" the problem of evil, in *The Lonely Man of Faith* the Rav portrays Halakhah as providing a practical means of mediating the unavoidable tension between the positions of Adam I and Adam II, without reaching a philosophical synthesis of these two approaches.[12]

---

11 See Chap. 23 for a fuller discussion of this issue, and Chap. 25 for its application on the national level.

12 See Chap. 14 below.

Thus, Halakhah responds to man's most urgent and deep-seated dilemmas – instead of being paralyzed by dichotomies and intractable problems, man is provided a means to respond to them practically and creatively. Halakhah does not deny man's desires and internal paradoxes. Rather, it confronts reality unblinkingly, providing man with a framework to help him negotiate his internal conflicts and to sanctify his natural urges (instead of delegitimizing them).

Cosmic Man and Origin-Questing Man

Having examined the concepts of *imitatio Dei* and dialectic, let us now explore how these concepts receive expression in the rest of the essay. Along the way, we will discover some of Rav Soloveitchik's views on the nature of man and the role of Halakhah in shaping it.

> The basic dialectic of man and his morality was beautifully captured in two midrashic homilies quoted by Rashi. In his comment to the verse, "And God created man dust of the earth" (Gen. 2:7), Rashi says:
>> "God gathered the dust [from which man was fashioned] from the entire earth – from its four corners.
>> Another explanation: He took the dust [from which man was made] from that spot which was designated by the Almighty, at the very dawn of creation, as the future site of the [Temple's] altar" (27).

On this basis, Rav Soloveitchik develops a dual typology of man: both types of personality – "cosmic man," who was fashioned out of dust from the four corners of the earth, and "origin-questing man," whose dust was drawn from the location of the altar – are inherent in human nature. The two *midrashim* regarding man's creation are thus complementary. I would first like to outline the characteristics of cosmic man and origin-questing man, and then analyze this description and its consequences.

I. Attitude to the World

Cosmic man is characterized by a sense of expansiveness, questing for vastness in all areas of endeavor. Intellectually, his curiosity is of universal dimensions; he believes nothing is beyond the grasp of his mind. Experientially, he wishes to be everywhere, to leave his familiar environs and experience the unknown. He is cosmic in his mobility and in his ability to adapt to new settings. "In short, cosmic man is mesmerized by the infinite numbers of opportunities with which his fantasy presents him. He forgets the simple tragic fact that he is finite and mortal" (29).

On the other hand, man was also created from the dust of a single spot. As origin-questing man, he is rooted in a particular place and looks not outward toward the uncharted vastness of the universe, but rather inward to the source of his being. No matter how far he travels, he is attached to his origin and strives to return to it.

II. Search for God

Both types of man search for God, even though they are not always aware of it. Cosmic man, in his feverish haste to leave home, quests for God within the vastness of the cosmic drama. "In times of joy and elation . . . when man is drunk with life, when he feels that living is a dignified affair, then man beholds God in infinity" (32). Origin-conscious man, in his yearning to return home, quests for God within the narrowness of finitude, within the roots of his very being. In times of crisis and suffering, he senses God not in His infinite vastness and distance, but rather in His nearness and relatedness. The Rav shares a personal example of this experience, from the time his wife lay on her deathbed:

> . . . I could not pray in the hospital; somehow, I could not find God in the whitewashed, long corridors among the interns and the nurses. However, the need for prayer was great; I could not live without gratifying this need. The moment I returned home I would rush to my room, fall on my knees and pray fervently. God, in those moments, appeared not as the exalted, majestic King, but rather as a close friend, brother, father: in such moments of black despair, He was not far from me; He was right there in the dark room; I felt His warm hand, *ki-veyakhol* (as it were), on my shoulder, I hugged His knees, *ki-veyakhol*. He was with me in the narrow confines of a small room, taking up no space at all (33).

In short, cosmic man experiences *majestas Dei* (the majesty of God), and origin-questing man experiences *humilitas Dei* (the humility of God).

III. Types of Morality

Perceiving God's majesty and kingship, cosmic man seeks to embody these qualities as well, and he consequently formulates a "morality of majesty" (33), also called an "ethic of victory" (34). This means that he sees himself as a creator, a conqueror, who seeks to subjugate the forces of nature to his own needs. Beyond this, he attempts to establish "a true and just society, and an equitable economic order" (34). Relying only on his intellect, he develops an orderly and rational system of ethics. His enterprise is based ultimately on the mystical doctrine that God purposely left creation incomplete so that man could join Him as co-creator.

However, when man experiences *humilitas Dei*, he formulates not an ethic of triumph but one of retreat, sacrifice and humility. He imitates the divine act of *tzimtzum*, self-contraction, by which the Infinite "makes room" for a finite world or is "contained" within the precincts of a temple or a supplicant's small room. In a similar fashion, humble man constrains himself and accepts his limitations – for example, by obeying *hukkim*, divine laws which the intellect cannot fathom.

The Ethic of Victory and the Ethic of Retreat

Asserting his sovereignty in every realm, cosmic man formulates a morality that is comprehensible to him and serves his needs. Historically, most philosophical treatments of ethics have been geared toward man's social functioning, not towards his metaphysical aspirations (such as sanctity). The human goals pursued by these systems include the development of regulated societies and dignified citizens. Aristotle's ethics is a good example of this approach.

Some theorists formulated concepts of natural law which assert that just as nature is orderly, so should man's life be. They failed to take into account that in nature there is also chaos, ugliness and cruelty. John Cardinal Newman (nineteenth century England) asserted that his belief in God was not based on the order he saw in nature; rather, he saw order in nature because he believed in God.[13] Not everything in the world is comprehensible to man, nor is the human intellect adequate to serve as an exclusive guide to one's actions.

The morality of cosmic man must be complemented by another morality, not only because it unjustifiedly asserts the absolute hegemony of the human intellect, but because it also does not encompass all of man's existential situations. There must be an ethic which takes into account human failure and helplessness. When one experiences one's own humility and vulnerability, one seeks God's nearness and support. In his total reliance on God, humble man willingly accepts God's authority to curtail and even defeat his own desires.

This dialectic of advance and recoil, of victory and defeat, is built into the structure of human existence and constitutes the essence of halakhic living. On the one hand, God desires that man move forward and attain mastery over

---

13 *Letters and Diaries of John Henry Newman*, eds. C. Dessain and T. Gornall, vol. 25 (Oxford, 1973), 97.

his surroundings. On the other hand, from time to time man must halt his headlong rush towards triumph and success, and be willing to retreat, to be defeated by a higher authority. "The movement of recoil redeems the forward-movement, and the readiness to accept defeat purges the uncontrollable lust for victory" (37). In other words, when left to itself, the human desire for victory can be an expression of egocentric interests and self-aggrandizement. The desire for victory can be regarded as a response to a divine summons only if man is willing to curtail his forward-movement when God so demands. If man conquers only to gratify himself, he will be unwilling to accept limitations; if man conquers because God desires it, he will desist when God tells him to do so. Through the readiness to withdraw from conquest, not only is man's retreat sanctified, but so is his advance.

The Rav expresses the idea thus:

> Man, in Judaism, was created for both victory and defeat – he is both king and saint. He must know how to fight for victory and also how to suffer defeat (36).

It is clear why victorious man is called "king," since kingship is expressed by ruling or conquest. But why does the Rav refer to defeated man as "saint"? The word "saint" derives from the Latin root *sanctus*, meaning sacred – the saint is a holy person. Why, according to the Rav, is holiness expressed in defeat? Rav Soloveitchik does not explain this here, but several (mutually acceptable) answers can be proposed.

(1) The holy person negates his will before God's.
(2) The holy person makes room for the wills of other people, not insisting on his own.
(3) The classic understanding of "You shall be holy" is, "You shall be separated (*perushim*)," i.e., you should separate yourselves from sinful desires and from situations which are likely to arouse them (Rashi, Lev. 19:2).

The upshot of all of these explanations is that the act of retreat is inherently endowed with holiness. The act of advance is not in itself holy, but can be imbued with this quality through the willingness to accept defeat.

It is precisely in those areas where one most fervently desires success that one must be willing to withdraw, to suffer defeat at one's own hands. This is true of sublime acts such as the *akedah* (the binding of Isaac), and of more mundane acts such as the regulation of sexual passion by the halakhic laws of separation. Only by refraining when the Halakhah so demands is the physical relationship between man and woman redeemed; it is purged of its "coarseness and animality" and becomes a sacred, divinely-mandated act.[14]

---

14 The specific examples of defeat mentioned by the Rav here – particularly regarding sexual restrictions and the limits of the intellect – are more fully treated in "Catharsis." I will therefore

In a very acute analysis, the Rav observes that modern society is marked by crisis because it is unable to deal with this duality of advance and retreat:

> Modern man is frustrated and perplexed because he cannot take defeat. He is simply incapable of retreating humbly. Modern man boasts quite often that he has never lost a war. He forgets that defeat is built into the very structure of victory, that there is, in fact, no total victory; man is finite, so is his victory. Whatever is finite is imperfect; so is man's triumph (36).

This tantalizing remark anticipates a theme developed at great length in *The Lonely Man of Faith*; in fact, to a great extent, it constitutes the main point of that essay.[15] We will therefore explore this idea further in Chapter 15.

Two Conclusions

We have seen that man must integrate both majesty and humility into his life. Is one of these primary? If so, we could raise two theoretical possibilities:
(1) Defeat only serves to purify the desire for victory, but it is the forward movement that is more important.
(2) The advance is only a means for one to accept defeat, but defeat is an end in itself (or is itself a victory).
Which is the ultimate goal – victory or defeat? Does Judaism champion a three-part movement (advance-retreat-advance) or a two-part movement (advance-retreat)?

I believe that, true to his general approach, the Rav maintains both these conceptions in dialectical tension. Perhaps we can state it differently: victory and defeat are of equal value. Majesty and humility are two basic facets of the human personality, and neither can be denied. The oscillation between the two is endless.

The essay "Majesty and Humility" has, if we look carefully, two different endings.[16] On the one hand, the Rav writes:

> What happens after man makes this movement of recoil and retreats? God may instruct him to resume his march to victory and move onward in conquest and triumph. The movement of recoil redeems the forward-movement, and the readiness to accept defeat purges the uncontrollable lust for victory. Once

---

delay discussion of them to Chaps. 5 and 7, respectively.

15 In the terms of *The Lonely Man of Faith*, modern man develops only the Adam I side of his personality and neglects the Adam II side.

16 I believe the phenomenon of dual endings recurs several times in the Rav's writings, as I will point out with reference to *The Lonely Man of Faith* in Chap. 18 (pp. 195–96) and "Redemption, Prayer, Talmud Torah" in Chap. 20 (p. 221).

man has listened and retreated, he may later be instructed to march straight to victory.

Abraham was told to withdraw, and to defeat himself, by giving Isaac away. He listened; God accepted Isaac but did not retain him. God returned him to Abraham: "And thy seed shall take possession of his enemies' gate" (Gen. 22:17). Abraham found victory in retreat (37).

Here the Rav portrays a three-part movement, ending in victory. Note, however, that he qualifies his statement: "God *may* instruct him to resume his march to victory . . . he *may* later be instructed to march straight to victory." Right after ending the essay on a note of triumph, the Rav adds a little footnote (#21), which explains the reason for his qualification:

> Moses was less fortunate. He withdrew; he gazed upon the land from afar; but his prayers were not fulfilled. He never entered the Promised Land which was only half a mile away. He listened, though his total obedience did not result in victory. God's will is inscrutable.

Who has the last word – Abraham or Moses? Which is the true ending of the essay – the final paragraph or the footnote following it? Does the essay end on a note of victory or defeat?

The answer is: both. True, the note of ultimate victory is sounded in a major chord and the note of defeat in only a minor chord (since the former is stressed in the main text and the latter in a footnote). But the Rav is honest enough to admit that there is not always a happy ending, and defeat is perhaps as valuable to man and as pleasing to God as victory. Man must know how to live with the tension between victory and defeat, advance and retreat, with no assurance of how it will ultimately end.

The next several chapters will discuss the essay "Catharsis," which elaborates the principle of withdrawal or self-defeat.

F OR F URTHER R EFERENCE

1. ***Imitatio Dei*:** R. David Shapiro, "The Doctrine of the Image of God and *Imitatio Dei*," in *Contemporary Jewish Ethics*, ed. M. Kellner (NY, 1978), 127–151; Shalom Rosenberg, *"Ve-Halakhta bi-Derakhav,"* in *Pilosophiah Yisraelit*, ed. M. Halamish (Tel Aviv, 1982), 72–91; translated into English as "You Shall Walk in His Ways," *The Edah Journal* 2:2 (Tammuz 5762), http://www.edah.org/backend/JournalArticle/rosenberg2_2.pdf. See also R. Walter Wurzburger, *"Imitatio Dei* in the Philosophy of Rabbi Joseph B. Soloveitchik," in *Hazon Nahum: Studies Presented to Dr. Norman Lamm*, eds. Y. Elman and J. Gurock (New York, 1997), 557–75; reprinted in R. Wurzburger's *Covenantal Imperatives* (Jerusalem, 2008), 172–90.

2. **Rambam's ethics:** This subject is very complex and has been subject to many conflicting interpretations. Some of the issues in dispute are the relationship between the Rambam's "middle path" and Aristotle's "golden mean," the relationship between the *hakham* and *hasid* (sage and saint) in Rambam's writings, the Rambam's different accounts of his ethical system in his various works (*Shemonah Perakim, Mishneh Torah, Moreh Nevukhim*), and the Rambam's ideal of human perfection. For a presentation of the various opinions on the last issue, and a treatment of the previous issues, see Menachem Kellner, *Maimonides on Human Perfection* (Atlanta, 1990).

3. **Repentance and suffering:** See *Kol Dodi Dofek*, trans. L. Kaplan, 9–11; *Out of the Whirlwind*, 6–8, 100–104, 127–150; *On Repentance*, 289–324; and the discussion in Chapter 23 below.

Section II

THOUGHT, FEELING
AND ACTION

Chapter 4

"Catharsis" (1): Halakhic Heroism

I regard "Catharsis" as one of Rav Soloveitchik's most important English essays, and it is likely that he also considered it as such. Its themes occupied his attention for a number of years, during which he returned to the essay repeatedly and revised it.[1] So many ideas are packed into such a small space that it is hard to do justice to this essay without simply quoting it in full.[2]

Who is a Hero?

Rav Soloveitchik presents the Halakhah's central demand in a striking formulation: Live heroically. Only by living heroically can one endow one's life with transcendent meaning. However, in the Rav's reading, heroism (or *gevurah*) is not what it is usually understood to mean. It consists primarily of the capacity of restraint, the power to overcome oneself, the ability to purge or to purify one's existence. In the familiar words of the Mishnah (*Avot* 4:1): "Who is a hero? He who conquers his desire."

In fact, the Rav explicitly draws a sharp contrast between the biblical (Jewish) and the classical (Greek) understandings of heroism. Classical heroism is an aesthetic category, to be admired for its beauty; it is a grand gesture designed to impress an audience, to attain renown and thus immortality. By identifying with the image of the hero "who dared to do the impossible and

---

1 Note, for example, that the Rav anticipates themes developed in "Catharsis" in his 1957 lecture "The Crisis of Human Finitude" and his 1961 lecture "A Halakhic Approach to Suffering," both of which appear in *Out of the Whirlwind* (see esp. 106–15 and 159). There are also several drafts of "Catharsis" among his manuscripts.

2 Once again, I urge readers to try to read in full all the works discussed in this book.

to achieve the grandiose," disenchanted and frustrated classical man could satisfy his vanity and imagine that he, too, shared in the reflected glory of the hero. "The mere myth of the hero gave the aesthete endless comfort . . . hero worship is basically self-worship" (42).

In contrast, biblical heroism is neither the product of an ephemeral mood, nor theatrical in nature.

> It is perhaps the central motif in our existential experience. It pervades the human mind steadily, and imparts to man a strange feeling of tranquility. The heroic person, according to our view, does not succumb to frenzy or excitement. Biblical heroism is not ecstatic but rather contemplative; not loud but hushed; not dramatic or spectacular but mute. The individual, instead of undertaking heroic action sporadically, lives constantly as a hero (42).

In practical terms, infusing all of one's life with heroism means living in accordance with Halakhah, with its perpetual dialectic of bold advance and humble retreat (as explained both here and in "Majesty and Humility").

To take one example (which I shall expand upon in the next chapter), the Rav portrays the heroism of a bride and groom who recoil from each other when the bride sees a speck of menstrual blood:

> Bride and bridegroom are young, physically strong and passionately in love with each other. Both have patiently waited for this rendezvous to take place. Just one more step and their love would have been fulfilled, a vision realized. Suddenly the bride and groom make a movement of recoil. He, gallantly, like a chivalrous knight, exhibits paradoxical heroism. He takes his own defeat. There is no glamor attached to his withdrawal. The latter is not a spectacular gesture, since there are no witnesses to admire and laud him. The heroic act did not take place in the presence of jubilating crowds; no bards will sing of these two modest, humble young people. It happened in the sheltered privacy of their home, in the stillness of the night. The young man, like Jacob of old, makes an about-face; he retreats at the moment when fulfilment seems assured (45–46).

The Absurd

One of the prerequisites for halakhic heroism is the ability to overcome, when necessary, one's pragmatic, utilitarian, success-oriented judgment. This is what the Rav, borrowing a term from the Danish philosopher Søren Kierkegaard,[3] refers to as the leap into "the absurd." By "absurd" the Rav

---

3 The "absurd" – specifically, the "absurdity of faith" and the consequent "leap of faith" – is

does not mean ridiculous or irrational (i.e., *against* reason), but rather *non-rational* or *meta*-rational. As we noted in "Majesty and Humility," the ethic of humility entails recognizing the limitations of one's intellect and accepting the dictates of a higher authority which we cannot always understand.[4]

True commitment to religion is total, embracing all aspects of human existence – of which the intellectual is but one. This commitment is based not on rational assent to various propositions, but rather on a basic, pre-rational and super-rational experience of God. It is this that gives one the courage to confront daunting opposition, as Jacob did in his nocturnal struggle with a mysterious foe (Gen. 32:25–31), and as the Jewish nation has throughout its existence. This total commitment also gives one the strength to recoil at the very edge of victory, just as Jacob paradoxically freed his foe after having overcome him.

Redefining Catharsis

We are now in a position to appreciate the irony implicit in the Rav's choice of a title for this essay. "Catharsis" is a Greek term denoting purifying or purging (as when one purges gold of its impurities in a crucible). In his *Poetics* (chapter 6), Aristotle defined the function of tragedy as catharsis of the emotions of terror and pity. Man is often troubled; he is full of anxieties that interfere with his social success. When he watches a tragic drama at the theater, he releases these emotions in a controlled and safe environment, emerging from the experience cleansed.

Although the Rav does not directly compare his notion of catharsis with that of Aristotle, the contrast is striking (and certainly intentional). For the Rav, catharsis is not the passive response of a theatergoer, but an active and demanding way of life. It is designed to attain not equanimity but redemption, to produce not an arrogant patrician unencumbered by anxiety but a sanctified personality balancing majesty and humility. While Greek tragedy teaches that man is an object acted upon by random forces and suffering an inexorable fate, Judaic catharsis is a means for man, as a subject, to connect himself actively to a meaningful higher destiny.

---

a major theme in Kierkegaard's *Fear and Trembling* (1843).

4 The Rav stresses in *The Lonely Man of Faith* that the fact that we cannot understand all of God's dictates does not mean that they lack reasons or that they are not beneficial to us.

Redefining Heroism

In contrast to the Rav's redefinition of catharsis, his redefinition of heroism is more subtle. He begins by presenting *gevurah* as military victory, then gradually changes the reader's understanding of it to include bold action taken contrary to pragmatic reasoning, and ends up by defining it as the paradoxical strength to withdraw, not to consummate victory.

This is a good example of a common phenomenon in Rav Soloveitchik's writings. He takes loaded terms that carry positive connotations in modern ears – heroism, boldness, creativity, mastery, autonomy, and others – and shows that they are really demanded by Judaism. Many people would consider these terms to be the very antithesis of Jewish religiosity, which they perceive as being conservative to the point of ossification, and submissive to the point of slavishness. What, then, is the Rav doing when he applies these epithets to halakhic life? One of two things: either

(a) informing us that these qualities, as we commonly understand them, are actually Jewish values; or

(b) reinterpreting them (sometimes subtly) and showing us that the new understanding is part of Judaism.

Clearly, we have here an instance of the latter. For the Rav, there is more heroism in humility than in majesty. If so, why does he use the term "heroic"? Again, there are two possibilities.

(1) This could be a pedagogical device geared to make halakhic life more attractive to modern man. The word "heroic" has positive associations for us, so we will be attracted to something described this way. Eventually, we will come to appreciate the values inherent in the new definition of heroism.

(2) He is uncovering a deeper or more authentic meaning of the term. At the core of the concept of heroism (or creativity, autonomy, etc.), there is a powerful idea which, over the generations, has been covered with layers of dross. If we remove some of our preconceived notions, if we perceive things within a frame of sanctity and service of God, then we will behold the positive root of the idea in its pristine purity. Or, perhaps, in another formulation: the idea itself is neutral and can be turned in better or worse directions, depending on the surrounding framework within which we see it.

I leave it to the reader to decide which possibility is most applicable here.

Another noteworthy aspect of Rav Soloveitchik's writing is his ability to reveal striking new meanings in familiar sources, often simply by placing them within a new frame of reference. For example, the Rav bases his thesis in this essay on rabbinic maxims such as, "The commandments were given to purify mankind" (Gen. Rabbah 44:1), and, "Who is a hero? He who conquers his desire" (*Avot* 4:1). But we had never really understood these aphorisms in quite this way before, and after reading the Rav's interpretation, it is hard to go back to our old way of understanding them.[5]

Retreat for the Sake of Advance?

Let us return briefly to a question raised in Chapter 3. Is the halakhic dialectic one of advance-retreat-advance, or one of advance ending in retreat? Once again, we find differing indications of the Rav's position. On page 43, he talks of a two-part dialectic, while on the very next page he discusses a three-stage dialectic. His statement that, "[M]an is called, following the movement of withdrawal, to advance once again, toward full victory" (46), stands in stark contrast to his statement in "Majesty and Humility" that, "defeat is built into the very structure of victory . . . there is, in fact, no total victory; man is finite, so is his victory" (36).

Although, overall, "Catharsis" does stress the importance of the third stage of resuming the forward march, it nevertheless ends on a note high-lighting retreat: "He showed thee, man, what is good, and what doth the Lord require of thee, but to move forward boldly, to triumph over and subdue thy environment, and to retreat humbly when victory is within thy grasp" (54). As I stressed previously, this duality in the Rav's approach does not reflect confusion but rather a dialectic within his concept of defeat.

Catharsis in Daily Life

Dividing our "total existential experience" into four realms (the aesthetic-hedonic, emotional, intellectual and religious), Rav Soloveitchik proceeds to show how the idea of catharsis applies to each. This next section of the essay is particularly fascinating not only because readers can directly apply it to their daily lives, but because the Rav provides powerful examples of catharsis in each realm. The themes developed here recur throughout the Rav's writings, testifying to their importance in his mind. Therefore, I will devote the next several chapters to the catharsis of these four realms, and to important issues raised by this discussion.

---

5 Yet another innovative aspect of the Rav's writing is the way he reshapes the reader's understanding of various *mitzvot* through his unforgettable descriptions of their emotional components. See Chaps. 6 and 8 for examples.

Chapter 5

"Catharsis" (2): Elevating Physical Existence

Pleasure and Holiness

The first area of human experience the Rav explores in the latter section of "Catharsis" is the aesthetic-hedonic realm, which encompasses one's physical drives and bodily pleasures.[1] Here the need for catharsis is clear and asserts itself more frequently than in any other realm. In this area, catharsis consists of withdrawal from an external temptation, or, stated differently, of restraining and channeling one's inner desire.

> The stronger the grip of the physiological drive is felt by man, the more intoxicating and bewildering the prospect of hedonic gratification, the greater the redemptive capacity of the dialectical catharsis – of the movement of recoil (45).

This is illustrated beautifully in a midrash quoted by the Rav:

> It often happens that a man takes a wife when he is thirty or forty years of age. When, after going to great expense, he wishes to associate with her, she says to him, "I have seen a rose-red speck [of menstrual blood]." He immediately recoils. What made him keep away from her? Was there an iron fence; did a serpent bite him; did a scorpion sting him? Only the words of the Torah, which are as soft as a bed of lilies . . .
> A dish of meat is placed before a man and he is told that some forbidden fat has fallen into it. He withdraws his hand from the food. What stopped him from tasting it? Did a serpent bite him; did a scorpion sting him? Only the words

---

1 Since the Rav's discussion in "Catharsis" is brief, the main source for our examination of this theme is *U-Vikkashtem mi-Sham*, 110–17. The Rav addresses this subject in a number of other works as well; see For Further Reference, #1.

of the Torah, which are as soft as a bed of lilies (Midrash Rabbah on Song of Songs 7:3).

The identification of *kedushah*, sanctity, with restraint of mankind's primal drives has a long history. For example, the Rambam (like the above midrash) groups together the laws of forbidden sexual unions and forbidden foods in his *Sefer Kedushah* (Book of Holiness).[2] What separates man from beast is that man controls his drives as opposed to having them control him. In this sense, the Torah's restrictions in these areas actually give him freedom; he is not a slave to his passions, but rather their master. I believe this is part of what is meant in the following celebrated maxim:

> Said Rabbi Yehoshua ben Levi . . . "And the writing was the writing of God engraved upon the tablets" (Ex. 32:16). Do not read "engraved" (*harut*), but rather "freedom" (*herut*), for no man is truly free except he who engages in the study of Torah (*Avot* 6:2).

Equating holiness with withdrawal from physical pleasure can lead to an ascetic approach that negates the value of man's physical existence, considering it a hindrance to his spiritual pursuits. Such a position, indeed, has been espoused by some Jewish thinkers (most prominently by the Rambam in his *Guide of the Perplexed*). Rav Soloveitchik, however, takes the opposite approach. The act of withdrawal purifies and redeems man's natural urges, endowing them with sanctity and allowing them to serve as a means for spiritual growth.

According to the Rav, God does not desire that man live an otherworldly ascetic existence, nor does He wish for man to adopt an ethereal and abstract spirituality. Rather, God wants man to lead a full and enjoyable natural life. However, man must instill it with meaning and direction, thus grounding his spirituality in his concrete physical life. For example, if unrestrained and unredeemed, the sexual act can be brutish and dehumanizing. Man succumbs to a frenzy of primitive passion and treats his sexual partner as an object, a mere means to fulfill his desire. However, within the framework of marriage (and at the permitted times), sexuality becomes something beautiful and sacred. Hedged in by prohibitions, it turns into an act conforming to God's will. Between husband and wife, it expresses love and commitment (which are also desired by God). Furthermore, it actually becomes a vehicle for fulfilling *mitzvot* such as procreation (*"peru u-revu"*) and the obligation of

---

2 Rav Soloveitchik groups a third drive with these two – the desire for acquisition, which similarly must be restrained and sanctified. See For Further Reference, #1.

conjugal relations (*onah*). Thus, one's physical life becomes the fountainhead of *kedushah*.[3]

The *Yetzer ha-Ra*

Although he does not state it explicitly, it seems that Rav Soloveitchik perceives the *yetzer ha-ra*, commonly translated as the "evil impulse," to be identical with man's natural biological drives. These in themselves are, of course, necessary for survival, but they can easily be turned to evil. If one gives in to them without recognizing any restraints or exercising any selectivity, they drag one down to, at best, a coarse and animalistic existence. At worst, in a relentless quest for gratification of one's ever-increasing desires, one can become criminal and depraved, almost satanic. On the other hand, if one exercises control over these natural urges, channeling them in the proper direction, they can be a force for good.

This approach is firmly rooted in talmudic sources. For example, an aggadic passage (*Yoma* 69b and *Sanhedrin* 64a) recounts that once the Sages managed to imprison the *yitzra de-aveirah* (impulse of sin). Three days later, however, they searched for a freshly-laid egg and could not find one in the entire Land of Israel. The Sages realized that if they would not free the *yitzra de-aveirah* at once, the world would be destroyed. This approach is also articulated in a midrash explaining why on the first five days of creation God beheld His works and "saw that they were good," while on the sixth day "God saw *everything* that He had created, and, behold, it was *very* good" (Gen. 1:31):

> "Very good" (*tov me'od*) – this refers to the *yetzer ha-ra* . . . for without it, one would not build a house, marry, or beget children (Eccl. Rabbah 3:3).[4]

The Mishnah (*Berakhot* 9:5) teaches that the commandment "to love the Lord your God with your *whole* heart (*be*-khol *levavkha*)" (Deut. 6:5) refers to "your two impulses: the good impulse and the evil impulse." It seems to me that the most plausible way to understand this teaching is along the lines suggested above, namely, that you must serve God through both your spiritual

---

3 The discussion of physical pleasure in "Catharsis" emphasizes only the aspect of withdrawal, but *U-Vikkashtem mi-Sham* fills out the Rav's position by adding that physical activity itself can become a source of sanctity.

4 A parallel midrash (Gen. Rabbah 9:7) derives this idea not from "*very* good" but from the "and" in "*and* behold, it was very good." This midrash also adds "engaging in business" to the list of activities one would not perform if not for the *yetzer ha-ra*.

and your physical impulses. The necessity of this approach and its attendant dangers are highlighted in the following aggadic passage:

> One's *yetzer* . . . should be pushed away with one's left hand and brought near with one's right (*Sotah* 47a, *Sanhedrin* 107b).

Sanctity and Morality in Eating

Rav Soloveitchik takes the Sages' approach a step further by stating that not only are man's natural urges necessary for his survival but, as mentioned above, they themselves can serve as a source of sanctity. In fact, the Halakhah insists that man's spirituality be based precisely on his physical existence and that it penetrate every aspect of that existence. Large portions of *Halakhic Man* and *U-Vikkashtem mi-Sham* polemicize against the type of spirituality that ignores or denies man's natural life.[5] Halakhic religiosity is focused on this world. As opposed to those who pine for the purity of the World-to-Come, the Halakhah abhors death, assigning anything connected with it to the realm of impurity.[6]

As the Rav points out in *Halakhic Man* (51), Halakhah is a realistic doctrine that takes literally the statement, "God saw all that He had created, and behold, it was very good." It affirms the value and dignity of man's physical existence by giving it direction and meaning. What Halakhah opposes is boundlessness and undirectedness, the darkness of untrammeled bestial drives, but not physicality per se. To the contrary, man must serve God with all the powers at his disposal, starting with his body.

This is why, for example, so many *mitzvot* revolve around the meal:

> The animalistic behavior of eating, upon which man's life depends, has been refined by the Halakhah and transformed into a religious ritual and an elevated moral act (*U-Vikkashtem mi-Sham*, 112).

> Eating is an act that realizes the idea of holiness, whose meaning is the sanctification of both body and soul. If man eats properly, in accordance with the requirements of the Halakhah, then he is eating before God, serving Him with this "despised" function, and cleaving to Him (ibid., 114).

Not only are there restrictions on what we may eat (*kashrut*), and not only are we obligated to pronounce blessings before and after eating, but many of

---

5 Regarding *Halakhic Man*, see Chap. 28, pp. 304–06 below; regarding *U-Vikkashtem mi-Sham*, see Chap. 33, pp. 357–58 below.

6 *Halakhic Man*, 31–37. See also the discussion of mourning at the end of Chap. 24 below.

the most sublime *mitzvot* are fulfilled through the consumption of food – e.g., eating *kodashim* (sacred offerings), *matzah*, *kiddush*, rejoicing on festivals, etc. These are not mysterious symbolic rituals, like the Catholic communion, but real acts of eating which one enjoys and which satisfy one's hunger. In fact, if one eats in a manner which is not pleasing, such as if one is already full and is now merely stuffing oneself (*akhilah gassah*), it is questionable whether one has fulfilled these *mitzvot*.

Furthermore, as the Rav points out, the Halakhah turns eating into "an elevated moral act." First, it is forbidden to eat stolen food, and any *mitzvah* utilizing it is disqualified. Second, one must invite the needy and unfortunate to participate in all halakhic feasts one may celebrate (e.g., eating *kodashim*, the Seder, a *se'udat mitzvah*, etc.). As the Rambam so memorably puts it:

> When a person eats and drinks [in celebration of a holiday], he must feed the stranger, orphan, widow, and other unfortunates who are destitute. In contrast, one who locks the gates of his courtyard and eats and drinks with his children and his wife, without feeding the poor and the embittered, is not engaging in the rejoicing of a *mitzvah* but rather in the rejoicing of his belly (*Hilkhot Yom Tov* 6:18).

Inviting the poor is not extrinsic to the *mitzvah* of rejoicing but rather is part of its very fulfillment. This is not only an act of charity, but, more importantly, an expression of community, fellowship and concern. One's own enjoyment cannot be complete if others are alone and suffering.

Halakhah's Non-Dualistic Approach

Having noted that Halakhah purifies our aesthetic-hedonic experience, we must ask: What is the nature of our enjoyment? The Rav writes:

> The Halakhah enjoins man to take no less pleasure than the hedonist in the glory and splendor of the creation. The pleasure of halakhic man, however, is refined, measured, and purified . . . The Torah has never forbidden man the pleasures of this world, nor does it demand asceticism and self-torture. . . . [However,] Halakhah abhors the chaos in pleasure. . . . The Halakhah enjoins man from the hysteria of desire and madness. The sort of pleasure that the Halakhah recommends avoids excessive intensity, stimulation of the nerves, and intoxication of the senses. Instead, it has the beauty of the refinement and splendor of life's aesthetic elements. When man takes pleasure in the world in accordance with the view of the Halakhah, his pleasure is modest and delicate, an enjoyment which avoids the mania of sexual desire and the frenzy of gluttony (*U-Vikkashtem mi-Sham*, 111–12).

Halakhah's belief that physical life can be sanctified stands, the Rav writes, in stark contrast to the dualistic approach of Western (i.e., Greek and Christian) thought. The latter "morally and metaphysically despairs of the natural element within man and devotes itself entirely to the spiritual and the rational" (*U-Vikkashtem mi-Sham*, 110). It creates an unbridgeable gap between the physical and the spiritual. While the Torah declares, "And you shall eat in the presence of the Lord your God, in the place where He will choose to establish His Name, the tithes of your new grain and wine and oil, and the firstlings of your herds and flocks, so that you may learn to revere the Lord your God always" (Deut. 14:23), Greek thought would not be able to fathom such a command:

> The beast eats; man thinks and cognizes the spiritual, the general, and the ideal. The intellect comes close to God, but the stomach does not. "You shall eat in the presence of the Lord" – can there be two more extreme opposites than these? But it is nevertheless so! (*U-Vikkashtem mi-Sham*, 112).

In Judaism, the Rav teaches, all spirituality is based on the real, the concrete, the physical. Anything holy must have a defined time and place.[7] In response to those who mock Halakhah's "excessive" attention to physical life, the Rav proudly and unabashedly declares:

> Yes, indeed, the Halakhah is a doctrine of the body; but there lies its greatness. By sanctifying the body it creates one whole unit of psychosomatic[8] man who worships God with his spirit and his body and elevates the beast [in him] to the eternal heavens (*U-Vikkashtem mi-Sham*, 117).

---

7 See his essay "Sacred and Profane."
8 *Psyche* = spirit, *soma* = body.

F OR F URTHER R EFERENCE

1. **Redeeming physical drives:** In various places, the Rav discusses three basic human biological drives that must be redeemed: sexuality, eating, and acquisition. As noted above, *U-Vikkashtem mi-Sham* discusses the first two at length. Very rich discussions of these themes can also be found in the following sources:
   (a) Sexuality – "The Redemption of Sexual Life," *Family Redeemed*, 73–104, and "The Tree of Knowledge and the Emergence of Sin," *The Emergence of Ethical Man*, 95–128;
   (b) Eating – "An Exalted Evening: The Seder Night," *Festival of Freedom*, 1–34;
   (c) Acquisition – "Pesah and the *Omer*," *Festival of Freedom*, 160–72, and "An Exalted Evening," 7–12.
   The more general issue of the sanctification of physical life is a major theme throughout *Halakhic Man*, *U-Vikkashtem mi-Sham*, and *The Lonely Man of Faith*.

2. **Jewish approaches to asceticism and pleasure:** See Moshe Z. Sokol, "Attitudes toward Pleasure in Jewish Thought: A Typological Proposal," in *Reverence, Righteousness and Rahmanut: Essays in Memory of Rabbi Dr. Leo Jung*, ed. R. Jacob J. Schacter (Northvale, NJ, 1992), 293–314.

3. **Natural Man and Spiritual Man:** This theme arises in many of Rav Soloveitchik's writings; see especially "Confrontation" and *The Emergence of Ethical Man*. While the former work has been analyzed in depth and from a variety of perspectives (see Chapter 18, For Further Reference, #2), the latter deserves further study; in the meantime, see the helpful introduction by the volume's editor, Michael Berger, and the review by Daniel Rynhold in *Religious Studies* 42:3 (2006), 364–68.

4. **Jewish vs. Greek view of eating:** In *U-Vikkashtem mi-Sham*, 113–14, the Rav contrasts the Jewish *se'udah* with the Greek *symposium*. See also *Festival of Freedom*, 4–7.

Chapter 6

"Catharsis" (3): Purifying the Emotions

After discussing the need for purifying the physical realm of man's existence, and the method of accomplishing this, the Rav moves next in his essay "Catharsis" to consider the purification of the emotional realm. While catharsis of the former requires that man refrain from certain acts, catharsis of the latter demands that he change his innermost feelings. As the Gemara tells us (*Sanhedrin* 106b), "God desires the heart."

> [T]he Halakhah thinks there is an ethic, not only of action, but of feeling, as well. Man is master over his own emotional world, capable of disowning feelings or emotions, however compulsive or powerful, if they seem to be disruptive; and, conversely, of assimilating redemptive emotion into his personality (47).

In other words, because our feelings are such an important part of us, and because they affect us so deeply, it is crucial that we exert control over them, that we shape and direct them in a positive fashion, and that we integrate them into our service of God. In fact, as we shall see in this chapter and in Chapter 8, the Rav believes that a person's main arena of religious struggle lies precisely within the internal-emotional realm.

Commanding Emotions

Although the assumption that one can be master over one's emotional world may seem foreign to the modern mind, it lies at the basis of many *halakhot*. While many *mitzvot* regulate a person's actions, e.g., the commandment to eat *matzah* or the prohibition of theft, some *mitzvot* seem to address themselves directly to a person's emotions, e.g., "You shall love the Lord your God"

(Deut. 6:5), "You shall not hate your brother in your heart" (Lev. 19:17), and "You shall not desire your neighbor's house . . ." (Deut. 5:18).[1] This corresponds to the famous distinction first posited by Rabbenu Bahya ben Yosef ibn Pakuda between *hovot ha-evarim* and *hovot ha-levavot*, duties of the limbs and duties of the heart.

The obvious question presents itself: how can a person be expected to control his feelings? Can he help it, for example, if he is jealous of someone wealthier than he is? Strikingly, only a few of our sages actually ask this question. Most seem to take it for granted that since one's emotions are a matter of halakhic concern, it is clear that one can and should be able to exert control over them.

One of the few *Rishonim* to deal with the question, the twelfth-century Bible commentator R. Avraham ibn Ezra, suggests that one can control one's emotions through an intellectual effort, i.e., through internalizing the laws of Halakhah. He writes:

> I will offer you a parable. Know that a peasant of sound mind who beholds a beautiful princess will not desire in his heart to lie with her, for this cannot be.[2] . . . Similarly, a wise person knows that all wealth . . . comes from God; therefore, he will not desire that which God has not given him. Additionally, since he knows that it is God who has forbidden his neighbor's wife to him, she will be even more exalted in his eyes than the princess in the eyes of the peasant (commentary to Ex. 20:13).

The unstated opinion of most *Rishonim*, however, is presented forcefully by the late-thirteenth-century halakhic-ethical work, *Sefer ha-Hinukh*:

> Do not wonder and ask: But how can it be in one's power to restrain his heart from longing for riches that he may see in his fellow man's possession, when he himself is lacking them all? How can a prohibition be given in the Torah about something which man cannot possibly obey?
> This matter is not so; none but wicked fools . . . would speak so. For it is indeed in one's power to restrain himself, his thoughts and his longings, from whatever he wishes. It lies within his free choice and his decision to repel his desire or draw it near, with regard to all matters, as he wishes; and his heart is given over into his control; however he pleases, he may turn it . . . There is

---

1 Note that I quoted the verse "You shall not desire" (*lo titaveh*), and not the verse "You shall not covet" (*lo tahmod*; Ex. 20:14 and Deut. 5:18), as an example of a *mitzvah* pertaining *solely* to the emotions. Many *Rishonim* interpret the latter prohibition as entailing some sort of action, while the former is only a feeling (e.g., Rambam, *Hilkhot Gezelah* 1:9–12).

2 Recall that he is writing in the context of a feudal society.

nothing so good for a man as a good, pure thought, since that is the beginning of all good deeds and their end. And this, as it seems, is the significance of the "good heart" which the Sages praise in *Avot* (2:9) (*Mitzvah* #416 in most editions; #424 in R. Chavel's edition).

As opposed to Ibn Ezra's theory of intellectual conviction, the *Hinukh* seems to think that controlling emotion is a matter of sheer willpower and force of habit.[3] Rav Soloveitchik, I think, would agree with both approaches. Like Ibn Ezra, he believes that emotions can be controlled and guided by human reason. He even offers criteria for evaluating the worthiness of emotions, based on which one can decide which emotions to accept or reject in various circumstances.[4] Like the *Hinukh*, who believes in the power of the will and in the potency of actions in influencing the will, Rav Soloveitchik advocates harnessing action and will (along with intellect) to foster identification with Halakhah.[5] Like both, he strenuously rejects the notion that Halakhah can mandate only action but not emotion. In fact, one of the Rav's most celebrated halakhic *hiddushim* revolves around the emotional component of *mitzvot*.

Action and Fulfillment

While the division of *mitzvot* into "duties of the limbs" and "duties of the heart" was well-known, the Rav identified a third hybrid category of *mitzvot*, defined it in strict halakhic terms, and devoted much attention to it. In this category, although the Halakhah demands the performance of a certain external action, the *mitzvah* actually is fulfilled through an internal experience. In "*lomdish*" parlance, the Rav termed this the duality of *ma'aseh* (act) and *kiyyum* (fulfillment or realization).

Often, *ma'aseh* and *kiyyum* go together: for example, one fulfills the *mitzvah* of eating *matzah* simply by ingesting it, regardless of one's inner

---

3 The Rav's great-grandfather, the *Beit Halevi*, offers an interesting variation on the *Hinukh*'s approach. In his Torah commentary (on the verse "You shall not covet" in *Parashat Yitro*, 48–50 in the Warsaw 1884 edition), he judges Ibn Ezra's explanation to be "pleasant but unnecessary." The *Beit Halevi* conjures the image of a person, inflamed by a sinful passion, hurrying across a frozen river on his way to an illicit rendezvous. If this person slips on the ice, the fright engendered by his fall will wipe away his sinful desire in a single moment. So, too, continues the *Beit Halevi*, a little bit of fear of God can extinguish covetousness and other sinful thoughts. It is unclear, however, how he would account for the Torah's commandments to experience certain positive emotions, instead of extinguishing negative ones.

4 See For Further Reference, #1.

5 See further discussion in Chaps. 8, 10, and esp. 35 below.

awareness of the liberation from Egypt.[6] However, the Rav focuses our attention on cases where the *ma'aseh* and the *kiyyum* exist on two different planes (both, however, necessary for the proper fulfillment of the *mitzvah*). For example, the *mitzvah* of prayer consists of reciting certain words (*ma'aseh*), but its essence (*kiyyum*) is "the service of the heart," the experience of standing before God and the feelings of gratitude and dependence. It is interesting that, in "Catharsis," the Rav draws his examples of purging the emotional realm from this category of *mitzvot*.[7]

Mourning and Joy

The Rav's first illustration of emotional catharsis is God's command to Aaron not to mourn the deaths of his two sons. On the day on which the *Mishkan* (Tabernacle) was to have been dedicated, the greatest day of Aaron's life, his sons Nadab and Abihu were suddenly struck down by a divine fire. Since Aaron, the high priest, was wholly consecrated to divine service, he had to continue fulfilling his duties despite his personal tragedy. Aaron was not permitted the basic human right to mourn; he had to deny one of man's most powerful emotions, the love for a child.[8]

Of course, God does not demand total commitment only from the high priest, but from the entire "nation of priests" (i.e., the Jewish People) as well. As an example, the Rav cites a common situation which is actually very similar to the predicament in which Aaron found himself. When major holidays fall during one's *shivah* mourning period, they cancel the mourning. This does not entail merely a change of clothes or other superficial differences; it somehow demands of the mourner that he forsake grief in favor of joy. Neither the

---

6 To be precise, the Rav develops a theory that there are two different fulfillments associated with the eating of *matzah*, one of which does not entail an awareness of the Exodus and one of which does. See For Further Reference, #2.

7 See the appendix to this chapter for a list of *mitzvot* that fall into this category, and Chap. 8 for further discussion of this important group of commandments.

8 Note that while Aaron's sense of mission as a representative of the people overcame his personal sorrow, the People of Israel performed the opposite gesture. They overcame their feelings of communal joy at the dedication of the *Mishkan* and mourned for the tragedy of the individual. "And Moses spoke to Aaron and to his sons Eleazar and Ithamar, saying: 'Do not bare your heads and do not rend your clothes . . . But your kinsmen, the entire House of Israel, shall bewail the burning that the Lord has wrought'" (Lev. 10:6; see Ramban and Hizkuni, *ad loc.*). In other words, the individual must sometimes overcome his personal interests and instead dedicate himself to the community, while the community must feel the pain of each individual. The Rav, however, focuses here on the dedication of the individual to serving God, not the dedication of the individual to serving the community.

halakhic laws of mourning nor the command to "rejoice in your festivals . . .
and you shall have nothing but joy" (Deut. 16:14–15) refer solely to actions.
As the Rav puts it:

> [Mourning] is an inner experience of black despair, of complete existential
> failure, of the absurdity of being . . . Similarly, the precept of rejoicing on
> a holiday . . . [refers] to an all-penetrating depth-experience of spiritual joy,
> serenity and peace of mind deriving from faith and the awareness of God's
> presence (48–49).[9]

If mourning (*avelut*) and holiday rejoicing (*simhat yom tov*) were merely
external observances, or if one were internal and one external, then perhaps
we could have found some way for them to coexist. But since they are both
primarily internal fulfillments, one must prevail over the other since the emotions of despair and joy are mutually exclusive.

In his halakhic discourses, the Rav develops at length this theory of the
internal *kiyyum* of both *avelut* and *simhat yom tov*. These are contrasted to the
rabbinic *mitzvah* of honoring and enjoying Shabbat (*kibbud ve-oneg*), whose
content is exhausted by external actions. Because the *mitzvah* of *kibbud ve-
oneg* does not mandate an internal *kiyyum*, Shabbat does not cancel *avelut*.[10]
On Shabbat one does not manifest mourning publicly but nevertheless continues certain practices of mourning in private.

Discipline and Feeling

Rav Soloveitchik is aware that catharsis of the emotions is very demanding,
and he does not hide this fact. Facing the situation realistically, he displays
uncharacteristic hesitance and diffidence in assessing the capacity of modern
man to attain emotional catharsis:

> Is it possible? As far as modern man is concerned I would dare not answer.
> But with respect to Biblical man we read that Aaron acted in accord with the
> divine instruction (48).
> Can one replace the experience of monstrosity (*avelut*) with the feeling of

---

9 I highly recommend that the reader examine the rest of the passage where the Rav so
beautifully describes these experiences. It is clear that one cannot write this way unless one has
personally experienced these feelings.

10 The Rav actually seems to contradict himself on this point. In *Shiurim le-Zekher Abba
Mari*, vol. 2, 191 (= *Out of the Whirlwind*, 72), he offers the explanation brought above.
However, in vol. 1, 64–68, he seems to say that there is indeed an internal *kiyyum* involved in
kibbud Shabbat, but it is not one that would preclude the internal *kiyyum* of *avelut*.

highest meaningfulness (*simhat yom tov*)? I have no right to judge. However, I know of people who attempted to perform this greatest of all miracles (49).[11]

In this realm, the Halakhah seems more intrusive than in any other. What can be more intimate and personal than one's feelings? Rav Soloveitchik himself admits that "The Halakhah, which at times can be very tender, understanding and accommodating, may, on other occasions, act like a disciplinarian demanding obedience" (49).

But it is important to remember that the Halakhah is not demanding that we quash all feeling. It wants us to feel, to experience the gamut of human emotions, the joys and sorrows of life. The Ramban states this strongly in the introduction to his masterpiece on *avelut*, *Torat ha-Adam*, where he polemicizes against those who adopt a stance of philosophic apathy towards the world. But, while we feel deeply, our emotions must be shaped and guided by Halakhah and must remain within our control. The Torah wants to purify our emotions and to redeem us by means of our emotions.

After exploring the last two forms of catharsis in Chapter 7, we will broaden our inquiry in Chapter 8 by examining the necessity of inwardness in all areas of religious life.

FOR FURTHER REFERENCE

1. **Halakhah and emotions:** The Rav's most detailed and profound treatment of the issue of Halakhah and emotion can be found in the last two essays in *Out of the Whirlwind*, "The Crisis of Human Finitude" and "A Theory of Emotions." See the discussion of these essays in Chapter 24 below. See also the Rav's comments at the end of "A Halakhic Approach to Suffering" (*Out of the Whirlwind*, 113–15) on the importance of catharsis for mental health.

2. **Two fulfillments in eating *matzah*:** The well-known *mishnah* (*Pesahim* 10:5), repeated in the *Haggadah*, reads: "Rabban Gamliel used to say: Whoever does not mention these three things [i.e., the paschal lamb, *matzah*, and bitter herbs] on Passover has not fulfilled his obligation."

---

11 Among the latter, the Rav may have had in mind his grandfather, Rav Eliyahu Feinstein of Pruzhan. Rav Soloveitchik writes in *Halakhic Man* (77–78) of his grandfather's presence of mind when, while his beloved daughter was about to die, he remembered to put on *tefillin* of Rabbenu Tam prior to becoming an *onen* (one whose relative has died but not yet been buried, who is exempt from performing *mitzvot*).

Most authorities (e.g., Rambam, *Hilkhot Hametz u-Matzah* 7:5) understand Rabban Gamliel to be referring to the obligation of *sippur yetziat Mitzrayim*, retelling the exodus; part of *sippur* is explaining the allegorical meaning of these three *mitzvot* (as we say in the *Haggadah*: "This *matzah* – why do we eat it? Because our ancestors' dough did not have time to become leavened before the King of kings ... appeared and redeemed them," etc.) However, Ramban (*Milhamot, Berakhot* ch. 1, p. 2b in the Rif) understands Rabban Gamliel as referring to these three *mitzvot* themselves; thus, one does not fulfill the *mitzvah* of *matzah* unless one explains its meaning.

Based on Ramban's insight, the Rav develops a theory that eating *matzah* involves two fulfillments. First, there is the *mitzvah* of "You shall eat *matzot* in the evening" (Ex. 12:18), which involves nothing more than the physical act of ingestion. Second, eating *matzah* is a fulfillment of *sippur* ("You shall tell your child on that day, saying: This is done because of what God did for me when I left Egypt," Ex. 13:8), for *sippur* entails both oral recounting and the performance of symbolic actions. This latter facet of the *mitzvah* of *matzah*, namely, as an expression of *sippur* via action, must be informed by an accompanying awareness of the Exodus.

See *Shiurim le-Zekher Abba Mari*, vol. 2, 161–63; *Festival of Freedom*, 55–58, 116–17; and the analysis by R. Daniel Wolf, "Digesting the Exodus Narrative: Rav Soloveitchik's Approach to the Seder Eve," *Tradition* 41:4 (Winter 2008), 87–98.

3. **Action and fulfillment in *mitzvot*:** While the Rav frequently discusses specific applications of this distinction (see the appendix to this chapter), he offers very evocative comments on the general issue of *ma'aseh* and *kiyyum* in *Worship of the Heart*, 13–19.

4. **Mourning and joy:** See R. Jacob J. Schacter's introduction to *Siddur Nehamat Yisrael: The Complete Service for the Period of Bereavement* (New York, 1995), xi–xiv.

Appendix to Chapter 6

Mitzvot which Require Action but whose Fulfillment is Experiential

(I) *Mitzvot* **where the experience is essential to the** *kiyyum*
1. **Repentance and Confession**: *On Repentance*, 77–81, 84–85.
2. **Prayer**: ibid., 81–84; *Worship of the Heart, passim*, especially 19–26.
3. **Fasting, Blowing Trumpets and Crying Out in Times of Distress**: *Shiurim le-Zekher Abba Mari*, vol. 1 (Jerusalem, 5743), 69–90, 191–99; *"Al ha-Tzar ha-Tzorer Etkhem"* and *"Ha-Evkeh ba-Hodesh ha-Hamishi,"* adapted by R. Yair Kahn, *Alon Shevut le-Bogrim* 9 (Sivan 5756), 131–42.
4. **Mourning**: See especially *Shiurim le-Zekher Abba Mari z"l*, vol. 2 (Jerusalem, 5745), 182–96 (English: *Out of the Whirlwind*, 49–85). Also: *"Peleitat Sofreihem,"* in *Divrei Hagut ve-Ha'arakhah*, 137–40 (English: *Shiurei Harav*, 46–48); *Out of the Whirlwind*, 1–30; *Shiurim le-Zekher*, vol. 1, 40–49; R. Eliakim Koenigsberg, *Shiurei ha-Rav al Inyanei Avelut u-Tishah be-Av* (Jerusalem, 1999), *passim*.
5. **Festival Rejoicing**: *Shiurim le-Zekher*, vol. 2, 188ff. (English: *Out of the Whirlwind*, 64ff.); ibid., vol. 1, 64–68; *U-Vikkashtem mi-Sham*, 193–98 (footnote 19).

(II) *Mitzvot* **where the experience is an aspect of the** *kiyyum*
6. **Reciting the *Shema***: *Shiurim le-Zekher*, vol. 1, 24–33; *Worship of the Heart*, 87–106.
7. **Shofar**: *Shiurim le-Zekher*, vol. 1, 191; B. David Schreiber, *Nora'ot Ha-Rav*, vol. 1 (New York, 1996); Arnold Lustiger, *Before Hashem You Shall Be Purified: Rabbi Joseph B. Soloveitchik*

on the Days of Awe (Edison, NJ, 1998), 18–29 = "*Be-Sod Siah ha-Shofar*," in *Yemei Zikkaron* (Jerusalem, 1996), 137–52.

8. ***Hallel***: *Shiurim le-Zekher*, vol. 2, 17–22.

9. **Honor and Fear of Parents**: *Family Redeemed*, 126–57.

10. **Retelling the Exodus**: *Shiurim le-Zekher*, vol. 2, 152–63; *Festival of Freedom*, 102–05.

11. **Taking the Four Species**: "*Be-Din Pesulei Etrog Kol Shivah*," in *Kovetz Hiddushei Torah*, 114–19; *U-Vikkashtem mi-Sham*, 193–94.

12. **Charity**: The Virtual Beit Midrash, "*Tzedaka*: Positive and Negative *Mitzvot*," based on a *shiur* by R. Aharon Lichtenstein, http://vbm-torah.org/archive/halak58/11tzeda2.doc.

13. **Torah Study**: *Shiurim le-Zekher*, vol. 2, 7–11.

14. **Torah Reading**: *Shiurim le-Zekher*, vol. 2, 207–13; *Out of the Whirlwind*, 14–15.

15. **Honoring and Enjoying the Sabbath**: *Shiurim le-Zekher*, vol. 1, 62–68.[12]

---

12 See n. 10 above.

Chapter 7

"Catharsis" (4): Intellectual and Religious Humility

Rav Soloveitchik discusses catharsis – the purification of man's personality and existence – with reference to four areas of human experience: the aesthetic-physical, the emotional, the intellectual, and the moral-religious. We examined the first two areas in Chapters 5 and 6, and in this chapter we will explore the last two. Subsequently, Chapters 8–10 will address important issues raised by our discussion of catharsis, namely, the interplay between emotion, intellect and action in Jewish religiosity.

Redeeming the Intellectual Experience

> Judaism has insisted upon the redeeming of the logos and maintained that there is an unredeemed cognitive gesture just as there is an unredeemed carnal drive ("Catharsis," 50).

The Rav does not mean by this that we should reject knowledge or withdraw from certain fields of inquiry. On the contrary, we must fearlessly seek the truth and must pursue this task in as precise a manner as possible. It is not knowledge that is potentially problematic, but rather our attitude towards it and the conclusions we draw from it. Therefore, the Rav continues, "Cognitive withdrawal is related, not to the scientific inquiry as a logical operation, but rather to the axiological experience of scientific work" (ibid.).

How, precisely, are we to understand the "axiological experience" of scientific inquiry, as well as its purification?

Here we encounter an important theme in the Rav's writing: the experience of knowing.[1] Clearly, this is a powerful feeling for Rav Soloveitchik:

---

1 See Chap. 9 regarding the experiential aspect of Torah study.

Knowing is not an impersonal performance which can be computerized, emptied of its rich, colorful, experiential content. It is, instead, an integral part of the knower as a living person, with all his complex emotional experiences and axiological judgments. Next to the religious experience, knowledge is perhaps the most vibrant and resonant personal experience. It sweeps the whole of the personality, sometimes like a gentle wave infusing the knower with a sense of tranquility and serenity; at other times like a mighty onrushing tide, arousing the soul to its depth and raising it to a pitch of ecstasy (ibid.).

The experience of knowledge is based upon, and intertwined with, value judgments regarding the significance of that knowledge. In our context, this means that the value one assigns to scientific inquiry will affect how one experiences it; and a distorted "axiology" (= value assessment) will lead to a distorted experience. Thus, it is precisely "the axiological experience of scientific work" – namely, the attitude arising out of one's evaluation of the meaning and significance of scientific activity – that may require purification. If man feels that he can master everything through his intellect, then his cognitive gesture is arrogant and unredeemed. Although his information may be accurate, his experience of knowledge is defective, misleading and even damaging.

The scientific experience can attain catharsis only through a proper assessment of what science can and cannot explain. This entails, first, recognition of the ultimate mystery of being. This recognition has two expressions. To begin with, the scientist must acknowledge that every problem he solves engenders a more complex and more encompassing problem than the first. This situation, while true of all scientific systems, takes on added significance in light of the indeterminacy principle, chaos theory, etc.[2]

Furthermore, once a certain phenomenon has been assigned a scientific explanation, this does not imply that there is nothing more to be said about it. According to a theory of science subscribed to by the Rav, modern science merely creates an abstract mathematical world which parallels the functioning of nature. This quantitative correlate is useful as far as technology is concerned, but it operates on a wholly different plane than the qualitative world experienced by us. We experience not a world of abstract quantities, but rather one of living qualities, of impressions and sensations. An equation describing the flight of a bird or the wavelength of a red flower cannot elucidate the great

---

2 While in the University of Berlin, Rav Soloveitchik studied physics and mathematics (in addition to philosophy) and was well-versed in early quantum theory, as is evident to anyone who reads *The Halakhic Mind*. Throughout his life he tried to keep abreast of developments in physics.

mystery of qualitative being in which we live our lives and to which we react with awe and wonder.[3]

For the scientist, awareness of the qualitative dimension of existence, and of his inability to account for it, introduces humility into his intellectual endeavor; and for everyone else, the qualitative awareness is no less important. Elsewhere, the Rav writes that it is through the qualitative dimension that we experience divinity within the world.[4] This immediate experience of God not only evokes the Jew's blessings over natural phenomena,[5] but, more broadly, it also inspires and enables praise of God within prayer.[6]

In order to attain catharsis of the intellect, the scientist (or the philosopher) must admit not only the ultimate mystery of being, but also that "the moral law can never be legislated in ultimate terms by the human mind" (52). We have already encountered this theme in "Majesty and Humility." Modern man, in his unredeemed majesty, is engaged in such an attempt, "which demonstrates pride and arrogance, and is doomed to failure" (ibid.). Although the Rav probably had in mind Marxism and similar pseudo-scientific systems of ethics, his stricture applies equally to any system which intends to supplant (rather than elaborate) the divine law.

Thus, the quest for knowledge in general must be marked by both daring advance and humble submission.[7] By acknowledging his limitations, man introduces a measure of humility into his intellectual experience and thereby redeems it.

---

3 In Chap. 28 we shall see that the Rav invokes this theory of science to describe the activity of the halakhist.

4 See chap. 2 of *U-Vikkashtem mi-Sham* and the discussion in Chap. 32, pp. 349–50 below. See also the brief but suggestive comments in *U-Vikkashtem mi-Sham*, 126–27, discussed in Chap. 35, pp. 379–81 below.

5 *U-Vikkashtem mi-Sham*, 19–22.

6 This is discussed in chap. 4 of *Worship of the Heart*. See For Further Reference, #2, in Chap. 20 below.

7 Intellectual boldness and humility are important regarding not only science, but also Torah study. Boldness comes to expression in *hiddushei Torah*, novel interpretations, while humility receives expression in acceptance of *hukkim*, commandments whose rationale we cannot comprehend. See, for example, "*Be-Inyan Seder ha-Parashiyot shel Rabbenu Tam*," in *Shiurei ha-Grid al Inyanei Tefillin, Ketivat Stam, ve-Tzitzit*, ed. R. Yair Kahn (Jerusalem, 2004), 219–23. Humility is also necessary in accepting the "autonomy of faith," as we shall see in Chaps. 16–18.

Multiple Demands

Before moving to the final form of catharsis, it is important to note a common feature of the previous three types of catharsis (those of the aesthetic, emotional, and intellectual realms). Since Rav Soloveitchik's discussion focuses on the need for retreat, it is easy to overlook the fact that the divine demand for withdrawal appears against the background of a divine mandate to advance. The latter is no less novel than the former.

Judaism does not discourage involvement in the "real" world, but, instead, promotes bodily existence, emotional engagement, intellectual endeavor, etc. The Halakhah is not otherworldly, apathetic, or obscurantist; rather, it demands that one employ all the powers at one's disposal within an overall framework of *avodat Hashem* (service of God), and this is expressed both in advance and in retreat. God wants man to be fully human, not angelic; but in order to attain his human potential, to realize his destiny, he must live his life as a servant of God. With this awareness, his worldly involvement will avoid becoming self-serving and egocentric. One's "advance," and not just his "retreat," will thereby be an expression of one's devotion to God.

Dialectic, complexity, plurality of demands – these are the fundamental difficulties in studying and teaching the Rav; but they also represent his greatness. People are often looking for simple, monochromatic answers to the great questions of life. In his unflinching honesty, the Rav does not, and cannot, provide these, for he does not believe they exist. In his eyes, man contains conflicting tendencies, God sets forth multiple demands, and the world must be perceived under differing aspects.

The complexity of Rav Soloveitchik's views leads to differing emphases in his various writings and addresses.[8] To an audience at the Massachusetts Institute of Technology (where "Catharsis" was originally delivered as a lecture), the Rav emphasized the importance of retreat and the heroism of withdrawal; to a more insular and traditionalist audience, he would have stressed the religious requirement of engagement in the cultural and technological arenas. Therefore, the need for a balanced reading of the Rav's writings is paramount. Problems arise when people undertake the opposite process: through a selective reading of the Rav, they pick out those themes congenial to them, and ignore the rest. Although such selective readings frequently result from someone's personal or communal agenda, they can also be innocent

---

8 When discussing differing emphases in the Rav's writings, the biographical factor should not be discounted (as we shall discuss on pp. 410–11), but in my opinion it also should not be overemphasized.

and unintentional. Part of the Rav's greatness is that he touches a chord in the hearts of many readers. However, while grasping an insight which resonates deep within us, we must not allow it to blind us to other, possibly opposed, strains in the Rav's oeuvre.

Redeemed Religiosity: The Ultimate Catharsis

In our day, the religious Jewish community concentrates most of its energies simply on the struggle to maintain observance. But by focusing mainly on the *quantity* of observance (the largest number of people keeping the largest number of *mitzvot*), we lose sight of the *quality* of observance. The Rav focuses attention on a crucial dimension of religious life: the need for humility, especially concerning the religious gesture.

> There is an unredeemed moral and religious experience, just as there is an unredeemed body and an unredeemed logos. Let us be candid: if one has not redeemed his religious life, he may become self-righteous, insensitive, or even destructive. The story of the Crusades, the Inquisition and other outbursts of religious fanaticism bear out this thesis (52).

Of course, there are less dramatic expressions of unredeemed religiosity than the Crusades. In our own lives, the Rav says, we must cultivate a sense of our own imperfection in order to avoid the pitfalls of religious arrogance.

> Perfect man has never been created. If a man is not conscious of the contradiction inherent in the very core of his personality, he lives in a world of illusion and leads an unredeemed existence. It matters not what we call such a complacent state of mind – self-righteousness, pride, haughtiness, stupidity – it is all a manifestation of a brutish and raw state of mind (54).

Because of man's limitations and weaknesses, his religious life takes a zigzag course, marked by ascent and descent, closeness to God and distance from Him.[9] Anyone who imagines that he experiences no falls is only fooling himself and impeding his personal development. (He will also quite often be insufferable to others and even dangerous due to his false certainties.) In fact, the descent frequently enables one to ascend even higher than before. In our context, this cathartic descent is identical with an awareness of sin and of God's distance. Thus, in a striking turn, the Rav identifies *teshuvah* (repen-

---

9 This forward-backward movement, which is so central to religious life, is the theme of what is perhaps the Rav's most significant philosophical work, *U-Vikkashtem mi-Sham.*

tance) as the true cathartic *experience*, and *viddui* (confession of sins to God) as the ultimate cathartic *act*.

We can say that, for the Rav, everyone should be a *ba'al teshuvah* (penitent). "Great is not the man who has never faltered but the man who tripped, fell and rose again to greater heights" (54).[10] The Rav explains the dynamics of this process in his *teshuvah* discourses.[11] One type of *teshuvah* is attained by a person erasing his sinful past and returning to his starting point. However, an even greater form of *teshuvah* can be attained by utilizing the negative energy of the past and converting it to a positive direction (as the Rav puts it, "changing the vectorial force of sin, its direction and destination").

The power of the latter form of *teshuvah* is based upon two factors:

(1) *The dynamism of sin*: Because of the powerful drives which lead one to sin, a person may discover while sinning that he possesses reserves of energy and stubbornness previously unknown to him. In the process of *teshuvah*, this new-found energy can be used to propel him to even greater heights than before.

(2) *The intensity of longing*: When a person realizes how low sin has led him to sink, it awakens in him a painful longing for a past state of relative wholeness and closeness to God. While experiencing God's nearness and a sense of personal wholeness, a person can become complacent and cease to aspire to further ascent. However, when one loses this sense, when one feels distant, forlorn and tarnished, one begins to appreciate the value of what one has lost.[12] This sense of contrast can become a springboard for spiritual ascent, thereby turning a sin into a powerful source of religious growth.

In an early memorial lecture for his father (1945, later printed as "Sacred and Profane"), Rav Soloveitchik connected these two forms of *teshuvah* to the ideas of acquittal and purification (*kapparah* and *taharah*).[13] Acquittal means that, although God "owes" one a punishment for his sin, God is willing to erase the "debt" due to the sinner's sincere remorse. However, despite the fact that punishment no longer hangs over one's head, the spiritual pollution of sin has not been cleansed. This spiritual cleansing is attained by means

---

10 As we saw, the Rav believes that "the man who has never faltered" does not exist. Given the reality of sin, the great person is one who afterwards rises to greater heights.

11 See For Further Reference, #4.

12 In a similar vein, the Rav would often say in eulogies that we can appreciate what a person meant to us only when he is no longer present.

13 The Rav had already developed the distinction between *kapparah* and *taharah* (expressed with different terminology) in a letter he wrote in 1929; see *Iggerot ha-Grid ha-Levi*, 23–25. It is also central to his discussion of *teshuvah* in *Halakhic Man*, 110–17.

of purification, which is not a supernatural process of forgiveness but rather a psychological remaking of one's personality. It entails not just regretting a sin, but leaving the entire "path of sin"; it necessitates soul-searching and redirection of energies. Acquittal parallels the *teshuvah* of erasing sin; purification parallels the *teshuvah* of elevating sin.[14]

The idea of the repentance of purification (*taharah*) brings us full circle, for what is catharsis if not purification? One offers up to God one's mundane existence, one's daily activities and self-awareness, and then receives these back in a purified and sanctified form. In the religious realm, a person's awareness of his own fallibility cleanses him of self-righteous intolerance; moreover, his recognition of his own sinfulness and distance from God brings him rushing back into God's arms. By performing an accurate and exacting self-assessment, he allows himself to grow in new directions. Although in other realms the Rav talks about how defeat is built into the structure of victory (since there is no full victory for finite man), in the religious realm we can say that victory is built into the structure of defeat. The recognition of defeat, of one's sinfulness, is itself a victory that brings one closer to God.

In truth, the statement that defeat is built into the structure of victory requires modification. The idea that the servant of God can never completely attain his own desires, that total commitment to God necessarily entails defeat of one's personal wishes, is true only at lower levels of the religious consciousness. At the very highest level, however, man overcomes the dichotomy between externally-imposed divine law and human freedom and creativity – an idea we shall explore in *U-Vikkashtem mi-Sham*.[15]

---

14 In later discourses, included in *On Repentance*, the Rav expanded upon these two sets of ideas and treated them separately. The key to linking them is found in the earlier essay. I urge readers to see these penetrating and inspiring *teshuvah* discourses in full, as I cannot possibly do justice to them in a few paragraphs.

15 See Chaps. 34–35 below.

FOR FURTHER REFERENCE

1. **The role of the intellect:** See *U-Vikkashtem mi-Sham*, 107–10 and 119–21, and the discussion in Chapter 35 below.

2. **Ethics in the Rav's thought:** R. Shalom Carmy, "Pluralism and the Category of the Ethical," *Tradition* 30:4 (Summer 1996), 145–63, reprinted in *Exploring the Thought of Rabbi Joseph B. Soloveitchik*, ed. R. Marc Angel (Hoboken, 1997), 325–46; R. Walter Wurzburger, "The Maimonidean Matrix of Rabbi Joseph Soloveitchik's Two-Tiered Ethics," in *Through the Sound of Many Voices*, ed. J. Plaut (Toronto, 1982), 172–83, reprinted in his *Covenantal Imperatives* (Jerusalem, 2008), 161–71.

3. **The danger of unredeemed religiosity:** See also "Sacred and Profane," in *Shiurei Harav*, especially 8.

4. **Using sin in the process of *teshuvah*:** *On Repentance* (essays entitled "Acquittal and Purification" and "Blotting Out Sin or Elevating It"); "Sacred and Profane," especially 25–31. See also Chapter 22 below.

5. **Religious tolerance:** This is a recurring theme in the writings of the Netziv, R. Naftali Zvi Yehudah Berlin, *rosh yeshivah* of Volozhin. See the introduction to the Book of Genesis at the beginning of his Torah commentary *Ha'amek Davar*, and the essay "On Right and Left" in his responsa *Meshiv Davar* I:44. For broad treatments of this subject, see Rav Aharon Lichtenstein, "The Parameters of Tolerance," in *Leaves of Faith*, vol. 2 (Jersey City, 2004), 85–116, and Aviezer Ravitzky, "The Question of Tolerance in the Jewish Religious Tradition," in *Hazon Nahum: Studies Presented to Dr. Norman Lamm*, eds. Yaakov Elman and Jeffrey Gurock (New York, 1997), 359–91.

Chapter 8

The Experiential Dimension of Judaism

The Importance of Inwardness

In Rav Soloveitchik's view, the inner, experiential realm is no less important in religious life than the domain of action, and it is perhaps the arena of one's greatest struggles. This explains the Rav's intensive focus on *mitzvot* such as prayer and repentance. It also accounts for the deeply passionate and personal tone of his writings. Even regarding Torah study, which would seem to be a purely intellectual pursuit, Rav Soloveitchik invariably emphasizes the experiential element.[1] When we recall that the Rav was a paragon of the abstract and highly intellectual Brisker approach to Torah study, his emphasis on the *experience* of "learning" becomes even more striking.

The reason for the Rav's emphasis on inwardness in religious life is twofold: it is central to Judaism, and it is so lacking in modern man. Rav Soloveitchik highlights this problem especially in his *derashot*. For example, in one of his discourses on repentance, he laments the disappearance of the "*Erev Shabbos* Jew" in America:

> Even in those neighborhoods made up predominantly of religious Jews, one can no longer talk of the "sanctity of Shabbat." True, there are Jews in America who observe Shabbat . . . But it is not for Shabbat that my heart aches; it is for the forgotten "*erev Shabbat*" (eve of the Sabbath). There are Shabbat-observing Jews in America, but there are no "*erev Shabbat*" Jews who go out to greet Shabbat with beating hearts and pulsating souls. There are many who observe the precepts with their hands, with their feet, and/or with their mouths

---

1 There are many facets to the experience of *talmud Torah*, as we shall explore in Chap. 9.

– but there are few indeed who truly know the meaning of the service of the heart! (*On Repentance*, 97–98).[2]

The emotional poverty of the religious life of most contemporary Jews greatly disturbed Rav Soloveitchik. Although he had no easy solutions to this fundamental problem, he did offer some speculations as to its cause:

> Much of this is due to the current religious atmosphere, suffused with shallow pragmatism; much is caused by the tendency towards the ceremonialization – and, at times, the vulgarization – of religion; and much is brought about by the lack of a serious ability to introspect and to assess the world and the spirit (*"Al Ahavat ha-Torah u-Ge'ulat Nefesh ha-Dor,"* 419).

The problem, according to the Rav, is not confined to those uneducated in Torah or to those whose religious commitment is weak. It affects even the young generation of *talmidei hakhamim* (Torah scholars), and its consequences are dire. Although they know the Torah intellectually, they have not experienced it by means of "living tangible sensation which causes the heart to tremble and to rejoice" (ibid., 408).

In a resonant kabbalistic metaphor to which he returns in later writings,[3] Rav Soloveitchik describes this as the dialectic of *"gadlut ha-mohin"* and *"katnut ha-mohin"* (lit., "greatness of mind" and "smallness of mind"). Rav Lichtenstein has paraphrased the former as "the depth and force of a powerful mind mastering its environment and impacting upon it," and the latter as "the simplicity of the child . . . the archetype of a helpless humble spirit groping towards his Father and finding solace in Him and through Him."[4] Although *"gadlut ha-mohin"* is the necessary starting point for a scholar, those who lack the child's "naive curiosity, natural enthusiasm, eagerness and spiritual restlessness," as well as the child's sense of dependence and unlimited trust, cannot truly pray or have faith. In effect, they cannot approach God.

> The adult is too clever. Utility is his guiding light. The experience of God is not a businesslike affair. Only the child can breach the boundaries that segregate the finite from the infinite. Only the child with his simple faith and fiery enthusiasm can make the miraculous leap into the bosom of God . . . The

---

2 Note, however, that religious experience is important and desirable when it is bound to and derives from religious observance (here, the arrival of the Sabbath), not when it is an amorphous and independent entity. We shall address this in Chaps. 9 and 10.

3 See For Further Reference, #1.

4 "The Rav at Jubilee: An Appreciation," *Tradition* 30:4 (Summer 1996), 50; reprinted in Rav Lichtenstein's *Leaves of Faith: The World of Jewish Learning* (Jersey City, 2003), 196.

giants of Torah – when it came to faith, became little children, with all their in-genuousness, gracefulness, simplicity, their tremors of fear, the vivid sense of experience to which they are devoted ("A Eulogy for R. Hayyim Heller," 63).

Returning to the young generation of *talmidei hakhamim* who are intel-lectually proficient but experientially lacking, the Rav writes that, aside from missing a fundamental dimension of Judaism, they are also generally unable to formulate a balanced and authentic approach to Torah:

> On the one hand, the young [*talmidei hakhamim*] of America occasionally tend to exaggerated extremism, which is frightening in its arrogance; frequent-ly, they move in the opposite direction and agree to concessions and the path of least resistance. In a word, they are perplexed in the pathways of Judaism, and this perplexity is the product of an imperfect grasp and experience of the world (*"Al Ahavat Ha-Torah,"* 408).[5]

The Halakhic Demand for Inwardness

Having posited the need for internal fulfillment of *mitzvot*, the Rav proceeds to fill his writings and discourses with memorable descriptions of those expe-riences.[6] However, aside from direct sermonizing and personal example, one of the Rav's main and most potent vehicles for promoting inwardness among his students was his halakhic scholarship. As we discussed in Chapter 6, he identified a category of *mitzvot* whose fulfillment (*kiyyum*) is internal but which require external action (*ma'aseh*) as well. It is evident from the sources listed in the appendix to Chapter 6 that the Rav devoted considerable atten-tion to this category of *mitzvot*, especially in his public lectures. To recall, some of the *mitzvot* which fall under this category are mourning, rejoicing on holidays, *keriat Shema*, fasting, prayer and *shofar*. What is important to note regarding this category is that the feelings are not merely "aggadic" or pietistic accessories to a formal halakhic act; rather, the emotions are part of the formal halakhic requirement itself. Indeed, they constitute the "realiza-tion" of the *mitzvah*.[7]

---

5 This, of course, is very relevant to our discussion in Chap. 6 of the catharsis of the religious experience.

6 For example, see the essays "An Exalted Evening: The Seder Night" and "Counting Time" in *Festival of Freedom* and "Jews at Prayer" in *Shiurei Harav*.

7 Note that the distinction between physical *ma'aseh* and experiential *kiyyum* can apply to prohibitions as well. See R. Michael Rosensweig, *"Lo Tahmod," Beit Yitzhak* 19 (5747), 214–27.

This distinction between outer action and inner fulfillment is a powerful tool in solving many halakhic conundrums. For example, in Chapter 6 we saw how it answered the question of why holidays interrupt mourning while Shabbat does not. Another famous question which this distinction answers relates to the opening of Rambam's *Laws of Repentance* (1:1): ". . . When a person repents and returns from his sin, he must confess before God." Many have asked: Isn't repentance itself a *mitzvah*? From the Rambam's formulation, it would seem that one is not *commanded* to repent, but if he *wishes* to do so, he must offer a verbal confession to God.

Rav Soloveitchik answers that here the Rambam is interested in detailing the performance of the law; however, in the heading to the *Laws of Repentance*, he sets out to define the law, to expose its essence, and therefore he writes, "The Laws of Repentance contain one commandment, namely, that the sinner should repent of his sin before God and confess." In other words, the *kiyyum* of the *mitzvah* is the long process of inner repentance, while the external *ma'aseh* is confession. Without the inner component, the outer action is meaningless. Similarly, the Rambam begins the *Laws of Prayer* by describing an action: "It is a positive commandment to pray daily." However, in the heading to this section, he defines the law in terms of its essence: "to *serve* God daily by means of prayer." The *kiyyum* of the *mitzvah* is the service of the heart; this must be manifested in the act of prayer.

Aside from shedding light on individual *halakhot*, the Rav occasionally employs this "*hakirah*" and others to draw broader conclusions about the nature of Judaism and of man's relationship to God. This is especially evident in his treatment of prayer, which we shall deal with separately.[8] But to return to our familiar example of a holiday canceling mourning, the Rav notes that a similar phenomenon applies to the *kohen gadol* (high priest): like a Jew during a holiday, he is exempted from mourning; however, his exemption applies all year round. On the other hand, a *metzora* (leper) and *menudeh* (excommunicate), who are required because of their status to observe mourning rituals, must do so even during holidays. The Rav connects these phenomena to form an overarching theory.

What is common to the Jew during a holiday and a *kohen gadol* year round is that they are standing in the presence of God.[9] Nearness to God is man's main source of joy, and therefore it is incompatible with the sadness of mourning. By contrast, the mourner, leper and excommunicate all experience

---

8 See Chaps. 20 and 21 below.

9 According to the Rambam (*Hilkhot Bi'at ha-Mikdash* 1:10), the *kohen gadol* has the status of "being perpetually in the Temple."

a sense of distance from God, and therefore must perform mourning rituals. The mourner, though he feels distant from God, is still part of the community, and therefore must join them in rejoicing in God's presence during the holiday. The leper and excommunicate, on the other hand, have been excluded from the community, and therefore do not fully experience the joy of God's presence even on a holiday.

This discussion is actually much more complex and nuanced than presented here.[10] It is a classic instance justifying Rav Soloveitchik's claim in *The Halakhic Mind* (91–102) that a philosophy of Judaism can and must be drawn from the sources of Halakhah.

The Teacher's Duty

Despite all of his efforts to enrich the religious and emotional lives of his students, the Rav lamented what he saw as his failure to convey adequately the experiential side of Judaism:

> Therefore, I hereby announce that I am able to identify one of those responsible for the present situation – and that is I myself. I have not fulfilled my obligation as a guide and teacher in Israel. I lacked the spiritual energies which a teacher and a rabbi needs, or I lacked the necessary will, and did not dedicate everything I had to my goal. While I have succeeded, to a great or small degree, as a teacher and guide in the area of *"gadlut ha-mohin"* – my students have received much Torah from me, and their intellectual stature has been strengthened and increased during the years they have spent around me – I have not seen much success in my efforts in the experiential area. I was not able to live together with them, to cleave to them and to transfer to them from the warmth of my soul. My words, it seems, have not kindled the divine flame in sensitive hearts. I have sinned as a disseminator of the Torah of the heart . . . Blame me for the mistake (*"Al Ahavat Ha-Torah,"* 420).[11]

Regarding this admission, Rav Lichtenstein poignantly comments:

> That, too, is part of the Rav's legacy. Not just spellbinding *shiurim*, magnificent *derashot*, electrifying *hiddushim*, but the candid recognition of failure – failure which is transcended by its very acknowledgement. In his own personal vein, so aristocratic and yet so democratic, he has imbued us with a

---

10 See the sources cited in Chap. 6, particularly *Shiurim le-Zekher Abba Mari z"l*, vol. 2, 182–96 (translated in *Out of the Whirlwind*, 49–85), and *U-Vikkashtem mi-Sham*, 193–98, n. 19.

11 This translation is based on that of Rav Lichtenstein in "The Rav at Jubilee," 55.

sense of both the frailty of majesty and the majesty of frailty. He has trans-mitted to us not only *Torat Moshe Avdi*, but the midrashic image of Moshe Rabbenu constructing and then dismantling the *mishkan* during *shivat yemei ha-milu'im* – whose import the Rav interpreted as the fusion of radical, almost Sisyphean frustration with ultimate hope.[12]

The above confession by the Rav can help us solve a riddle which has puzzled many. Given the esteem in which the Rav held the Lithuanian tradi-tion of emotional reticence, why did he discuss his feelings so openly in his public teaching? The Rav writes in numerous places of the need to maintain one's reserve, to shield one's deepest feelings from the prying eyes of the public. This is clearly imbibed from the scholarly Lithuanian milieu in which he was raised.

In fact, as is his wont, the Rav raises a personality he esteems into a general model, an ideal type. In his eulogy for the Mizrachi leader R. Ze'ev Gold, entitled "*Be-Seter u-ve-Galui*,"[13] the Rav develops the character of the *Ish Rosh Hodesh*, the "New Month Man." He is so called because Rosh Hodesh, the beginning of the month, is a day whose inner sanctity is almost completely shielded from public view. Although on Rosh Hodesh one goes about one's daily routine, merely adding some additional prayers, the Torah groups it along with the major holidays, and its inner sanctity is fully revealed only within the precincts of the Temple. Similarly, there are some personali-ties whose inner passion and sanctity are concealed beneath a solemn exterior (such as the Rav's father) or beneath a sparkling exterior (such as R. Gold). Rav Soloveitchik confesses that he has always been attracted to such person-alities, partially due to his upbringing:

> From childhood, I was taught to control my feelings and not to display what was taking place in my emotional world. Father *z"l* used to say: "The holier the feeling, the more intimate it is, the more it needs to be buried in the depths . . .." What is the holiest of places if not the Holy of Holies of the emotional life? If man is full of joy and happiness, let him reveal his feelings to God . . . but let him not exhibit them to others, lest a stranger's look desecrate his Holy of Holies. If, on the contrary . . . man is given over to suffering and torment . . . let him confess before the Master of the Universe . . . but let no stranger ap-proach the Holy of Holies, for he might desecrate with indifference the sanc-tity of mute suffering oppressing man ("*Be-Seter u-ve-Galui*," 174).

---

12 Ibid., 55–56. See also the discussion of the "ethic of defeat" in Chap. 3 above (pp. 59–61).
13 Printed in *Divrei Hagut ve-Ha'arakhah*, 163–86.

Why, then, did the Rav take the uncharacteristic step of revealing his emotions so passionately in his lectures and his writings, repeatedly sharing his innermost feelings with his audiences? I believe several factors can account for this.

(1) As he states in *The Lonely Man of Faith* (6), revelation of one's stormy inner feelings has a cathartic effect:

> All I want is to follow the advice given by Elihu the son of Berachel of old, who said, "I will speak that I may find relief;"[14] for there is a redemptive quality for an agitated mind in the spoken word and a tormented soul finds peace in confessing.

(2) It was a pedagogical necessity. As we saw above, the lack of religious feeling among many observant Jews greatly distressed the Rav, and he consciously set out to rectify the situation. R. Shalom Carmy reports: "The Rav once remarked in my hearing that old-time *Gedolim* refrained from talking about themselves, but that the disconnection of modern man from living exemplars of religious existence has made self-revelation an educational necessity."[15] This applied to more than just the need to communicate his experience of halakhic living. The centrality of crisis in his thought, and his focus on failure and insecurity leading to the virtue of humility, necessitated that he share his sense of personal vulnerability with us.[16]

(3) At all times, even when the community is not deficient in religious emotion, it is the role of the teacher to share his existential experience with his student – sometimes explicitly and sometimes implicitly. According to Rav Soloveitchik, the teacher must mold not only the student's mind but his soul as well. This goes far beyond the ancient tradition (to which R. Carmy alluded above) of students learning a way of acting and feeling by observing the behavior of their teacher. Rather, it is accomplished by self-revelation, a spontaneous, almost involuntary overflow of the teacher's inner self towards the student.

This colloquium of souls between teacher and student, and indeed between generations, is the essence of the *masorah* (passing on of the tradition). It is also the basis of the Rav's understanding of the nature of *Torah She-be'al*

---

14 Job 32:20.

15 "Of Eagle's Flight and Snail's Pace," *Tradition* 29:1 (1994), 31, n. 22.

16 See also Chap. 19 below, which addresses the question of why Rav Soloveitchik saw it as a pedagogical necessity to share not only his religious experiences, but also his family experiences. My article, "Hidden Man, Revealed Man: The Role of Personal Experience in Rav Soloveitchik's Thought," in *Ha-Har ha-Tov ha-Zeh: Essays in Honor of Yeshivat Har Etzion* (Alon Shevut, 2012), 46–54, expands on the pedagogical issue raised above.

Peh (Oral Law) and of prophecy. In fact, the Rav ends his *magnum opus* on the religious experience, *U-Vikkashtem mi-Sham*, by discussing this very theme – the teacher's overflow towards and merging with his student – and its manifold ramifications.[17] In light of the Rav's espousal of this idea, it becomes clear that, in his writing and teaching, he himself was engaged in such a process of sharing himself with others. And we are all the richer for it.

FOR FURTHER REFERENCE

1. ***Katnut ha-mohin*:**
   (a) *"Al Ahavat ha-Torah u-Ge'ulat Nefesh ha-Dor,"* in *Be-Sod ha-Yahid ve-ha-Yahad*, ed. P. Peli (Jerusalem, 1976), 403–32; reprinted in abridged form in *Divrei Hashkafah* (Jerusalem, 1992), 241–58. Quotations here (except for that of p. 420) are my translation, based on the former edition.
   (b) *"Peleitat Sofreihem,"* in *Divrei Hagut ve-Ha'arakhah*, 137–62; slightly abridged translation by R. Shalom Carmy, "A Eulogy for R. Hayyim Heller," in *Shiurei Harav*, ed. J. Epstein (Hoboken, 1994), 46–65.
   (c) *Abraham's Journey*, eds. David Shatz, Joel Wolowelsky and Reuven Ziegler (Jersey City, 2008), 184–92.

2. **On the inner fulfillment of *mitzvot*:** See the general explanation offered in *Worship of the Heart*, 15–19. For specific cases, see the sources quoted in the appendix to Chapter 6 of this book. Regarding *avelut*, see especially Chapters 1, 2 and 5 of *Out of the Whirlwind*.

3. ***Rosh Hodesh* man:** R. Shalom Carmy, "Anatomy of a *Hesped*: Reading an Essay by the Rav," in *Bein Kotlei ha-Yeshiva*, vol. 6 (5748), 8–20. Translations of passages from *"Be-Seter u-ve-Galui"* are taken from this essay.

---

17 For an elaboration of this topic, see Chap. 2 above (pp. 47–49) regarding the teaching community, and Chap. 35 below (pp. 381–83) regarding the Rav's understanding of *masorah*.

Chapter 9

Torah Study: Intellect and Experience

In the previous chapter, we explored Rav Soloveitchik's emphasis on inwardness, the experiential aspect of Judaism. However, two other indispensable elements of religious life must also be considered: thought and action. Only through the combination of these three aspects – thought, feeling and action – is one's religiosity complete. In fact, the Rav believes that one's religious experience itself is lacking if it is not based on knowledge of the Halakhah, and it must certainly be accompanied by – or better yet, stem from – observance of the Halakhah. Therefore, in this chapter we will discuss Torah study as both a prerequisite for the religious experience and as an experience in its own right, and in the following chapter we will turn our attention to the need for action to accompany thought and feeling.

The Effect of Knowledge upon Experience

In Rav Soloveitchik's view, which has its roots in both the teachings of *Hazal* and the theology of the *mitnaggedim* (such as R. Hayyim of Volozhin and the Netziv), *talmud Torah* (Torah study) is a central – perhaps *the* central – component of Jewish religiosity. Far more than being a guide to practical observance of Jewish law, *talmud Torah* allows us to penetrate God's infinite will and thus informs every aspect of our relationship to Him. Rav Lichtenstein sums up the Rav's approach as follows:

> Torah study gives the Jew insight – as direct and profound as man is privileged to attain – into the revealed will of his Creator. Through the study of Halakhah – the immanent expression of God's transcendent rational will – man's knowledge of God gains depth and scope. Further, religious study is a stimulus to the

total spiritual personality. Faith can be neither profound nor enduring unless the intellect is fully and actively engaged in the quest for God.[1]

In light of this, we can understand Rav Soloveitchik's insistence that one's sense of inwardness in *mitzvot* be based not on "cheap sentimentality or ceremonialism" (*Divrei Hashkafah*, 78), but rather on serious familiarity with halakhic sources. ". . . [W]ithout knowledge of Torah, the Jew cannot attain the proper religious experience, nor can he fully understand the beauty and splendor of *avodat Hashem* (divine service)" (ibid., 76). Recall also the Rav's claim that the laws of Halakhah are the basic data of Judaism, out of which any understanding of Judaism must be derived.

Rav Soloveitchik believed that the demand for a strong intellectual component in one's *avodat Hashem*, while proper at all times, is especially relevant in our generation. His disciple, R. Shalom Carmy, writes:

> With keen sensitivity to the malaise of commitment affecting contemporary Jewry, the Rav concluded that religious engagement of the intellect is essential to the cure . . . [T]he Rav deemed our time propitious for the intellectual quest:
>> The young American generation . . . is not totally engrossed in the pragmatic, utilitarian outlook . . . To the degree that average people in our society attain higher levels of knowledge and general intelligence, we cannot imbue them with a Jewish standpoint that relies primarily on sentiment and ceremony (*Divrei Hashkafah*, 78).
>
> If R. Kook witnessed the alienation of Jews from traditional religious commitment and decided that his generation needed exposure to a comprehensive Jewish philosophy deriving from the sources of Kabbala, the Rav offered a simpler, more startling solution: renew the covenant with the exoteric sources that directly confront our concrete experience.[2]

Talmud Torah is so central to the Rav's view of Judaism that he interprets many seemingly unrelated *mitzvot* as actually being fulfillments of *talmud Torah*. For example, he perceives *sippur yetziat Mitzrayim* (recounting the Exodus) on Passover night as being fulfilled through Torah study. We do not merely narrate a story. Rather, we recount the Exodus by means of exegesis of biblical verses (*midrash*), recitation of set laws (*mishnah*), and analysis and conceptualization of Halakhah (*gemara*). Similarly, he sees the recitation of

---

1 "R. Joseph Soloveitchik," in *Great Jewish Thinkers of the Twentieth Century*, ed. Simon Noveck (New York, 1963), 290.

2 R. Shalom Carmy, "Of Eagle's Flight and Snail's Pace," *Tradition* 29:1 (1994), 26–27; reprinted in *Exploring the Thought of Rabbi Joseph B. Soloveitchik*, 115–16.

Pesukei de-Zimrah (the psalms introducing the morning prayer) as an act of *talmud Torah* – understanding our position vis-à-vis God, thereby allowing us to petition Him.[3] In fact, according to Rav Soloveitchik, all prayer must contain a cognitive element; as we shall see in Chapter 20, he makes much of the fact that the word *tefillah* is derived from the root *pll*, denoting judgment or discrimination.[4]

The Experience of Knowledge

While he intellectualizes certain experiential *mitzvot*, Rav Soloveitchik also experientializes the intellectual *mitzvah* par excellence, namely, *talmud Torah*. In other words, he repeatedly presents *talmud Torah* not merely as a cognitive endeavor but also as a powerful experience. At first glance, this may seem somewhat strange: the intellect is characterized by cold, dispassionate analysis, precision and detachment, while emotion is characterized by warmth, fervor and involvement. However, this seeming contradiction dissipates when we realize that, for the Rav, pursuit of knowledge is a passionate and consuming quest, especially when the knowledge is that of Torah and ultimately of God.[5]

Although one must approach Torah study with the utmost seriousness and intellectual rigor, the process of the attainment of Torah knowledge becomes a vibrant, engaging and invigorating experience that reaches into the depths of the human personality:

> When a person delves into God's Torah and reveals its inner light and splendor
> . . . and enjoys the pleasure of creativity and innovation, he merits communion with the Giver of the Torah. The ideal of clinging to God is realized by coupling the intellect with the Divine Idea, which is embodied in rules, laws and traditions . . .[6] However, halakhic knowing does not remain sealed off in the realm of the intellect. It bursts forth into one's existential consciousness and merges with it . . . The idea turns into an impassioning and arousing ex-

---

3 See For Further Reference, #1 and #2.

4 *Tefillah*, prayer, is to be distinguished from *tze'akah*, outcry: "While *tefillah* is a meditative-reflective act, *tze'akah* is immediate and compulsive" ("Redemption, Prayer, Talmud Torah," 68). For more on prayer in the Rav's thought, see Chaps. 20 and 21 below. Regarding *tze'akah*, see pp. 220–21 below.

5 Regarding the experiential dimension of knowledge in general, as distinct from Torah knowledge, see the discussion of catharsis of the intellect in Chap. 7 above.

6 This is reminiscent of passages in R. Hayyim of Volozhin's *Nefesh ha-Hayyim* (4:10) and R. Schneur Zalman of Liadi's *Tanya* (*Likkutei Amarim*, chap. 5), though the Rav characteristically emphasizes *creativity* and *innovation*, and not simply *study* of Torah.

perience; knowledge into a divine fire; strict and exacting halakhic discipline turns into a passionate love burning with a holy flame. Myriads of black letters, into which have been gathered reams of laws, explanations, questions, problems, concepts and measures, descend from the cold and placid intellect, which calmly rests on its subtle abstractions and its systematic frameworks, to the heart full of trembling, fear and yearning, and turn into sparks of the flame of a great experience which sweeps man to his Creator ("*Al Ahavat Ha-Torah*," 410–11).

Love of God

The fusion of intellect and passion has a venerable history in Judaism (although the Rav puts his own individual stamp on it). For example, the Rambam writes that love of God depends on knowledge of Him:

> One only loves God with the knowledge with which one knows Him. According to the knowledge will be the love – if much [knowledge], much [love]; if little, little (*Hilkhot Teshuvah* 10:6).

Given such a seemingly intellectual and abstract conception of love, the following description may come as somewhat of a surprise:

> And what is the love which is befitting? It is to love the Eternal with a great and exceeding love, so strong that one's soul shall be knit up with the love of God, and one should be continually enraptured by it, like a lovesick individual whose mind is at no time free from his passion for a particular woman, the thought of her filling his heart at all times, whether he be sitting down or rising up, eating or drinking. Even more intense should be the love of God in the hearts of those who love Him . . . The entire Song of Songs is indeed an allegory descriptive of this love (*Hilkhot Teshuvah* 10:3).

This passage serves as a source of great inspiration to Rav Soloveitchik, and he cites it in *U-Vikkashtem mi-Sham* (81–82) as a description of the pinnacle of human religious attainment.[7]

---

7 It is important to note that, although the Rav follows the Rambam in asserting that "knowledge of God" leads to love of God, he deviates from the Rambam regarding the nature of this knowledge. For the Rambam, it is knowledge of philosophy (physics and metaphysics), while for the Rav it is knowledge of Halakhah. See For Further Reference, #4, and Chap. 34 below.

Revelation

Rav Soloveitchik often stresses the importance of love of Torah, and depicts Torah study as a form of passionate clinging to God. He believes that man bonds with God intellectually through studying Torah, and man strengthens his emotional connection to God via a mutual object of love, the Torah. Thus, the Rav frequently describes Torah study as an encounter with God, even a form of revelation.[8] Much of his scholarship regarding *keriat ha-Torah* (public reading of the Torah) revolves around this premise. For example, he champions the practice of Maharam of Rothenberg to stand during Torah reading in the synagogue,[9] since this is a re-enactment of the revelation at Sinai (where the Jews stood to receive the Torah).[10]

In revelation, there are two components: the contents (i.e., the actual message, namely the Halakhah) and the experience. Both aspects are crucial, and the Rav finds it necessary to stress each. Against those who accuse the Briskers of cold intellectualism, the Rav expounds the vital experiential aspect of *talmud Torah*. Against those (like Martin Buber) who focus only on the experience of the encounter while ignoring the contents of the revelation, he insists on the indispensability and centrality of the study and practice of the law.

Torah Lishmah

In discussing Torah study as a form of *devekut* (cleaving to God), we must take pains to distinguish the Rav's conception from that developed by certain branches of *Hasidut*. According to the latter approach, namely, learning Torah for the sake of attaining *devekut*, Torah study is to be viewed as a means to attaining some form of ecstatic experience. The method need not be one of intellectual rigor, and the actual content of the learning is of secondary importance.[11]

For the Rav, a staunch advocate of the ideology of *Torah lishmah* (Torah study for its own sake), one must adopt a method of strict intellectualism and innovative analysis in Torah study. Torah is not to be approached with less "sweep and scope of . . . creative thought, analytic acuity, subtlety of

---

8 See, for example, *Family Redeemed*, 176–78.

9 Cited by *Mordekhai, Shabbat*, 422, and Rema, OH 146:4.

10 See For Further Reference, #6.

11 See, for example, Joseph Weiss, "Torah Study in Early Hasidism," in his *Studies in Eastern European Mysticism*, ed. D. Goldstein (Oxford, 1985), 56–68.

abstraction, and systematic consistency" than any other field of intellectual endeavor (*U-Vikkashtem mi-Sham*, 108). The experiential aspect *accompanies* the learning and grows out of it, but it is not the *reason* to learn. Torah study is an end in and of itself.

A Multifaceted Experience

Apart from *devekut*, the experiential aspect of Torah study takes on many other expressions, including:
(1) the uplifting and majestic experience of cognition and creativity ("*Al Ahavat Ha-Torah*," 409–10);
(2) relating to Torah as a living personality, about whom one is fascinated and to whom one is committed ("*Mah Dodekh mi-Dod*," 70–75; "Remarks at a *Siyyum*," 182–83);
(3) the experience of a living tradition, of communion and dialogue with previous generations of the *masorah* (*U-Vikkashtem mi-Sham*, 143–46);
(4) purification and sanctification of one's personality:

> Torah study, aside from being an intellectual, educational endeavor, enlightening the student and providing him with the information needed to observe the law, is a redemptive cathartic process – it sanctifies the personality. It purges the mind of unworthy desires and irreverent thoughts, uncouth emotions and vulgar drives ("Torah and Humility").[12]

Based on the famous *aggadah* depicting a baby being taught Torah in the womb (*Niddah* 30b), according to which Torah remains latent in one's personality and is rediscovered through study, the Rav states that *talmud Torah* helps man find his true self and thereby redeems him ("Redemption, Prayer, Talmud Torah," 69). In fact, the public reading of the Torah on Monday, Thursday and Shabbat was instituted primarily for the purpose of purifying the Jew's personality by bringing him into contact with God's word (*Shiurim le-Zekher*, vol. 2, 205–07; vol. 1, 164–68, 175–78).

According to Rav Soloveitchik, there are additional dimensions to *talmud Torah* – for example, Torah study is a means of perceiving the world and not just a source of norms. We will deal with these in the chapters on *Halakhic Man* and *U-Vikkashtem mi-Sham*.

---

12 In *Shiurim le-Zekher Abba Mari*, vol. 2, 13–16, the Rav similarly develops the theme of Torah study bringing about personal holiness and purity. Earlier in the same *shiur* (7–9), he identifies Torah study as a form of prayer, acceptance of the yoke of Heaven, and praise of God.

For Further Reference

1. ***Sippur yetziat Mitzrayim* as Torah study:** *Shiurim le-Zekher Abba Mari z"l*, vol. 2, 152–63; *Festival of Freedom*, 25–27, 89–93. See also *Shiurim le-Zekher*, vol. 1, 2–3, n. 4; R. David Shapiro, *Rabbi Joseph B. Soloveitchik on Pesach, Sefirat ha-Omer and Shavu'ot* (Jerusalem, 2005), 15–32.

2. ***Pesukei de-Zimrah*:** *Shiurim le-Zekher*, vol. 2, 17–34.

3. **The experience of Torah study:**
   a. "*Al Ahavat ha-Torah u-Ge'ulat Nefesh ha-Dor*," in *Be-Sod ha-Yahid ve-ha-Yahad*, ed. P. Peli (Jerusalem, 1976), 403–32; reprinted in slightly abridged form in *Divrei Hashkafah* (Jerusalem, 1992), 241–58.
   b. "On the Love of Torah: Impromptu Remarks at a *Siyyum*," prepared by M. Kasdan, in *Shiurei Harav*, 181–85.
   c. "*Mah Dodekh mi-Dod*," in *Divrei Hagut ve-Ha'arakhah* (Jerusalem, 1982), 57–98.
   d. "Torah and Humility," http://www.vbm-torah.org/archive/rav/rav11.htm and rav11b.htm.
   e. "Torah and *Shekhinah*," in *Family Redeemed*, 158–80.
   f. "Redemption, Prayer, Talmud Torah," *Tradition* 17:2 (Spring 1978), 55–72.
   g. "*Be-Inyan Birkot ha-Torah*," in *Shiurim le-Zekher*, vol. 2, 1–16.
   Of course, this is also an important theme throughout *Halakhic Man* and *U-Vikkashtem mi-Sham*.

4. **Rambam's concept of love of God:** *Shemonah Perakim*, chapter 5; *Sefer ha-Mitzvot*, positive commandment 3; *Hilkhot Yesodei ha-Torah* 2:1–2; *Hilkhot Teshuvah* chapter 10; *Guide of the Perplexed* III:51.

5. **Love of Torah:** see reference 3 above, essays a–e.

6. **Torah reading as revelation:** *Shiurim le-Zekher*, vol. 2, 210–13; *U-Vikkashtem mi-Sham*, 139–40. On *keriat ha-Torah* in general, see the three relevant essays in *Shiurim le-Zekher* (vol. 1, 135–56 and 157–78; vol. 2, 197–213).

7. ***Devekut*:** "*Al Ahavat Ha-Torah*," 411–17; *U-Vikkashtem mi-Sham*, chapters 11ff.; "Torah and Humility."

Chapter 10

Mitzvot: The Need for Action

Given Rav Soloveitchik's emphasis on inwardness, which we have explored in several chapters, we might well be tempted to ask: why does Judaism require action at all? What is the point of the myriad commandments governing every aspect of our lives? Why should a religious person go beyond feeling and thought?

Much of Chapter 5, dealing with the sanctification of physical existence, dealt with this question. Before offering new answers, let us briefly review some of the conclusions reached there. Judaism wants man to live a full natural life, and the commandments relating to the physical side of his existence force him to involve himself with the natural world. In this manner, he can avoid the temptation of a purely ethereal, otherworldly spirituality that leads to a dualistic approach of affirming the spirit while rejecting the world.

On the other hand, while Halakhah demands involvement in natural life, it also demands that one actively sanctify one's physical existence. This is attained through the observance of *mitzvot*, which affect every facet of a person's worldly existence, from the moment of awakening until the moment of falling asleep. These *mitzvot* have the effect not just of sanctifying one's personality (e.g., by asserting control over one's physical drives), but of sanctifying one's very actions and physicality. By infusing every area of life with meaning and purpose, the individual avoids a divided existence. The all-encompassing demands of the *mitzvot* ensure that one will be conscious of God at all times, not just when one is in the synagogue or *beit midrash*. When one serves God by all means at one's disposal, one consecrates one's entire life to God, making one's service of God integrated and complete.

While Chapter 5 focused on the concrete ways in which observance of *mitzvot* sanctifies one's physical existence, I would now like to focus on the dangers inherent in a religious posture that ignores the arena of one's natural worldly existence, concentrating instead exclusively on religious feeling and contemplation. I believe that the Rav's objections to such an approach can be grouped under five headings. This form of religiosity is:

(1) otherworldly;
(2) unrealistic;
(3) purely subjective;
(4) overly individualistic;
(5) esoteric and undemocratic.

Let us examine each of these.

(1) Otherworldly

According to Rav Soloveitchik, what distinguishes halakhic man from the general *homo religiosus* (religious man) is his attitude to *olam ha-zeh* (this world, i.e., the physical world, as opposed to the world-to-come). While *homo religiosus* seeks to flee the impurity of the mundane world towards a supernal region of pure spirit, halakhic man seeks to do precisely the opposite: he attempts to bring the sanctity and purity of the transcendent realm *into* the material world. The existence of halakhic man is firmly centered in *olam ha-zeh*, which he tries to fill with sanctity by realizing the ideals of the Halakhah.

Religiosity which does not concern itself with man's physical activities, social interaction, etc., is thereby withdrawn from engagement with the outside world and, as a result, will not be able to sanctify it. It will encourage man to view his physicality with contempt, as a barrier between his soul and its ultimate felicity. Judaism, by contrast, believes that the world is "very good," and frowns upon monasticism.

Furthermore, an otherworldly religiosity leads one to adopt a quietistic mystical approach that looks inward while ignoring the reality of others' suffering. Judaism finds this morally repugnant, and instead enjoins man to engage in *tikkun ha-olam*, mending the world.

(2) Unrealistic

Ideally, a strong component of action in one's religiosity will strengthen the internal component; at minimum, it will preserve religiosity at times when the internal component is lacking. In Rav Lichtenstein's words:

> With its pervasive psychological realism, Halakhah has recognized that ordinary mortals need to be jogged out of their spiritual lethargy, and that unless

they are prodded to specific action, many will be quite content to neglect the religious life completely. Habitual observance ingrains moral and religious sensibility into the very fiber of the personality. It strengthens the inner power of spirit and, at a deeper level, human emotion is profoundly affected by the very process of externalization . . .

We should keep in mind, however, what we often tend to forget: the most legalistic ritualism is better than no worship whatever; and the individual who, within Halakhah, lapses into a formalistic rut, would very likely be bereft of religious awareness completely were he without it. At the very least, ritual establishes a floor for religion; at most, it leads man to the scaling – and holding – of the loftiest spiritual heights.[1]

The fact that it is more likely that actions will influence emotions than the reverse explains why Halakhah devotes its primary attention to actions:

Both the subjective [inner] as well as the objective [outer] component are indispensable for the self-realization of the religious personality. Yet Halakhah lays emphasis upon actions rather than upon experiences, for it is confident that, while actions are capable of stirring the soul, exciting the imagination and firing the heart, feelings – no matter how noble and dignified, no matter how strong and violent – may exhaust themselves in an inner tempest without breaking through to the surface at all (*Family Redeemed*, 40).

Thus, if religion does not provide man with an objective framework of action containing specific divine norms, it will – at best – be vague and transient. At worst, however, it will lead to the most horrible excesses, which brings us to our next point.

(3) Purely Subjective

Rav Soloveitchik believes that it is not only *undesirable* for man to try to escape his corporeality, but it also is *impossible* for him to accomplish this. Therefore, any ideology based on the premise that man can become a purely spiritual creature is inherently false and doomed to failure. By focusing solely on man's contemplative-spiritual side, it fails to acknowledge the strength of his inner drives and passions. Seeking to do the impossible – to eliminate or ignore man's physical nature – it lacks the power to do what is necessary, namely, to restrain and channel man's drives and thus use them positively.

---

1 "R. Joseph Soloveitchik," in *Great Jewish Thinkers of the Twentieth Century*, ed. Simon Noveck (New York, 1963), 294.

Religiosity lacking the objective-revelational element that obligates man to perform particular actions cannot conquer the beast in man. Subjective faith, lacking commands and laws, faith of the sort that Saul of Tarsus spoke about – even if it dresses itself up as the love of God and man – cannot stand fast if it contains no explicit commands to do good deeds, to fulfill specific command- ments not always approved by rationality and culture. The terrible Holocaust of World War II proves this. All those who speak of love stood silent and did not protest. Many of them even took part in the extermination of millions of human beings (*U-Vikkashtem mi-Sham*, 54–55).

Thus, despite the importance of the spiritual and contemplative sides of religion, "Limiting the religious experience to its spiritual aspects leads to the elimination of its grandeur and influence" (ibid., 54). In addition to its spiri- tual facet, religion also plays a practical role: "to rectify man's actions on this earth and impose upon him a tyrannical authority that will stand as a barricade in the face of attacks of boiling lust or evil instinctual cravings" (ibid., 53). Freedom from the authority of specific norms, and from a sense of coercion in following them, leads to moral anarchy and, eventually, degeneracy.[2]

In light of all the dangers expressed above, we can appreciate Rav Soloveitchik's memorable characterization of the Halakhah:

> The fundamental tendency of the Halakhah is to translate the qualitative fea- tures of religious subjectivity – the content of religious man's consciousness, which surges and swells like the waves of the sea, then pounds against the shores of reality, there to shatter and break – into firm and well-established quantities, "like nails well fastened" (Eccl. 12:11), that no storm can uproot from their place (*Halakhic Man*, 57).

By becoming concrete, objective, and specific, religion acquires the strength to affect man's entire life, to withstand the assaults of temptation, to endure regardless of the individual's mood, and to survive from generation to generation. This accounts (in part) for Judaism's attention to detail, its con- centration on standards and measures – times of the day (e.g., when to pray, when Shabbat begins), amounts of food and drink (how much wine to drink at *kiddush*, how much *matzah* to eat at the Seder), and so on.

Halakhah regulates not only man's actions, but even his internal states.

---

2 In the section on otherworldliness (p. 112) we noted that a purely contemplative-spiritual religiosity leads to an *amoral* position, namely, one that is indifferent to the world and uncon- cerned with alleviating human suffering. Here, however, the claim is stronger: the lack of objec- tive commands and limitations can lead to an *immoral* position, to human depravity, because subjective religiosity alone lacks defenses against man's barbaric impulses.

Thereby, "The objective halakhic mold . . . channels religious feeling into 'the depth, and not the tumult, of the soul.'"[3] In Rav Soloveitchik's words:

> The Halakhah wishes to objectify religiosity not only through introducing the external act and the psychophysical deed into the world of religion but also through the structuring and ordering of the inner correlative in the realm of man's spirit. The Halakhah sets down statutes and erects markers that serve as a dam against the surging, subjective current coursing through the universal *homo religiosus*, which, from time to time, in its raging turbulence sweeps away his entire being to obscure and inchoate realms (*Halakhic Man*, 59).

(4) Overly Individualistic

If religion focuses solely on inner experience, this can lead to an "extravagant religious individualism" (*The Halakhic Mind*, 79) that is not geared towards the formation of a community. Yet, the Rav notes, "The history and psychology of religion will attest to the fact that the force and effectiveness of religion grows commensurately with increasing participation of the entire society in the religious drama" (ibid.).

Furthermore, an inner religion that is not expressed as a way of life attenuates one's connection not only to the community of one's contemporaries, but also to one's historical community, as noted by Rav Lichtenstein:

> The objective character of the Halakhah helps the Jew transcend his own subjective existence. In one sense, the Halakhic way of life serves as a distinctive mark of identification. As a minimal, uniform tradition, it helps weld the organic whole of the community of Israel. Halakhah places the Jew's life in a total perspective: he can see his isolated efforts as part of Israel's timeless and universal enterprise.[4]

(5) Esoteric and Undemocratic

Apart from the above-mentioned impediments to community, there remains a fundamental problem with spiritual-contemplative religion. A purely internal religiosity based on a deep feeling of the sublime, or a purely intellectual religiosity based on serene contemplation, is by its very definition confined to a small elite of particularly gifted individuals. The average person is incapable of attaining the requisite state of mind, depth of experience and detachment from materialism.

---

3 "R. Joseph Soloveitchik," 294 (citing William Wordsworth's 1814 poem, "Laodamia").
4 Ibid.

However, by emphasizing the centrality of clear-cut action, which can be accomplished by anyone, Judaism maintains a "democratic" and "exoteric" character.[5] The Torah is the inheritance of *all* of Israel, not just a clique of spiritual adepts. One does not need to be privy to secret knowledge or mystical techniques in order to fulfill God's commandments. The simplest and most obtuse individual can observe the *mitzvot* to the same extent as the spiritual genius – both eat *matzah* on Passover, honor their parents, are bound by the same restrictions, etc.

Thus, in a normative religion like Judaism, all individuals are equally able to approach God. A religion lacking this common basis of connection to God becomes overly stratified; it

> gives rise to ecclesiastical tyranny, religious aristocracies, and charismatic personalities. And there is nothing that the Halakhah loathes and despises as much as the idea of cultic mediation or the choosing of individuals, on the basis of supernatural considerations, to be intercessors for the community (*Halakhic Man*, 43).

Of course, there are areas of Halakhah where individuals of differing talents will achieve different levels. Returning to our distinction between *hovot ha-evarim* (duties of the limbs), *hovot ha-levavot* (duties of the heart), and *mitzvot* which are performed externally (*ma'aseh be-yadayim*) but fulfilled internally (*kiyyum ba-lev*), the area of differential achievement would refer primarily to the latter two categories. For example, the level of one's love of God (a duty of the heart) or prayer (an external performance with an internal fulfillment) depends on one's emotional depth and spiritual capacity. To take another example, through hard work and innate ability, one person may reach greater attainments in Torah study than will another.

This, asserts the Rav, is as it should be. Halakhah must give a person the ability to express his or her individuality in the service of God. Likewise, it must allow everyone the opportunity to strive for ever greater heights in divine worship. However, the strong component of action in Jewish religiosity, emphasizing the simple *ma'aseh ha-mitzvah* (performance of the commandment), maintains the underlying basis of equality of individuals.[6]

---

5 "Esoteric" means restricted to a small group, while "exoteric" means accessible to everyone. This pair of terms appears repeatedly in the Rav's writings. By "democratic" the Rav means roughly the same as "exoteric." Though he doesn't employ a single term to denote its opposite, one could suggest "exclusive," "elitist," or "aristocratic."

6 As is evident from his repeated treatments of the question of exotericism and esotericism in religion (see For Further Reference, #2), the Rav felt strongly that "On the one hand, religion belongs to everyone," but "On the other hand, religion must also provide the opportunity for

Conclusion

In summary, religiosity focused solely on one's internal state and lacking commanded actions suffers from a number of problems:[7]
(1) It is uninterested in influencing the outside world and unconcerned with the suffering of other human beings.
(2) It is unlikely to influence one's actions and is liable to dissipate over time.
(3) It cannot stand fast in the face of human desires and may degenerate into moral depravity.
(4) It is by nature an individualistic enterprise and therefore unlikely to bind people into communities, either historically or with their contemporaries.
(5) It is confined to a small spiritual elite and inaccessible to the masses.

The actional and imperative components of Judaism avoid these problems, shaping a this-worldly and realistic religion that strikes a balance between subjectivity and objectivity, between individualism and community-mindedness, and between elitism and democracy. The commandments concretize religiosity, ground it in real life, channel religious feeling, provide restraint against desire, and regulate man's interactions with his surroundings. Halakhah combines action with feeling and thought to form a unified whole that engages the entirety of man. It begins as a discipline – of action, feeling, and thought – and only then turns into a sublime romance.[8]

---

individual spiritual ascent" (*U-Vikkashtem mi-Sham*, 58). Yet there seems to be an irreducible tension between these two assertions. This tension is especially pronounced in the Rav's discussion of prayer. Although the Rav took great pains to emphasize the accessibility of prayer to everyone (see *Worship of the Heart*, 26–28, 92–94, 120–21, 173–75), R. Joshua Amaru (162–63 of his review essay referenced on p. 222 below) nevertheless cogently questions the extent to which Rav Soloveitchik's conception of prayer is truly exoteric. Analogously, on p. 315 below, I question the Rav's assertion that halakhic man is democratic. Clearly, this was an issue with which the Rav struggled.

7 As indicated above, the Rav's main treatments of this question are found in *Halakhic Man*, 41–44, 57–60, and elsewhere; *U-Vikkashtem mi-Sham*, 53–57; and *The Halakhic Mind*, 78–81.

8 See For Further Reference, #3.

For Further Reference

1. **Halakhah as quantification of religious subjectivity:** *Halakhic Man*, 55–63; *The Halakhic Mind*, 85ff.

2. **Esotericism and exotericism:** *Halakhic Man*, 42–44; *U-Vikkashtem mi-Sham*, 57–60; *The Halakhic Mind*, 80. As discussed above, in these works the Rav identifies practical observance of *mitzvot* as the basis for equality between Jews, despite individuals' unequal attainments in the spiritual and intellectual realms. In other works, the Rav identifies additional factors that allow Jews of differing ability and accomplishment to achieve a measure of equality. Regarding Torah study, scholar and simpleton alike can be united in their love of Torah and their dedication to it (*Family Redeemed*, 177–78). Similarly, regarding *shelihut*, or the divine mission entrusted to each person, equality resides not in accomplishment but in devotion and effort (*Derashot Harav*, 157–63; see also *Out of the Whirlwind*, 148).

3. **Is action dictated by emotion?** In this chapter, we asked why the subjective inner component of religion alone is insufficient, and why it needs to be supplemented by outer performance. After answering this, we are left with another question: granting the need for the inner and the outer, for the subjective and the objective, which should shape the other? Which is the starting point for religious inquiry? Should we mold our outer actions on the basis of our religious feelings, or should our experiences be generated and guided by our objective religious practices? The Rav opts for the latter position, based on two considerations. First, emotion is mutable, and were it to dictate action, Halakhah would lack stability and continuity. Second, it is easy to mistake aesthetic or ethical emotion for religious emotion; were Halakhah to be dictated by subjective emotion, there is no guarantee that the emotion would be authentically religious. The Rav develops these ideas in a philosophical manner in *The Halakhic Mind*, 88–91, and in popular manner in a 1973 *derashah* on *Parashat Korah* (adapted by R. Abraham Besdin as "The 'Common-Sense' Rebellion against Torah Authority," in *Reflections of the Rav* [Jerusalem, 1979], 139–49, especially 142–46). In both places, this argument forms the basis of his critique of the religious subjectivism of Liberal Judaism. See also Chapter 31 below.

Section III

RELIGION IN THE MODERN WORLD: THE LONELY MAN OF FAITH

Chapter 11

Presenting the Problem

In this penetrating and original work, perhaps his best known and most influential, Rav Soloveitchik tackles a number of major issues, the central ones being man's dual role in the world, and the possibility of religious existence in modern, largely secular, society. Along the way, he offers startling insights into a host of other topics. Some of these ideas develop themes raised in his shorter writings; here he places them into broader perspective. Other ideas echo those of his longer works. In this sense, *The Lonely Man of Faith* occupies a central place in the Rav's writings and can be regarded as an overture to his entire oeuvre.

The essay's rich range of ideas makes reading it a challenging and exhilarating endeavor, but at the same time it often serves to obscure the essay's main point. *The Lonely Man of Faith* is finely crafted, with a clear structure and progression of ideas. In this chapter, I would like to examine closely the Rav's introductory comments, where he delineates both the goal and the method of this work. When we understand how the Rav himself defines the issue he wishes to address, we can use this understanding to guide our reading of the rest of the essay.

Adam I and Adam II

Let me start by doing something unpardonable: trying to sum up the main argument of *The Lonely Man of Faith* in a few short paragraphs. Although perforce this will be oversimplified, I think it will aid us greatly in understanding the Rav's characterization of the essay.

Rav Soloveitchik proposes that the two accounts of the creation of man (in chapters 1 and 2 of Genesis) portray two types of man, two human ideals.[1] One type, termed Adam the first (or Adam I), is guided by the quest for dignity, which is an external social quality attained by control over one's environment.[2] He is a creative and majestic personality who espouses a practical-utilitarian approach to the world. Adam II, on the other hand, is guided by the quest for redemption, which is a quality of the inner personality that one attains by control over oneself. He is humble and submissive, and yearns for an intimate relationship with God and with his fellow man in order to overcome his sense of incompleteness and inadequacy. These differences carry over to the type of community each one creates: the "natural work community" (Adam I) and the "covenantal faith community" (Adam II).

God not only desires the existence of each of these personality types and each of these communities, but actually bids each and every one of us to attempt to embody within ourselves both of these seemingly irreconcilable types. We must attempt to pursue both dignity and redemption. The demand to be both Adam I and Adam II leads to a built-in tension in the life of each person responsive to this dual call. Because one lives with a constant dialectic, a continual oscillation between two modes of existence, one can never realize fully the goals of either Adam I or Adam II. Unable to feel totally at home in either community, man is burdened by loneliness. Since this type of loneliness is inherent in one's very being as a religious individual, the Rav terms it "ontological loneliness."[3] In a sense, this kind of loneliness is tragic; but since it is willed by God, it helps man realize his destiny and therefore is ultimately a positive and constructive experience.

The contemporary man of faith, however, experiences a particular kind of loneliness due to his historical circumstances, and this "historical loneliness" is a purely negative phenomenon.[4] Modern man, pursuant to his great success in the realm of majesty–dignity, recognizes only the Adam I side of existence, and refuses to acknowledge the inherent duality of his being. Contemporary

---

1 In their approaches to God, the world and the self, these roughly parallel the two personae depicted in "Majesty and Humility"; see Chap. 3 above. We will discuss the Rav's methodology of studying ideal personality types in Chap. 12.

2 In contemporary usage, "dignity" often carries a connotation of passivity or stoicism, as in "He suffered with dignity." In ethical discourse, it is taken to refer to inalienable rights, as in the phrase "human dignity." It is important to note that in *The Lonely Man of Faith* the Rav uses "dignity" in a different sense, namely, as referring to majesty, a quality attained through conquest. In *Out of the Whirlwind* (104–15), the Rav uses "dignity" in yet another sense, one that incorporates defeat as well as victory.

3 Ontological = relating to being or existence.

4 The contrast between "ontological" and "historical" means that the first type of loneliness is part of what it means to be human, while the second is not a built-in aspect of human existence but rather the product of specific historical circumstances.

society speaks the language of Adam I, of cultural achievement, and is unable or unwilling to understand the language of Adam II, of the uniqueness and autonomy of faith. Worse, contemporary Adam I has infiltrated and appropriated the realm of Adam II, the world of religion; he presents himself as Adam II, while actually distorting covenantal man's entire message.

A Universal Message

We are now in a position to understand the Rav's characterization of *The Lonely Man of Faith* in its opening paragraphs. First, from its very title, it is evident that the essay's message is universal. *The Lonely Man of Faith* refers to any religious faith, not just Judaism; the dilemma of faith in the modern world applies to all religions.[5] It should also be noted that the essay addresses men and women equally; nowhere here does the Rav distinguish between them. The word "man" in the title should therefore be understood as "person."

The essay's universalistic bent is further expressed in the choice of the text that stands at its center: the story of the creation of Adam and Eve, the parents of humankind. Significantly, references to Judaism and Jewish sources appear almost exclusively in the footnotes. Finally, it is worth mentioning that the essay originated in a lecture to Catholic seminarians and in a series of lectures, sponsored by the National Institute of Mental Health, delivered to Jewish (including non-Orthodox) social workers.[6]

A Personal Dilemma

In the essay's opening sentence, Rav Soloveitchik informs us that he will not address the intellectual challenges which modernity poses to faith, but rather something much more basic: the challenge modernity poses to the *experience* of faith. He will focus on "a human life situation in which the man of faith as an individual concrete being . . . is entangled" (1).[7] In this sense, the essay is

---

5 At least, this holds true of Western religions, which were the Rav's concern. He had little interest in Eastern religion.

6 A note at the beginning of the Doubleday printing of the book reads: "The basic ideas of *The Lonely Man of Faith* were formulated in Rabbi Soloveitchik's lectures in the 'Marriage and Family' program of the National Institute of Mental Health at Yeshiva University in New York City." R. Walter Wurzburger reports that *The Lonely Man of Faith* "was first presented as an oral lecture at a Catholic seminary in Brighton, Massachusetts" (*Covenantal Imperatives* [Jerusalem, 2008], 146).

7 I will refer to *The Lonely Man of Faith* interchangeably as an essay and as a book, since it was originally published in essay form in the journal *Tradition* (7:2, Summer 1965) and

not a work of abstract speculation but rather "a tale of a personal dilemma," whose power derives from the fact that it is based on "actual situations and experiences with which I have been confronted" (ibid.). In a striking characterization of the essay, the Rav concludes:

> Instead of talking theology, in the didactic sense, eloquently and in balanced sentences, I would like, hesitantly and haltingly, to confide in you, and to share with you some concerns which weigh heavily on my mind and which frequently assume the proportions of an awareness of crisis (1–2).

Furthermore, he later confesses that he does not have a solution to the problem he will pose, "for the dilemma is insoluble" (8). Why, then, does he bother to present the problem at all? He offers two reasons:

(1) "All I want is to follow the advice given by Elihu the son of Berachel of old who said, 'I will speak that I may find relief;'[8] for there is a redemptive quality for an agitated mind in the spoken word and a tormented soul finds peace in confessing" (2).

(2) ". . . [T]he defining itself [of the dilemma] is a worthwhile cognitive gesture which, I hope, will yield a better understanding of ourselves and our commitment" (8).

Why is the dilemma insoluble? Let us first consider the Rav's definition of the dilemma, and then we will return to this question.

Being Lonely and Being Alone

> The nature of the dilemma can be stated in a three-word sentence. I am lonely (3).

Here we must distinguish between being alone and being lonely.[9] Aloneness means lacking love and friendship; this is an entirely destructive feeling. Loneliness, on the other hand, is an awareness of one's uniqueness, and to be unique often means to be misunderstood. A lonely person, while surrounded by friends, feels that his unique and incommunicable experiences separate him from them. This fills him with a gnawing sense of the seemingly insurmountable gap that prevents true communion between individuals.

---

subsequently in book form (Doubleday, 1992; Aronson, 1996; Three Leaves, 2006; Maggid, 2011). Page and chapter references will follow the Doubleday printing.

8 Job 32:20.

9 We noted this distinction in Chap. 1 above, when discussing the death of the Rav's wife. While in *The Lonely Man of Faith* the Rav is consistent in his use of these terms, this is not always the case in other lectures.

While painful, this experience can also be "stimulating" and "cathartic," since it "presses everything in me into the service of God," the Lonely One, who truly understands me.

As mentioned above, loneliness – the sense of the uniqueness and incommunicability of one's inner life – can have two possible causes: ontological and historical. These two forms of loneliness, while stemming from the same basic dichotomy in the human personality, are experienced differently and must be addressed separately.

Ontological Loneliness: Experiencing Inner Conflict

The ontological loneliness of the man of faith derives from the very nature of his religious experience. In a phrase that may seem surprising at first, the Rav describes the religious experience as "fraught with inner conflicts and incongruities." He also calls it "antinomic" and "paradoxical" (2).[10]

This portrayal of the religious experience initially strikes us as odd because modern man often equates religious belief with tranquility and peace of mind. However, bearing in mind the summary of the Rav's argument at the beginning of this chapter, it should be clear why Rav Soloveitchik totally disagrees with the "peace of mind" approach. In his view, God demands of man to live in two seemingly incompatible modes of existence – that of Adam I and that of Adam II. Thus, one who heeds God's dual demand lives a life full of dialectical tension.

No Enchanted Island

However, it is important to understand that this tension does not derive only from the requirement to be both Adam I and Adam II, but is inherent within Adam II himself, within "Religious Man" and the religious realm proper. Religious man himself, and not only the compound persona of majestic and religious man, is an antithetical character. He constantly grapples with dichotomous concepts and experiences located at the heart of religious existence: "temporality and eternity, [divine] knowledge and [human] choice (necessity and freedom), love and fear (the yearning for God and the flight from His

---

10 "Antinomic" means contradictory, or, in our context, self-contradictory. This is not to be confused with "antinomian," which denotes refusal to recognize the authority of moral law. (In theology, "antinomianism" is the position that salvation is attained through faith alone, not through obedience to a moral or religious code.) While the Rav loved a good antinomy (= contradiction or paradox), he hated antinomianism, which espoused rejection of Halakhah.

glorious splendor), incredible, overbold daring and an extreme sense of humility, transcendence and God's closeness, the profane and the holy, etc."[11]
Many contemporary popularizers of religion portray faith as offering ready comfort and easy inner harmony to believers, providing a refuge from the discord, doubts, fears and responsibilities of the secular realm. From his earliest writings until his latest, Rav Soloveitchik took umbrage with this shallow and false ideology, which he found to be particularly prevalent in America.[12] Religion does not provide believers with instant tranquility, but rather forces them to confront uncomfortable dichotomies; it is "a raging, clamorous torrent of man's consciousness with all its crises, pangs, and torments."[13] Religion is not less demanding than secularity, but rather more so. It does not offer an escape from reality, but rather provides the ultimate encounter with reality. It suggests no quick fixes, but rather demands constant struggle in order to attain spiritual growth. As the Rav so memorably put it, "*Kedushah* is not a paradise but a paradox."[14]

Historical Loneliness: The Contemporary Crisis

Thus far we have discussed the ontological loneliness of the man of faith, the crises and tensions inherent in religious existence. However, Rav Soloveitchik informs us that in this essay his "prime concern" is not ontological loneliness but rather the man of faith's experience of historical loneliness, in which "a highly sensitized and agitated heart, overwhelmed by the impact of social and cultural forces, filters this root awareness [of ontological loneliness] through the medium of painful, frustrating emotions" (6). Rav Soloveitchik does not wish to focus on a general, timeless theological issue, but instead to address the predicament of the *contemporary* man of faith who, "due to his peculiar position in our secular society . . . lives through a particularly difficult and agonizing crisis" (6). A sharp and prescient social critic, Rav Soloveitchik is here keenly sensitive to the changes society has undergone and the consequent need to reassess the role of the man of religion within it:

> Let me spell out this passional[15] experience of contemporary man of faith.

---

11 *Halakhic Man*, 142.

12 The Rav's two classic treatments of this theme are found in "Sacred and Profane" (reprinted in *Shiurei Harav* [Hoboken, 1994]) and n. 4 of *Halakhic Man*. This footnote is a small jewel of an essay in its own right.

13 *Halakhic Man*, 142.

14 "Sacred and Profane," 8.

15 Passional = expressing suffering.

He looks upon himself as a stranger in modern society, which is technically minded, self-centered, and self-loving, almost in a sickly narcissistic fashion, scoring honor upon honor, piling up victory upon victory, reaching for the distant galaxies, and seeing in the here-and-now sensible world the only manifestation of being. What can a man of faith like myself, living by a doctrine which has no technical potential, by a law which cannot be tested in the laboratory, steadfast in his loyalty to an eschatological vision whose fulfillment cannot be predicted with any degree of probability . . . – what can such a man say to a functional utilitarian society which is saeculum-oriented[16] and whose practical reasons of the mind have long ago supplanted the sensitive reasons of the heart? (6–7).

The Rav is certainly not anti-intellectual, nor is he opposed to technological advances. What he is asserting here is the autonomy of faith. Modern society speaks in pragmatic and utilitarian terms, and expects religion to justify itself in these categories. But the value of religion, the Rav believes, is independent of its practical utility, its usefulness in helping man attain dignity and majesty. Rather, faith is a response to a divine summons, a call to submit ourselves to God. Its meaning and value far exceed justification by the human intellect. However, pragmatic modern man – whether secular or religious – works only with categories of the intellect, not realizing their limited purview. The danger, then, is not just that secularists have ceased to understand the man of faith; it is that adherents of religion have ceased to understand themselves.

We can now appreciate the true import of the concluding sentences of the Rav's introduction:

If my audience will feel that these interpretations are also relevant to their perceptions and emotions, I shall feel amply rewarded. However, I shall not feel hurt if my thoughts will find no response in the hearts of my listeners (9).

The Rav is not being coy or diffident here. Rather, as Rabbi Jonathan Sacks points out, this is "an expression characteristic of the man of faith in the modern world. He no longer speaks the shared language of society. . . . How then is he to communicate? Simply by speaking out of his inner situation and hoping to find an echoing response in his audience."[17] Thus, the man

---

16 "Saeculum" is an Augustinian term denoting the world of human life within time.

17 *Tradition in an Untraditional Age* (London, 1990), 41. To be sure, any depiction of inner human experience is necessarily subjective and therefore it is difficult to convey; but the man of faith's alienation from contemporary society makes it even less likely that his words will strike a responsive chord in his listeners.

of faith's uncertainty about his ability to communicate lies at the very heart of his problem.

The Insoluble Problem

Returning now to our question of why the dilemma this essay poses is insoluble, we must offer a dual response.

(a) In terms of ontological loneliness, the answer should be clear. An essential dichotomy is woven into the very fabric of the religious experience. As such, this basic dialectic is not subject to "solutions;" it is part of the very definition of religious existence.

(b) There is no a priori reason why there should not be a solution to the problem of historical loneliness. This feeling does not stem from any inherent qualities or basic definitions of religiosity. Rather, it is the product of the confrontation of the man of faith with specific historical and cultural circumstances. Therefore, as you read *The Lonely Man of Faith*, keep in mind the following questions: What are the possible solutions to the problem of the man of faith's historical loneliness? Is it perhaps insoluble? Even if the problem admits of no solution, one must still respond to it somehow. What course of action does the Rav advocate? Consider these questions especially when reading the end of the book.

A Reading Guide

To assist you in following the Rav's argument, I would like to present two outlines of the book, one briefly tracing its overall structure and the other detailing the contents of each chapter.[18]

---

18 Note that I follow the chapter numbering in the Doubleday edition and subsequent publishings. While the original *Tradition* 1965 edition counts the introduction as chapter 1, the Doubleday edition does not number it. Therefore, chapter 1 in the Doubleday edition is chapter 2 in the *Tradition* version, etc. However, although the Doubleday edition does away with sub-chapter headings, e.g., 8.A, 8.B, etc., I will retain these in order to clarify the internal structure of chapters. These sub-chapter divisions are indicated in the Doubleday-Aronson edition by a blank line between paragraphs. They are restored in the Maggid edition.

The Overall Structure of the Book:

The Contents of Each Chapter:

Chapter 12

Defining the Two Adams

Once Rav Soloveitchik finishes delineating the problem he wishes to address, he sets up the framework from which to determine the answer. For the man of faith, he notes, self-knowledge means "to understand one's place and role within the scheme of events and things willed and approved by God" (8). The Rav turns, therefore, to an examination of the Bible's account of the creation of Adam and Eve, which should reveal to us the essence and purpose of humanity.

Biblical Anthropology

The biblical narrative, as is well-known, contains two versions of the story of man's creation. Biblical criticism attributes this to the existence of two different documents that were subsequently interwoven in the biblical text. *Hazal* and the *Rishonim* were aware of these same discrepancies,[1] but offered different solutions based on their vastly differing assumptions. Rav Soloveitchik offers a strikingly original solution which flows naturally from his general philosophic approach.

Since Jewish thought often takes the form of exegesis of canonical texts (whether biblical or rabbinic), it is often the case, as Rabbi Jonathan Sacks notes,[2] that new forms of Jewish philosophy entail new ways of reading

---

1 The Rav (10) lists several places where *Hazal* and the *Rishonim* take account of the discrepancies between Gen. chaps. 1 and 2 – *Berakhot* 61a, *Ketubot* 8a, Ramban on Gen. 2:7, and *Kuzari* IV.

2 *Tradition in an Untraditional Age* (London, 1990), 40. See also the sources cited in his footnote.

Jewish texts. In Rav Soloveitchik's case, this means extending the Brisker method of "*hakirah*"[3] from Halakhah to Bible and Aggadah. In keeping with this method, he highlights the differences between Genesis chapter 1 and chapter 2, offering a unique interpretation of their significance.

> [T]he answer [to the discrepancies] lies not in an alleged dual tradition but in dual man, not in an imaginary contradiction between two versions but in a real contradiction in the nature of man. The two accounts deal with two Adams, two men, two fathers of mankind, two types, two representatives of humanity, and it is no wonder that they are not identical (10).

Prior to examining the two Adams, let us review some comments about the Rav's methodology that appeared in Chapter 2 above. Much of Rav Soloveitchik's thought can be described as "philosophic anthropology," the description of different ideal types of personalities. They are "ideal" in the sense of being pure abstract types, not in the sense of being the best types. In fact, the Rav repeatedly emphasizes that these pure types do not exist in reality (*The Lonely Man of Faith*, 72; *Halakhic Man*, n. 1). We can compare them to certain chemical elements or subatomic particles which can be isolated only under laboratory conditions, but cannot be seen by themselves in nature.

Thus, due to the reality of human complexity, any specific real person will contain within himself or herself a conglomeration of various types. However, the point of separating an individual into his component parts is to demonstrate the internal coherence of each position, and thereby to understand better the nature of the complex hybrid produced by the coexistence of the various types. For example, every person is expected to embody the positions of both Adam I and Adam II, but in order to negotiate this dialectic successfully, one must understand each component by itself.

Two Accounts

I would now like to present selections from the two biblical accounts, and then the four major discrepancies which Rav Soloveitchik lists.[4]

I. Genesis 1:27–28:

> So God created man in His own image, in the image of God created He him, male and female created He them. And God blessed them and God said to

---

3 See p. 27 above.

4 Note that there are details of the stories with which he does not deal here, but which he addresses elsewhere – see For Further Reference, #1.

them: Be fruitful and multiply, and fill the earth and subdue it, and have dominion over the fish of the sea, over the fowl of the heaven, and over all the
beasts which crawl on the earth.

II. Genesis 2:7–8, 15, 22:
And the eternal God formed the man of the dust of the ground and breathed
into his nostrils the breath of life and man became a living soul. And the eternal God planted a garden eastward in Eden . . . And the eternal God took the
man and placed him in the Garden of Eden to serve it and to keep it . . . And
of the side, which the Eternal God took from the man, He fashioned a woman,
and brought her to the man.

The discrepancies:
(1) Regarding Adam I, the Torah states that he was created "in the image of
God" but mentions nothing about the creation of his body, while regarding Adam II, the Torah says that he was fashioned from dust and then God
breathed life into him.
(2) Adam I is told to "Fill the earth and subdue it," while Adam II is charged
to cultivate the garden.
(3) In the first account, male and female are created concurrently, while in the
second account, Adam is created alone and Eve appears later.
(4) The first account refers to God only by the name "*Elokim*," while the second account also uses the Tetragrammaton (the *Shem ha-Meforash*, the
four-letter sacred name).

Explaining the Discrepancies

The Rav's explanations of these discrepancies are spread throughout chapters
I–VI of *The Lonely Man of Faith*. I will present them here briefly, and will
then proceed to examine Adam I and Adam II in more detail.

(1) Chapters I–II: Adam I's creation "in the image of God" refers to his
capacity and desire to imitate God by becoming a creator, particularly in response to God's mandate to "fill the earth and subdue it." This is expressed by
man's practical intellect, i.e., his scientific ability to comprehend the forces
of nature and his technological ability to bend them to his will. Adam II, on
the other hand, does not have such a grandiose self-image; he is humble, realizing that he was created from the dust of the earth. He allows himself to be
overpowered and defeated by God. While Adam I maintains some distance
from God, relating merely to the divine endowment of creativity, Adam II

has a "genuine living experience" of God and is preoccupied with Him, as evidenced by the metaphor of God breathing life into his nostrils.

(2) Chapters III and IV.A: Told to subdue the earth, Adam I adopts an active, dignified and majestic posture. He is a conqueror in both intellectual and practical terms. Intellectually, he is able to take the bewildering array of natural phenomena and fashion scientific laws to explain their functioning. This is a conquest of the human mind over nature, or of order over chaos. Practically, Adam I overcomes nature's threats to his existence by draining swamps and discovering vaccines. He harnesses the forces of nature to serve his own ends by splitting the atom and extracting fuel from the earth. He fashions devices such as the automobile, airplane and spaceship to extend his hegemony. Adam II, on the other hand, is more passive and receptive. His goal is not to exercise mastery but to serve. God places him in the garden "to serve it and to keep it."

(3) Chapters III and IV.B: Adam I is a social creature; male and female are created together. His quest for dignity can be realized only within a community, since dignity entails impressing others by means of one's accomplishments. Furthermore, the quest for dignity requires the cooperation of others, because one person alone cannot master a hostile environment. Adam II, however, is created in solitude; loneliness is inherent to his very being. In order to redeem himself from this situation which God deems to be "not good" – meaning, to forge an existential community which will relieve him of his loneliness – he is required to sacrifice part of himself.

(4) Chapter VI: "*Elokim*" denotes God as the source of cosmic dynamics, while the Tetragrammaton indicates personal, intimate communion between God and man. Adam I is satisfied by an impersonal encounter with the former (the cosmic experience), while Adam II craves the latter (the covenantal experience).

Adam I – The Quest for Dignity

Adam I and Adam II seem to start at the same point: both are motivated by their encounter with the cosmos, both search for God, and both try to realize their full human potential. But because of their different needs, attitudes and goals, they approach these tasks in very different manners, so that they end up in very different places.

Adam I sees his main objective, the cultivation of his humanity, in the attainment of dignity.[5] "[B]y setting himself up as a dignified majestic being capable of ruling his environment," he distinguishes himself from and raises himself above the rest of nature.

> Dignity is a social and behavioral category, expressing not an intrinsic existential quality, but a technique of living, a way of impressing society . . . Hence, dignity is measured not by the inner worth of the in-depth-personality, but by the accomplishments of the surface-personality (25–26).

Why is the conquest of nature dignified? Why does majesty make one more fully "man"?

> The brute's existence is an undignified one because it is a helpless one . . . Man of old who could not fight disease and succumbed in multitudes to yellow fever or any other plague with degrading helplessness could not lay claim to dignity. Only the man who builds hospitals, discovers therapeutic techniques and saves lives is blessed with dignity (16–17).[6]

Hence, Adam I is completely utilitarian in motivation, and boldly aggressive in approach. When he confronts the cosmos, he asks only "how," not "why"; he wants to know how the cosmos functions so that he can master it. "The most characteristic representative of Adam the first is the mathematical scientist" (18), who conceptualizes natural phenomena into an abstract system of his own making.[7] He is concerned not only with the functionality of his creation, but also with its order, balance, pleasantness and beauty. This extends to his structuring of society: "[H]e legislates for himself norms and laws because a dignified existence is an orderly existence" (18–19).

All this should sound familiar: it echoes the approach of cosmic man in "Majesty and Humility."[8] He espouses an ethic of victory, seeking to master nature and to legislate orderly norms. And, as in "Majesty and Humility," the Rav here emphasizes that,

> Even this longing for vastness, no matter how adventurous and fantastic, is legitimate. Man reaching for the distant stars is acting in harmony with his nature which was created, willed, and directed by his Maker (19–20).

---

5 See n. 2 of the previous chapter regarding the Rav's use of the term "dignity."

6 Note that dignity does not derive from *helping* other people, but from *conquering* disease.

7 It is interesting to note that, in other works, the Rav presents the mathematical scientist as the model for halakhic man.

8 See pp. 57–59 above.

However, as in the former essay, the Rav will also inform us here that this approach must be balanced by that of humble, covenantal man.

Adam II – The Search for Redemption

Adam II also seeks to fully realize his humanity, but he interprets this in terms of attaining redemption. The Rav draws a series of contrasts between dignity and redemption. While dignity is a social quality of the surface personality, redemption is an existential state of the inner personality. Redemption is attained by control over oneself, dignity by control over one's surroundings; redemption expresses itself in surrender to God, dignity in defiance of nature; redemption is characterized by retreat, dignity by advance. The contrast between advance and retreat should clue us in to the fact that the dialectical oscillation between these two modes of living is a cathartic process.

The redemptive surrender to God gives Adam II a sense of "axiological security":

> The individual intuits his existence as something worthwhile, legitimate and adequate, anchored in something stable and unchangeable (35).

Ultimately, this experience serves as a basis for him to enter into an intimate relationship with God.

When confronting the cosmos, Adam II does not wish to master it or mathematize it, but rather to encounter it directly in all of its pristine splendor. This is the difference between what the Rav refers to as the quantitative and qualitative approaches to reality.[9]

> [Adam II] studies [the universe] with the naivete, awe and admiration of the child who seeks the unusual and wonderful in every ordinary thing and event … He looks for the image of God not in the mathematical formula or the natural relational law but every beam of light, in every bud and blossom, in the morning breeze and the stillness of a starlit evening (23).

The cosmic encounter propels Adam II to ask *why* the world exists (not *how* it functions), and to seek out God, Whose presence he senses behind all of creation. On the one hand, the natural religious response to this awe-inspiring encounter is to recite a benediction, praising and acknowledging

---

9 This distinction appears in many of the Rav's writings, and is especially important in *Halakhic Man, The Halakhic Mind* and "*Mah Dodekh mi-Dod.*" We discussed this distinction briefly in Chap. 7 above, in connection with the catharsis of the intellect. See also the sources cited in n. 4 there.

God as the source of cosmic dynamics (51, n. 1). On the other hand, Adam II recognizes that encountering God in nature is insufficient to attain redemption. There are two reasons for this. First, God is both hidden and revealed when one searches for Him in nature. Second, the message of the Heavens is impersonal.

> In short, the cosmic experience is antithetic and tantalizing. It exhausts itself in the awesome dichotomy of God's involvement in the drama of creation, and His exaltedness above and remoteness from this very drama. This dichotomy cancels the intimacy and immediacy from one's relationship with God and renders the personal approach to God complicated and difficult . . . Therefore, the man of faith, in order to redeem himself from his loneliness and misery, must meet God at a personal covenantal level, where he can be near Him and feel free in His presence (49–50).

It is the covenant, not the cosmic experience of God, which allows Adam II to attain redemption.[10]

The differences between Adam I and Adam II carry over to the type of community that each one forms. We will turn our attention to these two communities in the next chapter.

---

10 See For Further Reference, #2.

FOR FURTHER REFERENCE

1. **Other places where the Rav examines the creation story:** "Confrontation," "The Community," "Adam and Eve" (in *Family Redeemed*), and *The Emergence of Ethical Man*. There is also much material still in manuscript dealing with paradisiacal man. As I noted in Chapter 2, the Rav's habit was to examine a text afresh each time he encountered it, learning something new from it each time. This is well-known regarding his Talmud scholarship, and is no less true of his study of the Bible. See also Chapter 13, For Further Reference, #1.

2. **Cosmic experience of God:** This is a major theme in the opening chapters of *U-Vikkashtem mi-Sham* (where it is referred to as the "*Bereishit* experience" or the "natural ontological consciousness"). See especially chapter 3 of *U-Vikkashtem mi-Sham*, 19–27, which significantly expands the account in chapter VI of *The Lonely Man of Faith* of man's search for God in the cosmos and its ultimate failure. The account in *U-Vikkashtem mi-Sham* is examined in Chapter 32 below (pp. 349–53).

3. **Experience vs. proof:** In the fascinating and highly significant footnote at the end of chapter 6 of *The Lonely Man of Faith* (51–52), the Rav takes pains to distinguish between *apprehending* God *in* nature (the cosmic *experience*) and *comprehending* God *through* nature (the cosmological *proof*). The former is an experience, while the latter is an intellectual performance (whose validity has been undermined by modern philosophy, for reasons discussed in Chapter 32, p. 351 below). In a single stroke, the Rav does away with all medieval proofs for the existence of God, but then reinstates them when conceived as experiences and not as proofs. This has major ramifications, and is a good example of his translation of Maimonidean philosophy into more modern (generally existential) terms. In this manner, he saves many Maimonidean doctrines, which are dependent on a defunct philosophical framework, from irrelevance. He makes the same point in *U-Vikkashtem mi-Sham* (11–15), as discussed in Chapter 34, p. 370 below. See also the discussions of this issue in Chapters 17 and 32 below.

Chapter 13

Two Types of Community

According to Rav Soloveitchik, one cannot understand man exclusively as a solitary being; he must also be viewed as part of a community. This stems from the fact that existence in community is one of man's basic needs. Therefore, after delineating the features of Adam I and Adam II as individuals,[1] the Rav proceeds to examine the type of community each one creates.

Community of Majesty and Community of Faith

To further his quest for dignity, Adam I enters into a pragmatic partnership with others, creating a "natural work community." Existentially, Adam I sees himself as a complete, self-sufficient being. Although he does not suffer from loneliness and feels no yearning for soul-to-soul communication with others, he does require their cooperation in order to promote mutually beneficial action. Thus, he creates a community of shared labor, not of shared existence. Since he does not consider himself in need of catharsis or redemption, the community he forms does not elevate his inner self.

This kind of approach to the human need for community dominated political theory for centuries:

> The whole theory of the social contract brought to perfection by the philosophers of the Age of Reason reflects the thinking of Adam the first, identifying man with his intellectual nature and creative technological will and finding in human existence coherence, legitimacy and reasonableness exclusively. To the thinkers of the Age of Reason, man posed no problem. He was for them an

---

1 See Chap. 12 above.

understandable, simple affair . . . They saw man in his glory but failed to see him in his tragic plight (30).

Adam II, on the other hand, is sharply aware of "his tragic plight." Having been created alone, and subsequently becoming aware of his distinctness from the rest of nature,[2] he realizes that

"To be" means to be the only one, singular and different, and consequently lonely. For what causes man to be lonely and feel insecure if not the awareness of his uniqueness and exclusiveness? (40–41).

Adam II therefore seeks to create a "covenantal faith community" in which he will be able to overcome his sense of ontological incompleteness and loneliness by learning to communicate with others and to form a depth-connection with them. The recognition and validation of another person, who is as unique as oneself, entails relinquishing one's self-preoccupation and sense of all-inclusiveness. Therefore, for Adam II, forming a community is a sacrificial act, or what we have previously encountered in the Rav's writings as the act of *tzimtzum* (self-contraction or recoil).[3]

Covenantal Commitment

The covenantal faith community centers around shared commitments, not merely shared interests. Its members work together to "cleanse, redeem and hallow" their existences (33). The I and the Thou connect to each other by means of their mutual connection to the divine He.[4] This connection to God takes the form of an absolute commitment encompassing the totality of man's being: emotion, intellect, will and action. When two different people share this absolute and all-encompassing commitment to God, it allows them to overcome the barriers separating them from one another. Opening himself totally to God, man can open himself to other people as well, with shared values and goals serving as the basis for communication between them. Mutual commitment thus becomes the foundation of the existential community.

The overcoming of barriers that separate individuals takes place, as I described it when discussing "The Community," along both the horizontal

---

2 See For Further Reference, #1.

3 See Chap. 2 above.

4 The structure of A connecting to B through mutual connection to C figures prominently also in *U-Vikkashtem mi-Sham*, where God and man connect to each other through their mutual cognition of the world and of Halakhah. See Chap. 34 below.

and the vertical axes. Members of a covenantal community join their contemporaries (the horizontal plane) through sympathy, love and common action. They express concern for each other's welfare via, for example, prayer and charity. This sense of fellowship and friendship redeems man by relieving him of his feeling of isolation and incompatibility with others. The "other" is no longer a stranger, an "It," who concerns me only to the extent that he can bring me benefit or harm. Instead, he becomes a "Thou," a person of equal and independent worth to whom I am committed and whom I engage in true dialogue.

The gesture of friendship, however, does not characterize the community of Adam I.

> In the majestic community, in which surface-personalities meet and commitment never exceeds the bounds of the utilitarian, we may find collegiality, neighborliness, civility, or courtesy – but not friendship, which is the exclusive experience awarded by God to covenantal man who is thus redeemed from his agonizing solitude (69).

Within the covenantal community, moreover, Adam II overcomes his insecurity as a temporal being by infusing all his actions with meaning, linking them to the past in which the covenant originated and to the future in which it will ultimately be fulfilled. He joins the covenantal community of past and future generations (the vertical plane) through conveying the covenantal tradition.

> Within the covenantal community not only contemporary individuals but generations are engaged in a colloquy and each single experience of time is three-dimensional, manifesting itself in memory, actuality and anticipatory tension. This experiential triad, translated into moral categories, results in an awesome awareness of responsibility to a great past which handed down the divine imperative to the present generation in trust and confidence and to a mute future expecting this generation to discharge its covenantal duty conscientiously and honorably (71).[5]

Conceptually Distinct but Intertwining

When the Rav writes (at the end of chapter VII) that friendship or the three-dimensional time experience are categories of covenantal life, we should not mistakenly assume that he means that these can be found only among "religious" individuals. Rav Soloveitchik repeatedly stresses that his discussion

---

5 See For Further Reference, #2.

here is typological – it deals with simple, ideal personalities, not with real, complex people. The two Adams are theoretical constructs representing different aspects of life. Adam I, at this stage of our discussion, represents a life oriented purely to external accomplishment and success. Therefore, he lives in the moment and is capable only of shallow working relationships with others. Adam II, on the other hand, experiences the depth-dimension of existence and is inwardly oriented. This is why the Rav says that "Friendship – not as a social surface-relation but as an existential in-depth-relation between two individuals – is realizable only within the framework of the covenantal community" (68). In addition, since he continually searches for meaning beyond the here-and-now, only Adam II can regard the past and the future as "experiential realities."

Real people, of course, experience both the surface and depth-dimensions of life. The Rav's reason for separating these elements is to highlight the paradoxes implicit in our existence, stemming from the seeming incommensurability between these two dimensions of living. Furthermore, not only are real people complex, but the Rav acknowledges (in chapters VIII–X, primarily in chapter IX) that even according to his theoretical model, there must be interaction between the two communities, resulting in mutual influence and the borrowing of ideas from each other. For example, he writes:

> In reality there are no pure typological structures and hence the covenantal and majestic communities overlap. Therefore, it is not surprising that we come across the three-dimensional time experience, which we have presented as typically covenantal, in the majestic community as well . . . However, this time awareness was borrowed by majestic history from covenantal history (72–73).

> Certain aspects of the doctrinal and normative covenantal *kerygma* (message) of faith are of utmost importance to majestic man and are, in a paradoxical way, translatable into the latter's vernacular (93).

> Since majestic man is in need of a transcendental experience in order to strengthen his cultural edifice, it is the duty of the man of faith to provide him with some component parts of this experience (97–98).

We will deal with this subject more fully when addressing the last three chapters of the book.

God as a Member of the Community

The covenantal community includes not just Adam and Eve, but also God Himself, since both God and man are parties to the covenant.

> Of course, even within the framework of this community, God appears as the leader, teacher, and shepherd. Yet the leader is an integral part of the community, the teacher is inseparable from his pupils, and the shepherd never leaves his flock (45).

The section discussing God as a member of the covenantal community (chapter V) presents several difficulties. First, as I pointed out in an earlier chapter,[6] although the leader is connected to his community, he is not always *part* of the community. Moses, the leader of the Jewish people who lived in an isolated tent and covered his face with a veil, was quite remote from his compatriots; how much more so is this true regarding God!

Second, while the Rav emphasizes freedom and mutuality in the assumption of the covenant on the part of both God and man, we cannot ignore the fact that it is God who sets the terms of the covenant. Also, the "inalienable rights" of man to which the Rav refers were in fact granted to man by God!

Finally, although it would seem that there exists a basic dialectic in Jewish thought regarding freedom vs. coercion in divine service, the Rav here downplays coercion to the extent that he removes it almost entirely from the picture.[7]

While it is not easy to defend the Rav's one-sided preference for freedom over coercion here, we can attempt to offer two possible justifications for it. First, in *U-Vikkashtem mi-Sham* the Rav depicts a complex process whereby man can ultimately overcome the dialectic of coercion and freedom. While the details of this development lie beyond the scope of this chapter,[8] perhaps it is possible to read *The Lonely Man of Faith* in light of the final reconciliation

---

6 Chap. 2, p. 45 above.

7 While the Torah seems to indicate that the Jews accepted the Torah freely (most famously in the verse, "We shall do and we shall hear," Ex. 24:7), the Gemara (*Shabbat* 88a) cites an opinion that portrays the Jews as accepting the Torah under divine threat: "'They stood under the mountain' (Ex. 19:17): This teaches that the Holy One, blessed be He, held the mountain over them like a cask, and said to them, 'If you accept the Torah, it is good; if not, there shall be your burial.'" In the lengthy endnote on 45–46, Rav Soloveitchik radically reinterprets this Gemara to minimize the element of duress. It is important to note, however, that the Rav is not the only person who grapples with this Gemara's conclusion ("This [acceptance under duress] furnishes a strong protest against the Torah"); it has troubled commentators for generations. See also For Further Reference, #3.

8 See the discussion of *U-Vikkashtem mi-Sham* at the end of this book.

in *U-Vikkashtem mi-Sham*. Alternatively, perhaps we can suggest that Adam II experiences no coercion when confronted by the covenant, but Adam I does. The former sees it as the answer to his problem, while the latter sees it as an imposition. In other words, each of us is composed of both Adams; the dialectic of freedom and compulsion results from the responses of different parts of our psyche to the covenantal experience. To be honest, however, we must admit that while Rav Soloveitchik offers two interpretations of the sense of compulsion which *Hazal* discuss, neither of them matches the suggestions above.

Prophecy and Prayer

In the covenantal community, God and man communicate by means of prophecy and prayer: the first is communication initiated by God, and the second is communication initiated by man. Both the prophetic and the prayer communities are covenantal for three reasons.[9]

(1) In both, a confrontation between God and man takes place.

(2) The covenant is a threefold structure, linking I, Thou, and God. Thus, in their covenantal capacities, the prophetic and prayer communities link man both to God and to his fellow man (the Thou). The prophet who receives the divine message must convey it to the community; he serves as their representative before God. Likewise, prayer must include others: one should pray *with* others and *for* others.[10]

(3) Both encounters, which aim to redeem man, are "crystallized and objectified in a normative ethico-moral message" (61). Biblical prophecy is not merely a mystical vision; rather, God revealed Himself to Moses in order to give the Law, and to the other prophets in order to enforce it. The normative element of prophecy allows all members of the community to participate in the God-man encounter by taking part in the realization of the covenant. In other words, prophecy is relevant to everyone, not just to the select few.[11] Similarly, prayer entails committing oneself to God; it is only effective if a person is ready to cleanse himself in order to encounter God. In this manner, prayer becomes part of a total pattern of life, a "sub-

---

9 Since I will return in Chap. 20 to the Rav's discussion of prayer in *The Lonely Man of Faith*, I will treat it only briefly here.

10 Regarding prayer *with* and *for* others, see Chap. 20, n. 10, on p. 216 below.

11 The importance of action in the halakhic system was the subject of Chap. 10. See esp. the section on esoteric and undemocratic spirituality. See also the discussion of prophecy in Chap. 35 below.

lime prologue to halakhic action." Judaism centers on the entirety of one's daily life, not just on the synagogue.

Dedication

Although Chapters 12–13 of this book have not done justice to the wealth of ideas contained in the first seven chapters of *The Lonely Man of Faith*, they have hopefully highlighted their main themes and will enable you to read the Rav's essay more easily. Having set forth the conceptual framework of the essay – the dichotomy of Adam I and Adam II – we are now in a position to directly address the problems posed at the essay's beginning (elaborated in Chapter 11 of this book). Therefore, in the upcoming chapters, we will return to the ontological and historical loneliness of the man of faith, and will try to draw out the Rav's responses to these challenges.

Before closing this chapter, I would like to return to the Rav's beautiful dedication of the essay to his wife:

> To Tonya: A woman of great courage, sublime dignity, total commitment, and uncompromising truthfulness.

Why does he single out these four attributes? Now we should be able to grasp the deeper significance of this tribute. "Sublime dignity" and "total commitment" are the characteristics of Adam I and Adam II respectively. Here the Rav indicates that his wife both understands and embodies the dialectic of majesty and redemption. Consequently, "great courage" and "uncompromising truthfulness" are necessary in facing up to the dilemmas posed by this form of existence.

What makes these dilemmas "particularly difficult and agonizing" (6) for the contemporary man of faith is the fact that he is not understood by modern society. However, if the man of faith finds a partner who shares his multiple and complex goals, his overwhelming sense of loneliness can be mitigated and occasionally overcome. Together, the partners form an ideal community, united in both worldly endeavor and religious ideals.[12] Rav Soloveitchik's dedication indicates that he indeed found such a partner. Thus, although the essay's title highlights the author's loneliness, the dedication appearing be-

---

12 According to the Rav, every marriage union should strive to embody both Adam I and Adam II elements, constituting both a pragmatic partnership and a covenantal relationship. See Chap. 19 below on the Rav's book *Family Redeemed*, where this view of marriage is developed at length.

neath it shows that this loneliness is not as extreme as it could have been and offers hope for overcoming it.

For Further Reference

1. **"Confrontation" and *The Lonely Man of Faith*:** Rav Soloveitchik describes the unfolding of the I-awareness and man's alienation from nature in his essay "Confrontation" (*Tradition* 6:2 [Spring 1964], 5–29; reprinted in R. Norman Lamm, ed., *A Treasury of Tradition* [New York, 1967], 55–80). Although both "Confrontation" and *The Lonely Man of Faith* examine the same story, namely, the creation of man as described in the first two chapters of Genesis, they treat it very differently. While the former describes a *progression* of three existential positions, the latter depicts a *dialectic* of two approaches. What makes this particularly interesting is the fact that the two essays were published only a year apart!

   Despite the many differences between the two essays, it is important to note that they share a common theme: the autonomy of the faith commitment and the consequent difficulty in communicating it. However, they discuss this issue in different contexts. "Confrontation" deals with the problem of communication between different faith communities (in reply to the call for interfaith dialogue issued by the Second Vatican Council), while *The Lonely Man of Faith* deals with the problem of communication between religious man and secularized man. (Note that I say "secularized" and not "secular," because even a person who adheres to a religion can practice a secularized form of it.) Chapters 16–18 below are devoted to the crucial subject of the autonomy of faith in its many manifestations.

2. **Vertical and horizontal community; quantitative and qualitative time:** See "Sacred and Profane," *U-Vikkashtem mi-Sham*, "The Community," *On Repentance* ("Between the Individual and the Community"), and *Out of the Whirlwind* ("*Avelut Yeshanah* and *Avelut Hadashah*: Historical and Individual Mourning"). See also the discussion in Chapter 22 below.

3. **Freedom and coercion in halakhic observance:** In many contexts, the Rav opposed coercion in religious life and eschewed the exertion of authority. For example, he strongly felt that it was counterproductive for religious political parties in Israel to enact legislation enforcing religious laws; instead, he advocated religious education. And regarding education itself, he saw the teacher's role as sharing his spiritual wealth with his students and not as dominating or controlling them. On religious legislation,

see *Community, Covenant, and Commitment*, 187, 198, 210–11, and 224; on education, see, e.g., the Rav's letters to Dr. Milton Konvitz cited in R. Nathaniel Helfgot's supplement to the above book, "From the Rav's Pen: Selected Letters of Rabbi Joseph B. Soloveitchik," in *Rav Chesed: Essays in Honor of Rabbi Dr. Haskel Lookstein*, ed. R. Medoff, vol. 1 (Jersey City, 2009), 319–23.

Chapter 14

A Perpetual Dialectic

In Chapter VIII of *The Lonely Man of Faith*, the two parallel tracks we have been examining finally intersect.

> . . . Adam the first, majestic man of dominion and success, and Adam the second, the lonely man of faith, obedience and defeat, are not two different people locked in an external confrontation . . . but one person who is involved in self-confrontation. . . . In every one of us abide two personae – the creative, majestic Adam the first, and the submissive, humble Adam the second (84–85).

Thus, according to Rav Soloveitchik, each of us is fated to live in a perpetual dialectic, constantly oscillating between two modes of existence and between two types of community. This fact has several important ramifications which we shall now examine.

God Desires Both Adams

> God created two Adams and sanctioned both. Rejection of either aspect of humanity would be tantamount to an act of disapproval of the divine scheme of creation which was approved by God as being very good (85).

This is a radical message for a religious thinker. Clearly, any person animated by faith will proclaim to others that God calls upon them to live out the values of Adam II, covenantal man. But here Rav Soloveitchik additionally calls upon people of faith not to forsake the goals of Adam I, majestic man! The Rav grants powerful affirmation to this-worldly existence, reminding us that just as God wants us to strive for personal and communal sanctity, He also bids us to build and to create within the world.

In other words, contrary to the popular understanding, there is religious value not only to the actions of Adam II but to those of Adam I as well. He fulfills the divine mandate of "Fill the earth and subdue it" (Gen. 1:28) and displays his *tzelem Elokim* (divine image) through his creative involvement in the world of human affairs. Thus, he occupies a central position within the divinely-willed scheme of events.

Rav Soloveitchik's approach silences the Enlightenment critique of religion (still voiced in our day), which portrays religion as the enemy of human progress and cultural development. According to these critics, religion produces at best a quietistic and passive personality who has no interest in engaging the world around him. The Rav, in an about-face from this position, states that not only are science, technology and culture not inherently antithetical and challenging to religion, but they are in fact desired by God and therefore integrated into the broader religious worldview.

Furthermore, the Rav asserts what amounts to the independent value of man's creative cultural endeavor. Of course, he believes that these efforts must ultimately be within the bounds of Halakhah. But once this is assured, their value is not dependent on the service they render to that which is religious in the narrow sense. The attainment of dignity is a value in its own right. For example, we do not have to say that it is good that man lofts satellites into orbit because now we can broadcast rabbinic lectures around the globe. Rather, we value the human conquest of space because it is a breathtaking expression of man's majesty, his technical prowess and his creative spirit.

> Let us not forget that the majestic community is willed by God as much as the covenantal faith community. He wants man to engage in the pursuit of majesty-dignity as well as redemptiveness (81).

Complete Redemption is Unattainable

The perpetual dialectic between two modes of existence has another, more tragic, consequence:

> The dialectical awareness, the steady oscillating between the majestic natural community and the covenantal faith community renders the act of complete redemption unrealizable (80).

Had majestic man and covenantal man been two separate people, each abiding in his own community, all would have been well. Each one would have confronted a certain set of problems and would have been provided with the means to solve them. However, the fact that God bids man to adopt both modes of existence gives rise to insoluble difficulties, foremost among them being the problem of loneliness.

Adam I is unaware of his loneliness, while Adam II confronts this burdensome experience and is capable of redeeming himself from it (via his covenantal relationship with both God and man). However, the fact that man must oscillate between two ways of living and perceiving the world places him in a quandary. While living as Adam II, he becomes aware of his loneliness, but he is not afforded the opportunity to overcome it totally. The only way to defeat loneliness is to immerse oneself fully in covenantal existence, and God denies man this option by demanding that man participate in the majestic community as well.

> When man gives himself to the covenantal community the Halakhah reminds him that he is also wanted and needed in another community, the cosmic-majestic, and when it comes across man when he is involved in the creative enterprise of the majestic community, it does not let him forget that he is a covenantal being who will never find self-fulfillment outside of the covenant and that God awaits his return to the covenantal community (82–83).

This results in what we referred to earlier (Chapter 11) as the man of faith's "ontological loneliness," namely, the loneliness that is woven into the very fabric of the religious experience.

> Because of this onward movement from center to center, man does not feel at home in any community. He is commanded to move on before he strikes roots in either of these communities and so the ontological loneliness of the man of faith persists (87).

Contradictory or Complementary?

Throughout most of the book, Rav Soloveitchik portrays man's oscillation between majesty and redemption in dialectical terms. He depicts an unending tension between two conflicting modes of existence:

> [God] summoned man to retreat from peripheral, hard-won positions of vantage and power to the center of the faith experience. He also commanded man to advance from the covenantal center to the cosmic periphery and recapture the positions he gave up a while ago (81).[1]

However, in a brief but highly significant passage (82–84) which I would like to examine closely, the Rav paints a different picture.

---

1 Note that the Rav uses different metaphors to describe the relationship between majesty and covenant: in the above quote from p. 81, he refers to them as periphery and center, respectively, while in the preceding quote from p. 87, he terms them two alternating centers.

[M]any a time I have the distinct impression that the Halakhah considered the steady oscillating of the man of faith between majesty and covenant not as a dialectical but rather as a complementary movement . . . [T]he task of covenantal man is to be engaged not in dialectical surging forward and retreating, but in uniting the two communities into one community where man is both the creative free agent and the obedient servant of God (83–84).

Before addressing the contradiction between the previous two passages, let us first examine the meaning of the latter one.

Uniting the Natural and the Spiritual

The ability to view man's oscillation between majesty and covenant as a complementary movement is based upon Rav Soloveitchik's assertion that

[T]he Halakhah has a monistic approach to reality and has unreservedly rejected any kind of dualism. The Halakhah believes that there is only one world – not divisible into secular and hallowed sectors – which can either plunge into ugliness and hatefulness, or be roused to meaningful, redeeming activity, gathering up all latent powers into a state of holiness (84).

This statement should be understandable in light of our discussion in Chapter 5 of the sanctification of physical life. Much of medieval philosophic and religious thought was permeated by dualism, which viewed the physical and the spiritual as warring opposites, only one of which could prevail. The task of religion or of philosophy, according to this approach, was to ensure the victory of the spiritual over the natural by freeing man from the shackles of physicality as much as possible (via asceticism, contemplation and solitude). Dualists despaired of this-worldly existence. Believing that one should strive to become purely spirit, since physicality is the source of evil and hence irredeemable, they felt that one could come close to God only by abjuring the material world.

Rav Soloveitchik rejects this approach completely. According to him, Halakhah denies the dualist contention that the physical and the spiritual are mutually exclusive, and therefore Halakhah opposes the dualist conclusion that one must flee the physical if one wishes to attain spirituality.

The Halakhah has never despaired of man, either as a natural being integrated into his physical environment, or as a spiritual personality confronting God ("Catharsis," 38).

Rather, Halakhah believes that "God saw everything that He had created, and, behold, it was very good" (Gen. 1:31). Man must not attempt to escape to ethereal realms, contemptuously abandoning the world, but rather must infuse his this-worldly existence with sanctity. The task of the Halakhah is precisely to ensure that man lives this kind of life:

> Notwithstanding the huge disparity between [the majestic and covenantal] communities which expresses itself in the typological oppositions and conflicts described previously, the Halakhah sees in the ethico-moral norm [i.e., the *mitzvot*] a uniting force. The norm which originates in the covenantal community addresses itself almost exclusively to the majestic community where its realization takes place. To use a metaphor, I would say that the norm in the opinion of the Halakhah is the tentacle by which the covenant, like the ivy, attaches itself and spreads over the world of majesty (84).

In other words, *mitzvot* emanate from the covenantal realm, where man communes with God, but they can be fulfilled only by man who participates in the majestic realm: "When you build a new home . . . When you cut down your harvest . . ." etc. By addressing every aspect of man's mundane existence, Halakhah expresses its desire that man should (1) take part in the earthly endeavor, and (2) sanctify that endeavor. What Rav Soloveitchik is describing here is exactly the process of catharsis, which we have examined at length in previous chapters.[2] Catharsis results in the sanctification of natural man; seen differently, the cathartic dialectic assures that covenantal man does not become otherworldly and that majestic man does not become demonically unrestrained and egocentric. This opens the question: What is the central goal of Halakhah?

Halakhic Teleology

At the end of his book *The Halakhic Mind*, Rav Soloveitchik has the harshest words for Rambam's attempt at formulating a teleology of Halakhah.[3] He accuses the Rambam (in *The Guide of the Perplexed*, not in the *Mishneh Torah*) of trying to make Halakhah adhere to values derived from an external philosophical system, and thereby turning Halakhah into merely a means to attain some philosophically-determined end. The Rav counters that Halakhah is autonomous, a given; therefore, it must be understood in its own terms, and does not need to be justified by relating it to extrinsic values. In fact, the Rav continues, Halakhah's values must be derived from a study of its norms: the

---

2 Catharsis is the dialectic of advance and recoil we first encountered on pp. 59–60 above.

3 "Teleology" is an explanation of a phenomenon in terms of its ultimate purpose, derived from the Greek word *telos*, meaning goal.

proper procedure is to elicit our philosophy *from* Halakhah, and not to impose our philosophy *upon* Halakhah. As we have seen in previous chapters, the Rav discovered a basic pattern underlying various halakhic norms: the idea of catharsis, consisting of a dialectic of advance and retreat, the latter purifying the former.[4]

In *The Lonely Man of Faith*, the Rav offers his own teleology of Halakhah, finding it to lie precisely in the attainment of catharsis:

> If one would inquire of me about the teleology of the Halakhah, I would tell him that it manifests itself exactly in the paradoxical yet magnificent dialectic which underlies the halakhic gesture (82).[5]

God summons man to live both a majestic and a covenantal life, and by adhering to Halakhah man can answer both of these calls. This can be understood in two ways, both of which receive expression in *The Lonely Man of Faith*.

(a) Although the realms of majesty and covenant remain conceptually distinct and even incompatible, halakhic living provides a practical means of meeting God's dual demands. Analogously, the Rav writes in "Majesty and Humility" (26):

> [Halakhah] did not discover the synthesis [between majesty and humility], since the latter does not exist. It did, however, find a way to enable man to respond to both calls.

This is an example of a broader phenomenon that also can be said to constitute the telos of the halakhic system according to the Rav. In his understanding,

---

4 See, for example, the discussion of the halakhic attitude to sexuality in Chap. 5 above.

5 Several statements in articles we have already analyzed also point in this direction. For example, in "Catharsis" (42), the Rav writes:

> [Biblical heroism] is perhaps the central motif in our existential experience ... The individual, instead of undertaking heroic action sporadically, lives constantly as a hero.

As the Rav explains there, infusing all of one's life with heroism means living in accordance with Halakhah, with its perpetual dialectic of bold advance and humble retreat. Since "the central motif in our existential experience" is halakhic heroism, i.e., cathartic action, catharsis would seem to constitute the telos of the halakhic system.

In a related fashion, at the end of "Catharsis," Rav Soloveitchik designates catharsis as God's central demand of man. Paraphrasing Micah 6:8, he writes (54):

> He showed thee, man, what is good, and what doth the Lord require of thee, but to move forward boldly, to triumph over and subdue thy environment, and to retreat humbly when victory is within thy grasp.

Halakhah's goal is to help man take constructive action in the face of dichotomous demands and insoluble problems, without necessarily overcoming the conceptual dichotomies or solving the dilemmas.[6] According to this reading of *The Lonely Man of Faith*, Halakhah provides a practical means of negotiating the unavoidable tension between the positions of Adam I and Adam II, without reaching a synthesis between these two approaches.

(b) Alternatively, we can regard Halakhah as a unifying and even harmonizing force. Its telos is ultimately to unite the natural and the spiritual in man, not merely to provide a roadmap for an endless oscillation between contradictory modes of being. It enables man to live an integrated existence: a this-worldly life suffused with sanctity. This chord is more dominant in *U-Vikkashtem mi-Sham*, as exemplified in a passage we saw in Chapter 5:

> By sanctifying the body [Halakhah] creates one whole unit of psychosomatic[7] man who worships God with his spirit and his body and elevates the beast [in him] to the eternal heavens (*U-Vikkashtem mi-Sham*, 117).

Similarly, the goal of halakhic man is to bring sanctity down into this world. As we shall see when we study the book of that title, halakhic man sees no inherent problems in fulfilling this task, nor does he live a life of dialectical tension.

Tension and Harmony

To summarize: Halakhah can be seen either as a means to negotiate an irreconcilable dialectic (as in "Majesty and Humility") or as an ultimately unifying force (as in *U-Vikkashtem mi-Sham*). Both of these notions receive expression in *The Lonely Man of Faith*. How can this be? I think we can gain insight from a very significant endnote:

> Maimonides distinguishes between two kinds of dialectic: (1) the constant oscillating between the majestic and the covenantal community; (2) the simultaneous involvement in both communities, which is the highest form of dialectical existence and which, according to Maimonides, only Moses and the Patriarchs achieved. See *Yesodei Ha-Torah* 7:6 . . . (87–88).

This distinction can answer two questions we have raised in this chapter.

---

6 For an example of this, see the mention of *Kol Dodi Dofek* in Chap. 3, p. 56 above.

7 *Psyche* = spirit; *soma* = body.

(1) *The Telos of Halakhah:*

According to the first kind of dialectic described by the Rambam ("constant oscillating"), Halakhah is a practical response to an unending, insoluble tension. According to the second ("simultaneous involvement"), Halakhah is a unifying or harmonizing force.

(2) *The Nature of the Adam I / Adam II Dialectic:*

I pointed out above (p. 149) that the Rav generally portrays the dialectic between majesty and covenant in terms of conflicting movements, while on p. 83 he describes it as a complementary gesture. Now we can see that these two portrayals reflect the two types of dialectic cited by the Rambam. The first requires constant oscillation, since the two modes of living are seen to be contrasting and therefore they cannot easily abide together. The second, higher dialectic allows "simultaneous involvement in both communities" because the two are now perceived as being complementary.[8]

The continuation of this endnote makes an important point about the higher mode of dialectic:

> Maimonides is more explicit in the *Moreh* III:51 . . . "When we therefore find [the Patriarchs] also engaged in ruling others, in increasing their property and endeavoring to obtain possession of wealth and honor, we see in this fact a proof that when they were occupied in these things their bodily limbs were at work while their heart and mind never moved away from the name of God . . ." In other words, the Patriarchs were builders of society, sociable and gregarious. They made friends with whom they participated in the majestic endeavor. However, axiologically,[9] they valued only one involvement: their covenantal friendship with God. The perfect dialectic expresses itself in a plurality of creative gestures and, at the same time, in axiological monoideism[10] (88).

This passage significantly modifies our perception of the relationship between Adam I and Adam II. No longer are they on equal footing; no longer do they constitute equal and opposite poles of a dialectic. Rather, "The *perfect dialectic* expresses itself in a plurality of creative gestures and, at the same

---

8 *U-Vikkashtem mi-Sham* describes a similar progression of perception: the "natural" and the "revelatory" are first seen as contradictory, then as complementary, and finally as being united with one another.

9 "Axiologically" = in terms of values.

10 "Monoideism" = focus on one idea. The meaning of "axiological monoideism" in the context of this quote will be explained in the next paragraph.

time, in axiological monoideism."[11] This means that although a person should engage in different spheres of activity, ideally he should adopt only one set of values – and these are the values of Adam II.[12] Only they are of ultimate significance: "[A]xiologically, they valued only one involvement: their covenantal friendship with God."

When Adam I is uninformed by the values of Adam II, he does not factor God into all – perhaps any – of his considerations. (Recall that God is not a member of the Adam I natural work community.) Nevertheless, his existence has religious significance because it expresses his *tzelem Elokim* and manifests dignity, even if he is not directly motivated by a divine command. But while the *actions* of Adam I have religious worth, Adam I is not a religious *personality* because he is not interested in cultivating a personal relationship with God.

By contrast, when a person participates in the majestic realm in consonance with the higher mode of dialectic, it is with the self-conscious intention of fulfilling God's will. Whether engaged in politics or in prayer, one must possess a constant awareness of being involved in *avodat Hashem*;[13] and the desire to serve God is, of course, a value of Adam II. Living a life guided by the desire to serve God does not, for the Rav, entail a rejection of Adam I. Man's involvement in the cultural domain is mandated by God, and it is crucial to Jewish spirituality, which, as we have explained, is rooted in this-worldly existence. Furthermore, as we shall see especially in *Halakhic Man* and *U-Vikkashtem mi-Sham*, Judaism assigns great importance to human creativity and autonomy (which are Adam I categories), but Judaism desires that these should be incorporated into one's *avodat Hashem*. In short: one must always keep in mind that nothing is more important than one's relationship with God, and must gear all of one's actions accordingly.

We must remember, however, that according to the Rambam, this ideal of perpetual engagement with God was attained by only four individuals in the course of Jewish history – the three Patriarchs and Moses. Like the Rambam, Rav Soloveitchik does not expect every individual to be able to attain this high level of unification; in fact, he explicitly assigns the ultimate overcoming of the dialectic – resolving all contradictions and filling the world with harmony

---

11 Emphasis added. Of course, this implies that the *imperfect* dialectic – namely, that which can be realistically expected of most people – is not predicated on axiological monoideism.

12 Another way to phrase this would be that a person's *endeavors* should be those of both Adam I and Adam II, but, ideally, his *motivation* should be that of Adam II.

13 In the *Guide* (III:51), Rambam makes this point explicitly. See the end of Chap. 18 below.

– to the realm of an eschatological vision (87). Yet, he claims elsewhere, we can *begin* to fulfill the eschatological vision while still in this world:

> The state of cleaving to God,[14] whose essence is in the eschatological vision ... has begun to be realized even in this divided world, in the actual life of man with his flawed, sterile existence. Judaism has always known about the continuity between temporal and eternal existence, between the world that struggles to exist and the world that is redeemed, between the world that is polluted and the world that is all purity and goodness (*U-Vikkashtem mi-Sham*, 84–85).

The vision of unity cannot be fully realized before the messianic era, but it can at least point out a direction to us. Perhaps the Rav is saying that although most of us are fated to live in a world of dichotomies and dialectical oscil-lation, we must strive, to the extent of our ability, to approach the ideal of unifying the different aspects of our existence.

To conclude, what is most novel about Rav Soloveitchik's theory of the two Adams? I would highlight two points:

(1) Adam I's existence is willed by God and therefore his majestic and cre-ative actions have religious value.

(2) Nevertheless, Adam II is independent of Adam I and is ultimately more significant. Religion (the realm of Adam II) is not subservient to culture (the creation of Adam I); it is a primordial force that has no need to legiti-mize itself in other terms. This will be the focus of the next four chapters.

---

14 Cleaving to God, or *devekut*, is the pinnacle of religious achievement attained by unifying man's creativity and autonomy with his absolute religious commitment.

For Further Reference

1. **Affirmation of this-worldly existence:** See Chapter 5 above. This is also a major theme in *Halakhic Man*. For further analysis of Rav Soloveitchik's views concerning the relationship between religion (Adam II) and culture (Adam I), and the this-worldly attitude of Judaism, see Rabbi Sol Roth, *The Jewish Idea of Culture* (Hoboken, NJ, 1997). Much of the book focuses on *The Lonely Man of Faith*.

2. **Blessings:** It has long been noted that in our recitation of blessings, we switch in mid-blessing from addressing God in the second person (*"Barukh atah"*) to addressing Him in the third person (*"asher kide-shanu be-mitzvotav,"* instead of *"asher kidashtanu be-mitzvotekha"*). In a footnote here (80), Rav Soloveitchik attributes this change to "man's dialectical see-sawing between the cosmic and the covenantal experience of God" – the cosmic address being in the third person, and the covenantal address in the second person. Note, however, that in *U-Vikkashtem mi-Sham* (71) he attributes this switch to the dialectic of *ahavah* and *yirah*, love and fear of God. See Chapter 33, p. 361 below.

Chapter 15

The Subversion of Religion

Chapter IX of *The Lonely Man of Faith* is the climax towards which the entire book has been building. In this chapter, Rav Soloveitchik returns to address the questions he posed at the beginning of the book, revealing to us the full force of the crisis facing the man of faith today.

Recall that in chapter I, the Rav stated that the goal of this work is to examine the loneliness of the man of faith, which is experienced on two planes – the ontological and the historical.[1] These differ both in their cause and in their effect:

> While the ontological loneliness of the man of faith is due to a God-made and willed situation and is, as part of his destiny, a wholesome and integrating experience, the special kind of loneliness of contemporary man of faith referred to at the beginning of this essay is of a social nature due to a man-made historical situation and is, hence, an unwholesome and frustrating experience (91).

"Ontological loneliness," as we explained earlier, results from God's dual call to mankind, and therefore is the lot of all people of faith. While difficult and demanding, it is nevertheless a source of religious growth and creativity, since these can come about only as the result of struggle. However, "contemporary man of faith lives through a particularly difficult and agonizing crisis" (6) due to his "historical loneliness," namely, the loneliness resulting from his specific historical circumstances, from the particular society and culture in which he lives. Therefore, the Rav's "prime concern" in the essay is to examine the cause and nature of this latter experience.

In order to accomplish this, the Rav first had to establish the framework of

---

1 See pp. 124–28 above.

his discussion, the Adam I/Adam II dichotomy (chapters I–VII); then he examined the ideal relationship obtaining between these two components of the human personality (chapter VIII); and now he can finally discuss the contemporary crisis situation where these two components are no longer maintained in balance. Chapter IX diagnoses the distortion of faith in the modern world, offering a devastating critique of contemporary forms of organized religion and exposing the lonely and precarious position of the man of faith in all its tragic dimensions.

Rejecting Adam II

The historical loneliness of the contemporary man of faith stems from the fact that his faith commitment, as spelled out in the covenantal-redemptive terms of Adam II, is incomprehensible to modern man.[2] Modern man, due to his great success in the realm of majesty-dignity, has been enticed into believing that the Adam I side of existence is all there is to life. He refuses to acknowledge the inherent duality of man.

> By rejecting Adam the second, contemporary man, eo ipso,[3] dismisses the covenantal faith community as something superfluous and obsolete (91–92).

Since he embodies only Adam I, modern man thinks in limited, relativistic, human terms and is guided solely by criteria of utility and verifiability (i.e., what is useful and comprehensible to him). Adam II, by contrast, thinks in absolute terms which transcend human finitude, and is guided by a commitment that is "meta-logical and non-hedonic" (i.e., exceeding the human intellect and not necessarily designed to bring about pleasure). Therefore, when the few remaining genuine men of faith (who espouse the Adam II worldview) speak of the basic human need for redemption and issue a call for self-sacrifice and for total commitment to God, they are met by blank incomprehension, if not derision, on the part of modern man. Hence, the loneliness of the contemporary man of faith turns into social isolation, and is therefore a frustrating and unhealthy experience.

---

2 Note the distinction – both in *The Lonely Man of Faith* and in my discussion of it – between the "contemporary man of faith" and "modern man." The former suffers from historical loneliness, and the latter is the cause of it. This will be explained in what follows.

3 "Eo ipso" = by that very fact.

The Heart of the Crisis

Rav Soloveitchik is diagnosing not merely the isolation of the religious community within an increasingly secular world. He is addressing a far more tragic and dangerous situation – *the secularization of religion itself.* The great *hiddush* of the Rav's essay, its most striking and original point, is that even modern "religious" man rejects Adam II! Many contemporary forms of organized religion espouse not the faith commitment of covenantal man but rather the "religious culture" of majestic man; they practice the religion of Adam I.[4]

> [When I speak of modern man's rejection of Adam II], I am referring [not to atheists but] rather to Western man who is affiliated with organized religion and is a generous supporter of its institutions. He stands today in danger of losing his dialectical awareness . . . Somehow, man of majesty considers the dialectical awareness too great a burden, interfering with his pursuit of happiness and success, and is, therefore, ready to cast it off (92).

Successful Adam I has extended his drive for conquest even to the sphere of religion. He has infiltrated the religious realm and taken it over – and in the process, he has undermined and distorted its very meaning. His is a religion of convenience, not commitment; it is geared to suit his own needs, not to serve God's will. He does not comprehend the meaning of total devotion and does not sense the need for redemption, which are the essence of faith. Therefore, the words of the man of faith fall on deaf ears even among "religious" individuals, and the man of faith finds himself isolated even within the "religious" community. This is his true tragedy, and this presents the gravest peril to the future of faith.

In order to assess this situation accurately, we must first examine two issues. The remainder of this chapter will explore Adam I's attitude to religion, and the following chapters will be devoted mainly to the issue of the autonomy of faith, i.e., how Adam II's faith commitment cannot be interpreted in the practical-utilitarian categories of Adam I. Having addressed these two topics, we will then be able to examine the options open to the man of faith when confronted by majestic man's usurpation of religion.

---

4 I would add, as we shall see in Chap. 18, that the Rav means to include in his critique not only movements which he regards as heterodox, but also, and perhaps primarily, his own "Modern Orthodox" community. See especially the section entitled "Modern Orthodoxy in Theory and in Practice," and the sources cited in the For Further Reference section there.

The Religion of Adam I

Adam I adheres to some form of religion only to the extent that it is useful to him in his pursuit of dignity; he is not committed to religion in an ultimate sense, nor is he willing to sacrifice any of his majestic goals for its sake. In fact, religion for him is merely another manifestation of his search for majesty. Like everything else he does, it is an anthropocentric enterprise, designed to enhance his self-image and to increase his comfort. Sometimes this may express itself in a commendable sense of philanthropy and social activism (think of the United Jewish Appeal, Jewish National Fund, Israel Bonds, etc.). Adam I, after all, is not simply a crass and materialistic being; recall Adam I's conception that "humanity = dignity = *responsibility* = majesty" (20). But when Adam I adopts some of the outer trappings of religion – ceremony, ritual, etc. – he empties them of their transcendental content, since he is not in search of the redemptive encounter with God. We see, therefore, that belonging to a religious establishment does not make one into a man of faith. The Rav puts it this way:

> [Western man who is affiliated with a religious establishment] belongs not to a covenantal faith community but to a religious community. The two communities are as far apart as the two Adams. While the covenantal faith community is governed, as I emphasized, by a desire for a redeemed existence, the religious community is dedicated to the attainment of dignity and success and is – along with the whole gamut of communities such as the political, the scientific, the artistic – a creation of Adam the first, all conforming to the same sociological structural patterns. The religious community is, therefore, also a work community consisting of two grammatical personae [i.e., I and Thou, two humans], not including the Third Person [i.e., God]. The prime purpose is the successful furtherance of the interests, not the deepening and enhancing of the commitments, of man who values religion in terms of its usefulness to him and considers the religious act a medium through which he may increase his happiness. This assumption on the part of majestic man about the role of religion is not completely wrong, if only, as I shall explain, he would recognize also the non-pragmatic aspects of religion (93).

This passage deserves careful analysis. I would like to highlight several points.

1. *Adam I's Use of Adam II Categories:*

As mentioned above, Adam I is trapped within the natural order, interpreting his existence in cognitive and functional categories. Adam II, on the other hand, deals also with that which transcends him and his natural existence.

Thus, they possess fundamentally different perspectives. The Rav terms Adam I's domain the realm of "culture," culture being a purely human creation. But as such, its horizons are restricted to that which is humanly perceptible – and this, of necessity, lends the entire cultural enterprise only a limited and relative value (since man is a finite being). On his own, Adam I cannot find values which transcend himself. Only Adam II, who has an intimate relation with God, can speak in terms of absolutes.

Adam I therefore faces a problem. He is not satisfied with material success, but also "evaluates his creative accomplishments, making an effort to place them in some philosophical and axiological [i.e., value-related] perspective" (95). More importantly, he seeks to lend "fixity, permanence, and worth" (96) to his endeavors. But these can be attained only with reference to the conceptual world of Adam II. Thus, in order to "strengthen his cultural edifice" (97), Adam I must turn to Adam II for support. By borrowing conceptual categories from Adam II, majestic man can raise his aesthetic experience to the level of the sublime; he can find higher sanction for his ethical norm; he can have access to the therapeutic powers of belief in times of distress; etc. (94–98). In short: he can introduce into his frame of reference an element of the transcendent, which is not bound by time, place, or human finitude.

The metaphor of translation is very pertinent here. Let us regard the cultural-majestic and religious-covenantal realms as speaking two different languages. Rav Soloveitchik makes two important points: (1) the language of the covenantal realm is partially translatable into the language of the cultural realm, but (2) it is not wholly translatable. This act of translation, or of Adam I borrowing from the language of Adam II, is necessary, legitimate and possible. It is *necessary*, as we just saw, in order to lend higher value to Adam I's endeavors. It is *legitimate* because God Himself has willed Adam I's existence. It is *possible* because

> God would not have implanted the necessity in majestic man for such spiritual perceptions and ideas if He had not at the same time endowed the man of faith with the skill of converting some of his apocalyptic experiences – which are meta-logical and non-hedonic – into a system of values and verities comprehensible to majestic man . . . (98).[5]

The problem is that contemporary Adam I thinks that the language of Adam II is *completely* translatable into his terms. If this were so, then there would be nothing unique and autonomous about the covenantal realm. Adam

---

5 However, it is important to note that, once translated, these concepts bear little similarity to their original form. For example, see the footnote on p. 97 of *The Lonely Man of Faith*.

I thereby makes religion totally subsidiary to culture; he evaluates religion purely in cultural-majestic terms and does not recognize anything beyond that.

2. *Religious Pragmatism*

It is legitimate not only for Adam I to borrow concepts such as the sublime and the eternal from Adam II, but it is even legitimate for Adam I to regard the religious act itself as having practical benefits. Adam II's religious observance can indeed be advantageous in the realm of Adam I. The Rav explains:

> The idea that certain aspects of faith are translatable into pragmatic terms is not new. The Bible has already pointed out that the observance of the Divine Law and obedience to God leads man to worldly happiness, to a respectable, pleasant and meaningful life. Religious pragmatism has a place within the perspective of the man of faith (98–99).[6]

However, it is crucial that man not relate to faith *solely* in pragmatic terms. He must be committed to God even if this does not appear to bring him happiness and fulfillment, and even if the commitment is not always comprehensible to him.

> This assumption on the part of majestic man about the role of religion is not completely wrong, if only, as I shall explain, he would recognize also the non-pragmatic aspects of religion (93).

If majestic man fails to "recognize also the non-pragmatic aspects of religion," then he will miss out on all that is unique about religion, and his faith gesture "will forfeit its redemptive and therapeutic qualities" (106). He undermines his own interests, for religion can truly provide him with what he seeks only if it retains its integrity and its connection to its transcendental source.

3. *Sociological Patterns*

Since modern man uses religion to further his overall quest for majesty, not recognizing that faith makes independent and absolute demands upon him, he creates a religious community that is structurally identical to all other communities formed by Adam I. It is a community of interests, not a community of commitment. Its members are bound together not by a mutual devotion to

---

6 In a somewhat different but related sense, the Rav emphasizes elsewhere the legitimacy of religiosity that is based on simple fear of punishment and anticipation of reward ("*she-lo lishmah*," not for its own sake), instead of insisting solely on religious observance for its own sake. See *U-Vikkashtem mi-Sham*, 159–61, and For Further Reference, #1.

God and to the attainment of redemption, but rather by the shared pursuit of dignity and comfort.[7]

What does this mean in concrete terms? If man views religion merely as another method for him to attain happiness – not as an autonomous, transcendent and elemental force that makes demands upon him – then he approaches religion with the question, "What's in it for me?" Religion is forced to justify and sell itself to the public; it becomes part of our larger consumer society.

Let me bring one example from my childhood. I recall that during the Sunday morning cartoons, a particular commercial was broadcast frequently. The commercial showed a clean-cut, fresh-faced, all-American family dressed in its Sunday best on the way to church. When they return home, they sit down to a lavish meal, all smiling beatifically and showering each other with love. This heartwarming scene would fade out and be replaced with the legend:

The family that prays together – stays together.

What message is this conveying? That religion must be marketed just like detergent or toothpaste. That you should be religious because it is good for you. Are you afraid of divorce? Go to church. Do you want happy, smiling children? Go to church. Try it – you'll be pleased with the results.

Now, I certainly don't mean to downplay the value of family harmony. It happens to be a value that even Adam II can appreciate. What is problematic is the "What's in it for me?" attitude, whereby religion must prove its usefulness to the "religious consumer." Man puts up a demand that religion adapt itself to *his* needs, not vice versa. In a situation like this, religion loses its authenticity and its power. It waters itself down in order to attract followers; in fact, it often changes its message entirely. In the supermarket of ideas, religion must market itself on the basis of values which people *already hold*, even though these ideas are not necessarily derived from religious sources. It tries to *appeal* to the public instead of *teaching* them; it reinforces their (majestic) values rather than dictating new ones.

People don't usually want to hear about sacrifice, humility and loneliness. They want religion to be less demanding and to provide instant gratification. It should make them feel good about themselves instead of trying to change them. When people who lack an unwavering faith commitment don't like the message they are hearing, they will either simply and complacently ignore it, or they will pick themselves up and move to a more congenial environment. Under these circumstances, who rises to positions of leadership in the

---

7 See For Further Reference, #2.

religious community? Often it is not the most learned, sincere or pious individual, but rather the best salesman.

In the next chapter, we will examine the other side of this dilemma – Adam II's stubborn refusal to identify himself wholly with Adam I's goals and ideas. After further exploring the clash of conceptions between the religion of Adam I and the faith of Adam II, we will turn to the question – what now?

FOR FURTHER REFERENCE

1. **Ulterior motives in religion:** Rav Soloveitchik explicitly grapples with Immanuel Kant's philosophy throughout his writings (especially in *Halakhic Man*, as we shall see in Chapter 30). In *The Lonely Man of Faith,* the Rav cites Kantian ethics as an attempt to lend absolute validity to a human cultural creation (97). At the heart of Kant's system lies the "categorical imperative," which is a rational principle guiding moral action. Since, for Kant, this principle demands unconditional commitment, we can say that in this sense Kant's ethical realm parallels Rav Soloveitchik's religious realm. But if so, I would like to point out a striking and ironic contrast between them (without going into detail regarding Kantian philosophy).

   Kant is perhaps most famous for denying the legitimacy of ulterior motives in following the "categorical imperative"; one must obey its dictates purely out of a sense of duty. Yet Rav Soloveitchik, who follows norms deriving from super-human revelation and not only from finite human reason, admits that it is valid to follow these norms out of pragmatic motivation!

   Of course, as we saw above, Rav Soloveitchik demands that one's faith commitment not be based *only* on pragmatic considerations; but nevertheless a measure of pragmatism is warranted. Furthermore, although a religious quest due to pragmatic considerations ("*she-lo lishmah*") appears as a seemingly necessary component of man's religious development in *U-Vikkashtem mi-Sham*, it is important to note that this is only the first of three stages delineated there. As one's religious consciousness deepens, one's pragmatic considerations diminish – yet they do not disappear. Even those at the peak of religious development never completely lose sight of the elemental, physical fear and security which follow upon divine punishment and reward. These are "the background of religious life; without them no religiosity can exist" (*U-Vikkashtem mi-Sham*, 52).

   It seems to me that Rav Soloveitchik's "revelational" doctrine, with its frank recognition of the inevitability of human frailty, is more in touch with human reality than Kant's idealistic philosophical doctrine.

2. **Sociology of religion:** The assertion that Adam I's religious community structurally parallels other Adam I communities constitutes a foundation of modern sociology of religion. This discipline examines religion as a social phenomenon and finds it similar to other social groupings. See, for example, the pioneering work of Peter L. Berger, *The Sacred Canopy* (New York, 1967), especially chapters 6 and 7, as well as Berger's subsequent works on this subject (such as *The Heretical Imperative*). Note that the publication of *The Lonely Man of Faith* preceded that of *The Sacred Canopy* by two years.

Chapter 16

The Autonomy of Faith

Why is the contemporary man of faith "lonely in a special way" (6)? Let us briefly recapitulate the Rav's argument thus far. Faith (Adam II) and culture (Adam I) represent two independent sides of a dialectic eternally implanted within mankind. Modern man,[1] however, identifies only with one side of this dialectic: Adam I's values of dignity, majesty and responsibility that produce technology and other aspects of culture. Intoxicated by his success in the scientific-technological realm, modern man has constricted his inner world to include only those values and emotional responses which reflect and enhance his majesty. The humility and the gnawing sense of incompleteness that characterize Adam II are completely foreign to him. However, this does not mean that modern man discards religion entirely. He adopts some of its outer forms, but empties them of their covenantal-redemptive content, substituting majestic values instead.

Thus, the contemporary man of faith confronts a bold and assertive secularism which has infiltrated even into the realm of organized religion. Speaking the "foreign" language of redemption that frequently entails sacrifice and surrender, the man of faith – Adam II – seems to have lost the ability to communicate with his surrounding society. He experiences not an invigorating sense of uniqueness and a fruitful dialogue between the disparate forces within himself, but rather social isolation and agonizing loneliness. He is misunderstood and ridiculed, regarded by society as "superfluous and obsolete."

In the previous chapter, we explored one aspect of this problem: the religious posture adopted by Adam I. Now we shall deal with the second

---

1 As noted in the previous chapter, "modern man" refers to the representative of general society, as distinguished from the "contemporary man of faith," who is isolated and marginalized.

component: Adam II's insistence on maintaining his autonomy, his stubborn refusal to identify wholly with Adam I's goals and values and to accommodate himself to them. After setting forth the theoretical foundations of the autonomy of faith in the current chapter, we will examine some of its consequences, both in the intellectual realm (Chapter 17) and in the practical realm (Chapter 18). Thus, the next chapter will analyze Rav Soloveitchik's response to various intellectual attacks on Orthodoxy, and our closing chapter on *The Lonely Man of Faith* will consider, in light of ideas presented here, a number of the Rav's influential halakhic responsa and public policy decisions.

Cold Calculation or Passionate Commitment

What is the process by which religion becomes secularized? In the previous chapter, we saw that although Adam I and Adam II speak different languages and hold different values, Adam I needs to borrow numerous concepts from Adam II in order to support his own cultural edifice. This translation of some of Adam II's redemptive categories into Adam I's cultural terms is entirely legitimate. However, modern man is not satisfied with *partial* translation; rather, he evaluates religion *entirely* in terms of its compatibility with his majestic goals. He thereby makes religion subservient to his own majestic-cultural ends, not acknowledging that the religious domain of Adam II has its own independent demands of man. In truth, the faith experience issues a call to man which far exceeds his limited comprehension and his pragmatic goals. As cited previously, the Rav describes the faith experience as "meta-logical and non-hedonic" (98), meaning that it is beyond reason and is not designed to bring about simple pleasure.

Why is this so? Faith is rooted not just in reason, but in one's whole personality, affecting every level of his being (such as the aesthetic, emotional and moral dimensions, as we saw in the essay "Catharsis"). Therefore, the faith commitment cannot ultimately have a pragmatic or utilitarian basis, since pragmatism and utility are only functional categories, stemming from one narrow (albeit significant) component of man's being, namely, the intellectual. In Rav Soloveitchik's powerful words:

> There are simply no cognitive categories in which the total commitment of the man of faith could be spelled out. This commitment is rooted not in one dimension, such as the rational one, but in the whole personality of the man of faith. The whole of the human being, the rational as well as the non-rational aspects, is committed to God. Hence, the magnitude of the commitment is beyond the comprehension of the logos and the ethos.[2] The act of faith is ab-

---

2 "Logos" and "ethos" refer to logical and ethical reasoning.

original, exploding with elemental force . . . The intellect does not chart the course of the man of faith; its role is an a posteriori one. It attempts, *ex post facto*, to retrace the footsteps of the man of faith, and even in this modest attempt the intellect is not completely successful . . . The man of faith animated by his great experience is able to reach the point at which not only his logic of the mind but even his logic of the heart . . . has to give in to an "absurd" commitment. The man of faith is "insanely" committed to and "madly" in love with God (99–100).

When applied to the man of faith's commitment, the epithets "absurd," "insane" and "mad" denote merely that it is not based on considerations of cold logic or practical benefit. His commitment is non-rational or meta-rational, but not irrational. In other words, it is *unrelated* to reason or *above* reason, but it is not *opposed* to reason.[3]

Here we encounter in full force the Rav's break with the medieval rationalist tradition of Jewish philosophy, which based religious life on intellectual proofs of God's existence.[4] According to the Rav, the man of faith's God-awareness, or his God-experience, lies at the core of his perception of the world and his sense of self. This means that he cannot conceive of either himself or the world without sensing the presence of God. For him, faith is a basic awareness, an a priori axiom, and not a conclusion that can be reached on the basis of certain premises.[5] What is crucial for us at this stage of the argument is to recognize that faith is not a function or an outgrowth of man's other pursuits, but rather an "aboriginal" force, a basic calling in its own right. Therefore, it is not subservient to other goals or values, and, in the modern era especially, it must fiercely guard its independence.

Autonomy of Halakhah

The Rav's assertion of the autonomy of the religious realm in general, and of Halakhah in particular, is central to his thought. Before examining its ramifications as regards *The Lonely Man of Faith*, let us explore some other contexts in which this issue arises.

Halakhic Man (e.g., 17–29) and "*Mah Dodekh mi-Dod*" (70–85) deal specifically with the autonomy of the halakhic system. Rav Soloveitchik asserts that Halakhah constitutes an independent cognitive realm, and should

---

3 For an elaboration of this important point, see the Rav's footnote on pp. 107–08.

4 The Rav prefers to regard this as a reinterpretation, rather than a break. His relationship to medieval Jewish philosophy is complex and will be discussed in Chap. 34. See also Chap. 12 above, For Further Reference, #3.

5 This leads precisely to the problem of communicating faith to others, which we shall explore in Chap. 18.

be studied and applied according to the tenets of its own internal logic, not according to the foreign categories of historical, economic or sociological causation. For the Rav, of course, the Brisker method best reveals the "internal logic" of Halakhah. In his sharp and succinct formulation:

> Kant, in his day, proclaimed the autonomy of pure reason, of scientific-mathematic cognition. [Similarly, my grandfather] Rav Hayyim fought a war of independence on behalf of halakhic reason and demanded for it complete autonomy. Any psychologization or sociologization of the Halakhah strangles its soul, as such an attempt must also destroy mathematical thinking. If halakhic thought is dependent on emotional factors, it loses all its objectivity and degenerates to the level of subjectivity with no substance . . . ("*Mah Dodekh mi-Dod*," 78).

In other words, mathematics is a self-contained system in which our task is to ask how the system works and not why it is structured as it is. To offer psychological or sociological reasons for mathematical theorems would be absurd. So, too, the Rav believes that Halakhah is primarily a system of interlocking concepts. Our task is to define the concepts and nature of their interactions, and not to ask why they are as they are.[6] While historical, sociological and economic conditions may impact on the *application* of Halakhah in differing circumstances, they do not impact on the halakhic *concepts* themselves. Furthermore, Halakhah's responses to changing circumstances are built into the system, and as such historical change does not affect the integrity of the halakhic system. Thus, although Rav Hayyim and the Rav had their own reasons for developing this "a priori" and autonomous conception of Halakhah, it can also serve as a response to the relativizing historicist orientation espoused by both non-Orthodox movements and the academic world.[7]

Autonomy of the Religious Realm

Rav Soloveitchik's book, *The Halakhic Mind*, establishes the philosophical basis for his assertion of the cognitive and methodological autonomy of Halakhah. Actually, *The Halakhic Mind*, like *The Lonely Man of Faith*, focuses not just on Halakhah, but on the religious realm in general.[8] In this very technical work, the Rav claims that the "epistemological pluralism" of

---

6 In our discussion of *Halakhic Man* in Chap. 28 we shall elaborate on the Rav's view of Halakhah as a cognitive system.

7 See also Chap. 10, For Further Reference, #3, and Chap. 31 below.

8 The Rav did not choose *The Halakhic Mind*'s misleadingly particularistic title.

twentieth-century science allows us for the first time to develop a genuine and autonomous philosophy of religion.[9] Just as contemporary science, especially quantum physics (as opposed to Aristotelian and Newtonian physics), admits a variety of ways of viewing the world and a variety of sources of knowledge, so too must philosophy. Therefore, the elements of religion – in our terms, the details of Halakhah – can serve as the basis for formulating a worldview which is no less valid than any other.[10] Since science and philosophy no longer claim to describe everything knowable, there is now room to turn to religion as a source of knowledge – and religion is now free to explain itself in its own terms.[11]

The Lonely Man of Faith is based upon the same assumption of a plurality of worldviews (Adam I and Adam II), and upon the same assertion of the autonomy of religion. However, instead of treating the cognitive facet of this issue – religion as a source of knowledge – it addresses instead its existential and experiential dimensions. While recognition of the autonomy of religion opens up exciting theoretical possibilities, it can also lead to a sense of alienation from those who do not share this recognition (and who instead treat religion as just another facet of culture). Thus, in place of the optimism characterizing *The Halakhic Mind*, which looks forward to a new era in religious philosophy, *The Lonely Man of Faith* adopts a more sober and ultimately tragic tone in depicting the man of faith's isolation and his frustrating inability to break through the communication barrier separating him from his contemporaries. In an eloquent analysis, R. Jonathan Sacks draws a connection between the two essays, written two decades apart (*Halakhic Mind* in 1944 and *Lonely Man* in 1965):

> The pluralism of contemporary culture, which [Rav Soloveitchik] was the first to recognize, was both a liberation and a privation. It liberated tradition from having to vindicate itself in alien terms. But it [pried] tradition from its moorings in the collective order and made it seem as just one system among many, either consciously chosen (the *ba'al teshuvah* phenomenon) or validated by an act of faith which is "aboriginal, exploding with elemental force" and eluding cognitive analysis. Soloveitchik's genius and the poignancy of his intellectual development are both evidenced in this: that he was the first to explore the

---

9 Epistemology is the theory of knowledge (in Greek, *episteme* = knowledge), that branch of philosophy which deals with such questions as: How do we come to know things – for example, by senses, by reason or by intuition? Also, what can we know – are there limits to our ability to know? "Epistemological pluralism," as we shall see, refers to the doctrine that there is more than one legitimate way to view reality.

10 Of course, in philosophic terms, it is also no *more* valid than any other point of view.

11 For more on the idea of epistemological pluralism, see For Further Reference, #1.

positive possibilities of the liberation [in *The Halakhic Mind*], and the first to chart the tragic dimensions of the privation [in *The Lonely Man of Faith*].[12]

FOR FURTHER REFERENCE

1. ***The Halakhic Mind***: For centuries, science and philosophy had walked hand-in-hand, with philosophy following science's lead in adopting a single way of viewing the world. Medieval philosophy was beholden to Aristotelian science in determining the questions to be asked and the methods of answering them; early modern philosophy was beholden to Newtonian science for the same. This forced religious philosophy either to justify religion in rationalist-instrumentalist terms or to reject rationality altogether.

   However, twentieth-century science no longer posited a unified or intuitive view of the world. For example, light is regarded as both a wave and a particle, which would seem to contravene the tenets of Aristotelian logic: something cannot be A and not-A at the same time. To take another example, Euclidean geometry is applied at the normal level of our sense experience, while non-Euclidean geometry (which rejects one of the fundamental axioms of Euclidean geometry) is necessary in astrophysics and other situations where one must employ Einstein's general relativity.

   Since science has adopted a stance of epistemological pluralism, admitting a multiplicity of models and sources of knowledge, philosophy must follow suit. The quantitative scientific model must no longer be regarded as the sole cognitive method of viewing the universe. This opens the way for establishing religion as an autonomous domain of knowledge and truth. Because the philosophy of religion has now been liberated from naturalistic presuppositions, Rav Soloveitchik opens his book with the bold and optimistic claim, "It would be difficult to distinguish any epoch in the history of philosophy more amenable to the meditating *homo religiosus* than that of today" (3).

   For clarification of the major arguments of *The Halakhic Mind*, see R. Jonathan Sacks, "Rabbi Joseph B. Soloveitchik's Early Epistemology," in his book *Tradition in an Untraditional Age* (London, 1990), 287–301, and William Kolbrener, "Towards a Genuine Jewish Philosophy," *Tradition* 30:3 (Spring 1996), 21–43. Both of these essays also appear in the collection, *Exploring the Thought of Rabbi Joseph B. Soloveitchik*, ed. R. Marc

---

12 *Tradition in an Untraditional Age* (London, 1990), 299.

Angel (Hoboken, NJ, 1997), 179–225. See also the extended treatments in Reinier Munk, *The Rationale of Halakhic Man: Joseph B. Soloveitchik's Conception of Jewish Thought* (Amsterdam, 1996), and in Daniel Rynhold, *Two Models of Jewish Philosophy: Justifying One's Practices* (Oxford, 2005), as well as Chapters 10, 28 and 31 in this book.

Chapter 17

Intellectual and Existential Challenges to Faith

Unshakeable Faith

Having arrived at this stage of our analysis, we are now in a position to return to a striking statement at the beginning of *The Lonely Man of Faith* that has puzzled many readers.

> It would be worthwhile to add the following in order to place the dilemma in the proper focus. I have never been seriously troubled by the problem of the Biblical doctrine of creation vis-à-vis the scientific story of evolution at both the cosmic and the organic levels,[1] nor have I been perturbed by the confrontation of the mechanistic interpretation of the human mind with the Biblical spiritual concept of man. I have not been perplexed by the impossibility of fitting the mystery of revelation into the framework of historical empiricism. Moreover, I have not even been troubled by the theories of Biblical criticism which contradict the very foundations upon which the sanctity and integrity of the Scriptures rest. However, while theoretical oppositions and dichotomies have never tormented my thoughts, I could not shake off the disquieting feeling that the practical role of the man of faith within modern society is a very difficult, indeed, a paradoxical one (7).

How is it possible that these issues did not trouble the Rav? Surely it is not due to ignorance or obscurantism on his part. Anyone who attended the Rav's lectures, especially his philosophy classes, can testify to the Rav's familiarity with all these issues. Why, then, did they not disturb him?

---

1 Evolution at the cosmic level refers to the development of the universe, and evolution at the organic level refers to the development of life.

The answer flows directly from our discussion of the autonomy of faith. First, Halakhah possesses its own frame of reference and its own method-ological integrity. Therefore, it has no need to justify itself before challengers approaching it with outside assumptions. Additionally, since faith is a basic awareness and not a reasoned conclusion, it cannot fundamentally be shaken by cognitive dilemmas. This does not mean that the challenges mentioned above should not be addressed at all. But it does mean, I believe, that these questions should be kept in perspective – true faith will not rise or fall on them. The living sense of the divine is primary; matters of criticism are secondary.

In Rav Soloveitchik's words, the man of faith is "animated by his great ex-perience" (100), and only subsequently does his intellectual faculty come into play. This point is closely related to two issues touched upon briefly in previ-ous chapters, which we can now comprehend within a broader perspective.

(1) *Proof vs. Experience*

In Chapter 12, we saw that the cosmic *experience* of God renders the cosmo-logical *proof* of God superfluous. There are two reasons for this.

First, faith based on rational proof leads at best to intellectual assent to the existence of an abstraction termed "God." Faith stemming from experi-ence, on the other hand, can lead to an intimate personal relationship with the Creator.[2]

Second, if a person experiences God in a direct and unmediated man-ner, what need does he have for abstract proofs? Both in *The Lonely Man of Faith* (52) and *U-Vikkashtem mi-Sham* (16), the Rav approvingly quotes Kierkegaard's pointed remark on this subject:

> Does the loving bride in the embrace of her beloved ask for proof that he is alive and real? Must the prayerful soul clinging in passionate love and ecstasy to her Beloved demonstrate that He exists? So asked Søren Kierkegaard sar-castically when told that Anselm of Canterbury, the father of the very abstract and complex ontological proof, spent many days in prayer and supplication that he be presented with rational evidence of the existence of God.[3]

---

2 This resembles the distinction posited by R. Yehudah Halevi (*Kuzari* IV:16) between the God of Aristotle and the God of Abraham, or between the First Cause and the God of the Covenant. Unlike the Rav, however, R. Yehudah Halevi bases his faith on both personal experi-ence and the fact of historical revelation. The Rav's philosophy, by comparison, is less historical and more focused on the individual. Hence, he discusses the first of these bases of faith but not the second.

3 The quote above is from *The Lonely Man of Faith*. Its source is an 1853 entry in Kierkegaard's journal entitled "Curious Self-Contradiction" (X 5 A 120, cited in Søren Kierkegaard, *Papers*

(2) *Katnut ha-Mohin*

In Chapter 8, we discussed the dialectic of *gadlut ha-mohin* and *katnut ha-mohin* that characterizes *gedolei Yisrael*, great Jewish scholar-leaders (and, in a more moderate form, all Jews). Beside their "depth, scope and sharpness" of thought, beside their bold creative powers and intellectual maturity, the truly great scholars also possess the playfulness and innocence of a child, full of curiosity, enthusiasm and limitless faith. In one essay, the Rav painted a very evocative portrait of his grandfather as a "halakhic man-child," a portrait that can also describe the Rav himself:

> On the one hand, he was a great abstract thinker, who introduced basic conceptual transformations in the field of halakhic methodology. On the other hand, he was a child, unable to restrain his warm emotions, his yearning for something beautiful and elevated, his dreams and hopes. He, the man of iron discipline in the intellectual sphere, who captured the richness of Halakhah in its acute, exact, logical molds, was swept without reservation in a bold stream of simplicity, innocence, sensitivity, perplexity, childish confusion, but also immeasurable confidence . . . Whenever [Moses] fell before God, he cried like a child. Who can fall before his father, raise his eyes to him alone, to seek consolation and salvation, if not the child! . . . The mature, the adult, are not capable of the all-embracing and all-penetrating outpouring of the soul. The most sublime crown we can give a great man sparkles with the gems of childhood. ("A Eulogy for R. Hayyim Heller," 63–64).

Confronting Critics

In short, Rav Soloveitchik was not perturbed by the intellectual assaults on Judaism because of (1) the intensity of his faith experience, and (2) the methodological autonomy of Halakhah. This can account partially for why Rav Soloveitchik, despite his being the intellectual leader of Modern Orthodoxy, did not directly address in print conceptual assaults on faith such as evolution or historicism.[4] "He wrote," according to Dr. Moshe Sokol, "about matters

---

and Journals: A Selection, trans. Alastair Hannay [London, 1996], 556–57):
> Anselm prays to God in all sincerity that he may succeed in proving God's existence. He thinks that he has succeeded and throws himself down to thank God; curious, he does not notice that this prayer and thanksgiving are infinitely more proof of God's existence than – the proof.

4 In lectures, however, he occasionally offered brief comments that, instead of debating the evidence for or against the "Orthodox" position, cast the issues in a different light. Regarding evolution, see For Further Reference, #1. Regarding the historicity of biblical narratives, see

(a) that touched to the core of his own personal struggles with Jewish self-definition in the modern era; and (b) about which he believed that with his unique blend of Brisk and Berlin he had much to contribute."[5]

It is undoubtedly true that the Rav wrote out of a sense of deep intellectual and emotional engagement with a topic. This is what lends his writings a great deal of their power. However, I believe that several additional factors may account for why he wrote about certain issues and not about others.[6]

Let us take, for example, the question of biblical criticism. True, the Rav did not write a treatise on this topic because it held no great interest for him personally and because he felt that others, like Rav Hayyim Heller, had more specialized knowledge on the subject. However, he also makes a significant observation in *The Lonely Man of Faith* (10) that suggests that biblical criticism does not pose as great a challenge as one initially would assume. The critics base their case for multiple authorship on certain anomalies in the biblical text. Rav Soloveitchik points out in response that the Sages and the *Rishonim* were also sensitive to these textual anomalies, yet they offered different explanations for these phenomena because they were working with different assumptions than the critics. In other words, taking note of textual phenomena is one thing, but interpreting the phenomena is something else entirely.

For example, the fact that different names of God are recorded in chapter 1 and chapter 2 of Genesis does not necessarily lead to the conclusion that these chapters were penned by different authors. This fact can also indicate that the two chapters discuss distinct typologies of man (as Rav Soloveitchik believes), or different aspects of God (as the Kabbalists interpret), or a host of other explanations. The textual phenomena in themselves do not "prove" anything; they acquire significance only in light of one's preconceived notions about what the text can or should say.

Furthermore, R. Shalom Carmy[7] has pointed out that two approaches are possible when confronting critics:

(a) one can respond to them point-by-point, but then one is playing in their arena and is constantly on the defensive;

(b) one can offer a compelling alternate understanding.

Abraham's Journey, 1–7.

5 "'*Ger ve-Toshav Anokhi*': Modernity and Traditionalism in the Life and Thought of Rabbi Joseph B. Soloveitchik," in *Exploring the Thought of Rabbi Joseph B. Soloveitchik*, 133.

6 See also For Further Reference, #2.

7 "Of Eagle's Flight and Snail's Pace," in *Exploring the Thought of Rabbi Joseph B. Soloveitchik*, 113–14.

In *The Lonely Man of Faith*, the Rav takes the second path. Instead of undertaking a detailed critique of the critics' interpretation of the first two chapters of Genesis, he undercuts their arguments entirely by presenting a cogent alternative. Thus, he *does* actually confront the critics – in an indirect yet constructive manner, rather than in a direct but defensive manner.

Intellectual Autonomy

Related to this last claim is the assertion that the Rav did not engage in apologetics.[8] Apologetics (from the Greek *apologia*, meaning defense) results when a person accepts an external frame of reference as authoritative and tries to reconcile tradition with that external doctrine. When viewed this way, tradition becomes "problematic." By forcing tradition to fit into a preconceived and alien framework, one effectively places it into the proverbial *mitat Sedom*, or Procrustean bed. This inevitably leads to distortion of the tradition, either by assigning it unlikely meanings or by ignoring that which does not cohere with one's theory.

In contrast, Rav Soloveitchik had utter confidence in Jewish tradition and asserted its conceptual autonomy. He did not seek to "synthesize" or "harmonize" it with any other system of thought. Rather, he accepted Jewish tradition itself as his frame of reference, mining his vast erudition in fields of general knowledge for ideas that could shed new light on Judaism or enhance his understanding of man.

This non-apologetic approach characterizes the Rav's entire relationship to secular knowledge.[9] Imbued with strong faith and a secure sense of self, he was unafraid to expose himself to new ideas, nor did he place limits on his children's reading. The fact of divine revelation, entailing both belief in God and a system of norms, could not be changed by whatever he studied. But his understanding of tradition and his ability to communicate it could be enhanced through the study of "the best which has been thought and said in the world."[10]

---

8 See especially R. Yitzhak (Isadore) Twersky's discussion of apologetics and secular studies in sections 13 and 14 of his magisterial portrait of Rav Soloveitchik, "The Rov," in *Rabbi Joseph B. Soloveitchik: Man of Halacha, Man of Faith*, ed. R. Menachem Genack (Hoboken, NJ, 1998), 25–34.

9 While the Rav's thought is non-apologetic in the sense that "there is no attempt to demonstrate that traditional Judaism is completely congruent with philosophy (or any part of it)" (ibid., 29), he does set out in his earliest major work "to defend the honor of the Halakhah and halakhic men" (*Halakhic Man*, 137). See Chap. 30 below.

10 Matthew Arnold, Preface to *Culture and Anarchy* (1869), xiii.

Thus, the Rav's acceptance of Jewish tradition as his conceptual frame of reference justifies his selective use of concepts derived from Western thought. There are also internal philosophical reasons, as elaborated in *The Halakhic Mind*, that justify this selectivity. Unlike the "theories of everything" propounded by philosophers from Aristotle to Hegel, contemporary philosophy no longer trusts overarching and all-encompassing systems. As a good student of twentieth-century philosophy, Rav Soloveitchik realized that – philosophically speaking! – he was not beholden to any one school of thought. Therefore, he had the freedom to utilize insights from different philosophical schools without being enslaved to any one of them. This freedom afforded him much greater room for creativity than if the parameters and assumptions of a particular system had confined him.[11]

This consideration leads Prof. Twersky to conclude that "to quibble whether [the Rav's] premises and arguments are medieval or modern, rationalistic or pietistic, to argue whether his thought should be described as existentialist or dialectical, Kierkegaardian or neo-Kantian, is not very edifying."[12] Rav Soloveitchik was far from being an orthodox Aristotelian or Kantian who struggled to justify Judaism in light of an externally-conceived philosophy. Rather, he was a man of the *masorah* who creatively and critically utilized the most appropriate ideas he could find in order to understand and explain the Jewish tradition and the human condition.

Primary and Secondary Issues

Let us return to the question of why the Rav did not set out to address biblical criticism (and a host of other "burning" topics). We saw that (a) due to the intensity of his faith experience and the methodological autonomy of Halakhah, these issues did not trouble him personally; (b) the Midrash and medieval commentators had already addressed some of these "troublesome" phenomena, thereby demonstrating that the force of a question depends largely on one's presuppositions; and (c) by proposing a compelling alternative, he addressed the critics in a roundabout way. In his lectures, he wanted to expose his listeners to the intellectual and spiritual depth of Judaism, to open new vistas before them, and not to fight rearguard actions.

---

11 Interestingly, the Rav made the same point when comparing the Rambam to the Ramban (see For Further Reference, #3). While the former was somewhat straitjacketed by an Aristotelian philosophical framework and had to express his ideas in its narrow jargon, the latter was freer to exercise creativity in his religious thought.

12 *Op. cit.*, p. 34.

Beyond all this, I believe that the Rav's primary reason for not writing about these subjects was that he simply did not regard them as the most important issues or the main problems facing Judaism in the modern world. Judaism would be judged on what kind of person it produced, not on whether it could defend itself against these challenges. The battle between religion and secularism had to be fought in the human heart *before* it was fought in the human mind. Why is this so? We saw that the Rav believed that the God-experience lies at the core of faith, and the role of the intellect is only a posteriori – it is both ancillary and subsequent to the faith-experience. Therefore, there is no point in addressing questions of the intellect before one establishes within himself an experiential basis of faith. Conversely, once one has established this basis, then intellectual challenges become less urgent.

Thus, in *The Lonely Man of Faith* and many other writings, the Rav chose to address primarily issues related to the human existential situation: the possibility of experiencing faith within contemporary society, the relationship between the fundamental attitudes of modernity and religiosity, and the experiential crisis of the contemporary believer.[13] He states clearly at the outset of *The Lonely Man of Faith* that he does not want to deal with the abstract, intellectual side of the problem of faith and reason,[14] but rather with its existential dimension:

> Theory is not my concern at the moment. I want instead to focus attention on a human life situation in which the man of faith as an individual concrete being, with his cares and hopes, concerns and needs, joys and sad moments, is entangled (1).

I wish to stress that when the Rav says that he is "not troubled" by the phalanx of problems mentioned previously, this is not equivalent to saying that he is uninterested in them. He took science and philosophy far too seriously to be able to adopt such an approach. Rather, saying that these questions do not trouble him means that they do not shake his faith. Nevertheless, they are worthy of serious consideration. The epistemic autonomy of religion[15] provides an avenue in which to search for answers to these cognitive problems; and even if this avenue of inquiry fails to provide an adequate solution,

---

13 See also For Further Reference, #4.

14 However, in his early writings, especially *The Halakhic Mind*, the Rav does deal with the abstract side of the problem of faith and reason. In these writings, he does not try to harmonize faith and reason, as did the medievals. Rather, he establishes Halakhah as an autonomous cognitive discipline.

15 In our context, this refers to the recognition that Judaism operates with its own axioms and must be understood according to the rigorous tenets of its own internal logic.

the experiential foundation of faith provides us with the assurance that the questions need not be immediately answerable. If one has fundamental faith in the halakhic system and an inner experience of the truth of Torah, then one will relate differently to intellectual challenges, and will even be able to live more comfortably with unanswered questions.

Rav Soloveitchik saw his task mainly as helping the modern Jew understand his tradition, grasp its relevance and appreciate its desired effect upon his attitudes and lifestyle. The Rav's concern, thus, was far more with the crucial question of inner commitment to God rather than the secondary issues of intellectual critique. He had absolute intellectual confidence in Judaism, and was convinced that it could ward off all challengers. However, he had less confidence in man's soul, in his depth and strength of character, in his ability to transcend himself and his willingness to sacrifice. In Rabbi Sacks's penetrating formulation (49),

> It was not secular *knowledge*, encountered in the University of Berlin, that caused Soloveitchik such searing distress, but secular *man*, encountered in suburban-Jewish America.

In the next chapter, we will confront the results of the Rav's encounter with secular man.

FOR FURTHER REFERENCE

1. **Evolution:** In *The Emergence of Ethical Man,* Rav Soloveitchik writes that the crux of the "evolution versus creation" controversy is not the question of "divine creation and mechanistic evolution as such. We could find a solution of some kind to this controversy" (5). Rather, the essence of the problem is the seemingly contradictory views of man entailed by these two positions: is man's existence akin to those of plant and animal, or is he the bearer of the divine image? Modern science sees man as continuous with nature, while Greek philosophy, Christianity and "medieval and even modern Jewish moralists" (6) see man as separate and unique. Through an analysis of the first three chapters of Genesis and a variety of halakhic laws, the Rav concludes that Judaism – as represented by the foundational texts of the Bible and *Hazal,* and not by "the consensus of many [medieval and modern Jewish moralists], however great and distinguished" (ibid.) – takes a third position. Man is and must be continuous with the natural world. Yet, through his confrontation with God, he can *also* become – without forsaking his naturalness – a transcendent being.

2. **Bibliographical issues:** At this point, it is worth mentioning several bibliographical points which are crucial to gaining a comprehensive understanding of Rav Soloveitchik's literary output. First, with the possible exception of the three major early essays that we will discuss in the last section of this book, he had no preconceived publication plan. His major medium was the spoken word, and only occasionally would he consent to publish one of his lectures. (Note, however, that apart from his Talmud *shiur*, he generally spoke from a fully-written manuscript.) Many of his lectures/writings were connected to particular occasions and were not part of a project aforethought: eulogies, holiday sermons, *kinus teshuvah* lectures, addresses to various organizations, etc.

   Additionally, chance occurrences often determined which of his lectures were published and which not. Sometimes he would publish a lecture in response to someone's repeated entreaties, or working off a draft someone else prepared for him. If there was no one to prod him, a particular lecture might never be printed. This problem has largely been rectified by the fact that he bequeathed his unpublished manuscripts and taped lectures to his children, along with permission to publish them. These have been published in a steady stream in the years following his death; see the bibliography at the end of this book.

   Another factor to bear in mind is that Rav Soloveitchik was a thematic writer, not a system-builder. He wrote about individual topics that interested him, and would often return to and rethink these issues. In contrast to thinkers such as Aristotle or Kant, who set out systematically to address all the major philosophic issues of their generations, Rav Soloveitchik was neither systematic in his approach nor comprehensive in his scope. Partially, this was due to the aversion of twentieth-century philosophy to all-inclusive systems; other reasons are mentioned in the chapter above. For more on the problems of systematizing the Rav's thought, see the discussion of the relationship between *Halakhic Man* and *U-Vikkashtem mi-Sham* in Chapter 35 below, as well as the comments in Chapter 37 on the human perspective in the Rav's writings.

3. **Rambam vs. Ramban:** I heard this point in a tape of a 1968 lecture by the Rav on the Ramban's comments on *Parashat Lekh Lekha*. Subsequently, I saw it mentioned by Prof. Twersky in his article, "The Rov," *op. cit.*, 43–44, n. 17.

   Acceptance of a preconceived philosophical system affects not only creativity but also authenticity. In the taped lecture mentioned above, the Rav humorously calls the Rambam "overeducated"; therefore, in the

Guide the Rambam was prone to speak in philosophical clichés instead of letting the sources speak for themselves. The Ramban, on the other hand, was not beholden to Aristotelian categories and therefore could formulate a more authentic Jewish philosophy.

4. **Faith and reason:** We stated above that faith is prior to reason, and therefore the Rav felt that it was more crucial to address the former than the latter. Another way to view this issue is from within the perspective of reason itself. All reasoning must be conducted within a certain framework of presuppositions, or what in mathematics are called axioms. As we saw, the admissibility of a question depends on the validity of the assumptions behind it. The Rav, instead of dealing with the details of the questions, is addressing instead the far more crucial issue of defining one's governing assumptions. As he puts it in *The Lonely Man of Faith*, one must choose the framework from within which one will ask questions:

> Before beginning the analysis, we must determine within which frame of reference, psychological and empirical or theological and Biblical, our di-lemma should be described. I believe you will agree with me that we do not have much choice in the matter; for, to the man of faith, self-knowledge has one connotation only – to understand one's place and role within the scheme of events and things willed and approved by God . . . (8).

If one questions belief or tradition from the outside, using an alien set of assumptions, then this leads an unsatisfying, apologetic answer. If one asks from the inside – "I believe, but how am I to understand the follow-ing . . ." – then the question can be addressed more fruitfully. The Rav therefore devotes himself to elaborating the fundamental assumptions of the Halakhah – its views of God, man and the world, and the interaction between them.

Chapter 18

Practical Consequences of the Autonomy of Faith

Rav Soloveitchik as Community Leader and Halakhic Decisor

In Chapter 15, we saw that Adam I uses religion for his own majestic purposes. In Chapters 16 and 17, we saw that Adam II insists upon maintaining his own independent approach to religion, one based upon covenantal values. Yet contemporary Adam I is not content to live alongside Adam II; he seeks conquest, self-expansion and absolute hegemony over the whole of man's personality. In the modern era, Adam I attempts to usurp even the religious realm, recasting it from covenantal terms into his own majestic terms:

> He, of course, comes to a place of worship. He attends lectures on religion and appreciates the ceremonial, yet he is searching not for a faith in all its singularity and otherness, but for religious culture. He seeks not the greatness found in sacrificial action but the convenience one discovers in a comfortable, serene state of mind. He is desirous of an aesthetic experience rather than a covenantal one, of a social ethos rather than a divine imperative. In a word, he wants to find in faith that which he cannot find in his laboratory, or in the privacy of his luxurious home. His efforts are noble, yet he is not ready for a genuine faith experience which requires the giving of one's self unreservedly to God, who demands unconditional commitment, sacrificial action, and retreat. Western man diabolically insists on being successful. Alas, he wants to be successful even in his adventure with God. If he gives of himself to God, he expects reciprocity . . . Therefore, modern man puts up demands that faith adapt itself to the mood and temper of modern times (103–04).

It is precisely modern man's demand "that faith adapt itself to the mood and temper of modern times" – which are the mood and temper of Adam I – that most threatens the independence and legitimacy of Adam II's covenantal religiosity. As a leader of the Orthodox Jewish community, the Rav was sensitive to this threat and, on a number of fronts, he directed practical efforts at countering it. A unifying theme of many of the Rav's halakhic decisions and public activities is the need to preserve the autonomy of Judaism and of Halakhah in the face of external pressures to accommodate, water down or forego their demands and values. Let us examine a number of instances where the Rav gave concrete expression to the concern for religious autonomy, which has occupied our attention for the past several chapters.

1. Ritual Changes:

The Rav took especially strong public stands against changes in synagogue practice. The integrity of Halakhah was not a matter subject to public approval, he wrote: "It is ludicrous to argue against a religious law on the ground that the latter is not popular with the crowd."[1] In mid-twentieth-century America, Orthodox Judaism was perceived as being in retreat, and the Rav's resolute yet sensitive stand on issues such as the *mehitzah*, the barrier preventing intermingling between the sexes in the synagogue, helped turn the tide.[2]

The Rav objected to various proposed ritual changes in the synagogue because he believed they were not consonant with the legal principles of Halakhah. However, he also pointed out that, in their desire to make the synagogue service more "pleasing" or "acceptable," the changes reflected a lack of understanding of the Jewish philosophy of prayer (as derived from the sources of Halakhah). For example, regarding the innovation of having the cantor face the congregation during prayer, the Rav wrote:

> The departure corrupts every idea of prayer which calls for complete forgetfulness of man as a worthless and wretched being on the one hand, and unqualified surrender to God on the other. Watching the audience during recital of the prayers by the cantor is tantamount to a demonstration of the opposite sort – arrogance and haughtiness on the part of the congregation and its representative in giving preference to a social get-together over man's encounter with God.[3]

---

1 Cited in R. Louis Bernstein, *Challenge and Mission: The Emergence of the English Speaking Orthodox Rabbinate* (New York, 1982), 48. See also the collection of the Rav's letters entitled *Community, Covenant and Commitment: Selected Letters and Communications*, ed. R. Nathaniel Helfgot (Jersey City, 2005), 141.

2 Regarding the *mehitzah*, mid-twentieth-century Orthodoxy and the Rav's position, see For Further Reference, #1.

3 Cited in Bernstein, ibid. For a related explanation regarding *mehitzah*, see *Community,*

When dealing with the halakhic realm, it was imperative to be guided by Halakhah's internal logic and values, and not by other considerations.[4]

2. New Rituals and Rabbinic Autonomy:

The Rav was consulted on a number of occasions about the propriety of creating new rituals, such as commemorating the Holocaust at the Passover Seder, instituting a formal prayer service for *Yom ha-Atzma'ut* (Israel's Independence Day), and conducting a religious service to mark the 300th anniversary of Jewish life in America. The Rav felt that each of these events should be marked, but in time-honored and halakhically approved forms. He objected to the creation of new and hybrid pseudo-religious ceremonies that did not respect the autonomy of the halakhic process and the integrity of religious rituals.[5] The Rav had harsh words about the newfangled ceremonies. For example, regarding the last example cited above, he wrote:

> [T]he whole service concocted by some rabbi of the Synagogue Council should not and cannot be accepted by the RCA.[6] The service suggests to me both religious infantilism and Christian-Methodist sentimentalism which exhausts itself in hymn singing and responsive reading. As a matter of fact, an order of service by the Methodist church is by far superior to the approach employed by the Synagogue Council. I am ... disturbed ... by the whole character and structure of the service, which contains very few Jewish themes and a lot of high school commencement nonsense (*Community, Covenant and Commitment*, 115–16).

As an extension of his desire to preserve the autonomy of Halakhah, the Rav also wanted to preserve the autonomy of the rabbinate, and not have laymen dictate to it. This was another reason for his objection to the newly proposed ceremonies, such as that prepared by the Religious Zionist political organization Mizrachi for Israel's Independence Day:

Covenant and Commitment, 134–35.

    4 See the Rav's *derashah* on Korah cited above in Chap. 10, For Further Reference, #3.

    5 See *Community, Covenant and Commitment*, letters 12–15 (109–24), for the specifics of his objections to each of these proposals.

    6 The RCA is the Rabbinical Council of America, a major Orthodox rabbinic organization. Rav Soloveitchik chaired its Halachah Commission for many years. The Synagogue Council of America was an interdenominational Jewish group that included Orthodox, Conservative and Reform rabbinic associations.

I do not feel that the RCA ought to mail out to its members the program prepared by the Mizrachi. My feelings on this matter were prompted by a twofold
reason. First, the order of the service was arranged in a non-halakhic and non-
scholarly fashion and breathes meaningless ceremonialism, which is not only
alien but also contrary to our halakhic tradition . . .
Second, I do not believe that a rabbinical body like the RCA should dissemi-
nate any kind of material dealing with a religious subject which was prepared
by a different organization, especially a lay group. The first prerogative of
the rabbinate is full and unlimited sovereignty in all matters pertaining to Halakhah and observance. It is below our dignity to serve in the capacity of a
mailing agency for any group, regardless of the latter's distinct merits and
accomplishments (ibid., 123–24).

3. Interfaith Dialogue:

The principle of the autonomy of faith applies not only in the confrontation
of covenant with majesty, but also in the relationships of different religions
with each other. Historically, each faith community has developed its own
unique way of relating to God, and the Rav felt that each must respect the
other's integrity. While the Rav wrote that Jews can and should work together
with other faiths on matters pertaining to "the general welfare and progress
of mankind, [such as] combatting disease . . . alleviating human suffering . . .
protecting man's rights . . . helping the needy, et cetera,"[7] it is pointless (at
best) to engage in dialogue on matters of creed. Each faith speaks its own language, and it would be illegitimate for one to request of the other to interpret
itself in alien categories.

> [T]he mere appraisal of the worth of one community in terms of the service
> it has rendered to another community . . . constitutes an infringement of the
> sovereignty and dignity of even the smallest of faith communities.[8]

At the core of this position lies the idea that, as we have seen explicated
in *Lonely Man*, faith is a basic awareness and not a conclusion that can be
explained on the basis of certain premises. This fact prevents the possibility

---

7 "Confrontation," *Tradition* 6:2 (Spring–Summer 1964), 20–21. However, an addendum to
"Confrontation" entitled "On Interfaith Relationships" (*Community, Covenant and Commitment*,
letter 51, 259–61) expands the range of subjects open to dialogue to include matters of universal
religious concern, but not matters pertaining to "our private individual commitment." (Both
"Confrontation" and the addendum are also available at http://traditiononline.org/archives.) The
discrepancy between "Confrontation" and "On Interfaith Relationships" has been the subject of
much discussion; see For Further Reference, #2.

8 Ibid., 23. See also *Community, Covenant and Commitment*, letters 51 and 53.

of communication at the level of faith, since the religious experience of each community is specific to it and "does not lend itself to standardization or universalization" (ibid.). In short, the Rav believed in cooperation and dialogue on the level of Adam I, but not on the level of Adam II.

4. Interfaith Services:

For similar reasons, the Rav strongly objected to holding interfaith services.

> As to interfaith celebrations [marking 300 years of Jewish life in America], we are ready and willing to encourage such projects as long as they will be held within the confine of secular activities. No joint worship, however, can be encouraged. We are loyal citizens of our great country and we are committed to all its institutions, political, economic and educational, without any reservation or qualification, as are all other Americans. Hence, joint action and common effort are commendable in all areas of mundane endeavor. Yet one's relationship to, worship of and dialogue with God is an inner experience most intimate, most personal, most unique. Each community worships God in its singular way. "*Gleichschaltung*" [i.e., making equivalent] distorts the very essence of the religious experience (*Community, Covenant and Commitment*, 114).

The Rav explained the last point elsewhere:

> I am fully aware of the great American heritage of religious tolerance and I cherish this ideal with all my heart and soul. However, true tolerance expresses itself not in *Gleichschaltung*, as in equating two incommensurate systems of values and principles as Judaism and Christianity present, but in granting opportunity to all faiths to promote their world views and practices within unique historic and theological dimensions and to thrive in an atmosphere of mutual understanding and respect. Yet while practicing this great virtue, we must be constantly mindful that the very essence of religion expresses itself in individual character and singularity which can not be obliterated if religion is not to be stripped of its soul.[9]

5. Jewish Interdenominational Activities:

In an analogous sense (but clearly with a far greater awareness of fraternity and mutual responsibility), the Rav recommended cooperation with Reform

---

9 Bernstein, 61–62. This is taken from a letter by the Rav to R. Israel Klavan (May 23, 1954) on holding a joint telethon and appeal with Protestant and Catholic churches. See also the Rav's objection to interfaith chapels in *Community, Covenant and Commitment*, 8–10.

and Conservative organizations in matters relating to Jewish welfare and survival, but not in matters related to creed and observance. For example, he stated in a 1954 interview:

> The principle of [Jewish] unity expresses itself in two ways. First, the unity of Jews as members of a spiritual community, as a congregation which was established through the conclusion of the covenant at Mt. Sinai . . .
>
> Secondly, unity manifests itself also in our unique political-historical lot as a nation . . . The enigma of our existence is primarily revealed through our loneliness and our affliction in all times, the current era included . . . No Jew can renounce his part of the unity, which is based upon a fate of loneliness of the Jewish people as a nation . . .
>
> The conclusion above is very simple. When we are faced with a problem for Jews and Jewish interests toward the world without, regarding the defense of Jewish rights in the non-Jewish world, then all groups and movements must be united. In this area, there may not be any division, because any friction in the Jewish camp may be disastrous for the entire people . . .
>
> With regard to our problem within [the Jewish community], however, – our spiritual-religious interests such as Jewish education, synagogues, councils of rabbis – whereby unity is expressed through spiritual-ideological collectivism as a Torah community, it is my opinion that Orthodoxy cannot and should not unite with such groups which deny the fundamentals of our *weltanschauung* (*Community, Covenant and Commitment*, 144–46).

To use terms developed in this interview and, two years later, in *Kol Dodi Dofek*, Orthodoxy must act together with other Jewish denominations on the level of fate, but it cannot cooperate on matters of destiny. Jewish denominations function together as an *am* (nation), but not as an *edah* (congregation).[10]

6. Religion and State in Israel:

In Israel, there was an even greater danger of the encroachment of the state into religious affairs – a subject which greatly vexed the Rav. Halakhic decisions of the Chief Rabbinate, he felt, were often subjected to political

---

10 Despite his deep ideological differences with non-Orthodox denominations, Rav Soloveitchik always treated their representatives with respect: "I use the term 'battle' always in the ideological vein, and never in the personal sense. I may attack a certain point of view which I consider false, but I will never attack a person who preaches it. I have always a high regard for the individual who is honest and moral, even when I am not in agreement with him. Such a relation is in accord with the concept of *kevod ha-beriyyot*: 'Beloved is man, for he was created in the image of God' (*Avot* 3:14)" (*Community, Covenant and Commitment*, 146). See also the letter excerpted in For Further Reference, #1.

pressures by the government, which did not respect the sovereignty of the rabbinate. For example, regarding two controversies whose details need not concern us,[11] the Rav said:

> [T]he Marbek and Benei Israel issues should have been resolved five years ago by the rabbinate. However, the intervention of the state, the emergency session of the Knesset to deal with the [decision] of the rabbinate is a blow to the independence of the rabbinate. The United States court system [like the Chief Rabbinate] is an arm of the state. However, the separation of powers between the legislative branch and the judicial branch is so pronounced that no senator or congressman would dare challenge a ruling of the Supreme Court and certainly a special session of Congress would never be called to apply pressure on the Supreme Court. This greatly upset me and demeaned the honor of the rabbinate (ibid., 225–26).

In fact, one of the reasons Rav Soloveitchik did not accept the job of Chief Rabbi of Israel when it was offered to him was that he had concluded that the Chief Rabbinate was not autonomous.[12]

Modern Orthodoxy in Theory and Practice

As a leader of Orthodox Judaism, the Rav defended it not just from external encroachments on the uniqueness and irreducibility of its faith commitment, but also from tendencies from within to smooth over or discount elements conflicting with integration into the broader majestic society. In order to understand this, it is worth pausing for a moment to consider where *The Lonely Man of Faith* has taken us so far. First, it posits that covenantal man must bring his unique message to majestic man, leading, the Rav hopes, to an oscillation between the majestic and covenantal modes of living that will prove fruitful and even complementary. However, such is not the case in the contemporary age:

---

11 For an account of these controversies, see R. Helfgot's introduction to *Community, Covenant and Commitment*, xxx–xxxiii.

12 See *Community, Covenant and Commitment*, letters 29–34 and 40–42, as well as the article cited above in Chap. 1, n. 32. Prof. Gerald Blidstein recounts an interesting story he heard from the Rav in this regard: "He told me that David Ben-Gurion had sent an emissary to assure him that if he agreed to be nominated for the job, he – Ben-Gurion – would ensure that he was elected. In reply, he told the emissary that it was precisely Ben-Gurion's ability to ensure who was elected Chief Rabbi of the State of Israel that kept him from accepting the office" ("Rabbi Joseph B. Soloveitchik's Letters on Public Affairs," *The Torah U-Madda Journal* 15 [2008–09], 19).

In a word, the message of translated religion[13] is not the only one which the man of faith must address to majestic man of culture. Besides this message, man of faith must bring to the attention of man of culture the *kerygma* [i.e., message] of original faith in all its singularity and pristine purity, in spite of the incompatibility of this message with the fundamental credo of a utilitarian society. How staggering this incompatibility is! This unique message speaks of defeat instead of success, of accepting a higher will instead of commanding, of giving instead of conquering, of retreating instead of advancing, of acting "irrationally" instead of being always reasonable. Here the tragic event occurs. Contemporary majestic man rejects his dialectical assignment [i.e., combining majesty with covenant] and, with it, the man of faith (*The Lonely Man of Faith*, 101–02).

In fact, the man of faith confronts something even more alarming: the secularization of religion itself. In the parts of the world that have undergone modernization, the predominant forms of organized religion are those geared towards the attainment of success and dignity, not redemption. Modern man adopts only those elements of religion that are useful to him in his pursuit of majesty, without recognizing the autonomous and absolute claims of faith.

In this sense, *The Lonely Man of Faith* can be read as a powerful social and religious critique not only of modern organized religion in general, but specifically of tendencies within Rav Soloveitchik's own American Modern Orthodox community.[14] In other works, Rav Soloveitchik makes this critique explicit. For example, the Rav bitingly characterizes the world of Modern Orthodoxy, when compared with earlier exemplars of Adam II religiosity, as "shorn of wings to soar and bereft of roots to penetrate the depth of religious experience."[15] Instead of soaring to the heights and penetrating the depths of

---

13 This refers to the Rav's assertion that "the message of [Adam II's] faith, if translated into cultural categories [of Adam I], . . . is pertinent even to secular man" (96). For elaboration, see the discussion of "Adam I's Use of Adam II's Categories" in Chap. 15 above.

14 "Modern Orthodoxy" can refer to an ideology or a sociological grouping. This section, in fact, is devoted to the gap between these two: the ideology, as espoused by the Rav, is often not embodied by the community. R. Aharon Lichtenstein refers to this as the difference between Modern Orthodoxy *lekhathila* or *bediavad*, the former being an ideal choice stemming from dialectical tension and the latter a pragmatic default resulting from tepid indifference. See R. Lichtenstein's articles, "Centrist Orthodoxy: A Spiritual Accounting," in *By His Light: Character and Values in the Service of God*, ed. Reuven Ziegler (Jersey City, 2003), 220–52, and "The Future of Centrist Orthodoxy," in *Leaves of Faith*, vol. 2 (Jersey City, 2004), 309–30.

15 "*Peleitat Sofreihem*," in *Divrei Hagut ve-Ha'arakhah*, 148. See also, for instance, *On Repentance*, 148: "[D]espite his being a good, faithful Jew, the American Jew . . . does not sense the presence of the Master of the Universe. Possibly he 'believes,' and it is imperative to do so, but it is hardly enough; one must personally experience the reality of the Creator in an intimate

religiosity, instead of experiencing the dialectic of *The Lonely Man of Faith* in all its rigor and grandeur, Modern Orthodoxy can tend towards religious complacency, focusing on the here-and-now and preoccupied with material and cultural self-enhancement. Does one seek in its synagogues a covenantal encounter with the Almighty, entailing both a profound sense of dependence and a commitment to accepting the yoke of the commandments, or does one seek a social-aesthetic experience of comfortable community?

This insight can serve as a corrective to a prevalent misreading, or partial reading, of the message of *The Lonely Man of Faith*. True, in its advocacy of a life lived on the planes of both dignity and covenant, the book constitutes a defense or articulation of the *theory* of Modern Orthodoxy. But in pointing out that modern organized religion falls far short of the ideal whereby Adam I and Adam II live in dialectical counterpoise – or, even better, Adam II guides the endeavors of Adam I – the book is also a critique of Modern Orthodoxy in *practice*. When lived to its fullest, the Adam I-Adam II dialectic can produce a vision of sublime beauty. Yet in the contemporary world, exemplars of such beauty, whether on an individual or a communal level, are hard to find, and this results in Rav Soloveitchik's loneliness.

Engaging the World, Upholding the Covenant

The Rav's activities as "defender of the faith" – or, more accurately, as defender of the uniqueness of covenantal religiosity – should not overshadow the fact that he advocates active engagement with society and recognizes the religious worth of Adam I's attainments. Both sides of the Adam I-Adam II dialectic must be maintained, without one being allowed to eradicate or overwhelm the other. Just as he urges moderns, and perhaps especially the Modern Orthodox, to remember the covenant, so too does he emphasize that covenantal life need not fear majesty. The role of covenantal religion is not to retreat into a corner, on the one hand, nor simply to provide Adam I with the validation he seeks, on the other hand. Rather, it is to bring sanctity into all realms of existence, including those of Adam I. For example, regarding the founding of Yeshiva University's medical school, the Rav writes:

> The Orthodox community can win the respect of others by focusing on and excelling in three areas: (1) living their personal lives on a higher ethical-religious level; (2) defending their principles and ideals in a forthright and

---

manner." This is not to say that he had no criticism of other groups. However, as the leader of the Modern Orthodox camp, he saw his duty primarily as tending to the spiritual welfare of the members of his community, and not as pointing out to others their shortcomings.

uncompromising manner; (3) demonstrating to the world that the Torah Jew need not cower in a corner and gaze with sadness and resignation as life and the world pass him by. The Orthodox Jew must demonstrate that he navigates with pride the flow and currents of the modern world and participate in a life that is racing ever more rapidly towards new horizons and great accomplishments in the domains of science of technology. We must demonstrate that in all cultural, social and scientific situations a Jew can study Torah and live as a faithful Torah Jew. We must show the world that not only doesn't the Halakhah restrain the intellectual and emotional capacities and worldly knowledge of the Jew, [but] on the contrary, it deepens and broadens them greatly. Once and for all we must demonstrate the falsehood of the complaints of all the non-religious and pseudo-religious movements and organizations that proclaim that Halakhah limits the individual and estranges him from the world around him. We should not respond to their claims with theoretical arguments. Instead we should present practical examples and deeds. If the Yeshiva will endeavor to produce a first-class medical school, and thereby enable students to combine a Torah lifestyle with the medical profession, it will have accomplished a great deal to enhance the honor of Torah and the prestige of Orthodoxy (*Community, Covenant and Commitment*, 90–91).

Similarly, he expresses his affinity with Religious Zionism in broad and sweeping terms:

For me, Mizrachi is not only a political organization to whom we must gratefully acknowledge its contribution to the building of the Land of Israel, but also an ideological movement with an all-embracing philosophy that is no less relevant for Jewish life in the Diaspora, outside of *Eretz Yisrael*. This ideology that is an expression of our belief in the eternity of Judaism, affirms our staunch position within the modern world, with all of its attendant beauty and ugliness, greatness, power and cruelty, the torrential currents of life within it, the desire and conquering might, its great scientific and technological prowess, along with the audacity and haughtiness, moral corruption and spiritual contamination of modern man.

We have not removed ourselves from such a world, nor have we withdrawn into a secluded corner. We are unwilling to become a religious sect that forfeits the general public for the benefit of individuals. We will not build a Noah's Ark – our prayers are for everyone. It is our desire to purify and sanctify the modern world by means of the eternal vision, constant in its purity and grandeur, expressing the transcendental perspective and Divine calm within the stormy seas of change and metamorphosis that is known as progress. It is our belief that Judaism has the means to give meaning and significance, value and refinement, to the multi-faceted existence of modern life. We do not fear progress in any area of life, since it is our firm conviction that we have the ability to cope with and redeem it. I personally subscribe to this outlook with every fiber of my being (ibid., 203–04).

Perhaps the overarching message of the Rav's public activity, as set forth above, is the need for Orthodox Judaism to have the courage of its convictions, to proclaim forthrightly and to live out its dual commitment to majesty and covenant. The Rav believes that Orthodoxy need not fear confronting the challenges and opportunities of the modern world, for he has absolute confidence in the Torah's ability to "cope with and redeem" all realms of human endeavor. Nor, when confronted with majority groups holding a different viewpoint, does Orthodoxy have to try to ingratiate itself and compromise its principles in order to curry favor with them. By setting forth its principles with dignity and humility, it will only gain respect.

Yet this engagement with the realm of majestic man is valid only if Orthodoxy maintains sight of its covenantal foundations. The Jew must always remain aware that he is *both* a "stranger and a resident" (Gen. 23:4) – *ger ve-toshav* – in his surrounding society.[16] He is united with others in the majestic endeavor, but unique in his faith commitment. If engagement with the surrounding world cannot be conducted while maintaining the integrity of Orthodox principles, then there is no need to be afraid of retreating for a period of time from broader society and turning inward, as he counsels the head of a rabbinic organization:

> I noticed in your letter that you are a bit disturbed about the probability of being left out.[17] Let me tell you that this attitude of fear is responsible for many commissions and omissions, compromises and fallacies on our part which have contributed greatly to the prevailing confusion within the Jewish community and to the loss of our self-esteem, our experience of ourselves as independent entities committed to a unique philosophy and way of life. Of course, sociability is a basic virtue and we all hate loneliness and dread the experience of being left alone. Yet at times there is no alternative and we must courageously face the test. Maimonides of old was aware of such bitter experiences (vide Code, *Hilkhot De'ot* 6:1).[18]

---

16 The *ger ve-toshav* motif recurs often in the Rav's writings and speeches. See, for example, "Confrontation," 26–27, and *Out of the Whirlwind*, 37–40.

17 The project under discussion was a new translation of the Bible being prepared by the Jewish Publication Society. The Rav felt that Orthodox representatives could not participate in this project unless it would be guided by the principles and interpretations of the Oral Law.

18 *Community, Covenant and Commitment*, 111. In the passage the Rav references, the Rambam writes: "Man is created in such a way that his character traits and actions are influenced

What is to be Done?

This leads directly into the conclusion of *The Lonely Man of Faith*. Due to Adam I's rejection of Adam II, the man of faith confronts not just a breakdown in communication with his majestic counterpart, but also Adam I's hijacking of religion itself. This poses not an intellectual challenge, but rather a spiritual and experiential one. Rav Soloveitchik cannot overcome this problem by explaining how to become a man of faith, since (as noted in Chapter 16) no cognitive categories can contain faith, nor can faith be fully translated into cultural terms. He can *describe* what it is like to *be* a man of faith, but he cannot *explain* how or why to *become* one. Faith is a basic awareness, an a priori axiom, and not a reasoned conclusion. Faced with this situation that does not merely frustrate the man of faith but threatens his covenantal commitment, he may feel that he has no choice but to withdraw from such a society or – more fundamentally – from the majestic component within himself.

> It is here that the dialogue between the man of faith and the man of culture comes to an end. Modern Adam the second, as soon as he finishes translating religion into the cultural vernacular, and begins to talk the "foreign" language of faith, finds himself lonely, forsaken, misunderstood, at times even ridiculed by Adam the first, by himself. When the hour of estrangement strikes, the ordeal of man of faith begins and he starts his withdrawal from society, from Adam the first – be he an outsider, be he himself . . . He experiences not only ontological loneliness but also social isolation, whenever he dares to deliver the genuine faith-*kerygma*. This is both the destiny and the human historical situation of the man who keeps a rendezvous with eternity, and who, in spite of everything, continues tenaciously to bring the message of faith to majestic man (106–07).

Actually, Rav Soloveitchik ends the essay in two ways. Chapter IX concludes with an air of finality, asserting that the man of faith seemingly must withdraw from society. Chapter X, however, introduces the story of Elisha's transformation from a farmer (Adam I) into a prophet (Adam II). This story holds out the possibility that, after withdrawing from majesty and going to the limits of religious achievement available to him, Adam II, like Elisha, will

---

by his neighbors and friends, and he follows the custom of the people in his country. Therefore . . . if there are evil men and sinners who do not let him live in the country unless he mingles with them and follows their evil customs [and he cannot escape to a better country], he shall go off to [dwell in] caves, thickets or deserts, and not accustom himself to the way of sinners."

eventually return to majestic society "as a participant in state affairs, as an adviser of kings and a teacher of the majestic community" (112).

Elisha ultimately bridged the worlds of the two Adams. The Rav ends the book on a more positive note than one would expect at the end of chapter IX: the man of faith succeeds, despite the attendant difficulties and frustrations, in engaging and influencing the world from within a theocentric context.

Since the entire essay focuses on both the individual and the community, it is important to stress the communal dimension of the conclusion. Like the three Patriarchs and Moses, who founded a community that knows God, the man of faith is animated by the goal of developing and sustaining such a community. In a passage where many themes of *The Lonely Man of Faith* resonate, the Rambam portrays this as a human ideal:

> It also seems to me that the fact that these four [i.e., the Patriarchs and Moses] were in a permanent state of extreme perfection in the eyes of God, . . . even while they were engaged in increasing their fortune [i.e., tending to the world of Adam I], . . . was necessarily brought about by the circumstance that in all these actions their end was to come near to Him [i.e., the goal of Adam II] . . . For the end of their efforts during their life was *to bring into being a religious community* that would know and worship God, . . . to spread the doctrine of the unity of the Name in the world and to guide people to love Him (*Guide of the Perplexed* III:51).[19]

How does this translate into practice in our lives? Now that several decades have passed since its writing, how relevant does *The Lonely Man of Faith* remain? The Rav's analysis of God's call to man to embody both Adam I and Adam II should apply under all circumstances, since it describes something fundamental to the human condition. However, the rejection of Adam II is a function of society and its mores, and may or may not be relevant in different times and places.[20] What, then, is the correct path for the man of faith to follow today: withdrawal or engagement? Like the Rav in his dual conclusion, I leave this to the reader to decide.

---

19 In this passage, Rambam highlights the necessary interaction between the material and spiritual aspects of community building. When the Patriarchs and Moses "were occupied with governing people, increasing their fortune and endeavoring to acquire property," they did so in order to strengthen the material basis of a community of believers, who would in turn influence others. Therefore "these actions were pure worship of great import." Thus, "the end of *all their efforts*" – in the spheres of *both* Adam I and Adam II – was indeed "to spread the doctrine of the unity of the Name in the world and to guide people to love Him."

20 In other words, ontological loneliness is an unchanging facet of the human condition, but historical loneliness is contingent and changing. See For Further Reference, #3.

FOR FURTHER REFERENCE

1. **The *mehitzah* controversy, Orthodoxy and the Rav:** For histori-
   cal background on Orthodoxy in mid-twentieth-century America, see
   Lawrence Grossman, "American Orthodoxy in the 1950s: The Lean
   Years," in Rafael Medoff, ed., *Rav Chesed: Essays in Honor of Rabbi
   Dr. Haskel Lookstein*, vol. 1 (Jersey City, 2009), 251–69. On the *mehitzah* controversy, see Baruch Litvin, *The Sanctity of the Synagogue*, 3rd
   ed. (New York, 1987). Regarding the Rav's position on *mehitzah*, see
   Community, Covenant and Commitment, letters 16–20, 125–42. Letter 16
   is an outstanding example of the Rav's ability to proclaim his principles
   forthrightly while displaying both sensitivity and humility, and therefore, I
   would like to cite a lengthy excerpt. The occasion of its writing was an invitation extended to the Rav to a dinner at Temple Bnai Moshe (Brighton,
   MA) in honor of his friend Rabbi Joseph Shubow, a Conservative rabbi,
   at which Rabbi Shubow's mixed-seating synagogue would be dedicated.
   The Rav responded to the president of the congregation:

   > Frankly speaking, I was faced with a very unpleasant situation. On the one
   > hand I was eager to accept your invitation. I cherish my long association
   > with Rabbi Shubow and I consider him a dear and distinguished friend
   > whom I hold in great esteem because of his many talents and fine quali-
   > ties. It is self-evident that if the dinner were being given only in honor of
   > Rabbi and Mrs. Shubow I would consider it a privilege to serve as one of
   > the sponsors.
   >
   > On the other hand, however, this reception, to my regret, will also serve
   > as an occasion to celebrate the completion and dedication of the new tem-
   > ple. Let me say unequivocally that I do recognize the importance of this new
   > house of worship for the Jewish population of Brighton as a means of com-
   > munal organization and unification. I also appreciate the unselfish efforts
   > on the part of the members and leaders which made such an undertaking
   > possible. Their pride in having attained their goal is fully warranted. You
   > in particular have manifested a strong sense of community awareness and
   > devotion to Jewish causes for which you should be congratulated.
   >
   > Yet, all this does not justify my serving as a sponsor of a dinner at which
   > the dedication of this temple will be celebrated since the latter will, in all
   > probability, have a mixed seating arrangement which is in my opinion not
   > in consonance with our time-honored Law. The requirement for separate
   > pews is almost a truism in our religious code and I have neither the right
   > nor the desire to sanction either by word or by silence a departure from this
   > tradition. My presence at the celebration or the appearance of my name as

a sponsor would be tantamount to a tacit approval of mixed pews, a thing which would greatly disturb my conscience. Therefore, after I had given the matter considerable thought, I arrived at the unavoidable conclusion that my role in connection with this affair would prove to be absurd, and so I respectfully decline.

I wish to impress upon you that my words are not to be interpreted in the sense of criticism or censure. I am not a preacher by nature, and I have never tried to convert others who are committed to a different philosophy to my viewpoint. I write this letter with a sense of deep humility, explaining to you my feelings on the matter. I hope that you realize and fully understand my position and appreciate my hesitance in accepting an honor which would be in direct opposition to my inner convictions.

Please convey my regards to Rabbi and Mrs. Shubow and wish them, on my behalf, many years of joy and happiness.

2. **Interfaith dialogue:** The Rav's essay "Confrontation" and his position on interfaith dialogue have been subject to extensive discussion. See R. David Hartman, *Love and Terror in the God Encounter: The Theological Legacy of Rabbi Joseph B. Soloveitchik* (Woodstock, VT, 2001), 131–65; Daniel Rynhold, "The Philosophical Foundations of Soloveitchik's Critique of Interfaith Dialogue," *Harvard Theological Review* 96:1 (2003), 101–20; the online proceedings of a conference at Boston College's Center for Christian-Jewish Learning on "Rabbi Joseph Soloveitchik on Interreligious Dialogue: Forty Years Later," http://www. bc.edu/dam/files/research_sites/cjl/texts/center/conferences/soloveitchik/ index.html; and Yigal Sklarin, "Rushing in Where Angels Fear to Tread: Rabbi Joseph B. Soloveitchik, the RCA, Modern Orthodox Jewry and the Second Vatican Council," *Modern Judaism* 29:3 (Oct. 2009), 351–85.

Note that the Rav felt that just as Jews should not allow Christians to dictate Jewish belief, Jews also should not dictate to Christians what they should believe: "The Church is within her rights to interpret our history in her own theological-dogmatic terms. We are the ones who have transcended the bounds of historical responsibility and decency by asking for a theological document on the Jews as 'brethren' in faith instead of urging the Church to issue a strong declaration in sociological-human terms affirming the inalienable rights of the Jew as a human being" (*Community, Covenant and Commitment*, 264).

3. **Applying the Rav's thought:** For reflections on the continuing relevance of *The Lonely Man of Faith*, see the symposium sponsored by ATID on the fortieth anniversary of its publication (http://www.atid.org/resources/

lmof40.asp), as well as David Shatz's preface to the 2006 reprint of the book. Much has also been written regarding the educational application of the Rav's thought. See, for example, R. Moshe Simkovich, "Teaching Rabbi Soloveitchik's Thought in the High School Classroom," in *Wisdom from All My Teachers*, eds. R. Jeffrey Saks and Susan Handelman (Jerusalem, 2003), 341–59, and the papers from ATID's seminar on "Translating the Torah and Philosophy of Rabbi Soloveitchik to Contemporary Jewish Education," http://www.atid.org/journal/journal05/default.asp.

Section IV

DOCTRINE OF MAN

Chapter 19

Family Relationships and Religious Life

The Parental and Matrimonial Communities

In earlier chapters, we examined the question of why the Rav discusses his personal experiences in his philosophical writings.[1] We established that, in forming a relationship with God and developing a full religious personality, the experiential dimension of Judaism is crucial. The teacher can convey this dimension of Judaism only by means of his or her self-revelation to the student, thereby achieving a sharing of hearts and not just a meeting of minds.

The need to train students in Judaism's experiential dimension can account for the appearance in the Rav's writings and speeches of passages that discuss his own religious experience. Yet the Rav's oeuvre also contains many personal passages dealing with his family relationships, particularly those with his parents and his wife. What can account for these?

The answer becomes clear in *Family Redeemed*, a posthumous collection of the Rav's essays, which sets forth a fascinating doctrine regarding the connection between human family relationships and man's relationship to God.[2] The Rav claims that establishing appropriate family relationships is a necessary component of, or perhaps even a precondition for, establishing a relationship with God.[3]

---

1 See above, pp. 47–48 and 102–03.

2 All page references in this chapter will refer to *Family Redeemed*.

3 While *Family Redeemed* contains expositions of Judaism's views on these familial relationships, exposition alone is not enough. Therefore, in other places the Rav shares his own experience of family relationships, in order to teach the experiential dimension in this area too.

> . . . [T]he relationship of God to us and our relationship to Him lend them-
> selves to description and interpretation in finite human categories. The Jew has
> learned to confess his faith in and his impassioned love of God by telling the
> story of people whom he loves and with whom he seeks to identify himself.
> Judaic faith and theology are linked with finite experiences and meaningful
> human relations. *By developing proper human relations structures, the Jew*
> *learns how to love, revere and serve God* (167).[4]

Of which "human relations" is he speaking? The Rav specifies two relationships: that with one's parents and that with one's spouse.

> When the child finds his finite-conditioned origin in his father or his mother,
> he *ipso facto* discovers his infinite and ultimate origin in God. However, it is
> impossible to discover the mysterious transcendental origin if the individual is
> not acquainted with the origin-perception of belonging to and being rooted in
> something or someone within the range of the finite and tangible world.
> . . . [W]e realize that on the strength of the comparisons, indeed equation, of
> the matrimonial community with that of the parental,[5] the former is as inter-
> woven [as the latter] in the texture of man's metaphysical nature and his theo-
> logical quest for relations which cross the frontiers of finitude. Not only the
> parental, but also the matrimonial community, is a reflection of and prologue
> to the exalted community of man and God.[6]

Before explaining these pivotal but dense paragraphs, we must review
some basic terms in the Rav's writings. Much of Rav Soloveitchik's thought
constitutes a philosophy of man, and the foundation of his concept of man is
the claim that every human being is *incomplete*. There are two causes of this
incompleteness: humans are finite in relation to God, and male and female
need each other in order to attain wholeness.[7] Awareness of this incompleteness is termed *loneliness*.[8] Dealing with this condition and even overcoming it

---

4 Emphasis mine. There is a similar passage in *Family Redeemed*, 149.

5 He is referring to the verse, "Therefore a man shall leave his father and his mother and
he shall cleave to his wife, and they shall be one flesh" (Gen. 2:24), in which the matrimonial
community supplants the parental community.

6 The first paragraph appears in *Family Redeemed*, 149. The second paragraph follows in the
manuscript, but was removed from the published version due to editorial considerations.

7 *Family Redeemed*, 68: "The incompleteness of being is a result of two ontic [= built into
our existence] situations: finitude-infinity and manhood-womanhood singularity."

8 As we saw in *The Lonely Man of Faith*, "loneliness" also refers to an awareness of one's
uniqueness, and hence of one's incommensurability with others. This leads to the attempt to
establish a basis for communication with others, founded upon a shared commitment, which
leads back to the concept of *redemption*.

is called *redemption*.[9] The building of connections to others – parents, spouse, children, *Klal Yisrael* – overcomes loneliness partially, and points to the ultimate overcoming of incompleteness via the connection to God.

With this background, we are in a position to comprehend the passages above. The key to understanding them lies in the following sentence, which encapsulates their message:

> Not only the parental, but also the matrimonial community, is *a reflection of and prologue to* the exalted community of man and God.

It therefore behooves us to explain each of these characterizations, a "reflection" and a "prologue." Let us approach this task by ordering comments scattered throughout *Family Redeemed* into a cohesive whole.

Family Relations as a Reflection of the God-Man Relationship

The Rav defines the sense in which the parent-child community is a *reflection* of the man-God community in the following passage:

> *What is transient fatherhood and motherhood if not a reflected beam of light coming to us from beyond the frontiers of the cosmos, and what is paternal or maternal concern if not an echo of the great concern of the Almighty?* Whenever R. Yosef heard the footsteps of his mother, he would say: Let me rise because the *Shekhinah* is coming (*Kiddushin* 31b). Behind every mother, young or old, happy or sad, trails the *Shekhinah*. And behind every father, erect or stooped, in playful or stern mood, walks *Malka Kadisha*.[10] This is not mysticism. It is Halakhah. The awareness of the *Shekhinah* results in the obligation to rise before father and mother (168).[11]

Similarly, the marriage covenant is bound up indissolubly with the covenant between God and His people:

> The Bible equated the great historical covenant binding the charismatic community to God with the limited private covenant that unites two individuals in matrimony. On the one hand, the great covenant has been compared by the prophets time and again to the betrothal of Israel to God; on the other hand, the

---

9 Part of redemption is transforming oneself from a passive object into an active subject (as we shall see in *Halakhic Man* and *Kol Dodi Dofek*). Once one has accomplished this, one can properly enter relationships with other subjects, whether God or man.

10 In Kabbalah, *Shekhinah* and *Malka Kadisha* are "female" and "male" aspects of divinity, respectively.

11 Emphasis added.

ordinary betrothal of woman to man has been raised to the level of covenantal commitment (41).

Family relations reflect the God-man relationship if they exhibit qualities that transcend normal human relations, or qualities that would seem to be unique to a transcendental relationship. This is the case with both the parent-child relationship and the husband-wife relationship. In the former, the parents exhibit a totally selfless love, and the child a sense of absolute identification.

> The bond between parent and child, once the latter reaches maturity, is completely divorced from any hedonic, egocentric motivation and can only be interpreted in terms of love of a higher quality, which is rooted in the awareness of unqualified unity on the part of both parent and child. There is a steady outpouring of the heart of the parent toward the child, and conversely there is a continual act of identification of the child with the parent (147).

A person naturally feels compelled to search for the roots of his being, to find its source and anchor. This search brings him first to his parents and then to God.

> Judaism, with its characteristic sense of realism, considers the root quest [i.e., the search for one's roots] within here-and-now reality to be the reflection of the primary search for the absolute origin or source beyond the bounds of sensuous reality (149).

The discovery of a sense of dependence and of rootedness highlights the unique shared characteristics of the parent-child and God-man relationships:

> The Halakhah has emphasized time and again the unique nature of the parent-child relationship. In fact, it has introduced into it a transcendental motif and equated it with the relationship binding man to God. The origin perception is characteristic of both (148).

The unique aspects of the child's relationship to his or her parents receive halakhic expression in laws such as the special observances of mourning for parents,[12] the severe punishments for striking or cursing a parent, and, most of all, in the obligations of *kibbud u-mora*. These terms are usually translated as "honor and fear," but the Rav interprets them more along the lines of "love

---

12 E.g., tearing one's clothes above the heart and observing a one-year mourning period. See also the Rav's comments on the difference between mourning for children and mourning for parents in *Out of the Whirlwind*, 33–34.

and awe," which makes the parallel between the child-parent and man-God relationships even more apparent:

> In a word, the norm [of] *kibbud* is interpreted in categories of love: to honor means to love; and the latter manifests the experience of ontic unity [i.e., unity of being], of a thou union (147).

> What the Torah meant with its commandment of *mora* is an inner relationship of admiration, profound veneration and awe. One must revere his parents; they should arouse in his soul a craving, a longing, a deep, fearful love, a tremor and a great joy. These characteristics do not belong to the sphere of human mundane experiences. They stem from our transcendental awareness and are exclusively within the realm of man-God confrontation (154).

Similarly, the husband-wife relationship embodies elements that are otherwise unique to the God-man relationship, thus serving as a reflection of the latter:

> . . . [W]ithin the matrimonial covenantal community, a relationship prevails that is similar to the characteristic of the metaphysical-covenantal [community]: total commitment and unchangeability. In other words, the two unique traits of the [man-God] covenant are indicative of the matrimonial community as well (46).

By "total commitment," Rav Soloveitchik means that marriage is not merely a contractual agreement regulating property rights, but encompasses the deepest recesses of the personality, a sense of absolute belonging and togetherness.[13] The "unchangeability" of covenantal marriage refers to the fact that it transcends the whimsicality and capriciousness of eros and "teach[es] man to find love in identity and continuity" (47)[14]

To summarize: Man's relationship to God is based upon his *origin* in God and his *covenant* with God. The "origin" aspect is reflected in one's relationship with one's parents, giving rise to unique halakhic responsibilities, and the "covenant" aspect is reflected in one's relationship with one's spouse, which transcends other human contractual relationships.

---

13 Although the Rav speaks in this passage of the "personal bond which reaches deeply into the most hidden spheres of the human personality" (46), he later asserts that it is only the outer-directed ("kerygmatic") aspect of the personality that contracts a marriage agreement, while the inner-directed ("numinous") aspect remains aloof (62–63). It is unclear where to draw the line between these two assertions. Just how deeply does the marriage bond reach?

14 This, however, does not preclude the possibility of divorce, as explained on 61–67.

Family Relations as a Prologue to the God-Man Relationship

Given the unique characteristics shared by human family relationships and the God-man relationship, it now becomes clear how family relationships serve not just as a *reflection* of the latter but as a *prologue* to it as well. As Rav Soloveitchik asserted, "By developing proper human relations structures, the Jew learns how to love, revere and serve God" (167).[15] In other words, one builds a relationship with God via one's relationships with people, and this in two senses.

First, by exercising certain emotions with regard to other people, one learns how to exercise these emotions regarding God. For example, *mora* for one's parents points to reverence for God, while the fidelity and devotion of husband and wife train them to practice these virtues with regard to God. That which brings one to feel connected to one's parents – love, reverence, gratitude, recognition of dependence – should also awaken these same feelings with regard to one's ultimate source, the Creator and Sustainer of mankind. The sanctity entailed in the relationship of husband and wife develops the *kedushah* necessary for the God-man relationship, and a couple's mutual commitment to one another and to commonly-held values intensifies and paves the way for commitment to God.

In fact, the very sense of loneliness that leads one to search for completeness through marriage, and the ability to open one's closed existence and share it with another, are important components in developing a relationship with the divine. Although in this context the Rav does not reference the Song of Songs, one could point to its relevance here. The Song of Songs utilizes the *mashal* (allegory) of love between man and woman in depicting the *nimshal* (application) of divine-human love. Based on the Rav's insight regarding the relevance of family relationships in fostering one's relationship with God, one could say that the Song of Songs employs this allegory for a dual purpose. Of course, the allegory of the man-woman relationship illuminates the *nimshal* of divine-human love by comparing it to an intense and passionate relationship

---

15 Defining family relationships as a prologue to the man-God relationship raises the obvious question of whether this is a necessary prologue, or just one way among many to build a relationship with God. The question takes on added urgency for those from dysfunctional families. When teaching *Family Redeemed*, I am invariably asked: In Rav Soloveitchik's view, can one have a good relationship with God even if one has a poor relationship with one's parents? Can one use religious growth in order to mend family relationships, instead of the reverse? Although I would like to respond that the Rav posited family relationships as merely *one* means of developing a relationship with God, the text often seems to indicate that he believed that proper family relationships are a *necessary* prerequisite to a proper relationship with God.

with which people are familiar. Furthermore, by allowing the love between woman and man to stand in for the sublime love between human and God, the Bible shows the great significance of the man-woman relationship, both in itself and as a pointer and stepping stone to a higher relationship with God.

Moreover, it may often be impossible to make the leap to the metaphysical realm before one has established a basis for it within the domain of the physical, as the Rav writes with regard to the sense of dependence:

> Yet, the encounter of man and God can only occur if man, in his quest for the great ultimate and eternal root, is also concerned with his little, conditioned and transient this-worldly roots. Only after finite man recognizes and acknowledges his dependence upon someone in the here-and-now world, does God bestow upon him the illuminating consciousness of the dependence upon the One and Only root. The quest for the root is not only a transcendental adventure, but a human adventure as well (148–49).[16]

It is important to note that the Rav is referring not merely to one's childhood dependence on one's parents for one's creation and sustenance, but also to one's ongoing dependence on their approval, esteem and affection.

The Intertwining of Relationships

The second sense in which one builds a relationship with God via one's relationships with people is that these human relationships themselves become bound up with one's relationship to God. With regard to the child's relationship to his or her parents, the Rav writes:

> By commanding the child to fear his father and mother, the Torah introduced a new dimension into an interpersonal human relationship, namely, the transcendental. It whisks us far from the array of modes of action, thought and feeling of the material-human universe, into the transcendent pure realm of a higher consciousness, by which we become aware of the great mystery of being . . . Relationship and relatedness to a parent hides in its essence man's longing and craving for God; there is a final oneness in our surrender to parent and God. In fearing the parent, one stands in awe and tremor before God

---

16 In a related vein, Rav Soloveitchik writes in *The Halakhic Mind* (45) and elsewhere that knowledge of the world must precede knowledge of God: "The central theme of the religious experience, however, is not the Absolute, but the immediate and phenomenal reality in all its variegated manifestation. Universal knowledge of the Absolute is possible only after the 'world of shadows' has been thoroughly explored."

Himself, before the . . . source of his existence; in giving parents respect and reverence one adores and worships God (154).[17]

When the child marries, he or she creates a new primary bond, dethroning the old parental community in favor of the new matrimonial one. However, the child's own matrimonial community does not remain one with two partners; rather, once a child is born, it

> is elevated to a parental threefold one which, in turn, will be disrupted again by . . . the succeeding generation [when his own child eventually marries]. Through experiencing this dramatic flow of events of destroying in order to build and building in order to be destroyed, man realizes his quest for the origin or source and gradually moves closer and closer to God (35).

Since religion is the search for *redemption*, as defined above, marriage as a community of two does have religious value, and not merely psychological or pragmatic usefulness: "[T]he goal of marriage is the redeeming experience of life in fellowship" (33). Nevertheless, marriage reaches its most complete fulfillment as a community of three, in which the partners share a common devotion not only to values and to each other, but also to a third party: their child.[18] Herein we find the link between the matrimonial and the parental communities.

Within the threefold community, man and woman can imitate God most closely and become His partners (38–39). The begetting and raising of children entails *imitatio Dei* on several levels: creating, teaching, and practicing unconditional and boundless *hesed*, loving-kindness. By building a family based on values of sanctity and religious commitment, one worships and draws closer to God. Parents induct their children into the eternal *masorah* community, transforming them into part of the chain of tradition and thereby granting them not only temporal life but eternal life as well (29–30, 57–58).

---

17 To be precise, the Rav (149–52) distinguishes between *kibbud* and *mora*. The former demands that we treat our parents as we ourselves would want to be treated, and is an interpersonal category. The latter demands even more: unqualified commitment, self-denial and sacrifice, and is essentially a religious category.

18 While in *The Lonely Man of Faith* the third partner in the covenantal community is God, in *Family Redeemed* it is the child. The reason for this is that, although *The Lonely Man of Faith* uses the image of marriage, it is really discussing any human religious community, while *Family Redeemed* deals specifically with the community of husband and wife.

Dedications

In light of our discussion, it is no surprise that, of the three major works the Rav published himself, the first is dedicated to his father and the latter two to his wife. Although it is common for authors to dedicate books to beloved family members, the Rav's dedications, I would claim, are not merely tributes of this routine kind, but rather integral components of, or comments on, the works themselves. In one way or another, each of these works deals with the religious experience, and the latter, for the Rav, is mediated through family relationships.

As indicated in the epigraph to *Halakhic Man*,

> At that moment the image of his father came to him and appeared before him in the window (*Sotah* 36b),

the Rav intended that work to be, among other things, a book-length portrait of his father's religious sensibility, and a son's attempt to draw out its implications.[19] As I pointed out in Chapter 13, the dedication of *The Lonely Man of Faith*, on the other hand, is a reflection on and counterpoint to the essay.[20] It reads:

> To Tonya: A woman of great courage, sublime dignity, total commitment, and uncompromising truthfulness.

While the essay's stress on loneliness, highlighted in the title, offers little solace to the religious personality, the dedication contrasts with this bleakness. The dedication suggests that the loneliness experienced by the man of faith can be overcome, at least partially, by living in community with a partner who shares one's values and commitments.

The dedication of *U-Vikkashtem mi-Sham*,

> "Like a hind yearning for water brooks, my soul yearns for You, O God" (Ps. 42:2): In memory of my wife Tonya *z"l*, a woman of refinement,

further intertwines the two levels of questing for redemption and ontological completeness. By linking the psalmist's yearning for God with his own yearning for his wife's presence, Rav Soloveitchik subtly indicates that the search for redemption through God is intimately tied to the search for completeness in marriage. Thus, all three of these dedications highlight the religious and

---

19 See Chap. 29 below.
20 See pp. 144–45 above.

human value of family relationships, which are both redemptive in themselves and lead to ultimate redemption through God.

FOR FURTHER REFERENCE

1. **Betrothal and marriage:** See "*Mah Dodekh mi-Dod*," 71–73, where the Rav utilizes a *hiddush* of his grandfather R. Hayyim to demonstrate that while *eirusin* (betrothal) creates a formal-legal connection between husband and wife, *nissuin* (marriage) creates an existential unity.

Chapter 20

Prayer (1): Prayer as Encounter and as Self-Acquisition

Mystics and philosophers alike have wondered what effect our prayers can have on an infinite and omniscient God, and many thinkers have sought to understand why God accepts some prayers and not others. Yet, in his very rich and multifaceted discussions of prayer, Rav Soloveitchik eschews these questions. Instead, he focuses, as always, on the human side of the equation and not on the divine side. What, he asks, is the precise nature of the activity we call prayer? What are the inner states that it requires? What effect does it produce on the praying individual? In other words, what is the meaning and function of prayer *for humanity*?

The Rav offers several answers to this question, each of which constitutes the focus of a different essay:[1]

(a) prayer is an encounter with God (*The Lonely Man of Faith*);

(b) it is a means for man to find and shape himself ("Redemption, Prayer, Talmud Torah");[2]

(c) it is a form of self-sacrifice to God ("Reflections on the *Amidah*").[3]

---

1 Although some of these essays present more than one theme, I will focus on the dominant theme in each essay. In addition to the essays mentioned here, there is an entire book of the Rav's, published posthumously, on the subject of prayer: *Worship of the Heart: Essays on Jewish Prayer*, ed. R. Shalom Carmy (Jersey City, 2003). This book treats a number of themes and does not have a single focus. I will reference it when its themes overlap with those under discussion. Since I will focus mainly on the petitional aspect of prayer (*bakkashah*), I will omit *Worship of the Heart*'s very important discussion of the praise of God (*shevah*) and the redemption of the aesthetic; see For Further Reference, #2. For the same reason, I will also omit *Worship of the Heart*'s discussion of the *Shema*, except to contrast it with the *Amidah*.

2 This essay was delivered at a faculty colloquium at the University of Pennsylvania in May 1973, and was published in *Tradition* 17:2 (Spring 1978), 55–72.

3 This essay, originally entitled "*Ra'ayonot al ha-Tefillah*," appears as chap. 10 of *Worship*

In this chapter and the next, we shall examine each of these themes in turn, as well as the relationships between them. First, though, it is necessary to define what we mean by "prayer." The quintessence of Jewish prayer, with its tripartite structure of *shevah*, *bakkashah* and *hoda'ah* (praise, petition and thanksgiving), is the *Shemoneh Esreh*, also known as the *Amidah*. It is this prayer to which *Hazal* generally refer when they use the Hebrew term *tefillah*, and it is to this – and especially its core, *bakkashah* – that we will devote our inquiry.

Prayer as Encounter

Hazal debate the following question: must one have *kavvanah* (conscious intention) when performing a given *mitzvah* act in order to be credited with having fulfilled one's obligation? Or is it sufficient merely to perform the *mitzvah* action even without intending thereby to fulfill a divine command?[4] In the case of prayer, says the Rav, there is no dispute – everyone agrees that *kavvanah* is indispensable. The reason is that "*Kavvanah*, related to prayer, is, unlike the *kavvanah* concerning other *mitzvah* performances, not an extraneous addendum but the very core of prayer" (*The Lonely Man of Faith*, 74). Specifically, whereas the *kavvanah* pertaining to other *mitzvot* is merely "the normative intention on the part of the *mitzvah*-doer to act in accordance with the will of God" (ibid.; this intention is called *kavvanah latzeit*), the *kavvanah* that defines prayer is of an entirely different order:

> What is to be understood by *kavvanah* [in prayer]? One should free his mind from all extraneous thoughts and see himself as if he is standing before the Divine Presence (Rambam, *Hilkhot Tefillah* 4:16).[5]

Echoing the Rambam's description, the Rav writes that prayer is essentially an encounter with God:

---

of the Heart. However, since the other nine chapters of the book derive from two courses the Rav gave at Yeshiva University's Bernard Revel Graduate School in the late 1950s, and constitute a unified whole in themselves, I will treat this essay separately from them. "*Ra'ayonot al ha-Tefillah*" was published in 1978 (in *Hadarom* 47 [Tishrei 5739], 84–106), but the date of its composition is unknown.

4 For example, the Gemara in *Rosh Hashanah* (28a-b) discusses whether a person who blows a *shofar* in order to make music has fulfilled the *mitzvah* even though he did not intend to do so.

5 R. Hayyim of Brisk actually understands the Rambam as positing three distinct types of *kavvanah* in prayer, while the Rav sees the Rambam as positing a single type of *kavvanah*. Regarding this rare interpretive disagreement between the Rav and his revered grandfather, see For Further Reference, #3.

> Prayer is basically an awareness of man finding himself in the presence of and addressing himself to his Maker, and to pray has one connotation only: to stand before God (*The Lonely Man of Faith*, 56).

As such, *tefillah* differs from the recitation of *Shema*, for the latter is not a personal encounter but rather a declaration of commitment to *kabbalat ol malkut Shamayim*, "accepting the yoke of Heavenly dominion." In the *Shema*, one speaks *of* God in the third person; in *tefillah*, one speaks *to* God in the second person.

The Rav develops this distinction between *Shema* and *tefillah* by analyzing not only their respective texts and the aggadic material concerning them, but also, characteristically, the *halakhot* governing them.[6] For example, the *Amidah* must be recited while standing, facing Jerusalem, assuming the physical posture of a slave, wearing appropriate clothes, standing in a proper location (e.g., not on top of a wall), sober, and without interruptions and long pauses. However, none of these requirements applies to the *Shema*.[7] These laws reveal a clear pattern: the *Shema* is a declaration or dedication, directed at oneself or perhaps at other people, while in *tefillah*, one stands in God's presence and speaks to Him directly.[8]

The central and longest part of the *Amidah* is *bakkashah*, petition: the first three blessings of the *Amidah* praise God, the last three offer thanks to Him, and the middle thirteen are requests, petitions. Nevertheless, the primary function of the *tefillah* encounter is not procuring God's favorable answers to our entreaties. Rather, it is forming a fellowship, or community, between human beings and God:

---

6 See *Worship of the Heart*, 103–05, regarding the appropriate methods for uncovering the subjective experiences underlying religious performances. *Worship of the Heart*'s systematic examination of the experiential building blocks of prayer (praise, petition, thanksgiving) and of *kabbalat ol malkut Shamayim* is a sterling application of the methodology elaborated in that book, and, in greater detail, in *The Halakhic Mind*, for "reconstructing" the subjective (inner) elements of religion out of its objective (external) manifestations. See also Chap. 31 below.

7 The Rav analyzes the contrast between *Shema* and the *Amidah* in *Worship of the Heart*, 94–103, as well as in *"Be-Inyan Semikhat Ge'ulah li-Tefillah," Shiurim le-Zekher Abba Mari z"l*, vol. 2, 35–57.

8 Rashi formulates this succinctly, in the context of explaining why one has to wear a shirt when reciting the *Amidah* but not when saying the *Shema*: "But in prayer, he must present himself as one who stands before the king, and stands with fear, but [in] *keriat Shema*, one is not speaking before the king" (*Berakhot* 25a, s.v. *aval li-tefillah*). For more on the *Shema*, see For Further Reference, #4.

Acceptance of prayer is a hope, a vision, a wish, a petition, but not a principle or a premise. The foundation of prayer is not the conviction of its effectiveness but the belief that through it we approach God intimately and the miraculous community embracing finite man and his Creator is born. The basic function of prayer is not its practical consequences but the metaphysical formation of a fellowship consisting of God and man (*Worship of the Heart*, 35).

The discussion of prayer in *The Lonely Man of Faith* focuses on prayer's role in forming a covenantal community – a central goal of Adam II, who is plagued by loneliness. First, the prayer encounter creates a community between man and God, and, as such, it is a counterpart to and continuation of the God-man community engendered by the prophetic encounter. The only difference between the prophetic and prayer communities is that in the former, God initiates communication, and in the latter, man initiates it.[9]

Second, prayer creates a community between people. This is indicated by the halakhic emphasis on praying with the *tzibbur* (community), as well as by the fact that all requests in the *Amidah* are formulated in the plural – "Grant us," "Return us," "Forgive us," etc. – even though the *Amidah* is initially recited quietly by each individual. The Rav explains:

When disaster strikes, one must not be immersed completely in his own passional destiny, thinking exclusively of himself, being concerned only with himself, and petitioning God merely for himself. The foundation of efficacious and noble prayer is human solidarity and sympathy or the covenantal awareness of existential togetherness, of sharing and experiencing the travail and suffering of [others] (*The Lonely Man of Faith*, 59).[10]

Thus, the community of man and God formed in prayer must include one's fellow human being as well, instead of remaining focused selfishly on one's own personal requests or personal religious experience.

---

9 For an examination of several consequences of the Rav's understanding of prophecy and prayer in *The Lonely Man of Faith*, see R. Yitzchak Blau, "Dialogue, Community and Morality: The Prayer-Prophecy Parallel," http://www.atid.org/resources/lmof40/blau.asp.

10 Note that while in *The Lonely Man of Faith* the Rav discusses both praying *with* others and praying *for* others, elsewhere he conflates these two categories: when one prays *for* others because one shares their pain, then one naturally prays *with* them. See the Rav's handwritten comments cited by Lawrence Kaplan, "On Translating *Ish ha-Halakhah* with the Rav: Rabbi Joseph Soloveitchik's Supplementary Notes to *Halakhic Man*," in *Mentor of Generations: Reflections on Rabbi Joseph B. Soloveitchik*, ed. Zev Eleff (Jersey City, 2008), 339: "People who share distress together share also in the act of praying. . . . To pray for each other means to live through a common passional [= suffering] experience which urges, which impels man [*sic*] to pray together."

Yet, the prayer encounter is incomplete and not of optimal worth unless it is accompanied, or preceded, by a commitment to a godly way of life.[11] Indeed, says the Rav, "Any encounter with God, if it is to redeem man, must be crystallized and objectified in a normative ethico-moral message" (*The Lonely Man of Faith*, 61). The Rav explains this idea in a powerful passage:

> Who is qualified to engage God in the prayer colloquy? Clearly, the person who is ready to cleanse himself of imperfection and evil. Any kind of injustice, corruption, cruelty, or the like desecrates the very essence of the prayer adventure, since it encases man in an ugly little world into which God is unwilling to enter. If man craves to meet God in prayer, then he must purge himself of all that separates him from God. The Halakhah has never looked upon prayer as a separate magical gesture in which man may engage without integrating it into the total pattern of his life . . . Prayer is always the harbinger of moral reformation (*The Lonely Man of Faith*, 65).[12]

While the concept elucidated in this passage may not seem surprising at first, its consequence is indeed unexpected:

> This is the reason why prayer per se does not occupy as prominent a place in the Halakhic community as it does in other faith communities, and why prayer is not the great religious activity claiming, if not exclusiveness, at least centrality. Prayer must always be related to a prayerful life which is consecrated to the realization of the divine imperative, and as such it is not a separate entity, but the sublime prologue to Halakhic action (*The Lonely Man of Faith*, 65–66).[13]

This demotion of prayer from the central position it holds in other religions – or, rather, the integration of prayer into a broader framework of religious activities – is a recurring theme in the Rav's writings.[14] The Rav's

---

11 Within the prayer service, this is indicated by the halakhic requirement of *semikhat ge'ulah li-tefillah*, juxtaposing the *Shema* and its blessings to the *Amidah*. "One has no right to appear before the Almighty [in the *Amidah*] without accepting previously all the covenantal commitments implied in the three sections of *Shema*" (*The Lonely Man of Faith*, 75).

12 In a lengthy footnote (*The Lonely Man of Faith*, 76–78), the Rav clarifies that, "The privilege and right of prayer cannot be denied to anyone, not even to the most wicked." Rather, he means to say "that prayer requires a clean heart and that the prayer of a sinful person is imperfect."

13 Regarding "the prayerful life," see For Further Reference, #5.

14 There is precedent for this attitude in Jewish tradition. For example, Rav Aharon Lichtenstein points out that the traditions of Volozhin and Brisk, to which the Rav was heir, favored Torah study over prayer ("Prayer in the Teachings of Rav Soloveitchik *zt"l*," *Alei Etzion* 9 [Adar Bet 5760], 23–24). On the tension between Torah study and prayer in the time

book-length treatment of prayer, *Worship of the Heart*, opens by pointing out that, for Judaism, prayer is not the only means of reaching out to God. Judaism recognizes four separate media of religious experience – the intellectual (Torah study), the emotional, the volitional (*mitzvah* observance) and the dialogical (prayer) – and therefore, prayer must be understood within its proper context. Furthermore, following the *Sifrei* and the Rambam,[15] the Rav points out that the term *avodah she-ba-lev*, worship or service of the heart, refers not only to prayer, but to Torah study as well.[16] The heart serves God through both of these activities, and perhaps by means of integrating them. Let us now turn our attention to the second answer to the question I posed at the beginning of this chapter – what is the meaning of prayer for the human being? – and examine an essay that links the two forms of worship of the heart.

Prayer as Self-Acquisition

An interesting relationship prevails between the three terms appearing in the title of the essay, "Redemption, Prayer, Talmud Torah": redemption of the individual comes about not through divine intervention, but rather through the other two activities mentioned there. In other words, instead of a two-step process, in which one engages in prayer and *talmud Torah* so that God, in turn, will bring redemption, the Rav portrays a one-step process: a person redeems himself by praying and studying Torah. How so? Like the Rav's essay itself, we shall focus on the issue of prayer.

Although prayer is addressed to God and stems from recognition of one's dependence upon Him, it is a process that starts within the self: one must consider and weigh one's needs, and then present them before God.[17] A person can know what he truly needs only if he knows who he truly is and

---

of *Hazal*, see Yaakov Elman, "*Torah ve-Avodah*: Prayer and Torah Study as Competing Values in the Time of *Hazal*," in *Jewish Spirituality and Divine Law*, eds. Adam Mintz and Lawrence Schiffman (New York, 2005), 61–124. The aforementioned article by Rav Lichtenstein contains many valuable insights that could not be addressed within the space of this chapter. It can be accessed online at http://www.vbm-torah.org/alei/9-3tef-ral.rtf.

15 *Sifrei, Ekev*, 41, on Deut. 11:13; Rambam, *Sefer ha-Mitzvot*, positive commandment 5.

16 *Worship of the Heart*, 25–26; "*Be-Inyan Birkot ha-Torah*," in *Shiurim le-Zekher*, vol. 2, esp. 7–11; "Redemption, Prayer, Talmud Torah," 70. Regarding Torah study as *avodah she-ba-lev*, see also R. Aharon Lichtenstein, "*U-le-ovdo – Zeh Talmud*," in *Be-Darkhei Shalom: Studies in Jewish Thought Presented to Shalom Rosenberg*, ed. Binyamin Ish-Shalom (Jerusalem, 2007), 181–91.

17 This is true whether one regards oneself as an individual or as part of a community. We shall focus here, as does the Rav, on the prayer of the individual.

what are his goals. The prayer process, then, entails discovering and refining one's genuine need-awareness, and it is therefore a self-educational and self-transformative activity.

Thus conceived, prayer emerges as an important part of man's broader project of self-creation: "God wills man to be creator – his first job is to create himself as a complete being" ("Redemption, Prayer, Talmud Torah," 64). This view of prayer helps us understand the logic of presenting our requests before One who knows all our needs. Through prayer, man clarifies his need-awareness and thereby changes himself; and by transforming himself, he becomes more worthy of God granting his requests.[18]

How is this process redemptive? Based on a passage in the *Zohar*,[19] the Rav distinguishes between three stages in the progress from slavery to redemption. The Jews enslaved in Egypt were at first mute, feeling the pain of the lash but not the indignity of the servitude. The slave has no sense of self, no concept of his goals or his destiny. Therefore, he can feel *pain*, which is an instinctive reaction man shares with the animal, but he cannot *suffer*, for suffering is an existential experience resulting from a threat to one's sense of self. Because they lacked direction and knowledge of their genuine needs, because they could not yet conceive of another kind of existence, the Jews did not protest. Only when Moses defended the helpless Jew against the Egyptian taskmaster did they realize the injustice of their situation. This led them, for the first time, to cry out to God (Ex. 2:23), marking their emergence from muteness to sound.

Yet, though they now had the *awareness* of need, they still lacked the *understanding* of need. They sensed that their existence was defective, that they were being treated unjustly, but they did not yet know how to fill their lives with positive content. Upon arriving at Sinai, they gained an understanding of their deeper needs based upon their covenantal destiny spelled out in the Torah. This marked the third stage of their redemption, namely, the emergence from sound to speech. Redemption from slavery "is identical with communing . . . i.e., the emergence of speech" (56), for only one fully in possession of himself has a meaningful message to convey.

Slavery is not just a political institution, but a state of being.[20] Man is a

---

18 This application of the Rav's position is pointed out by R. Shalom Carmy, "Destiny, Freedom and the Logic of Petition," *Tradition* 24:2 (Winter 1989), 20–21. In broad outline, a similar solution to the philosophical problem of petition was presented by R. Yosef Albo in his *Sefer ha-Ikkarim* (4:18).

19 *Vaera*, 25b. The *Zohar* discusses communal redemption, but this does not matter for our present purposes.

20 See also the chapter "Slavery and Freedom" in *Festival of Freedom* (Jersey City, 2006),

slave whenever he lacks a sense of self and an accompanying awareness of his needs. Although man may think he knows his needs, an accurate assessment can stem only from a proper understanding of his destiny.

> Man is surely aware of many needs, but the needs he is aware of are not always his own. At the very root of this failure to recognize one's truly worthwhile needs lies man's ability to misunderstand and misidentify himself, i.e., to lose himself. Quite often man loses himself by identifying himself with the wrong image. Because of this misidentification, man adopts the wrong table of needs which he feels he must gratify. Man responds quickly to the pressure of certain needs, not knowing *whose* needs he is out to gratify. At this juncture, sin is born. What is the cause of sin, if not the diabolical habit of man to be mistaken about his own self? (62).

The antidote to this appears in prayer:

> Prayer is the doctrine of human needs. Prayer tells the individual, as well as the community, what his, or its, genuine needs are, what he should, or should not, petition God about. Of the nineteen benedictions of our *Amidah*, thirteen are concerned with basic human needs, individual as well as social-national.[21] Even two of the last three benedictions (*Retzeh* and *Sim Shalom*) are of a petitional nature . . . [Prayer] tells man the story of his hidden hopes and expectations. It teaches him how to behold the vision and how to strive in order to realize this vision, when to be satisfied with what one possesses, when to reach out for more. In a word, man finds his need-awareness, himself, in prayer. Of course, the very instant he finds himself, he becomes a redeemed being (65–66).[22]

In personal redemption, as in the Jews' liberation from Egypt, two stages succeed the mute unawareness of needs. The first of these is designated *tze'akah*, outcry, indicating the inchoate burgeoning of need-awareness – "sound" without "speech," in the *Zohar*'s terms. The next stage is *tefillah*, which derives from the Hebrew root *pll*, denoting "thinking, judging, discrimination" – in other words, to filter one's need-awareness through one's intellect, or "to ask intelligently" (67). In *tefillah*, one defines goals, evaluates desires and establishes a hierarchy of needs.

35–54.

21 Here the Rav references the Rambam: "The intermediate [thirteen] benedictions are petitions for the things which may stand as prototypes (Heb., *avot*) of all the desires of the individual and the needs of the community" (*Hilkhot Tefillah* 1:4).

22 In other words, man is redeemed from his ignorance about himself and from his servitude to false needs.

Though *tefillah* is of a higher order than *tze'akah*, both coexist in our liturgy, with *tze'akah* represented by *Selihot* and *tefillah* by the *Amidah*.

> Prayer as *tze'akah* lacks the gradual development of theme, the structural formalism, and the etiquette-like orderliness which Halacha required of the *mitpallel*, the prayerful person. While *tefillah* is a meditative-reflective act, *tze'akah* is immediate and compulsive (68).

Man has need of both heartfelt outcry and measured request.

The Rav then turns briefly to the redemptive role of Torah study in the process of self-acquisition. The Gemara teaches that a baby studies the entire Torah in utero (*Niddah* 30b). This means that Torah is part of one's very being, and when one studies Torah, one is, in effect, uncovering one's own self. Prayer and Torah study share the same structural pattern of discovery of the self, leading the Rav to note the aforementioned *Sifrei* that defines both prayer and Torah study as *avodah she-ba-lev*.

The introduction of the term *avodah* allows the Rav to execute a sharp turn-about at the very end of the essay. In rabbinic Hebrew, "*avodah*" generally refers to the sacrificial service in the Temple, and the Rav suddenly introduces a new, seemingly contradictory, theme regarding the *avodah she-ba-lev* of *tefillah*: prayer as self-sacrifice. The Rav himself notes the contradiction, or dialectic, between the presentation of prayer as self-acquisition earlier in the essay and the presentation of prayer as self-sacrifice toward its end:

> Judaic dialectic plays "mischievously" with two opposites, two irreconcilable aspects of prayer. It announces prayer as self-acquisition, self-discovery, self-objectification and self-redemption . . . Yet there is another aspect to prayer: prayer is an act of giving away. Prayer means sacrifice, unrestricted offering of the whole self, the returning to God of body and soul, everything one possesses and cherishes (70).

These two aspects of prayer stand in a sequential relationship:

> Initially, prayer helps man discover himself, through understanding and affirmation of his need-awareness. Once the task of self-discovery is fulfilled, man is summoned to ascend the altar and return everything he has just acquired to God (71–72).

Although the idea of prayer as self-sacrifice comes as a surprise at the conclusion of "Redemption, Prayer, Talmud Torah," it stands at the heart of the next essay we shall examine, "Reflections on the *Amidah*."

For Further Reference

1. **Prayer in Jewish thought:** See Gabriel Cohn and Harold Fisch, eds., *Prayer in Judaism: Continuity and Change* (Northvale, NJ, 1996), and especially the article there by Shalom Rosenberg, "Prayer and Jewish Thought: Approaches and Problems (A Survey)," 69–108.

2. **Prayer as praise of God (*shevah*) in the Rav's thought:** See R. Joshua Amaru, "Prayer and the Beauty of God: Rav Soloveitchik on Prayer and Aesthetics," *The Torah u-Madda Journal* 13 (2005), 148–76; and R. Elyakim Krumbein, "*Im Yesh Bo Davar Asher Tukhal Lekayyemo: Al Hashivuto shel ha-Sefer 'Avodah she-ba-Lev' me'et ha-Rav Y. D. Soloveitchik,*" *Akdamot* 18 (5767), 141–63.

3. **The need for *kavvanah* – solutions to the contradiction in the Rambam:** In *Hilkhot Tefillah* 4:1 and 4:15, the Rambam states the need for *kavvanah* in the *Amidah* without any qualifications: "Any prayer that lacks *kavvanah* is not prayer; and if one prayed without *kavvanah*, one must go back and repeat the prayer with *kavvanah*" (4:15). It would seem from here that one must maintain *kavvanah* throughout the entire *Amidah*. However, in *Hilkhot Tefillah* 10:1, the Rambam qualifies his statement and says that one must repeat one's prayer only if one lacked *kavvanah* in the first *berakhah* of the *Amidah*. R. Hayyim, the Hazon Ish and the Rav propose three different solutions to this seeming contradiction.

   A. **R. Hayyim** (*Hiddushei Rabbenu Hayyim ha-Levi, Hilkhot Tefillah* 4:1) proposes that Rambam is referring to different types of *kavvanah* in the two chapters. Chapter 4 is discussing the "*kavvanah* of standing before God," without which one's action is not defined as praying but merely as *mitasek* (coincidentally performing an action, but without any intention of doing so); therefore, it is required for the entire *Amidah*. Chapter 4 is also discussing *kavvanah latzeit* (intention to fulfill a *mitzvah* through one's purposeful action), which the Rambam believes is required for all *mitzvot*. However, chapter 10 deals with a *kavvanah* that is unique to the laws of *tefillah*, namely, "*kavvanah* to the meaning of the words"; and since it is difficult to focus on the words for the entire length of the *Amidah*, the Sages said that as long as one had this intention during the first blessing of the *Amidah*, one need not repeat the entire prayer.

   B. **Hazon Ish** (*Gilyonot* to *Hiddushei Rabbenu Hayyim ha-Levi*, ad loc.) answers that both chapter 4 and chapter 10 are talking about the same type of *kavvanah*, but chapter 4 sets forth the general rule while chapter 10 specifies the minimal amount of prayer for which *kavvanah* is necessary. In other words, chapter 10 is merely filling in details missing from chapter 4.

C. **The Rav** (*The Lonely Man of Faith*, 74, *Shiurim le-Zekher*, vol. 1, 25, and vol. 2, 39), like the Hazon Ish, believes that both chapter 4 and chapter 10 are talking about the same type of *kavvanah*, namely, the *kavvanah* of standing before God. He makes no mention of "*kavvanah* to the meaning of the words" and explicitly adds that *kavvanah latzeit* is not applicable to prayer. However, he explains the limitation of mandatory *kavvanah* to the first blessing of the *Amidah* differently than does the Hazon Ish. The latter believes that while *kavvanah* is desirable throughout *tefillah*, the Sages (as they so often did) gave a minimal *shiur* (quantity) for the fulfillment of the *mitzvah*, namely, intention during the first blessing. The Rav, however, believes that *kavvanah* is *necessary* throughout the entire *Amidah*, but the Sages, recognizing the difficulty of sustained concentration, decided to extend one's *kavvanah* in the first blessing to the rest of the *Amidah* as well.

4. **The *Shema***: For an articulation of the themes and laws of the *Shema* and its blessings, see chapters 6–9 of *Worship of the Heart*, as well as the Rav's "*Kuntras be-Inyanei Keriat Shema*," *Shiurim le-Zekher Abba Mari z"l*, vol. 1, 1–39.

5. **The "prayerful life"**: The Rav develops the idea that prayer "is not a separate entity, but the sublime prologue to Halakhic action" in numerous places. See *Halakhic Man*, 92–95; *The Lonely Man of Faith*, 76–78; *Worship of the Heart*, 164–68; *Days of Deliverance*, 41–46.

6. ***Tze'akah* and *tefillah***: For more on the concepts of *tze'akah* and *tefillah*, see *Before Hashem You Shall Be Purified: Rabbi Joseph B. Soloveitchik on the Days of Awe*, adapted by Arnold Lustiger (Union City, NJ, 1998), 43–58. In his article, "Destiny, Freedom and the Logic of Petition" (see n. 18 above), R. Shalom Carmy cogently develops these ideas beyond what the Rav himself taught.

Chapter 21

Prayer (2): Self-Sacrifice
and the Audacity of Prayer

Crisis and Prayer

While prayer redeems man, the Rav opens "Reflections on the *Amidah*" with the claim that prayer itself was redeemed by a man, namely, the Rambam. He accomplished this redemption, continues the Rav, on both the halakhic and the philosophical planes. First, while most authorities ruled that daily prayer is mandated only by a rabbinic enactment, the Rambam ruled that it is a commandment ordained by the Bible itself.[1] The majority position could lead one to regard prayer as a kind of afterthought to the halakhic system, while the Rambam's position clearly situates prayer in a more central halakhic position. Second, the Rambam elaborated a conception of *avodah she-ba-lev* as an all-pervasive attachment to God,[2] and, as we have seen, prayer is one form of *avodah she-ba-lev*.

These two claims on the part of the Rambam amount to a recognition that prayer is "the expression of the soul that yearns for God via the medium of the word, through which the human being gives expression to the storminess of his soul and spirit" (*Worship of the Heart*, 146). Everyone acknowledges that Judaism commands "love and fear of God, total commitment to Him and cleaving unto Him" (ibid.) – yet these religious experiences would have remained mute and internalized were it not for the verbal expression given to them in prayer. Prayer thus functions as "the mirror of the lovesick religious soul" (*Worship of the Heart*, 86). Therefore, even the Ramban (Nahmanides), in defending those who regard daily prayer as a rabbinic command, admits

---

1 *Hilkhot Tefillah* 1:1.
2 *Guide of the Perplexed* III:51.

that "the substance of prayer and its essence are derived from the Torah" (*Worship of the Heart*, 146). In other words, the Torah recognizes the institution of prayer, but does not demand it on a daily basis.[3]

In a different essay, the Rav offers an intriguing explanation of the dispute between the Rambam and the Ramban.[4] Both, he says, acknowledge that the Torah mandates prayer when an individual or a community encounters an *et tzarah*, a time of distress. Jewish prayer stems from the twin feelings of crisis and of man's total dependence on God: "Out of the straits, *min ha-metzar*, I have called upon the Lord" (Ps. 118:5); "Out of the depths, *mi-ma'amakim*, I have called to You, O Lord" (Ps. 130:1); "Behold, as the eyes of servants unto the hand of their master, as the eyes of a maidservant unto the hand of her mistress, so our eyes look unto the Lord our God until He be gracious unto us" (Ps. 123:2). Yet these two authorities differ on the question of what kind of *tzarah* engenders prayer. Ramban believes that "*et tzarah*" refers to external, obvious, surface crises, such as war, famine or disease. These occur only occasionally, and therefore, the Torah does not require daily prayer. Rambam, however, believes that man is perpetually in crisis, for "*et tzarah*" refers to the inner, existential, depth crisis that stems from an awareness of man's constantly looming defeat due to his human limitations, frailties and finitude.[5] As the Midrash states, "One does not leave the world with even half his desires fulfilled" (Eccl. Rabbah 1:13).

The awareness of one's utter dependence on God comes to expression mainly in *bakkashah*: we realize that we are lacking and incomplete, and that only God can fill our needs. One could even say that the Rav describes a circular relationship between prayer and crisis. *Bakkashah* not only serves as a *response* to the crisis awareness, but it is also meant to *engender* the crisis awareness, by bringing to our attention the magnitude of our insufficiency. This, in turn, leads one to beseech God even more fervently.[6]

---

3 Comments to Rambam's *Sefer ha-Mitzvot*, positive commandment 5.

4 *Worship of the Heart*, 29–33. See also "Prayer as Dialogue" in R. Abraham Besdin, *Reflections of the Rav*, vol. 1 (Jerusalem, 1979), 79–82.

5 Regarding prayer and crisis, as well as further analysis of the concept of "depth crisis," see "The Crisis of Human Finitude" in *Out of the Whirlwind*, esp. 159–67, and chaps. 2–5 of *Worship of the Heart*. See also Chap. 24 below.

6 This point is made by R. Joshua Amaru on p. 156 of his article cited in Reference #2 of the previous chapter.

Permission to Pray

Positing the centrality of crisis and *bakkashah* raises what the Rav considers a crucial question: how dare man bring his paltry requests before the Almighty God? This question is not philosophical, but religious: given the Rav's lofty conception of a transcendent God, and the *yirat Shamayim* (fear of Heaven) proceeding from it, is it not presumptuous for finite man to approach the infinite God, before Whom all recedes into insignificance, with his personal needs? In halakhic terms, the Rav is searching for a *mattir*, something that will permit man to engage in the audacious enterprise of prayer.

Before we turn to the *mattir* for the whole enterprise of prayer, let me add that the Rav also sees the need to procure a *mattir* every time we pray. This is, in fact, a cornerstone of many of his *shiurim* on prayer.[7] The Gemara establishes that before one makes requests of God, one must first offer praise to Him:

> R. Simlai expounded: One should always recount the praises of the Omni-present and then offer one's supplications. Whence do we learn it? From [the prayer of] our teacher Moses, which is recorded thus (Deut. 3:24–25): "O Lord God, You have begun to show Your servant Your greatness, etc.," and only thereafter [Moses requests], "Let me go over, I pray, and see the good land" (*Avodah Zarah* 7b).[8]

The Rav sees this not just as a matter of etiquette, but as permission to supplicate.[9] Hence, he concludes that the praise contained in *Pesukei de-Zimrah* and in the blessings of *keriat Shema* allow us to recite the *Amidah*, and the praise contained in the first three blessings of the *Amidah* permit us to continue with the requests in the next thirteen blessings. In halakhic terms, *shevah* is a *mattir* for *bakkashah*.[10] Thus, the need for a *mattir* is not merely a

---

7 See especially the *shiurim* on *Pesukei de-Zimrah* and on *semikhat ge'ulah li-tefillah* in vol. 2 of *Shiurim le-Zekher Abba Mari z"l*, 17–57.

8 This passage also appears in *Berakhot* 32a. A different talmudic passage (*Berakhot* 31a) determines the proper order of prayer from Solomon's plea that God should "hearken unto the *rinah* and unto the *tefillah*" (I Kings 8:28), understanding *rinah* as praise and *tefillah* as request.

9 The *mattir* is necessary from the *human* perspective so that man can enter the proper frame of mind before making requests of God. Praising divine greatness helps man understand the audacity of his undertaking to approach God, while praising divine goodness helps man appreciate God's grace in listening to his petitions.

10 See *Shiurim le-Zekher Abba Mari z"l*, vol. 2, 9–10, 18–22, 38–50. In fact, the Rav says that even *shevah* itself requires a *mattir*, as do additional types of prayer, such as *tefillat nedavah*, voluntary prayer, and *tashlumin*, compensatory prayer. These issues are discussed at length in the aforementioned *shiurim*.

philosophical question, but part of the very structure and experience of prayer itself.

It is not only *bakkashah* that requires a *mattir*; in his early *shiurim* on *tefillah*, the Rav adduced two *mattirim* for the very possibility of prayer itself, and he cites them in "Reflections on the *Amidah*" as well:

> The Talmudic dictum, "The prayers were established by the Patriarchs," does not contradict a second statement of the Sages, "The prayers were established to correspond to the fixed daily sacrificial offerings, the *temidim*" (*Berakhot* 26b). Rambam quoted both opinions, for they are mutually complementary.[11] Prayer is justified by both factors, historical precedent and the ceremonial law of the Temple cult (*Worship of the Heart*, 151).

The Rav's focus on the need for a *mattir* presents a powerful religious message: our ability to stand before God is a privilege that should not be taken for granted. A pervasive sense of *yirat Shamayim* must lead one to be cautious and circumspect in one's approach to God. However, in "Reflections on the *Amidah*," he adds an additional *mattir* of a very different tenor:

> [P]rayer is a vital necessity for the religious individual. He cannot conceal his thoughts and his feelings, his vacillations and his struggles, his yearnings and his wishes, his despair and his bitterness – in a word, the great wealth stored away in his religious consciousness – in the depths of his soul. Suppressing liturgical expression is simply impossible: prayer is a necessity. Vital, vibrant religiosity cannot sustain itself without prayer. In sum, prayer is justified because it is impossible to exist without it (*Worship of the Heart*, 150).[12]

This is a significant departure from the Rav's earlier conception of prayer, since it is a *mattir* that essentially does away with the need for *mattirim*. Prayer is now seen as inevitable, for it is a basic human need. Is it not natural to speak to God, as did the great biblical figures and, indeed, Jews throughout the generations? Is God not *Shome'a tefillah*, the Hearer of prayers?

Rav Lichtenstein has observed that, because of these questions, the Rav grew troubled over time by the focus on the *mattir*, leading him to de-emphasize it in his subsequent thought. Rav Lichtenstein attributes this change to

---

11 *Hilkhot Tefillah* 1:5 and *Hilkhot Melakhim* 9:1.

12 We may add to this that the Rav understands that the Torah desires man to live in this world, and therefore it sees man's this-worldly needs as legitimate. "Whoever permits his legitimate needs to go unsatisfied will never be sympathetic to the crying needs of others . . . Hence Judaism rejected models of existence which deny human need, such as the angelic or the monastic. For Judaism, need-awareness constitutes part of the definition of human existence" ("Redemption, Prayer, Talmud Torah," 65).

three factors. First, the Rav always rethought matters. Second, in many areas his thought moved over the years in a more humanizing direction, from the epistemological to the existential, engaged with and sensitive to human needs, agonies and hopes. Third, in Wordsworth's phrase, "a deep distress hath humanized my soul" (*Elegiac Stanzas* I.36) – his wife's illness led him to soften and ameliorate his position on the availability of prayer to man.[13]

Prayer as Self-Sacrifice

Yet Rav Soloveitchik's decreasing emphasis on the need for a *mattir* in prayer does not mean that he moved away from a view of God's transcendence towards one of God's immanence. Rather, in "Reflections on the *Amidah*," the Rav presents the daily *Shemoneh Esreh* as maintaining both of these conceptions in dialectical tension. This tension makes the *Shemoneh Esreh*, in the Rav's reading, into an emotional roller-coaster that takes one through a crisis experience thrice daily. The reason for the volatility of prayer is rooted in man's complex soul:

> Prayer, which is like a mirror reflecting the image of the person who worships God with heart and soul, is shot through with perplexity, for worship itself is rooted in the human dialectical consciousness. Hence prayer is not marked by monotonous uniformity. It is multi-colored: it contains contradictory themes, expresses a variety of moods, conflicting experiences, and desires oscillating in opposing directions. Religious experience is a multi-directional movement, metaphysically infused. Prayer too does not proceed slowly along one straight path, but leaps and cascades from wondrous heights to terrifying depths, and back (*Worship of the Heart*, 148).

According to the Rav, the *Amidah* has a chiastic structure of a-b-c-b-a.[14] This structure can be perceived most easily in the following diagram, portraying a descent into the depths and an ascent therefrom:

1. *Avot*	**19.** *Sim Shalom*	love, grace	*gadol*
2. *Gevurot*	**18.** *Modim*	fear, dependence	*gibbor*
3. *Kedushah* **4-16.** *Bakkashah* **17.** *Retzeh*		paradox, sacrifice	*nora*

---

13 R. Lichtenstein presented this thesis in an address at Yeshiva University's Gruss Institute in Jerusalem on May 26, 2006 entitled, "The Limits of Prayer."

14 The Rav's analysis of the experiential structure of the *Amidah* unfolds over the course of thirty pages (152–81) and will be given only the briefest summary here.

The first blessing, *Avot*, opens the *Amidah* with a joyous sense of divine *hesed* and human adequacy. These are replaced in the next blessing, *Gevurot*, by a dread-filled sense of divine strength and human weakness. The following blessing, *Kedushat ha-Shem*, presents the paradox of divine transcendence and human worship: "You are holy and Your name is holy, and holy ones praise You daily." How can man approach the Infinite? Only by means of self-sacrifice, which is accomplished in the next thirteen petitional blessings. While, in its most straightforward sense, *bakkashah* means pleading with God for the fulfillment of our needs, it also entails a sacrificial admission of our dependence and incompleteness:

> The very gesture of falling before God and acknowledging His unlimited sovereignty and man's utter impotence, constitutes an act of sacrifice. Service of the heart is expressed in the middle benedictions (*Worship of the Heart*, 175).

The capstone of the middle blessings is *Shema Kolenu*, in which we ask God to "accept our prayer" – i.e., the previous twelve petitional blessings – "in mercy and favor." This is a general request to accept our requests. The next blessing, *Retzeh*, ostensibly seems similar to *Shema Kolenu*, yet the Rav sharply distinguishes between them. *Retzeh* connects prayer to the sacrificial service (176–79), and, according to the Rav, constitutes the culmination of the theme of self-sacrifice, to which one has been building up throughout the previous fourteen blessings (*kedushat ha-Shem* and *bakkashah*). This is why he claims that "*Retzeh* is perhaps the central benediction in the text of *avodah she-ba-lev*" (*Worship of the Heart*, 177), understanding *avodah* specifically in the sense of sacrifice.

In other words, the thirteen middle blessings contain a dual theme: petitioning God for one's needs, and sacrificially admitting one's inadequacy. The first theme is highlighted by *Shema Kolenu*, the second by *Retzeh*. In *Retzeh*, one asks God not to accept one's supplications, but rather to accept one's offering:

> When a Jew says *Retzeh* he does not refer to the satisfaction of needs and the fulfillment of the desires about which he poured out his heart in the middle, petitionary section. For this he has already prayed in the previous benediction, *Shema Kolenu* ("Hear our voice"). When he reaches *Retzeh* these "petty" matters no longer concern him. His soul is bound up in a great, profound, world-embracing request. He asks God to accept the great sacrifice he has just offered,[15] to accept his being that is returned to God, cleaving unto the Infinite and connecting itself to the Divine throne (*Worship of the Heart*, 178–79).

---

15 It is unclear whether "the great sacrifice he *has just offered*" refers to the recitation of

This sacrificial element in this prayer can be understood in light of a passage in *Out of the Whirlwind*:

> Prayer flowing from a heart filled with the inner misery and despair of this contradictory experience[16] is not intercessory petition, which is intended to relieve one of his trouble, but rather has more of a subjective character. It does not ask for help, nor does it try to resolve the crisis. The prayer consecrates the defeat, redeems the misery and elevates it to the level of sacrifice. Prayer flowing *mi-ma'amakim*, from the depths, is a sacrificial service. The supplication imparts meaning and directedness to the crisis experience. The majestic personality of a while ago (at the hour of triumph) acquires dignity, and, of course, greatness through prayer, during which the free surrender is brought about or the defeat accepted. What this prayer accomplishes is remarkable (*Out of the Whirlwind*, 167).

In the Rav's various discussions of the structure of prayer, we discover differing, yet perhaps complementary, conceptions. "Redemption, Prayer, Talmud Torah" presents the *bakkashah* section of the *Amidah* as a journey of self-acquisition, followed by a concluding note of self-sacrifice in *Retzeh*. By contrast, "Reflections on the *Amidah*" portrays *bakkashah* as a form of self-sacrifice, capped by *Retzeh*; yet in "Reflections on the *Amidah*," self-sacrifice is then *followed by* self-acquisition:

> God is "satisfied" with this offering. He receives it and restores it to the one who has offered it. The praying individual annuls himself in order to acquire himself. From his prayer man emerges firm, elevated and sublime, having found his redemption in self-loss and self-recovery (*Worship of the Heart*, 179).

This contrast between "Redemption, Prayer, Talmud Torah" and "Reflections on the *Amidah*" harks back to the tension between the two forms of catharsis we discussed in Chapter 3: advance-retreat vs. advance-retreat-advance. Is the focus of prayer self-acquisition or self-sacrifice? Is self-sacrifice the terminus, or is it followed by reacquisition of the self? The answer is, of course, that both are true. When we consider the Rav's various works as a whole, we see that he constantly maintains a balance between affirmation and denial, majesty and humility. In the two essays just mentioned, the Rav finds

---

Retzeh itself or to the sacrificial element implicit in the previous thirteen blessings.

16 "This contradictory experience" refers to the self-assertion and self-negation that express one's depth crisis, which flows from "the steady awareness of an incomplete existence and an unfulfilled destiny" (*Out of the Whirlwind*, 164). See n. 5 above.

this dichotomy within the *Amidah* itself, while in *The Lonely Man of Faith* he discovers it in the contrast between the *Shema* and the *Amidah*:

> During the recital of *Shema*, man ideally feels totally committed to God and his awareness is related to a normative end, assigning to man ontological legitimacy and worth as an ethical being whom God charged with a great mission . . . In contrast to the *Shema* awareness, the *Tefillah* awareness negates the legitimacy and worth of human existence. Man, as a slave of God, is completely dependent upon Him . . . When the Talmud (*Berakhot* 14b and 15a) speaks of *kabbalat ol malkhut Shamayim shelemah*, the unitary acceptance of the Kingdom of God [attained by reciting *Shema* and *Tefillah* together], it refers to the two awarenesses which, notwithstanding their antithetic character, merge into one comprehensive awareness of man who is at the same time the free messenger of God and His captive as well (*The Lonely Man of Faith*, 75).

In "Reflections on the *Amidah*," *tefillah* presents not just two approaches to man, but a movement from affirmation to negation and then back to affirmation. "The order of the last three benedictions is the reverse of the opening three" (*Worship of the Heart*, 179), climbing out of the depths back into the sunlight, and ending on a note of grace:

> [A]fter all the transformations and oscillations from love and mercy to the experience of dread and human helplessness, after man comes crashing down from the heights of yearning and aspiration to the depths of confusion and terror, after self-negation and self-recovery, after the sacrifice, the binding and the offering on the altar, and after the return to existence – comes again the delightful, joyous and confident experience: God appears as a safe haven and secure abode . . . Man does not flee from God, but rather races towards Him and resides in the bosom of the *Shekhinah*. All is blanketed in the serenity of peace and quiet. Over all, there flows the blessing of the Infinite; the *hesed* of God descends "like the dew on Mount Hermon" (Ps. 133:3). The world is illuminated with the precious light that flows from the Infinite (*Worship of the Heart*, 181).

Conclusion: Why a Fixed Text?

If prayer is indeed the verbal expression of the stormy religious soul, why do we pray from a standardized text? Why not just express whatever is in one's heart? The Rav offers three different answers to this question, and these neatly reflect the three functions of prayer we have identified in his writings.
(a) In *The Lonely Man of Faith*, where the Rav presents the essence of prayer as an experience of encounter with God (meant to overcome loneliness),

the need for standardization is not specific to prayer. Rather, it reflects the general tendency of Halakhah to attempt to transcend the fleeting subjectivity of experience and to give it an objective dimension (56).

(b) According to "Redemption, Prayer, Talmud Torah," where prayer is seen as a medium for self-creation, *Hazal* penned a standardized text in order to teach man the hierarchy of needs (67), as well as to provide him with a framework for personal meditation and supplication.

(c) In "Reflections on the *Amidah*," with its stress on self-sacrifice and its focus on the paradox of how finite man can approach the infinite God, a set text is necessary because, otherwise, it would be impossible to pray; the endeavor of prayer would have been too bold to consider (151).

Thus, Rav Soloveitchik's complex view of prayer presents a dialectic between sacrifice and acquisition, between divine distance and nearness, between self-nullification and self-assertion. The reason for this dialectic is his dialectical view of man, which we will explore in the next few chapters.

FOR FURTHER REFERENCE

1. **Rambam's approach to prayer:** For a historically sensitive analysis
   of halakhic aspects of Rambam's approach, see Yaakov Blidstein, *Ha-
   Tefillah be-Mishnato ha-Hilkhatit shel ha-Rambam* (Jerusalem, 1994).
   For a penetrating and thought-provoking analysis of the philosophical dimension of Rambam's approach, connecting his views on prayer to those
   on human perfection, see Ehud Benor, *Worship of the Heart: A Study in
   Maimonides' Philosophy of Religion* (Albany, 1995). (Benor cites Rav
   Soloveitchik's views, though his book was published before the Rav's
   work of the same title. Both titles are influenced by Prof. Twersky's pre-
   ferred translation of *avodah she-ba-lev*.)

2. **The structure and wording of the *Amidah*:** For a close reading of the
   Shemoneh Esreh, written in the spirit of Rav Soloveitchik even if not
   always following the Rav's own interpretations, see R. Ezra Bick's series
   Understanding the Shemoneh Esreh on the Yeshivat Har Etzion's Israel
   Koschitzky Virtual Beit Midrash: http://www.vbm-torah.org/archive/18/.
   For an analysis of a broader range of prayers, based on a curriculum developed in consultation with Rav Soloveitchik at the Maimonides School,
   see R. Isaiah Wohlgemuth, *A Guide to Jewish Prayer* (Brookline, MA, no
   date).

3. **Commentary on prayer:** The Rav was a close reader of prayer and
   liturgical poetry and offered many insights into specific texts. These are
   much in evidence in the commentaries culled from the Rav's teachings by
   Dr. Arnold Lustiger in *Mahzor Mesorat ha-Rav* (Yom Kippur: New York,
   2006; Rosh Hashanah: New York, 2007) and *Siddur Koren Mesorat ha-
   Rav* (Jerusalem, 2011), and by R. Simon Posner in *Kinot Koren Mesorat
   ha-Rav* (Jerusalem, 2010).

Chapter 22

Repentance (1): Self-Creation or Self-Return?

The Challenge of *Teshuvah*

The subject of repentance, or *teshuvah*, captivated the Rav's imagination and preoccupied his thought – and it is easy to understand why. As a transformation of the personality in response to God's will, *teshuvah* reveals much about two of the Rav's main concerns: human nature and man's relationship with God. In addressing *teshuvah*, the Rav confronted questions such as: Can a person change? Is one's personality static or dynamic? What is the relationship between reason and emotion, between sin and suffering, between guilt and growth, past and future, free will and causality? How is one to approach God – with love or fear, as an individual or as part of a community, appealing to grace or justice, with a sense of self-nullification or self-worth? Given the issues raised, it is no wonder that some of the Rav's most powerful and penetrating insights appear in his discussions of repentance.

From his earliest writings until his latest, the Rav was drawn again and again to explore the dynamics of *teshuvah*. In 1929, he corresponded on this subject with his uncle,[1] and two of his earliest published works – *Halakhic Man* (1944) and "Sacred and Profane" (1945) – present profound analyses of repentance.[2] At the other end of his career, for a period spanning more than two decades, the Rav annually delivered highly-anticipated *Kinus Teshuvah*

---

1 *Iggerot ha-Grid ha-Levi*, 23–25.

2 *Halakhic Man*, 110–23; "Sacred and Profane," 25–31. *The Halakhic Mind* (written in 1944), 47–50, discusses the related topic of time perception, which, as we shall see later in this chapter, is crucial in allowing for the possibility of repentance.

lectures between Rosh Hashanah and Yom Kippur to the members of the Rabbinical Council of America.[3]

The *Kinus Teshuvah* lectures are works of art, aimed at both the heart and the mind. They generally begin with a difficult text in the Rambam's *Hilkhot Teshuvah*, asking question after question until all is resolved with a single blinding flash of insight. This insight or, more precisely, this *hakirah*[4] – for example, the distinction between *kapparah* and *taharah* (atonement and purification) – is then amplified through application to halakhic and philosophical issues, analysis of liturgical texts, sensitive psychological readings of biblical and midrashic tales, and instantiation through examples drawn from everyday life. The combined effect of all this is to convey the exaltedness of repentance and its ultimate attainability, without promising that it will be an easy or smooth process.

In fact, it is precisely the Rav's squarely confronting the complexity and pitfalls of *teshuvah* that sets him apart from many other thinkers. R. Walter Wurzburger comments on the *Kinus Teshuvah* lectures:

> Analysis in depth of the various components of halakhic norms yields a rich harvest of psychological, ethical, metaphysical, and religious insights. Especially striking is the complete avoidance of all apologetics and the unabashed willingness to face up to the complexities which are so frequently overlooked by philosophers in quest of a master formula designed to unify all experience.[5]

What R. Wurzburger asserts of the *Kinus Teshuvah* lectures holds true regarding the Rav's philosophy generally. At the Rav's *sheloshim*, R. Shalom Carmy observed:

> What did I learn from the Rav that I could not learn anywhere else? Conventional religion tends to edit reality, to soft-pedal existential conflict, to make the ugly aspects of reality disappear behind a rosy glow. More than any other Jewish thinker, the Rav's memorable and sometimes brutal honesty taught us what both conventional piety and fashionable liberalism seemed intent to conceal: that religion is no escape from conflict, but the ultimate encounter with reality. Facing reality, for the Rav, meant striving to penetrate the meaning

---

3 These lectures were delivered from the mid-1950s until 1980. Those from 1960 and 1967–1972 were adapted by Pinhas Peli in *Al ha-Teshuvah* (Jerusalem, 1975), translated as *On Repentance* (Jerusalem, 1980). The lectures from 1973–1980 were adapted by Arnold Lustiger in *Before Hashem You Shall be Purified* (Edison, NJ, 1998). (See also For Further Reference, #1.) Prof. David Shatz has commented that, for many of the attendees, these *derashot* became part of the *teshuvah* process itself.

4 See p. 27 for a definition of this term.

5 Preface to the 1984 reprint of *On Repentance*, x.

of Torah and the challenges of human existence, not distracting oneself from these tasks by cultivating doubts about the reality.[6]

To comprehend Rav Soloveitchik's views on *teshuvah*, it will be instructive to compare them with those of another twentieth-century titan of Jewish thought, Rav Avraham Yitzhak Hacohen Kook. Though Rav Kook, like Rav Soloveitchik, is a complex and dialectical thinker, his approach leads in a very different direction.

Two Giants

At first glance, the outlines of Rav Kook's biography (1865–1935) seem roughly similar to those of Rav Soloveitchik's. He received his Torah training in Eastern Europe, mastering both Halakhah and Jewish thought, before moving to a more modernized and secularized milieu, where he functioned as a communal leader, teacher and thinker. Eventually, he became the key authority and inspiration for an entire socio-religious way of life that creatively engaged the world as an expression of its commitment to Torah and *mitzvot*. Yet these points of convergence reveal important contrasts as well.

Whereas Rav Soloveitchik's thought was primarily philosophical and halakho-centric, with only occasional appropriations of Kabbalistic motifs, Rav Kook's was heavily mystical. Thus, when confronted with the growing secularization of Jewish society, Rav Soloveitchik's solution was to uncover the philosophical depth of the halakhic tradition, while Rav Kook's was to reveal Judaism's hidden mystical tradition. Both were dialectical thinkers; however, Rav Kook, with his mystical orientation, sought to synthesize dialectical positions, while Rav Soloveitchik, with his focus on the human perspective, often did not. In other words, Rav Kook searched for harmony, but Rav Soloveitchik saw the human situation as one fated to live with tension.[7]

Other differences are no less important. In 1904, Rav Kook settled in the Land of Israel, which was then under Ottoman rule, and eventually became Chief Rabbi of *Eretz Yisrael* under the British Mandate. This environment presented an entirely different set of opportunities and challenges than those faced by Rav Soloveitchik in mid-twentieth-century America.[8] Connected to

---

6 "A Three-Part Tribute," in *Memories of a Giant*, ed. Michael Bierman (Jerusalem, 2003), 142.

7 In terms that we presented in Chap. 3, Rav Kook engaged in Hegelian dialectic and Rav Soloveitchik in Kierkegaardian dialectic.

8 As we shall see in Chap. 27, there is also great significance to the fact that Rav Kook never witnessed the Holocaust and the establishment of the State of Israel, while Rav Soloveitchik did.

this is the fact that, for Rav Kook, national questions were far more prominent and pressing than in the thought of Rav Soloveitchik, which focused mainly on the individual.[9]

Although both rabbis were interested in the world around them and appreciated the value of secular studies, only Rav Soloveitchik was acquainted with these texts firsthand.[10] Furthermore, Rav Kook's statements about secular studies are riddled by ambivalence and contradiction, and may have changed over time, whereas Rav Soloveitchik's embrace of secular studies would seem to be a constant.[11] The literary genres they employed also differed. As is quite evident in their writings on *teshuvah* and elsewhere, both Rav Kook and Rav Soloveitchik possessed sensitive, poetic souls and were writers of great eloquence; only Rav Kook, however, wrote actual poetry.

Rav Soloveitchik and Rav Kook both place *teshuvah* at the center of their respective philosophical systems.[12] Both assign it very broad significance, far beyond the common understanding of *teshuvah*, but they disagree about the meaning of this broader conception. Generally, repentance is taken to mean regret over a past sin, accompanied by resolve not to return to it in the future. Rav Soloveitchik and Rav Kook recognize this as but one aspect of a more general, systemic, lifelong process that does not relate only to atoning for a sin. In a word, for Rav Soloveitchik *teshuvah* means creation of the self, while for Rav Kook it means return to the inner self (which, as we shall see, is connected to the general striving for perfection in all of existence).

---

9 Despite Rav Soloveitchik's focus on the individual, he does not ignore the importance of the community. See the discussions in Chaps. 2, 26, and 35.

10 R. David Hacohen, Rav Kook's disciple and editor of many of his writings, testified that Rav Kook's secular knowledge came from secondary sources: see *Orot ha-Kodesh* vol. 1, 18.

11 Regarding Rav Kook's complex relationship with secular culture and knowledge, see, for example, Jonathan Garb, "'Alien' Culture in the Circle of Rabbi Kook," in *Study and Knowledge in Jewish Thought*, ed. Howard Kreisel (Beer Sheva, 2006), 253–64, and the literature cited there in the footnotes.

12 Each wrote and lectured extensively about *teshuvah*, and these thoughts were compiled by others into book form during each rabbi's lifetime. Rav Soloveitchik read and granted post-facto approval to the adaptations of his lectures appearing in *On Repentance*, while Rav Kook charged his son with compiling *Orot ha-Teshuvah* (Jerusalem, 1924; translated by Ben Zion Bokser, *The Lights of Penitence* [New York, 1978]) out of passages drawn from his personal philosophical journals. This highlights an important stylistic difference between these books. *Orot ha-Teshuvah* is a collection of generally brief ideas arranged by the editor (except for its first three chapters, which were written as a unit by Rav A.Y. Kook). It therefore reads very differently than the highly structured public sermons in *On Repentance*.

Rav Kook: Cosmic Return to Divinity/Selfhood

For Rav Kook, *teshuvah* is not only something in which the individual engages; it is a cosmic process, the inner movement of all of creation towards perfection (*Lights of Penitence* 6:1). It is expressed in the life of the individual and of the nation, in cultural development and governmental improvement, in the return of Israel to its land and in the evolution of species.[13] All these are manifestations of the same force:

> General penitence, which involves raising the world to perfection, and particularized penitence, which pertains to the personal life of each individual, . . . all constitute one essence. Similarly, all the cultural reforms through which the world rises from decadence, the improvements in the social and economic order through this redress of every form of wrongdoing . . . all of them constitute an inseparable whole (4:3).

This striving for perfection is, of course, a striving to connect with God. Yet it is not an attempt to unite with God Who is outside of oneself; it is, rather, an effort to uncover and draw out the divine root within. For Rav Kook, whose conception of God is immanent rather than transcendent, divinity pervades and lies at the core of everything that exists.

> When one forgets the essence of one's own soul . . . everything becomes confused and uncertain. The primary role of penitence . . . is for the person to return to himself, to the root of his soul. Then he will at once return to God, to the Soul of all souls . . . This is true whether we consider the individual, a whole people, or the whole of humanity, or whether we consider the mending of all existence, which always becomes damaged when it forgets itself (15:10).

Sin alienates us from our selves, thereby obscuring our connection to God. Thus, while "*teshuvah*," or return, is generally understood to mean either returning from *sin* or returning to *God*, Rav Kook explains it differently: it means returning to the *self*, which contains Godliness at its core.

> Adam's sin [was] that he was alienated from his selfhood, for he followed the opinion of the serpent and lost himself . . . and he could not give a clear answer to the question of "Where are you," for he did not know his own soul . . .
> "The breath of our nostrils, God's anointed (*meshiah*)" (*Eikhah* 4:20) . . . is not external to us; he is "the breath of our nostrils" [i.e., he comes from with-

---

13 For the sake of comparison to Rav Soloveitchik, we shall focus only on the *teshuvah* of the individual.

in]. We shall seek out God our Lord and David our king . . . we shall seek out our "I"; we shall seek and find ourselves (*Orot ha-Kodesh* 3:97, 140–41).[14]

The idea that repentance and the messianic redemption mean a return to the self, which is also a return to God, leads Rav Kook to the striking conclusion that the depressing sense of sin is really a source of joy. Sin becomes conspicuous only when seen against the background of God's perfection; if one cannot perceive the divine, then one will not take notice of sin. Thus, the very awareness of sin is due to divine illumination, and "this very thought engenders endless joy and exaltation" (*Lights of Penitence* 15:9). In other words, the feeling of sinfulness is really a hint of the divine peeking out from within the deep recesses of the self!

Rav Soloveitchik: Living Time and Self-Creation

Rav Soloveitchik is perturbed by the fact that, rationally considered, the notion of repentance seems absurd. Time is linear, and the past cannot be undone. Remorseful or not, one deserves punishment for one's misdeeds, for actions have consequences. Only a supernatural act of grace can break the causal chain between crime and punishment.

Nevertheless, the human experience of time can differ from physical, unidirectional, clock-measured time. If one so chooses, says Rav Soloveitchik, one can abide within "living time," where all three tenses – the experienced past, the awareness of the present, and the anticipated future – are present within one's consciousness at every moment. In this mode of living, the meaning of the past depends on the direction one gives it in the present and future.[15] If the past is dead and determined, then causality works in one direction only: the past influences the future, but not vice versa. However, one can also choose to regard the past as alive, its meaning undetermined until the last

---

14 In Rav Kook's comments on prophecy, we find another striking passage equating inner selfhood with Godliness. This passage was so radical, in fact, that its editor censored it. The original, uncensored passage reads: "Prophecy and *ru'ah ha-kodesh* come *from a person's inwardness*, and from within him, he overflows to everything related to the world as a whole" (*Shemonah Kevatzim* 5:127, vol. 2, 250). The revised passage, which conceals Rav Kook's idea by adding several words, is entirely uncontroversial: "Prophecy and *ru'ah ha-kodesh* come *by the word of God to a person's inwardness*, and from within him they overflow to everything related to the world as a whole" (*Orot ha-Kodesh* 1:16, 23). For a treatment in English of the editing and censorship of Rav Kook's writings, see Avinoam Rosenak, "Hidden Diaries and New Discoveries: The Life and Thought of Rabbi A. I. Kook," *Shofar* 25:3 (2007), 111–47.
15 See *Halakhic Man*, 121–23.

chapter of one's life has been written. In this case, causality can work in the opposite direction, from future to past:

> The past by itself is indeterminate, a closed book. It is only the present and the future that can pry it open and read its meaning. There are many different paths, according to this perspective, along which the cause can travel.[16] It is the future that determines its direction and points the way. There can be a certain sequence of events that starts out with sin and iniquity but ends up with *mitzvot* and good deeds, and vice versa. The future transforms the thrust of the past (*Halakhic Man*, 115).

This is the essence of repentance:

> The main principle of repentance is that the future dominate the past and there reign over it in unbounded fashion (ibid.).

In this conception of time, "cause" and "effect" interact and affect each other. Since causality now has no predetermined meaning, "causality" is transmuted into "creation":

> When the future participates in the clarification and elucidation of the past – points out the way it is to take, defines its goals, and indicates the direction of its development – then man becomes a creator of worlds (*Halakhic Man*, 116–17).

This clarifies how the highest form of *teshuvah*, i.e., "repentance out of love," can transmute "deliberate sins into merits" (*Yoma* 86b). The transmutation is not a metaphysical process but a psychological one, wherein the penitent "becomes his own redeemer and releases himself from captivity in the pit of sin" (*On Repentance*, p. 183).[17] By reassessing past events in light of future goals, the past takes on new meaning and propels the penitent toward his chosen destination or destiny.[18]

---

16 Here the Rav is referring to "the cause" in the sense of "cause and effect." He means that, while we are accustomed to locating the cause in the past and the effect in the future, it is also possible for a cause in the future to have an effect in the past, as he goes on to explain.

17 The precise techniques of transmuting sins into merits by reappraising the past were detailed above in Chap. 7, pp. 93–94. In that chapter, we linked the "repentance of purification" to the "repentance of elevating evil." Here they are linked to yet another concept developed in *On Repentance*, namely, the "repentance of redemption." (These appear, respectively, in the first, sixth, and fourth discourses in *On Repentance*.)

18 For example, if one committed a sin, it is possible that this sin will simply ease one's path to further deterioration and dissipation. However, it is also possible that this sin will arouse in the sinner a sense of dissatisfaction, leading to an assessment of his future goals and where he is located in relation to them, and thereby to growth and improvement. The sin, then, can

Now we are in a position to resolve a seeming contradiction in Rav Soloveitchik's writings on *teshuvah*. Basing himself on the Rambam (*Hilkhot Teshuvah* 2:4), the Rav says in a number of places that by means of repentance one becomes a new person:

> The desire to be another person, to be different than I am now, is the central motif of repentance. Man cancels the law of identity and continuity which prevails in the "I" awareness by engaging in the wondrous, creative act of repentance. A person is creative; he was endowed with the power to create at his very inception. When he finds himself in a situation of sin, he takes advantage of his creative capacity, returns to God, and becomes a creator and self-fashioner. Man, through repentance, creates himself, his own "I" (*Halakhic Man*, 113).[19]

Yet the Rav also claims that the superior and healthier form of *teshuvah* is one in which a person does not cut himself off from his past and become a completely new person. Rather, it is preferable to maintain a connection with one's past identity and use it as a positive force in the present (*On Repentance*, 269–86). How are we to understand this discrepancy? Should one become a new person or not?

In light of the Rav's view on man's ability to reshape the significance of the past, it should be clear that when he talks about the formation of a new personality, he doesn't mean something created *yesh me-ayin*, out of nothingness. Rather, he is referring to rejecting or superseding the self formed by habit, thoughtlessly and passively. Man must take an active role in shaping his personality, changing himself from an object to a subject, from a person of fate to a person of destiny. While rejecting his earlier understanding of his actions, the penitent maintains continuity with his past self and reassesses the meaning of his past, thereby forming a new self-understanding, a new personality, that makes use of the old instead of cutting it off altogether. Creation of the self thus means active shaping of the raw material of the personality, or reshaping of a sinful personality. God commands man to make himself, to form himself into an ideal personality. This is a central theme in the Rav's philosophy, and in his mind it is the central thrust of the *mitzvot*: "The most fundamental principle of all is that man must create himself. It is this idea that Judaism introduced into the world" (*Halakhic Man*, 109).

---

take on different meanings – as a spur to decline or a catalyst for ascent – depending on its future ramifications. Thus, by shaping one's present in light of one's future, one can change the meaning of the past.

19 See also, for example, *On Repentance*, 67, 198–99.

Points of Contrast

Rav Kook's and Rav Soloveitchik's respective views on repentance have many ramifications and can be contrasted at many levels. Let us explore a few of the differences between them.

(A) *Image of God*

For Rav Kook, as we have seen, the image of God is implanted in man and his task is to let it burst forth. For Rav Soloveitchik, on the other hand, the image of God "is a challenge to be met, not a gratuitous gift" ("Redemption, Prayer, Talmud Torah," 64). This means that "Man comes into our world as a hylic,[20] amorphous being . . . It is up to man . . . to impress form upon a latent formless personality" (ibid.).

(B) *Always in the heart*

Rav Kook writes: "Penitence is always present in the heart. At the very time of sin, penitence is hidden in the soul, and it releases its impulses, which become manifest when remorse comes summoning to repent" (6:2). The self is predisposed to penitence; in fact, the life-force of penitence is always present in man, waiting to emerge. This makes sense when one views *teshuvah* as returning to the inner self.

For Rav Soloveitchik, however, there is no inborn inner self, and therefore one cannot speak of *teshuvah* as being "always present in the heart." Rather, *teshuvah* means remaking oneself, actively forming the self one should be. Hence, *teshuvah* cannot emerge from within, but must be chosen by man in a creative decision.

This contrast is reminiscent of a similar disagreement regarding prayer. Rav Kook writes that the soul is perpetually at prayer; this prayer is always striving to emerge, and when a person prays he is simply allowing the prayer of the soul to rise to the surface (*Olat Re'iyah*, vol. 1, 11–13). As we saw in Chapters 20 and 21, however, Rav Soloveitchik paints a very different picture of prayer by emphasizing the audacity of approaching God, the consequent need for a *mattir*, and the dimension of active self-creation in prayer instead of the self-revelation posited by Rav Kook.

---

20 "Hylic" comes from the Greek term *"hyle,"* meaning matter. Many medieval Jewish writers, adapting Aristotelian terminology, used the term to denote specifically matter without form – i.e., something amorphous (like the biblical *"tohu va-vohu"*). Aristotle himself referred to formless matter as "prime matter," or *"prote hyle."*

(C)   Pain

For Rav Kook, the pangs of *teshuvah* are like the pain entailed in treating a disease, but ultimately *teshuvah* should be joyous and not sad or morbid (e.g., 8:1, 9:10). In fact, as we saw above, the pain of *teshuvah* is itself a source of joy.[21] Rav Soloveitchik agrees that sin is a sickness, and as such, it causes suffering (*On Repentance*, 212ff.). He also concurs in the belief that penitence should not lead one to become morose or melancholy (*Halakhic Man*, 113). However, he adds an additional reason for the pain of repentance: *teshuvah* is a creative activity, and pain necessarily accompanies creativity.[22]

(D)   Ease

Although Rav Kook recognizes that many people experience repentance as a difficult process, he claims that since it is natural, it can be relatively easy if one approaches it with the proper perception: "When one wishes to embark on penitence, one must realize that there is nothing to thwart this objective. Even the twenty-four offences that impede repentance (Rambam, *Hilkhot Teshuvah*, chapter 4) – *immediately* when one desires and comes to repent for them, they are no longer impediments" (14:3). "Most falls come about because one does not believe in the ease of repentance" (14:4a).[23] Therefore, his writings are full of encouragement, both to the individual[24] and to the community: "Nothing is more certain than penitence, and in the end everything will be redressed and perfected" (6:2).

Rav Soloveitchik, however, does not believe that repentance is easy. It is not a matter of removing the barrier and letting out our inner purity, but rather a struggle to remake oneself. Therefore, Rav Soloveitchik brings a promise of hope only to the community, but not to the individual. The Community of Israel is assured forgiveness; however, there are no guarantees for the individual.[25]

---

21 15:9. See also 8:2, 13:13, and 16:7–8.

22 For more on role of suffering in the Rav's thought, see Chaps. 23 and 24.

23 Here I follow the numbering of the 8th Hebrew edition of *Orot ha-Teshuvah* (Merkaz Shapira, 1987), and have translated these two passages myself.

24 See throughout chap. 14 of *Lights of Penitence* (e.g., passages 15, 23, 26 in the Hebrew edition; add one for the equivalent passages in the English translation), as well as the lengthy description in *Iggerot ha-Ra'ayah*, vol. 2, #378, esp. 36–37.

25 In Chap. 2, pp. 43–44, we saw how this accounts for difference between the anxiety surrounding the individual's confession in the silent prayer on Yom Kippur and the assurance surrounding the communal confession in the *hazzan*'s repetition of the *Amidah*.

Two Conceptions of Human Nature

Rav Kook's and Rav Soloveitchik's understandings of repentance, with all their differences, are clearly predicated on divergent views of the nature of man.

For Rav Kook, the categories of sin and repentance apply not to man in relation to God, but to man in relation to himself: one sins against one's "self" and returns to one's "self." This, in turn, is based on the idea of the God-man unity in the inner self, symbolized by the perpetual inner *teshuvah* of the soul. In Rav Kook's thought, everything begins and ends with God. Repentance means revealing the divine within man and, ideally, uniting it with divinity in its fullness.[26]

Rav Kook's is thus an encouraging and uplifting approach. Man is essentially good and holy, and must merely remove the impediments in order to allow himself to join the soul of the world in its upward movement.

Rav Soloveitchik believes that God is God and man is man, and there is a chasm between them; man must create himself if he wants to draw closer to God. Man begins as a formless mass and must either shape himself actively or be shaped passively by circumstances. He has great potential, but must work hard to actualize it.[27]

The difference between their approaches is nicely encapsulated in their differing approaches to the relationship between Torah study and *teshuvah*. Rav Kook writes that the clarity of one's Torah learning increases in accordance with the *teshuvah* that precedes it (14:28).[28] Rav Soloveitchik says the

---

26 Sin "disrupts the unity between the individual person and all existence" (8:3); one perceives oneself as a discrete entity and not as part of an encompassing divine whole.

27 In a number of places (e.g., *On Repentance*, 201–02), the Rav writes that there is an inner part of the personality that is not sullied by sin. How are we to understand this in light of his portrayal of man as either a self-created being or as one created by circumstance? It is possible that he is being inconsistent; it is possible that he is using homiletical license; or it is possible to read these passages about the pure inner personality as referring to the Rav's understanding that a basic trait of human nature is to seek the good.

28 "The brighter the light of penitence shines before study, the clearer will be one's understanding of his study. The potency of the intellect rises as the potency of the will rises, and it attains clarity in proportion to the clarity of the will." (This appears as 14:27 in the original Hebrew.) In order to grasp the full meaning of this passage, I believe that one must know the metaphysical basis of Rav Kook's conception of *teshuvah*, as elaborated above. However, in a letter to a British educator, Rav Kook makes a similar point that can be understood in purely psychological terms: "[A]ny success in Torah . . . depends on the measure of fear of heaven and the depth of pure and holy faith that is implanted in one's soul. For the broadening and deepening of the intellectual faculty . . . depends on the depth of emotional will that awakens to

reverse: Torah study brings about a purification of the personality! For Rav Kook, *teshuvah* reveals the divine within a person, which helps that person understand the Torah;[29] for Rav Soloveitchik, *teshuvah* is a process of building oneself, and Torah gives one guidelines and ideals to emulate.[30]

Unity or Division?

At this point, one may well ask whether Rav Soloveitchik's focus on the division between the divine and the human and Rav Kook's focus on their inner unity are necessarily contradictory; perhaps they merely address different dimensions of experience. Rav Soloveitchik engages in phenomenology, the study of *human* experience, and this experience, to his mind, entails division, dichotomy, tension, and anxiety. Rav Kook, however, engages in metaphysics, focusing on the *divine* essence of things, which is harmonious. Thus, the difference between them might be merely one of perspective.

Before answering this question, we can note that the very motivation to harmonize different positions is itself characteristic of Rav Kook, while Rav Soloveitchik – in his *shiurim*, philosophy and life – did not see a need for this. Addressing the question directly, this attempt at harmonization fails when we consider that for Rav Kook, the human experience of division is illusory, a product of sin, and must be overcome, while for Rav Soloveitchik this experience is part of the human condition, insurmountable by finite beings.

This returns us to the notion that Rav Soloveitchik views man as burdened by irresolvable dichotomies: he is both great and lowly, victorious and

---

value what is being studied" (*Iggerot ha-Ra'ayah*, vol. 3, #798, 77–78). In other words, if one values what is being studied, one will be motivated to work harder at understanding it.

29 While I focus above on R. Kook's statement in *Orot ha-Teshuvah* regarding the effect of repentance on Torah study, it is only fair to mention that elsewhere R. Kook discusses the purifying effect of Torah study upon the personality. Note that the reason he gives for Torah study's purificatory power (see *Orot ha-Torah* 11:6) fits in precisely with his general theory of personality stated above: by bringing man's capacities into contact with their source of life and holiness, Torah study draws out the genuine inner divinity of the personality. Thus, Rav Kook believes that *teshuvah* and *talmud Torah* energize each other, because both have the same essential function of drawing out divinity. In *Orot ha-Torah* 13:1, he brings prayer into this circle, claiming that, under certain circumstances, it improves Torah insight by eliciting the divine spirit.

30 Additionally, as we saw in Chap. 9, by focusing the mind on that which is truly significant, and by bringing a person into contact with God's wisdom and will, Torah study "purges the mind of unworthy desires and irreverent thoughts, uncouth emotions and vulgar drives."

defeated, natural and transcendent,[31] numinous and kerygmatic,[32] subject and object.[33] Uncomfortable with acknowledging his finitude and uneasy with dialectical tension, man often seeks ways of escaping this awareness.[34] Yet the maintenance of this dialectical awareness, Rav Soloveitchik believes, is crucial to man's psychological and religious well-being, for it reflects the true nature of reality. "The existential awareness must not mirror ideal conditions, but everyday realities. Therefore, it should not reflect only one or two of the multiple aspects, but the total adventure of man, which contains both affirmation and negation, triumph and loss" (*Out of the Whirlwind*, 176). Maintaining this broad perspective allows one to overcome self-preoccupation and acknowledge others, avoid excessive dependence on finite goods and values, gain the consequent ability to sacrifice, experience life in a deep yet balanced fashion, and commit oneself exclusively to God.[35]

In this regard, repentance parallels prayer. Prayer, as we saw in Chapter 21, entails a dialectical awareness. On the one hand, it requires that man acknowledge his insufficiency and engage in self-sacrifice. Yet, at the same time, only if he feels that his life has significance, purpose, and value can he engage God in dialogue and enumerate his needs. Similarly, in *teshuvah* man gazes upon his failures, yet the very fact that God has granted him free will and the ability to remake himself validates his worth and signifies that his service is desired. On this point Rav Soloveitchik and Rav Kook concur: having been placed in the world at a certain place and time, and granted certain talents and abilities, every person can fulfill a mission unique to himself or herself.[36] It is up to each person to listen for the divine summons, and to discover or to create the personal resources to accomplish this task.

---

31 This is a major theme in *The Lonely Man of Faith* and *Family Redeemed*.

32 See especially *Family Redeemed*, 62–63.

33 See the Rav's 1964 *yahrzeit* lecture and his 1974 *teshuvah* lecture, both adapted by Arnold Lustiger: *Derashot Harav* (Union City, NJ, 2003), 66–75; *Before Hashem You Shall be Purified*, 17–42.

34 In various essays, the Rav utilizes Job and Kohelet (representing Philistine vs. Daemonic Man), the Generation of the Flood and the Generation of the Tower of Babel (representing Orgiastic vs. Arrogant Man), and Ahasuerus and Haman (representing the same) to exemplify the different ways of fleeing the dialectical awareness of human finitude. See *Out of the Whirlwind*, 151–57 and 165–66, and *Days of Deliverance* (Jersey City, 2007), 30–39.

35 *Out of the Whirlwind*, 172–78 and 179–214. See Chap. 24 below for a more detailed discussion of the consequences of the dialectical awareness.

36 Rav Soloveitchik: *Out of the Whirlwind*, 147–50, and *Days of Deliverance*, 43–46; Rav Kook: *Olat Re'iyah*, vol. 2, 356.

FOR FURTHER REFERENCE:

1. **Repentance and the High Holidays:** In addition to *On Repentance* and *Before Hashem You Shall be Purified*, adaptations of some of the Rav's lectures on *teshuvah* and the *Yamim Nora'im* can be found in *Yemei Zikkaron* (Jerusalem, 1986) and *Divrei Hashkafah* (Jerusalem, 1992), both adapted by Moshe Krone; the *Nora'ot Ha-Rav* series, adapted by B. David Schreiber; and the *Mahzor Mesorat Ha-Rav* on Rosh Hashanah (New York, 2007) and Yom Kippur (New York, 2006), edited by Arnold Lustiger with R. Michael Taubes.

2. **Time awareness:** According to the Rav, the sense of a living past forms the basis for our observance of holidays and fast days. For example, at the Seder we re-experience the Exodus, and on Tishah be-Av we re-experience the destruction of the Temples. Similarly, Torah reading returns us to Sinai. The "unitive time consciousness" also explains the strength of our connection to our historical heroes and to the Land of Israel. See, among many sources, *Out of the Whirlwind*, 14–17, *The Emergence of Ethical Man*, 164–65, and *The Lord is Righteous in All His Ways*, 25–26. See also Chapter 13 above.

3. **Philosophical influences on Rav Soloveitchik's concept of repentance:** Scholars have noted the influence of several philosophers – most notably Hermann Cohen, Henri Bergson and Max Scheler – on Rav Soloveitchik's views on time and repentance. A number of studies explore the nature of this influence: where the Rav creatively utilizes their ideas, where he develops them, and where he differs. See R. Yitzchak Blau, "Creative Repentance," *Tradition* 28:2 (1993), 11–18, reprinted in R. Marc Angel, ed., *Exploring the Thought of Rabbi Joseph B. Soloveitchik* (Hoboken, 1997), 263–74; Eliezer Goldman, *"Teshuvah u-Zeman be-Hagut ha-Rav Soloveitchik,"* in Avi Sagi, ed., *Emunah bi-Zemanim Mishtanim* (Jerusalem, 1996), 175–90; Lawrence Kaplan, "Hermann Cohen and Rabbi Joseph Soloveitchik on Repentance," *Journal of Jewish Thought and Philosophy* 13:1–3 (2004), 213–58. As Kaplan notes, "A truly great thinker is more than the sum total of the intellectual influence operating upon him. Rather, he draws upon these influences in a creative and innovative way, always maintaining his own identity, uniqueness, and originality" (240).

    In this context, it would be interesting to compare the Rav's doctrine of man not only to that of Rav Kook but also to those of twentieth-century Protestant theologians with whose work the Rav was familiar, e.g.,

Max Scheler (*Man's Place in the Universe*), Emil Brunner (*The Divine Imperative*; *Man in Revolt*) and Reinhold Niebuhr (*The Nature and Destiny of Man*).

4. **Rav Soloveitchik and Rav Kook:** See the brief historical account and the bibliography in R. Jeffrey Saks, "Rabbi Soloveitchik Meets Rav Kook," *Tradition* 39:3 (Fall 2006), 90–96.

Chapter 23

Repentance (2): Responding to Distress and Evil

The Problem of Pain

The most basic question addressed by religious philosophy is the problem of evil: If God is wholly good, all-powerful and all-knowing, how can He allow the righteous to suffer? This question, of course, is not just a plea for understanding; it is also a cry of the wounded heart. Since this question is so emotionally and intellectually fraught, the Rav asserts that, "No religion can afford the luxury of ignoring the most disturbing of all problems, the problem of suffering."[1]

One possible solution is to deny the basic premise about God's nature: perhaps evil occurs because God is limited in some way and unable to control it. However, such an assertion is problematic from a Jewish standpoint, and is uncommon in Jewish literature.[2] A more common solution – propounded, for example, by the Rambam in his *Guide of the Perplexed* (III:10–12) – is to deny the metaphysical reality of evil: In the big picture, from God's point of view, everything is good. What we perceive as evil is merely an illusion, due to our limited perspective.[3] A different solution, articulated in the Talmud,[4] claims that the righteous suffer in this world precisely to maximize their reward in the world-to-come, a reward compared to which this-worldly suffering is insignificant.[5]

---

1 *Out of the Whirlwind*, 92.

2 However, some thinkers – especially kabbalists – believe that God sometimes *chooses* to limit Himself. See For Further Reference, #1.

3 The Rav elaborates on this viewpoint in *Out of the Whirlwind*, 96–100, 125–27.

4 *Kiddushin* 40b and elsewhere.

5 See *Out of the Whirlwind*, 96–98.

Rav Soloveitchik refuses to treat evil as either unreal or inconsequential.[6] For him, suffering is an undeniable human experience, and it cannot be swept under the rug by fancy theories. Explaining away suffering on philosophical or mystical grounds is problematic for intellectual, moral and practical reasons.

First, this enterprise is intellectually shaky, for how can our finite intellects know the infinite "big picture"?

Second, it is morally objectionable, for it denies the legitimacy of a person's suffering. If someone has experienced a loss or is in pain, how dare we tell him that evil is an illusion and suffering a misperception? Rather, the moral response is to acknowledge his pain, respect his suffering, and offer support and sympathy. Furthermore, if evil is an illusion or if suffering is for the victim's ultimate benefit, why, logically speaking, should we act to alleviate it?

Third, today such explanations are practically useless for, even if they brought comfort and solace to pre-modern man, they do not help the contemporary person cope with his or her suffering.[7]

Beyond all these problems with theodicy, or the metaphysical explanation of evil, there lies a more fundamental problem. Even if all the above-mentioned objections were dismissed, we are still left with the fact that philosophical speculation about evil is an essentially passive enterprise. By not requiring any action or response on man's part, the philosophical approach deprives man of the opportunity to utilize the redemptive power of suffering.

Instead of a passive, theoretical *explanation* or justification of suffering, the Rav advocates an active, practical, halakhic *response*. Accepting the reality of suffering, this response does not ask *why* it exists, but rather *what* one should do once one encounters it: "How shall a person act in a time of trouble? What ought a man to do so that he not perish in his afflictions?"[8]

---

6 Unlike many thinkers, Rav Soloveitchik does not distinguish between "natural evil," such as earthquakes or famines, and "human evil," such as crime and cruelty. The reason for this is that he is not concerned about the *cause* or *source* of evil, but rather about its *effect* on man.

7 In *Out of the Whirlwind* (99–100), the Rav describes how, presumably early in his career, he tried to employ the metaphysical dismissal of evil, but to no avail: "I can state with all candor that I personally have not been too successful in my attempts to spell out this metaphysic in terms meaningful to the distraught individual who floats aimlessly in all-encompassing blackness, like a withered leaf on a dark autumnal night tossed by wind and rain. I tried but failed, I think, miserably, like the friends of Job." The reference to the friends of Job may also indicate that the metaphysical explanation of evil did not bring solace to biblical man either.

8 *Fate and Destiny*, trans. Lawrence Kaplan (Hoboken, 2000), 8. Henceforth I shall refer to this by the more familiar Hebrew title, *Kol Dodi Dofek*. For the history of this work and its various translations, see Chap. 25, For Further Reference, #1.

Indeed, this is the way of Halakhah: not to speculate about insoluble questions or tensions, but to provide a means of living with them.[9]

The Halakhic Response

What response, then, does Halakhah demand of suffering man? In a nutshell, the halakhic response is *repentance*: When faced with suffering, one should choose to utilize this painful experience as a catalyst for self-improvement or self-creation.[10] Changing oneself from an object into a subject – or, as the Rav puts it in *Kol Dodi Dofek*, from a person of fate to one of destiny – is perhaps the central theme in his philosophy, and what he sees as the central thrust of the *mitzvot*.[11] God commands man to create himself in the image of his own ideal personality. Instead of being buffeted by external forces in random directions and having one's personality shaped passively and unthinkingly (fate), one should chart the course of his development and use his circumstances to reach that destination (destiny).

In *Kol Dodi Dofek*, the Rav rejects the metaphysical approach to evil entirely, going so far as to call it "self-deception" (4). This unequivocal rejection is quite bold, for the metaphysical approach to evil was a staple of Jewish philosophical and mystical thought for generations! The Rav was aware of this, and in two other major treatments of the problem of evil – "A Halakhic Approach to Suffering" and "Out of the Whirlwind"[12] – he gives the metaphysical approach its due by acknowledging that there are indeed two complementary dimensions to the Jewish approach to evil: the metaphysical-theoretical and the halakhic-practical.[13] Yet even in these essays, it is clear

---

9 See Chap. 3, pp. 56–57 above.

10 It is important to note that the Rav is *not* saying that a specific sin or shortcoming caused suffering to befall one, and therefore one should repent for that specific sin. Absent prophecy, such knowledge of direct cause and effect, he believes, is beyond human capacity. Rather, he is saying that since suffering – whatever its cause may be – has shaken one out of one's routine, one should utilize the opportunity to consider ways of self-improvement. This is not a *causal* argument but a *normative* one.

11 See our discussion in Chap. 22 above.

12 Both of these essays appear in the volume *Out of the Whirlwind*, 86–115 and 116–50 respectively.

13 In "A Halakhic Approach to Suffering," the Rav terms these two dimensions "thematic" and "topical," deriving from the Greek words for root (*theme*) and surface (*topos*). In other words, a theoretical approach aims to find the root of the matter, while a practical approach remains on the surface, not bothering to delve into deeper dimensions. In "Out of the Whirlwind," the Rav (somewhat counterintuitively) calls the two dimensions "cosmic" and "covenantal," for within the framework of the created world, one seeks understanding, while within the framework of

that his heart is with the active "halakhic" approach. In fact, when the Rav summarized one of his lectures on this subject, he completely omitted any mention of the metaphysical approach. This summary is worthy of examination for its succinct presentation of the Rav's major arguments:

> The gist of my discourse was that Judaism did not approach the problem of evil under the speculative-metaphysical aspect. For such an inquiry would be a futile undertaking. As long as the human mind is unable to embrace creation in its entirety and to gain an insight into the very essence and purposiveness of being as such it would not succeed in its attempt to resolve the dilemma of evil ... Therefore, Judaism has recommended that the metaphysical inquiry be replaced by the halakhic ethical gesture. Man should not ask: Why evil? He should rather raise the question: What am I supposed to do if confronted with evil; how should I behave vis-à-vis evil? The latter is a powerful challenge to man and it is the duty of man to meet this challenge boldly and courageously. Suffering, in the opinion of Judaism, must not be purposeless, wasted. Out of suffering must emerge the ethical norm, the call for repentance, for self-elevation. Judaism wants to convert the passional,[14] frustrating experience into an integrating, cleansing and redeeming factor.
>
> Man was summoned to defy evil and try to eliminate it. However, if he fails temporarily to defeat evil he must see to it that the confrontation be a courageous one, heroic and useful. In a word, instead of philosophizing about the nature of evil within the framework of a theodicy, Judaism wants man to fight it relentlessly and to convert it into a constructive force.[15]

In this summary, as in his essays, the Rav presents two "halakhic" responses to evil.

First, man must actively combat evil and try to eliminate it. God gave him the talents and abilities to fight both natural and human causes of suffering – such as disease, famine, war, poverty and oppression – and he must make full use of them.

Second, suffering should be a spur "for repentance, for self-elevation," thereby allowing the suffering to be converted into "an integrating, cleansing and redeeming factor." Clearly, suffering shakes people out of their complacency and routine. Yet how, exactly, can they utilize the experience of suffering to elevate and cleanse themselves? The Rav offers three lessons of suffering, to which we will devote the rest of this chapter.

---

the covenant, one seeks to know how to act. (The Rav sometimes uses the word "apocalyptic" instead of "covenantal," since apocalypse means revelation.)

14 "Passional" means "relating to suffering."

15 *Community, Covenant and Commitment*, 331–32.

Empathy

According to the Rav's compelling reading of the story of Job in *Kol Dodi Dofek*, the major lesson of suffering is empathy and solidarity with one's fellow human being. Initially, Job is an upright and God-fearing man, yet concerned only with himself and his family. Every time his children gathered for a feast, he "rose up early in the morning, and offered burnt-offerings according to the number of them all; for Job said: It may be that my sons have sinned, and blasphemed God in their hearts" (1:5). *Hazal* sharpen this perception by suggesting, for example, that Job was an advisor to Pharaoh, and remained silent when another advisor suggested casting Jewish boys into the Nile (*Sotah* 11a). Since the biblical text does not tell us when Job lived, the Gemara (*Bava Batra* 15a–b) lists a number of possibilities;[16] the Rav notes that these were all destiny-charged moments in the struggle for Jewish survival, yet Job did not lift a finger to help the Jewish people.

After Job is struck with tragedy, he bemoans his fate and questions God's justice. His friends gather to comfort him and try in various ways to justify God's actions. Eventually, God speaks to Job out of the whirlwind, informing him that he will never understand the metaphysics of suffering: "Who is this that darkens counsel by words without knowledge? . . . Where were you when I laid the foundations of the earth?" (38:2, 4). Job acknowledges his limitations: "Therefore I have uttered that which I did not understand; things too wonderful for me, which I knew not" (42:3). Yet even if Job does not understand the reason for his suffering, he does learn how to identify with the pain of his fellow sufferers, how to feel fraternity with the broader community, and how to respond to their suffering with *hesed* and concern. It is precisely when Job discovers empathy – thereby reversing the self-centered piety he had displayed at the book's opening – that the turning point occurs: "And the Lord restored the fortunes of Job, *when he prayed for his friends*" (42:10).

Awakening from Illusions of Immortality

While the Rav presents the first lesson of suffering (namely, empathy) in terms of his reading of Job, he draws powerfully on his own experience in presenting the other two lessons. In 1959, Rav Soloveitchik was diagnosed

---

16 For example, various opinions suggest that he was a contemporary of Jacob, Joseph or Ezra. The Gemara also cites an opinion, not mentioned by the Rav, that Job "never existed, but is a parable."

with cancer and had to undergo risky surgery.[17] The operation, to his and our good fortune, was successful. During several months of recovery, he had occasion to reflect on his experience, drawing from it a number of lessons that he put into writing and discussed in a closed forum in May 1960. These reflections remained concealed in manuscript for decades until their posthumous publication in 2003 in the title essay of his volume *Out of the Whirlwind*.

In this essay, the Rav specifies two additional ways that suffering can be utilized to purify the human personality. First, the confrontation with nihility, with the reality of one's own end, should shock a person out of his illusions of immortality. Although everyone knows intellectually that he will die, seldom do people internalize this fact. Consequently, their desires and frustrations assume overblown proportions. When people truly grasp their own mortality, they gain a truer perspective on life, relieving them of petty worries and anxieties and allowing them to focus on what is truly significant.

> Whenever I started to think of death [before my illness], my thoughts were dashed back and they returned to their ordinary objective, to life . . . Then sickness initiated me into the secret of non-being. I suddenly ceased to be immortal; I became a mortal being.
>
> The night preceding my operation I prayed to God and beseeched Him to spare me. I did not ask for too much. All I wanted was that He should make it possible for me to attend my daughter's wedding, which was postponed on account of my illness – a very modest wish in comparison with my insane claims to life prior to my sickness. The fantastic flights of human foolishness and egocentrism were distant from me that night.
>
> However, this "fall" from the heights of an illusory immortality into the valley of finitude was the greatest achievement of the long hours of anxiety and uncertainty. Fundamentally, this change was not an act of falling but one of rising toward a new existential awareness which embraces both man's tragedy and his glory, in all its ambivalence and paradoxality. I stopped perceiving myself in categories of eternity . . . A more logical self substitutes himself for a self who was intoxicated to the extent of insanity with the vision of being . . .
>
> When one's perspective is shifted from the illusion of eternity to the reality of temporality, one finds peace of mind and relief from other worries, from his petty fears and from absurd stresses and nonsensical nightmares (*Out of the Whirlwind*, 131–32).

Furthermore, when a person becomes aware that he is mortal and has a limited time on earth, this awakens his time-awareness and sensitizes him to the value of each passing moment. This newfound awareness requires one to

---

17 See Chap. 1, pp. 32–33 above.

assess what he wants to accomplish in his remaining time, to clarify to himself his unique role in the world, to listen for God's summons and to determine the mission that only he can fulfill.

> When we experience the swing back from an illusory eternity to a temporal reality, a new category is discovered, namely, that of service . . . Our existence is not just a coincidence, a mechanical fact, a meaningless caprice on the part of nature or providence, but a meaningful assignment which abounds in re-sponsibility and commitment . . .
>
> Judaism believes that every individual is capable of qualifying himself for Divine service . . . Every person possesses something unique, by virtue of which he differs from the thou, making him or her irreplaceable and indis-pensable – the inner worth of a one-timely, unique, never-to-be-duplicated existence, which can and must serve God by self-involvement in the drama of redemption at all levels. This is Judaic humanism, or Judaic democracy . . .
>
> If one lives in an illusory eternity, he may miss the call; he may not hear the voice which addresses itself to him; he may not realize that God Himself turns to him and summons him to His service. For in eternity nothing passes, nothing is lost; there is no time which lies behind us; everything persists and endures. There is eternal repetition. Yet if the time awareness is awakened in me, . . . I [may] realize that I have missed the call, that I am late for the execu-tion of my task, for the fulfillment of my mission. I also begin to comprehend the responsibility which my time-experience entails, the norm of vigilance and alertness every moment, since the call comes through often, at very short intervals. I anticipate the future with trepidation and anxiety, because it is the time in which I may act and serve. Every fraction of the infinite stream of time becomes precious. For this moment I am alive and capable of action; what will happen the next minute I do not know.
>
> . . . Judaism believes that each person has a fixed place in creation. If I find myself thrust in here and now, it is because God thinks that I can act here and now efficiently. If I had been born a hundred years ago or if I would come into this world a century later, my contribution as a servant would be nil. God wills me to act right here and now (*Out of the Whirlwind*, 147–49).[18]

The Sufferer's Loneliness

In "Out of the Whirlwind," the Rav specifies a further way that one can uti-lize the trauma of suffering to elevate and purify one's personality, thereby converting the ordeal into a redemptive force. In addition to conveying the awareness of mortality, suffering opens the individual to the experience of

---

18 See For Further Reference, #4.

loneliness. The person who suffers feels singled out from the crowd and cut loose from his social moorings.

> When the blow strikes, the first question which pops up upon the lips of the sufferer is: Why me? Why should I be different from others? Why was I selected to explore the valley of sorrow? A feeling of envy fills out the heart of the afflicted. He envies everybody, pauper and prince, young and old. They were spared, while I was picked out.
>
> When I eulogized my uncle, R. Velvel Soloveitchik, *zt"l*, in the auditorium of Yeshiva University while knowing of my affliction, one nagging thought assailed my mind. All these thousands of people are healthy and expect to live a long and happy life, whereas I am not certain that I will be able to accompany my daughter to the wedding canopy. While these thoughts are passing through one's mind with the speed of lightning, one feels forsaken, forlorn and lonely. I am different; I have met with a strange destiny. No one else is like me (ibid., p. 133).

On the eve of his operation, the Rav recounts, he felt alienated even from those who were closest to him. He alone faced death, and they could not participate in that confrontation. Only then did he comprehend the meaning of the verse, "When my father and my mother forsake me, the Lord will take me up" (Ps. 27:10).

> I had never understood this verse . . . Yet in certain situations, one is cut off even from his parents or his beloved wife and children. Community life, togetherness, is always imbued with the spirit of cooperation, of mutual help and protection. Suddenly one realizes that there is no help which his loved ones are able to extend to him. They are onlookers who watch a drama unfolding itself with unalterable speed. They are not involved in it . . . I stand before God; no one else is beside me (ibid., 134).

Yet, when he grasped that his dependence on other people and his connections to them – no matter how strong and ennobling – are ultimately limited, the Rav experienced an overpowering feeling of absolute, unrestricted and solitary connection to God. Therefore, he concludes, "A lonely being meeting the loneliest Being in utter seclusion is a traumatic but also a great experience" (ibid.).

Utilizing the Tragic

For the Rav, repentance means self-creation: not mere "spiritual maintenance" or correction of faults, but rather converting oneself from a passive object into an active subject and remaking one's personality. In *Kol Dodi Dofek* and "Out of the Whirlwind," he suggests three lessons of suffering – empathy, mortality and loneliness – that can lead to this transformation and elevation of the self.

People have an understandable tendency to try to bury the experience of suffering and repress it from their consciousness. However, such repression would be doubly tragic, for in that case not only did one suffer, but one then "wasted" this potentially redemptive experience. If a person can integrate the experience and lessons of suffering into his selfhood, he thereby responds actively and constructively to his misfortune. He draws out its redemptive power, bringing about moral and religious growth, increased closeness to the divine, and a heightened sense of personal mission. Hence, the Rav concludes that even if the period of one's travail has passed, the experience and its lessons "must not be forgotten" (ibid.).

FOR FURTHER REFERENCE

1. **Theodicy in Jewish thought:** For a brief and engaging survey, see Shalom Rosenberg, *Good and Evil in Jewish Thought* (Tel Aviv, 1989).

2. **The Rambam's approach to evil:** We saw above (p. 249) that in the *Guide* the Rambam offers a metaphysical explanation of evil as an illusion. Yet in his *Mishneh Torah*, the Rambam advocates repentance as a halakhic response to evil:

   > Whoever does not mourn, as enjoined by the sages, is hard-hearted. Rather, one should fear, worry, investigate his conduct and repent. If one of a company dies, all the members thereof should worry; during the first three days of mourning, one should think of himself as if a sword is resting upon his neck . . . Reflections of this sort should prepare him, and he will repent and bestir himself from his slumber, as it says, "You have stricken them, but they were not affected; [You have consumed them, but they have refused to receive correction; they have made their faces harder than a rock; they have refused to return]" (Jer. 5:3) – from here we learn that one should awaken and be moved [when confronted with suffering] (*Hilkhot Avel* 13:12).

   (Oddly, the Rav does not quote this Rambam, even though it would seem to bolster his argument. Elsewhere, however, he does quote *Hilkhot Ta'aniyot* 1:1–3, which speaks of prayer and repentance as mandated responses to communal distress.)

   How can the Rambam adopt such different approaches in the *Mishneh Torah* and in the *Guide of the Perplexed*? One explanation might lie in the Rav's presentation of two dimensions of the Jewish response to evil, as explained above. Additionally, in *The Halakhic Mind* (92–98), the Rav elaborates on the differing methodologies for finding religious meaning that the Rambam employs in his two masterpieces. For a broader treatment of the differences between the *Mishneh Torah* and the *Guide*, see R. Isadore Twersky, *Introduction to the Code of Maimonides* (New Haven, 1980), 430–47.

3. **Suffering in the Rav's thought:** For analyses of the Rav's approach, see David Shatz, "'From the Depths I Have Called to You': Jewish Reflections on September 11th and Contemporary Terrorism," and Moshe Sokol, "Is There a 'Halakhic' Response to the Problem of Evil?", in Roberta Rosenberg Farber and Simcha Fishbane, eds., *Jewish Studies in Violence* (Lanham, MD, 2006), 195–225 and 227–38.

4. **The concepts of service and divine mission:** For more on the concept of service, see the end of Chapter 22 above, as well as "The Doctrine of Assignment," in *Derashot Harav*, 45–75. For broader reflections on the concepts of leadership and mission, see *The Emergence of Ethical Man*, 183–92; *Festival of Freedom*, 149–59; and *Days of Deliverance*, 70–78.

Chapter 24

Suffering: Halakhah and the Human Condition

In the previous chapter, we saw that the Rav derived two crucial lessons from his brush with death. This might lead one to think that these lessons can be learned and applied only under the most dire and tragic of circumstances. I believe, however, that the Rav meant for these same messages to be relevant even in less extreme situations, and therefore we can hear their echoes in other teachings of the Rav and his disciples.

Yamim Nora'im and the Lessons of Suffering

The lessons of suffering are especially relevant to our annual encounter with judgment, namely, the High Holidays, when God decides our fate for the coming year: "On Rosh Hashanah they are inscribed, and on Yom Kippur they are sealed."

For example, upon learning that he had cancer, Rav Soloveitchik experienced a sharp sense of loneliness that dissolved the social threads connecting him to others. However, this radical loneliness brought him to stand wholeheartedly before God. This idea can help explain a custom which has baffled many. Why do we commence Yom Kippur, the most exalted and awesome day of the year, with a prosaic declaration of renunciation of vows, *Kol Nidrei*? The incongruousness of this situation led some, such as Rav Samson Raphael Hirsch, to go so far as to eliminate the recitation of *Kol Nidrei* in their congregations.

The Rav's lesson of loneliness clarifies the concept behind *Kol Nidrei* and grants its recitation new significance. On Yom Kippur, one comes before God and pleads for continued life. Yet, what right does a person have to ask God to grant him life if he has not committed himself wholly and unreservedly to

God's service? If one is bound by all sorts of extraneous commitments and obligations, if one is in thrall to one's desires and ambitions, if one is enslaved by public opinion, then one still serves "foreign gods" and cannot stand before God. Only as free and unencumbered beings can we dedicate ourselves exclusively to His service. Therefore, we cannot enter the Day of Judgment without declaring that all our oaths and obligations are null and void, that there are no claims upon us other than God's. We accomplish this through the solemn declaration of *Kol Nidrei*.[1]

The second dimension that suffering opens to us is what the Rav calls "non-being," or mortality. Once a person stops perceiving himself as immortal, he can assess his unique mission in life and take stock of where he stands in relation to its fulfillment. While Rav Soloveitchik discusses this stock-taking in the context of the traumatic encounter with death, Rav Aharon Lichtenstein finds it embedded in our annual calendar. If one must repent year-round for any sin he has committed, Rav Lichtenstein asks, what need is there for a special *mitzvah* of *teshuvah* during the Ten Days of Repentance? Rav Lichtenstein suggests that "while generally one relates to specific sins within the context of his spiritual existence, between Rosh Hashanah and Yom Kippur the obligation is to examine that existence proper."[2]

In other words, one generally proceeds through life operating with certain goals and values, and along the way one tries to mend any personal flaws one may discover. Yet, one does not normally bring into question the very premises and assumptions guiding one's path. However, the Ten Days of Repentance demand precisely this kind of fundamental reassessment. Instead of focusing only on specific sins, one must reconsider the entire direction of one's life.

Instead of waiting for misfortune to prompt a broad examination of one's goals and aspirations, Rav Lichtenstein suggests that one use the *Yamim Nora'im* as an opportunity for radical repentance.[3] Rav Soloveitchik, on the other hand, believes that it is suffering that forces a person to assess his

---

1 See *On Repentance*, 244–45.

2 Rav Aharon Lichtenstein, *By His Light: Character and Values in the Service of God*, ed. Reuven Ziegler (Jersey City, 2003), 223.

3 It is "radical" in that it relates to the root (*radix* in Latin) of one's very existence. Note that in the lengthy n. 3 of *Kol Dodi Dofek* (75–79), Rav Soloveitchik likewise links the repentance prompted by suffering to that required by Yom Kippur, albeit in a somewhat different fashion. He suggests that while one must always repent for sins of which one is aware, both suffering and Yom Kippur mandate that one seek out hidden and unknown sins in an effort to reshape and purify one's personality. This is not quite the far-reaching questioning of premises and goals delineated by Rav Lichtenstein, but it is still much broader than the standard form of repentance.

mission in life. However, the Rav's definition of "suffering" is not limited to its most acute forms, such as pain or death. Because of his expansive definition of suffering, which we shall soon explore, his teachings on this subject extend to the *Yamim Nora'im*, and even beyond them into broader realms of human experience.

Depth Crisis

Admittedly, "Out of the Whirlwind" assigns suffering a surprisingly significant role in religious life, perhaps one of the strongest found in Jewish thought. However, if we read "Out of Whirlwind" in the context of the two essays that follow it in the book, which were originally part of the same series of lectures,[4] we get a more moderate impression of Rav Soloveitchik's views on this subject. According to the Rav, "depth crisis"[5] is also a form of suffering, and ideally *everyone* should come to be aware of the "depth crisis" underlying his or her own existence.

Surface crisis, such as a disease or a natural disaster, is visible to all and is therefore an obvious form of suffering. Depth crisis is a private and unique experience, which the mature personality must voluntarily choose to confront. This crisis stems from the realization of our finitude: "The incompleteness of our existential experience at all levels is rooted in the nature and destiny of man. He is a creature and, as such, a part of a finite reality – and finitude is incomplete, deficient and impregnated with paradoxes and absurdities" (*Out of the Whirlwind*, 158).[6] Everything we desire is ultimately bounded by its antithesis, such that none of our victories is complete: life is bounded by death, knowledge by ignorance, beauty by ugliness and morality by evil.

Though we can never attain wholeness, we can relieve ourselves of the burden of despair brought on by this realization "by consecrating this incompleteness as an offering to God" (ibid.). This "offering" can be accomplished in two ways: "first, at the subjective experiential level, as a crisis awareness spelled out in prayer; second, at the objective level, as a sacrificial decision" (159). The former, an acceptance of our utter dependence on God, was

---

4 From 1957 to 1960, Rav Soloveitchik gave a series of over forty lectures, entitled "Judaism's Conception of Man," to an interdenominational group of Jewish clergy under the auspices of the New York Board of Rabbis and the National Institute of Mental Health. "The Crisis of Human Finitude" and "A Theory of Emotions" were lectures delivered near the beginning of the series, while "Out of the Whirlwind" was the series' conclusion.

5 We discussed "depth crisis" briefly in Chap. 21 above (p. 225).

6 All subsequent page references in this chapter will be to *Out of the Whirlwind*, unless specified otherwise.

discussed in our chapter on prayer and sacrifice. The latter refers to our accepting divinely-mandated limitations, thereby hallowing all our actions – a theme we developed in our discussion of "Catharsis."

Surface crisis and depth crisis are not the only sources of human suffering. Any time one's will is thwarted, the Rav believes, the sense of frustration and limitation one experiences is a form of suffering. Therefore, due to the self-restraint and the sacrifice demanded by religion, the Rav goes so far as to state that "The religious act is essentially an experience of suffering"![7] Religion means placing God's will before one's own, or accepting defeat by God.[8] In light of this, it is clear why the Rav says, "I am repulsed by all those sermons revolving around a single topic: observing the commandments is good for one's digestion, restful sleep, domestic harmony and social standing."[9] Although *mitzvah* observance may indeed benefit us, it is first and foremost an act of obedience to God and a response to His summons.[10]

The Dialectical Experience of Life

The mature decision to confront the depth crisis implicit in human existence can lead one to "the dialectical experience of life."[11] The Rav uses the word "experience" in a very specific way, distinguishing it from a feeling or mood. For example, he says that the depth crisis is not "a *mood* of defeat and forlornness, but . . . an *experience* in which the affirmation is indissolubly bound up with the negation, the thesis with the antithesis" (167). A feeling or mood

---

7 "*Al Ahavat ha-Torah*," 427. The Rav here is describing the essence of religion as he understands it. Not all religions would necessarily agree.

8 As we shall see in *U-Vikkashtem mi-Sham*, at the very highest reaches of religious attainment one may experience a sense of identification with God's will instead of defeat by God's will. But this level is attained by few. Most people experience a dichotomy between their own will and God's, and they must choose which one to follow.

9 "*Al Ahavat ha-Torah*," 427.

10 In *Out of the Whirlwind*, 113–15, the Rav notes an important and ironic benefit of regarding *mitzvot* as a way of serving God and not a way of serving ourselves. By training us to take defeat at our own hands (i.e., to thwart our wills in response to God's will), *mitzvah* observance prepares us to take externally-imposed defeat with dignity. "[I]f man is trained gradually, day by day, to take defeat at his own hands in small matters, in his daily routine, in his habits of eating, in his sex life, in his public life . . . then, I believe, when faced with evil and adversity and when he finds himself in crisis, he will manage to bear his problem with dignity" (114–15). While in *Kol Dodi Dofek* and elsewhere the Rav discusses the Halakhah's view of how one should *respond* to suffering, here he discusses how halakhic living *prepares* one to cope with suffering.

11 The meaning of this phrase will become clear over the next few pages.

is an immediate, almost instinctive, emotional reaction to some stimulus. It lacks "intellectual insight, intuition of higher values and direction of spiritual energy into the right channels" (168). An experience, on the other hand, is consciously chosen and constructed out of emotions that one deems desirable and appropriate. One can take a mass of fleeting, disorganized and amorphous moods, winnow out the disjunctive ones, cast the remaining ones into a broader framework of values, and mold them into a great experience that possesses both constancy and direction.

Accordingly, notes the Rav, Judaism does not value religious moodiness, such as sudden conversion. Instead, it views the religious experience as the product of a long inner development.

> Judaism is interested in a religious experience which mirrors the genuine personality, the most profound movements of the soul, an experience which is the result of true involvement in the transcendental gesture, of slow, painstaking self-reckoning and self-actualization, of deep intuition of eternal values and comprehension of human destiny and paradox, of miserable sleepless nights of dreary doubt and skepticism and of glorious days of inspiration, of being torn by opposing forces and winning freedom (169).

Hence, Judaism does not try to allure man with charming externals – darkened naves, stained glass, organ music – for these would produce merely a fleeting mood.

While moods are subject to the principle of contradiction – e.g., a person cannot feel both a happy and a sad mood at the same time – an experience, when properly constructed, can contain dichotomies. This is what enables the dialectical experience advocated by Judaism. Asking, like the *Midrash Tehillim* (102:1), how David can call himself both king and pauper in the Psalms, Rav Soloveitchik answers that David's existential awareness encompassed both poles of existence: victory and defeat, majesty and humility.

> The experience of life is ambivalent because existence itself abounds in dichotomies and contradictions . . . The existential awareness must not mirror ideal conditions, but everyday realities. Therefore, it should not reflect only one or two of the multiple aspects, but the total adventure of man, which contains both affirmation and negation, triumph and loss (176).

Everyone, indeed, must be honest and mature enough to admit that he is both king and pauper, magnificent and abject, self-transcendent and finite. This is one major aspect of "the dialectical experience of life."

Benefits of the Dialectical Awareness

In "A Theory of Emotions," the final essay of *Out of the Whirlwind*, Rav Soloveitchik explains the process by which one can subject one's emotions to critical review and thereby decide whether to incorporate them into one's existential experience. While I do not want to delve into the mechanics of this process here,[12] I do want to note the psychological consequences of the dialectical awareness advocated by Judaism. The view of man as both king and pauper is not only more realistic than the alternative one-sided views, but also more beneficial to man as a spiritual being. Therefore, in enumerating the consequences of this awareness, we will come to understand some of the reasons why dialectic plays such a central role in the Rav's thought.

First, by advocating a broad and dialectical vision of reality, Judaism promotes *the totality of emotional life*. This means that we must not absolutize and prioritize one emotion and disqualify all others. Christianity, for instance, declares that it bases itself solely on love, but this curtailment of emotional activity both impoverishes human creativity and distorts one's view of the world. Life, according to Judaism, is too rich and multifaceted to be captured by a single emotional response; as the Rav puts it, "A changing destiny cannot be appreciated by an unalterable emotional activity" (186). Hate is sometimes as necessary as love – for example, when the need arises to fight entrenched evil.

Second, when filtered through our dialectical awareness, each of our emotional experiences takes into account past and future, and thereby merges with the state of mind antithetical to it. The Rav refers to this as *the continuity of emotional experience*. For example, at the level of uncritical emotion, one reacts to a wedding celebration with unrestrained joy. Yet when placed in a critical and all-encompassing life-perspective, "the unchecked reverberating joy passes gradually into calm and quiet, touched with that solemn melancholy which befits one attending a great festival at which two destinies merge into one" (193). This more measured experience is called forth by the breaking of the glass, which Tosafot (*Berakhot* 31a, s.v. *aytei*) attribute not to remembrance of the destruction of Jerusalem, but rather to the principle of "Rejoice with trembling" (Ps. 2:11) set forth in the following Gemara:

> What is meant by "rejoice with trembling?" Rabbi Ada the son of Matna said in the name of Rav: In the place where there is rejoicing, there should also be trembling . . .

---

12 See For Further Reference, #2.

Rabbi Ashi made a marriage feast for his son. He saw that the rabbis were growing very merry, so he brought a cup of white crystal and broke it before them, and they became serious.

The rabbis said to Rabbi Hamnuna Zuti at the wedding of Mar the son of Ravina: Please sing us something. He said to them: "Woe unto us, for we are to die; woe unto us, for we are to die . . ." (*Berakhot* 30b–31a).

Marriage represents not only the "sacred union of two strangers," but also their mutual attempt "to combat a dreaded fiend – death" by perpetuating their existences through a child. It is thus inseparable from an awareness of man's tragic destiny; hence Rabbi Hamnuna Zuti's perplexing refrain, "Woe unto us, for we are to die."

Note, however, that Halakhah does not reject raw emotions, emotions that have not yet been subjected to critical review. In fact, Halakhah demands that we rejoice with the bride and groom in an exuberant and unrestrained fashion.[13] Yet, Halakhah also desires that this joyfulness be juxtaposed with its opposite, a solemn consciousness of human destiny. In this manner, we place each of our emotions in a broader and more meaningful framework, thereby creating a balanced and critical experiential awareness.[14]

Hesed: Transcending Emotional Egotism

The third, and main, benefit of Judaism's dialectical approach to emotion is ethical. The dialectical awareness directs our attention not only to past and future events, and not only to emotions antithetical to those we are experiencing now, but also to other people. Feelings tend to focus on oneself: How do *I* feel about this, what does this mean to *me*? Judaism believes that emotions must leave their egotistic shell. For example, it often happens that when a young person falls in love, he will focus all his attention and affection on his beloved, to the exclusion of everyone else – even (or especially) his parents. Judaism believes that, instead of raising barriers, love should tear them down, enabling the young person to understand how much and how unselfishly his parents love him, and how important it is for him to reciprocate that love. The way to accomplish this is through the critical evaluation of emotions, which

---

13 See, e.g., *Ketubot* 17a.

14 In our examination of *aninut* and *avelut* below, we will encounter another instance where Halakhah finds a place for both uncritical and critical emotions, or raw and filtered emotions, each at its appropriate time.

shifts emotion into the perspective of one's total life experience and points one's attention to the feelings of others.

The Torah thus summons the "I" to recognize the "thou" when the "I" is least inclined to do so. For example, although a farmer feels secure and joyful at the conclusion of a successful harvest, this should not lead him to self-centered satisfaction, but rather to a desire to share his bounty with those less fortunate. Precisely when he wishes to shut himself up with his family and celebrate the harvest festival, the Torah calls upon him to open his doors to the widow and orphan, to offer portions of his harvest to the *kohanim, levi-yyim* and the indigent, and, most importantly, to open his heart to them.

> ... Judaism saw to it that this festival gladness and enthusiasm would not fortify man in his separateness and existential isolation but, on the contrary, would bring him into closer contact with his fellow man. Sympathy – which is intrinsically an experience of pain, the apprehension of misery, destitution and want – was infused into the glorious joy. Only through the critical interpretation, interweaving the antithesis into the experience-texture, does joy ascend from merely selfish, instinctive, harvest merrymaking into the higher, humane, existential sphere, where emotions are provided with values, and joy is socialized as a service to one's fellow man (205–06).

The Rav broadens his point to encompass a central Jewish concept. "The critical interpretation of our emotional experiences and their ethicization expresses the most uniquely Jewish ethical idea, namely, *hesed*" (207). In Hebrew, *hesed* denotes excess or overflow. When raised to the existential level, this means opening a closed-in existence, or transcending the bounds of the self. While the norm of *hesed* is demonstrated first via deeds, it also extends to cultivating an all-inclusive awareness, sharing others' feelings and sharing one's own feelings with others – in other words, expanding one's own existential sphere. The Rambam (*Guide* II:37) bases both his theory of education and of prophecy on this notion: the teacher or prophet is impelled by an inner drive to impart his message; his personality is so full that it overflows to others. In Jeremiah's powerful words, "For the word of the Lord . . . was in my heart as a burning fire, enclosed in my bones; and I wearied myself to keep it in, but did not prevail" (20:8–9).

However, prior to such reaching out, one must retreat within oneself to perfect one's personality, contracting one's egotistic existence and moving one's ego from the center of reality to its periphery. Only then will *hesed* express regard for others and not just self-glorification. This movement of contraction and expansion is "the great ethical drama which the dialectical experience unfolds before us" (214).

Two Types of Mourning

Several subjects we have examined – suffering, dialectical emotion and repentance – all come together in the Rav's discussion of the two phases of
mourning in the first essay of *Out of the Whirlwind*, "*Aninut* and *Avelut*." A
mourner is in a state of *aninut* from the moment of his relative's death until
the latter's burial. During this period, the mourner is exempt from all halakhic
obligations unconnected with the funeral arrangements, such as prayer, *tefillin*, etc. *Avelut*, on the other hand, which commences after burial, is marked
by a sudden imposition of halakhic obligations.

The Rav opens his discussion of these two stages with a characteristic
question: "What is the halakhic and the experiential distinction between these
two phases of mourning?" (1). The human psyche confronts the world with
different, even contradictory, perceptions. Halakhah, insistent on a truthful
and realistic appreciation of these human reactions, gives expression to all
of them. An understanding of Halakhah, then, requires an understanding of
human nature.

Allegiance to Halakhah requires an appreciation of human self-worth, an
awareness of the significance and importance of one's actions. A confrontation with death, however, undermines that self-conception. How can our existence have significance over that of the animals when death makes us realize
that we are just another one of the living creatures, like the beasts in the field,
facing the same cruel end?

> In a word, man's initial response to death is saturated with malice and ridicule
> toward himself. He tells himself: If death is the final destiny of all men, if
> everything human terminates in the narrow, dark grave, then why be a man at
> all? Then why make the pretense of being the choicest of all creatures? Then
> why lay claim to singularity and *imago Dei* (the divine image)? Then why be
> committed, why carry the human-moral load? (2).

The Halakhah does not try to gloss over these "crazy" torturing thoughts
and doubts that contradict the basic halakhic doctrine of man's election as
a singular being. Instead, it insists on giving expression to "the spontaneous
human reaction to death." For the Rav, the rule that the mourner at the initial
stage of *aninut* is exempt from performing positive *mitzvot* flows naturally
from the realities of life, not only from the exegesis of texts.

If the exemption from *mitzvot* is a natural reaction, the immediate reim-
position of obligation when *aninut* abruptly comes to an end with burial is an
imposed reaction. Free will extends not only to actions, says the Rav, but to
thoughts and feelings as well. Just as the Halakhah demands that people give

expression to their devastation when they confront the inevitable end of life, so too it demands that they give expression to their strength and their ability to triumph in their encounter with the "self-devastating black despair" that accompanies the "hideous darkness" of a confrontation with death.

In the stage of *aninut*, man mourns "in total darkness and confusion," unable to acknowledge his greatness and chosenness. But after burial, in *ave-lut*, he mourns "in an enlightened mood" in which he can acknowledge his unique human status. This is not a return to the pre-*aninut* stage wherein man might have been oblivious to the possibility of the bottom falling out of the meaningfulness of life. Rather, "death gives man the opportunity to display greatness and to act heroically; to build even though he knows that he will not live to enjoy the sight of the magnificent edifice in whose construction he is engaged" (4). In lieu of the shock and despondency of *aninut*, man learns during *avelut* "to transcend his physical self and to identify with the time-less covenantal community. Death, the Halakhah warns the mourner, not only does not free man from his commitment but, on the contrary, enhances his role as a historic being and sensitizes his moral consciousness" (ibid.) – pre-cisely the lesson of suffering we saw in "Out of the Whirlwind." The mourner thereby transforms "despair into intelligent sadness, and self-negation into self-affirmation" (5).

The ceremonial turning point at which *aninut* becomes *avelut* is the re-cital of *Kaddish*. This prayer is a praise of God, an awareness that, far from being insignificant like the beasts of the field, man is important enough for God Himself to be concerned with his praise. Saying *Kaddish*, then, is a state-ment not only about the greatness of God, but about the greatness of man. "Through the *Kaddish* we hurl defiance at death and its fiendish conspiracy against man," as "grief asserts itself in the awareness of human greatness and human election" (ibid.).

We find here a classic example of the continuity of emotional experience, and of Halakhah's accommodation of both uncritical and critical emotion. *Aninut* represents raw emotion, focused only on the present and feeling only pain. *Avelut* marks the critical or filtered stage of mourning, where it is placed within a broader perspective; therefore, *avelut* incorporates elements of its antithetical emotions – consolation and hope. The latter do not replace grief, but rather interpenetrate with it to form a broader, more integrated experience.

The critical mourning awareness is also tied to repentance, and, indeed, many of the *shivah* prohibitions (such as those against washing, the use of cosmetics and ointments, wearing shoes and marital relations) are reminiscent of Yom Kippur. The act of mourning becomes an act of expiation. In both mourning and repentance, it is loss that makes us aware of what we had. The consequence of sin is God's departure from our lives; only then do we realize the opportunities lost and potential unfulfilled. The same holds true for the death of a loved one. "During the mourning stage we ask the questions we should have asked before: Who was he? Whom did we lose? His image fascinates us from afar, and we ask with guilt and regret the questions that are now overdue, the questions to which only our lives can provide the answers" (8).

These questions, again, connect us back to the lessons of suffering. By responding actively and self-critically to suffering, one may use the painful experience of loss as an engine for self-improvement and self-dedication. Thus, we can now understand the Rav's brief encapsulation of his view in another essay in *Out of the Whirlwind*, "Abraham Mourns Sarah":[15]

> Mourning, if observed with restraint and in compliance with the Halakhah, enhances the status of man. It is an experience of great dignity; it is a sacrificial act enlightening the sufferer as to the meaning of life as well as the destiny of mankind. This axiological critical analysis enriches his personality. It purges him of the ugly and contemptible in life (34).

Tragedy and Creativity

For all its focus on suffering, crisis and "the tragic destiny of man," Rav Soloveitchik's vision is not a pessimistic one. It proceeds from and affirms a sense of the value of each individual and the meaningfulness of his or her life. In fact, it is only in light of the meaningfulness of a person's life that the Rav pronounces death absurd by contrast. As the Rav frequently pointed out, the halakhic requirements of mourning and eulogizing are predicated upon a recognition of each person's uniqueness, for only this recognition permits a proper assessment of the irreplaceable loss we have suffered with his or her passing.[16] Studying Judaism's attitude towards mourning therefore enhances our esteem for man, notwithstanding his inevitable and tragic end. Furthermore, reflecting on one's mortality awakens a person's sensitivity to the flow of time, pressing him to ascertain his task in life and to strive to accomplish it.

The very act of creative confrontation with the subjects of mortality and human vulnerability can help one overcome his fear of them. In *Halakhic Man*, Rav Soloveitchik explains that by subjecting these topics to creative

---

15 Incidentally, the autobiographical undertones of this essay, written ten years after the death of Dr. Tonya Soloveitchik, are impossible to miss.

16 See, for example, the opening of Rav Soloveitchik's eulogy for R. Hayyim Heller in *Divrei Hagut ve-Ha'arakhah*, 137–142 (Hebrew); *Shiurei HaRav*, 46–50 (English).

analysis, by making them into materials for one's mind to act upon, one in effect becomes their master, and his fear of them dissipates. He relates that his grandfather, Rabbi Hayyim of Brisk, would overcome his dread of death by studying the laws of corpse defilement: "And these laws ... would calm the turbulence of his soul and would imbue it with a spirit of joy and gladness ... The act of objectification overcomes the subjective terror of death" (73). Analogously, the Rav continues, Tolstoy conquered his fear of death by "transforming death into an object of his artistic creativity" when writing *The Death of Ivan Illich* (154, n. 86). Rav Soloveitchik himself turned death into an object of his philosophical and halakhic creativity, thereby not only objectifying it, but using it positively as a spur to reflection and growth. Thus, the very study of the subjects of death and suffering can be a constructive, cathartic and redemptive act.[17]

---

17 Parts of this chapter are adapted from the introduction to *Out of the Whirlwind*, which I wrote together with the other editors of that volume.

For Further Reference

1. **Suffering in Jewish thought:** See R. Shalom Carmy, ed., *Jewish Perspectives on the Experience of Suffering* (Northvale, N.J., 1999).

2. **Critical review of emotions:** We saw in this chapter and in Chapter 6 that, according to Rav Soloveitchik, Judaism requires that man control his emotional life, integrating into his personality those emotions he finds worthy and rejecting those he finds unworthy. This does not require dampening his emotional responses, but rather approaching them with a critical eye. In "A Theory of Emotions," Rav Soloveitchik elaborates the criteria according to which one should evaluate the worthiness of his emotional responses.

   If I love my neighbor, that entails two components: first, an intellectual assertion that there exists a person I call my neighbor; second, a value judgment that this person is worthy of my love. (It is because of this second component that Rav Soloveitchik says, "Emotions are the media through which the value-universe opens up to us" [181], thus highlighting the importance of emotions and of the employment of our critical faculties with regard to them.) A worthy and character-building emotion would be one where both the cognitive and the value judgments are accurate. An unworthy and damaging emotion would be one generated by a false perception of reality (e.g., the object of my fear does not really exist) or by a mistaken value judgment (e.g., this person is really not worthy of my friendship). The worthiness of an emotion is to be assessed not by its intrinsic qualities, but by the context in which it arises.

   Far from being just a collection of fleeting moods, man's personality can have depth, wholeness and constancy if man remains ever mindful of the dialectical experience of life. Thus, by maintaining a critical attitude towards one's emotional responses and incorporating them into a broader perspective, one can shape them according to his values.

Section V

JEWISH HISTORY AND DESTINY:
KOL DODI DOFEK

Chapter 25

From the Holocaust to the State of Israel

Fate and Destiny

Kol Dodi Dofek, one of Rav Soloveitchik's best-known discourses, is often read for what it is not. Some study it as an example of "Holocaust theology"; however, it claims that a theological understanding of the Holocaust is neither possible nor desirable. Others, especially in Israel, celebrate it as a classic statement of Religious Zionism; yet its powerful affirmation of God's hand in the founding of the Jewish state can obscure the fact that its vision of Religious Zionism differs significantly from that espoused by most of its Israeli readers. Between the charged poles of the Holocaust and the State of Israel, one of its most innovative and important ideas – finding a place within a religious framework for secular Jewish identity – often gets lost. Nevertheless, within the essay's rich blend of genres – ranging from theoretical analysis, biblical exegesis and halakhic discourse to socio-political observation, personal confession and communal directive – a central theme emerges: the distinction between fate (*goral*) and destiny (*yi'ud*), and the role of each in Jewish communal life.

This distinction posits that there are two levels of human existence: fate, wherein man is a passive object, acted upon by external forces, his life not animated by meaning and lacking direction; and destiny, wherein man is an active subject, charting his course in accordance with values he has chosen, and imbuing his life with purpose and direction. "Man's task in the world," says the Rav, "is to transform fate into destiny; a passive existence into an active existence; an existence of compulsion, perplexity, and muteness into an existence replete with a powerful will, with resourcefulness, daring, and imagination" (6).[1] By doing so, "man becomes transformed into a partner with the Almighty" (ibid.).

In Chapters 23 and 24, we encountered the distinction between fate and destiny as applied to the individual. Instead of asking the passive and unanswerable "fate" question – "*Why* did this misfortune befall me?" – one should approach suffering from the point of view of "destiny," asking "*How* can I *respond* constructively to this misfortune?" and then using the suffering as a catalyst for moral and religious self-improvement. In a broader sense, the move from fate to destiny, from object to subject, underlies the Rav's entire doctrine of self-creation, which we explored at length in our chapters on prayer and repentance. Through these activities, one makes oneself into a new and better person by clarifying one's true needs and attempting to shape oneself according to the image of what one ideally should be.

In *Kol Dodi Dofek*, Rav Soloveitchik applies to the nation the categories we have seen developed with regard to the individual: self-creation, object and subject, fate and destiny. On a national level, however, we shall see that they take on a new twist, for "fate" is a given in Jewish communal existence and cannot be transcended.

Holocaust and Israel

Kol Dodi Dofek addresses two of the most momentous events in Jewish history: the Holocaust, in which a third of the Jewish people was systematically murdered, and the birth of the State of Israel, in which Jewish sovereignty was restored in the Land of Israel following nearly two thousand years of exile. When *Kol Dodi Dofek* was first delivered as a speech in 1956, these two events were still fresh in the minds of the listeners: the Holocaust had ended in 1945 and the State of Israel had been founded in 1948.

The proximity of these two overwhelming events almost begged one to connect them. At the extremes, some saw the connection in terms of strict causality. For example, the Satmar Rebbe believed that the Holocaust was a divine punishment for the sin of attempting to establish Jewish sovereignty before the coming of the Messiah, and the success of the Zionists in establishing the State of Israel was to be attributed to the *sitra ahra*, the metaphysical forces of evil.[2] At the opposite end, Rabbi Zvi Yehudah Kook believed that the Holocaust was divine "surgery" necessary to sever the Jews' connection

---

1 For bibliographical information on *Kol Dodi Dofek*, see For Further Reference, #1.
2 R. Yoel Teitelbaum, *Vayoel Moshe*, 2nd ed. (New York, 1961), 122–25.

to the Diaspora and bring them to the Land of Israel as part of an inexorable process of national revival and messianic redemption.[3]

Rav Soloveitchik does not provide causal explanations, nor does he offer metaphysical speculation as to the reasons God brought about these events.[4] In his view, the human's finite mind cannot fathom the ways of divine providence, and the only question one can and should ask oneself is how to respond to one's given circumstances. The Rav emphasizes that is it as important to respond properly to goodness as it is to evil. We must redeem our good fortune and not only our suffering:

> Judaism has deepened this concept [of using suffering to forge self-improvement] by combining the notion of the mending and elevation of suffering with that of the mending and elevation of divine loving-kindness, divine *hesed*. God's acts of *hesed*, Judaism declares, are not granted to man as a free gift. Rather, they impose obligations, make ethico-halakhic demands upon their beneficiary . . . The bestowal of good is always to be viewed as a conditional gift – a gift that must be returned – or as a temporary gift. When God endows a person with wealth, influence, and honor, the recipient must know how to use these boons, how to transform these precious gifts into fruitful, creative forces, how to share his joy and prominence with his fellows, how to take the divine *hesed* that flows toward him from its infinite, divine source and utilize it to perform, in turn, deeds of *hesed* for others (9–10).

Turning to his audience of American Orthodox Jews, and including himself in his rebuke, the Rav then asks: Did we respond properly when our brothers in Europe were in need? Given that we did not, have we learned anything from our failure? Now that God has provided us with a miraculous gift in the form of the State of Israel, will we again miss the moment and fail to respond? We cannot know why the Holocaust happened, the Rav says, but we

---

3 R. Zvi Yehudah Kook, *Sihot ha-Rav Zvi Yehudah al ha-Moadim*, vol. 1, ed. R. Shlomo Aviner (Jerusalem, 2006), 230–49. In English, see *Torat Eretz Yisrael: The Teachings of HaRav Tzvi Yehuda HaCohen Kook*, ed. R. David Samson (Jerusalem, 1991), 259–74. Regarding Satmar, R. Zvi Yehudah Kook, and the spectrum of Religious Zionist approaches to the connection between the Holocaust and the State of Israel, see For Further Reference, #2.

4 When Rav Soloveitchik refers to the Holocaust as "*hester panim*," the hiding of God's face (25, 29 and 35), I believe he is using this term to describe the way it is perceived and experienced by human beings, not as a theological explanation for divine inaction. Other thinkers, however, do use *hester panim* as a theological basis for understanding the Shoah. For example, see R. Eliezer Berkovits, *Faith after the Holocaust* (New York, 1973), 94ff., and R. Norman Lamm, "The Face of God," in *Theological and Halakhic Reflections on the Holocaust*, eds. R. Bernhard Rosenberg and R. Fred Heuman (Hoboken, 1992), 119–36.

can know what it demands of us: to help our fellow Jews wherever they may be, and to seize the opportunities God presents before us.

"My Beloved Knocks!"

The central image the Rav employs is drawn from the biblical Song of Songs. The maiden and her beloved, both lovesick, search for each other but are repeatedly frustrated. Traditionally, this poem's story line has been understood in two different ways: as an allegory for the relationship between the individual and God, or as an allegory for the relationship between the Jewish people and God.[5] *U-Vikkashtem mi-Sham* develops the former interpretation, while *Kol Dodi Dofek* develops the latter. As a consequence of their differing interpretations, *U-Vikkashtem mi-Sham* starts with the maiden's search for her beloved, while *Kol Dodi Dofek*, as its title indicates, focuses on the beloved's search for the maiden.

In *Kol Dodi Dofek*, the Rav emphasizes that we don't know why the Beloved hides (as in the Holocaust), but we do have to open the door when He knocks. Clearly, the Rav continues, the founding of the State of Israel is not a natural event. It is, in fact, a divine gift, a divine opportunity, the sound of God knocking at our door:

> Eight years ago [in 1948], in the midst of a night of terror filled with the horrors of Maidanek, Treblinka, and Buchenwald, in a night of gas chambers and crematoria, in a night of absolute divine self-concealment . . . – in that very night the Beloved appeared. "God who conceals Himself in His dazzling hiddenness" suddenly manifested Himself and began to knock at the tent of His despondent and disconsolate love, twisting convulsively on her bed, suffering the pains of hell. *As a result of the knocks on the door of the maiden, wrapped in mourning, the State of Israel was born!* (25).

God's knocks on the maiden's door – His summons to the Jewish people – were expressed in six significant and even miraculous aspects associated with the founding of the State of Israel.
1. *Political*: "No one can deny that from the standpoint of international relations, the establishment of the State of Israel . . . was an almost supernatural occurrence. Both Russia and the Western countries jointly supported the establishment of the State" (26).

---

5 The Rav elaborates on the two interpretations of the Song of Songs and their sources in *U-Vikkashtem mi-Sham*, 151–53, n. 1. Interestingly, he notes there that the kabbalistic interpretation of the Song of Songs combines both motifs.

2. *Military*: "The small Israeli Defense Forces defeated the mighty armies of the Arab countries" (27).
3. *Theological*: "[A]ll the claims of Christian theologians that God deprived the Jewish people of its rights in the land of Israel, and that all the biblical promises regarding Zion and Jerusalem refer, in an allegorical sense, to Christianity and the Christian church, have been publicly refuted by the establishment of the State of Israel and have been exposed as falsehoods, lacking all validity" (28).[6]
4. *Assimilation*: "Many of those who, in the past, were alienated from the Jewish people are now tied to the Jewish state by a sense of pride in its outstanding achievements. Many . . . are now filled with fear and concern about the crisis overtaking the State of Israel . . . It is good for a Jew not to be able to hide from his Jewishness . . . The very fact that people are always talking about Israel serves to remind the Jew in flight that he cannot run away from the Jewish community" (30).
5. *Self-defense*: "For the first time in the history of our exile, divine providence has surprised our enemies with the sensational discovery that Jewish blood is not free for the taking, is not *hefker*!" (31).
6. *Refuge*: "A Jew who flees from a hostile country now knows that he can find a secure refuge in the land of his ancestors. This is a new phenomenon in our history" (34).

Opening the Door?

Clearly, then, these wondrous developments demand an appropriate response on the part of the Jewish people. In the imagery of the Song of Songs, the maiden must cease tarrying, arise from her bed, and open the door. But what does this mean in concrete terms? After such a dramatic buildup, the natural response to this divine call would seem to be *aliyah*: emigrating to the State of Israel and actively participating in the building of its institutions and the shaping of its character. Indeed, the Rav initially does seem to draw this conclusion (36–39). However, he then segues into a request for philanthropy and the extension of aid to the State of Israel. In something of an anticlimax, the latter line of argument persists until the end of the essay.[7]

6 For an account of Rav Soloveitchik's own encounters with missionaries, see his *The Lord is Righteous in All His Ways: Reflections on the Tish'ah be-Av Kinot*, ed. R. Jacob J. Schacter (Jersey City, 2006), 158–60.

7 To be sure, in this essay the Rav is speaking of God's call to the Jewish *nation*, and of a commensurate *national* response that is demanded. Thus, he says the Jewish people should "open the door" through national projects (settling the Negev), and the Orthodox community

Undoubtedly, this shift away from calling for *aliyah* is due in part to the Rav's knowledge of his audience. He felt that few American Jews, even Orthodox ones, would be enticed to leave their comfortable lives and become pioneers in a struggling and embattled country. Furthermore, he writes elsewhere, the unresponsiveness to calls for *aliyah* is attributable not just to inertia or convenience, but to a deficiency in religious experience. Even the Torah-oriented youth in America relate to the Land of Israel in purely intellectual terms, lacking an emotional connection to the land and to the "yearning of generations" (*"Al Ahavat ha-Torah,"* 418). The Rav felt that the decision to pursue *aliyah*, while subject to numerous considerations, was to be taken for idealistic reasons deriving from Torah values; in a 1975 interview, he commented:

> In truth, the Jewish Agency and governmental representatives are mistaken [in their approach]. You do not need to tell people: "Come on *aliyah*, and if you remain [in the Diaspora] you are putting yourselves in danger just as German Jews did before the rise of Hitler to power." This is not the right way. One must educate and teach towards a lifestyle that will bring people to *Eretz Yisrael*. This is what we are doing.
> *Do you see in this a national Zionist mission?*
> This is the mission of the Torah and Divine Providence.[8]

Nevertheless, it is undeniable that *aliyah* is not a major theme in the Rav's writings – not even in his annual addresses to the Religious Zionists of America! This poses the almost unavoidable question of why, given the powerful call of the six knocks, Rav Soloveitchik himself did not make *aliyah*. This question is so obvious and insistent that an Israeli high school class, studying *Kol Dodi Dofek* six years after its publication, asked their teacher to put this question to the Rav. Writing several months after his wife's passing, Rav Soloveitchik replied:

> I thank you for your words, and accept your rebuke willingly. Indeed, I sinned against the Holy Land. I am amongst those who have fallen back [in not coming to the Holy Land]. Of course, many factors that were out of my control

---

should undertake community projects (starting religious kibbutzim, building housing for religious immigrants, and establishing a network of schools). It could be argued that as long as the nation and community undertake these projects, the individual can participate through philanthropy, or can turn his attention to other worthy causes, such as Jewish education. Although this may indeed be in line with the Rav's thinking, it does not, to my mind, do away with the question of individual *aliyah*.

8 *Community, Covenant and Commitment*, 238–39.

prevented me. In spite of this, I am not searching for an excuse, nor am I justifying myself. I am guilty, and the blame rests on my shoulders. Last year, we – my wife *z"l* and I – decided to come to Israel and remain for about six months, to see the land and the people who dwell therein. However, "many are the plans in a man's heart" (Prov. 19:21), what happened, happened, and "my sighs are many and heart is sick!" (Lam. 1:22).[9]

This, of course, is not the whole story. I think it is safe to say that Rav Soloveitchik felt that since he had built up a great enterprise of Torah learning in the United States and had contributed significantly to the strengthening of Orthodoxy there, it would be dangerous and irresponsible for him to leave his community without a leader. Although in the above-mentioned interview the Rav testified that he encouraged *aliyah*, his distinguished disciple R. Hershel Schachter reports that this encouragement did not extend to rabbis and teachers who had proven their effectiveness in educating Diaspora communities.[10] Indeed, this is the gist of the closing of the Rav's letter to Miriam Shiloh, the Israeli teacher whose students in Givat Washington had been puzzled by the Rav's remaining in the United States:

> I, too, a simple Jew, would say, in the words of the rabbis of Yavneh (*Berakhot* 17a): "I teach, and many others who work in the field of Torah education teach; my work is in the large city of New York, in an institution with great numbers of students, and they, their work is in Givat Washington or some other *moshav* in a similarly small institution. One may do much or one may do little; it is all one, provided he directs his heart to Heaven. All our work is dedicated to the flourishing of the values of Judaism, the tradition of our forefathers and our sages, the bearers of the tradition and its scholars."[11]

Clearly, the message of *Kol Dodi Dofek* is not exhausted by the "six knocks," and it is necessary to understand the Rav's position within a broader context. In the next chapter, we will examine the continuation of the essay where the Rav presents his theory of the covenants of fate and destiny, and we will examine its ramifications regarding the basis of Jewish identity in our day. This background will enable us in Chapter 27 to gain a deeper understanding of the nature of the Rav's multifaceted commitment to the State of Israel.

---

9 Ibid., 228.

10 R. Hershel Schachter, *Nefesh HaRav* (Jerusalem, 1994), 98.

11 *Community, Covenant and Commitment*, 229.

FOR FURTHER REFERENCE

1. ***Kol Dodi Dofek***: This essay originated as a Yiddish address at Yeshiva University on Israel's Independence Day in 1956. Rav Soloveitchik published a Hebrew version in 1961, which has been reprinted numerous times, including in *Divrei Hagut ve-Ha'arakhah*, 9–55. It has been translated into English twice, by Lawrence Kaplan and by David Gordon. This book references Kaplan's translation as it appears in *Fate and Destiny: From the Holocaust to the State of Israel* (Hoboken, NJ, 2000), though I refer to the work by its more familiar Hebrew title. Much has been written about this essay, including a symposium on *"Kol Dodi Dofek* at Fifty" in *Tradition* 39:3 (Fall 2006), 15–96.

2. **Confronting the Holocaust:** Regarding the opposing approaches of Satmar-Munkacz and R. Zvi Yehudah Kook, see Aviezer Ravitzky, *Messianism, Zionism, and Jewish Religious Radicalism* (Chicago, 1996), 40–144. For a survey of Religious Zionist views on the connection between the Holocaust and the State of Israel, with a focus on the powerful ideas of Rav Yehuda Amital, see Moshe Maya, *A World Built, Destroyed and Rebuilt: Rabbi Yehuda Amital's Confrontation with the Memory of the Holocaust*, trans. Kaeren Fish (Jersey City, 2005), 45–87. Regarding the fascinating question of how Orthodox Jewish thinkers understood the Holocaust *while it was occurring*, see Mendel Piekarz, *Hasidut Polin: Megamot Ra'ayoniyot bein Shtei ha-Milhamot u-vi-Gezerot 5700–5705* (Jerusalem, 1990); Eliezer Schweid, *Bein Hurban li-Yeshuah* (Tel Aviv, 1994); Esther Farbstein, *Hidden in Thunder: Perspectives on Faith, Halachah and Leadership during the Holocaust* (Jerusalem, 2007). For a broad survey of Orthodox approaches to the Holocaust, both contemporary to it and retrospective, see R. Tamir Granot's online course "Faith and the Holocaust," archived on Yeshivat Har Etzion's Israel Koschitzky Virtual Beit Midrash: http://www.vbm-torah.org/shoah.html. For a broad selection of writings by Orthodox and non-Orthodox thinkers, see Steven Katz, Shlomo Biderman, Gershon Greenberg, eds., *Wrestling with God: Theological Responses during and after the Holocaust* (Oxford, 2007).

Chapter 26

Fate, Destiny and Jewish Identity

The Covenant of Fate

We saw in the previous chapter that the individual is summoned to transform an existence of fate into one of destiny. However, on the national level, the Jewish people cannot transcend fate; they must live both a fate and a destiny existence, for God has entered with them into covenants of both fate and destiny.

The covenant of fate sealed in Egypt bound all Jews together in solidarity due to common persecution. This covenant set the Jewish people apart from the rest of the world, with or without their consent: "I will take you to Me for a people, and I will be to you a God" (Ex. 6:7).[1] At Mt. Sinai, on the other hand, the Jews freely entered into a covenant of destiny with God, wherein they accepted His commandments in order to become a holy people: "And [Moses] took the book of the covenant, and read in the hearing of the people; and they said: 'All that the Lord has spoken will we do, and obey;' and Moses took the blood, and sprinkled it on the people, and said: 'Behold the blood of the covenant, which the Lord has made with you in agreement with all these words'" (Ex. 24:7–8). The covenant of fate creates the fact of Jewish distinctness and even isolation; the covenant of destiny gives meaning and content to this separateness, adding the dimensions of uniqueness and sanctity.

---

1 In *Five Addresses* (139–52), the Rav terms this "the Patriarchal covenant," but it is essentially identical to what he calls "the covenant in Egypt" in *Kol Dodi Dofek*. Even in *Kol Dodi Dofek* the Rav admits that the covenant of fate existed before the servitude in Egypt – bringing examples of this covenant from the lives of Abraham and Joseph – and it was "crystallized" in Egypt (44). See For Further Reference, #1, regarding the origins of idea of the covenants of fate and destiny.

The Rav applies the fate/destiny distinction in different – perhaps inconsistent – manners on the individual and communal levels. For the individual, fate is not chosen but rather compelled; it is a passive mode of existence; and for these reasons, it must be transcended. For the Jewish community, fate is likewise coerced; however, fate need not be passive, and it cannot be transcended.

Jewish separateness and solitude are givens that cannot be changed since they are based on the covenant in Egypt. Even if a Jew wishes to flee his people, he will be reminded by non-Jews of his national origin. This coerced identification can have both negative and positive aspects. The fate dimension of Jewish existence is a negative force if one regards it passively or struggles against it in vain. However, if freely acknowledged and accepted, it can lead to positive feelings that ameliorate its oppressiveness. When one becomes aware that one is bound by fate to all other Jews, one develops a fellowship-consciousness with four components.

First, all Jews, no matter what their social station or land of residence, share a common history and a common fate; all will rise or fall together. This was Mordecai's message to Esther: "Do not think in your heart that you shall escape in the king's house any more than all the other Jews" (Esther 4:13), and this is one of the themes the Rav highlights in his discourses on Purim.[2] Purim, of course, is a classic example of the common fate suffered by all Jews; the holiday is even named after fate (*goral*)! "Because Haman the son of Hammedatha, the Agagite, the enemy of *all the Jews*, had devised against the Jews to destroy them, and had cast a *pur*, that is, the *goral* (lot), to discomfit them, and to destroy them . . . wherefore they called these days Purim, after the name of the *pur*" (Esther 9:24, 26).

Second, if all Jews share common circumstances, they must share each other's suffering as well. When a Jew in Yemen is in distress, a Jew in London must feel his pain. This sense of sympathy receives expression in the fact that our prayers for those in need and our consolation of mourners are formulated in the plural. We cannot relate to the needs of the individual without relating to those of community, and, conversely, the entire community must grieve for the pain of the individual.[3]

Third, shared suffering leads to shared responsibility. This is both a halakhic principle – "All Jews are guarantors for one another" (*Shevuot* 39a) – and a historical fact: the entire Jewish community has always been held

---

2 See, e.g., "The Duality of Purim," in *Days of Deliverance*, 1–24.

3 See also the section on mutual commitment in Chap. 2 above, and the discussion of prayer and community in Chap. 20 above.

responsible for the actions of its individual members. While this fact, which is inexplicable other than as a manifestation of the covenant of fate, has often been employed to our detriment by antisemites, it is also the basis of the commandment of *kiddush ha-Shem* and the prohibition of *hillul ha-Shem*: when an individual Jew behaves properly, he or she sanctifies God's name, and when a Jew behaves improperly, he or she desecrates God's name.

Finally, common suffering and responsibility give rise to common action, to acts of charity and mutual aid that stem not only from duty but from a sense of compassion and connection. Both objective charitable action and subjective feelings of empathy and kindheartedness (what the Rav calls elsewhere the character trait of *rahmonus*) lie at the heart of Jewish morality.[4] The most exalted manifestations of the covenant of fate, when the latter is recognized and accepted, are *hesed* and love of one's fellow Jew:

> We have stated that it is the consciousness of the fate imposed upon the [Jewish] people against their will and of their terrible isolation that is the source of the people's unity, of their togetherness. It is precisely this consciousness as the source of the people's togetherness that gives rise to the attribute of *hesed*, which summons and stirs the community of fate to achieve a positive mode of togetherness through ongoing, joint participation in its own historical circumstances, in its suffering, conscience, and acts of mutual aid. The lonely Jew finds consolation in breaking down the existential barriers of egoism and alienation, joining himself to his fellow and actively connecting himself with the community. The oppressive sense of fate undergoes a positive transformation when individual personal existences blend together to form a new unit – a people. The obligation to love one another stems from the consciousness of this people of fate, this lonely people that inquires into the meaning of its own uniqueness. It is this obligation of love that stands at the very heart of the covenant made in Egypt (53–54).

Two Components of Jewish Identity

The covenant of destiny enacted at Sinai requires less explanation than the covenant of fate. It means, simply, the Jews' free acceptance of *mitzvot* and of the consequent goals of attaining sanctity and imitating God. Jewish nationhood, which in the fate dimension is merely an unalterable condition, gains meaning, content and direction when viewed from the perspective of destiny:

---

4 The Rav develops this theme at length in his discourses on Passover, where he discusses the foundational impact of servitude in Egypt upon the Jewish psyche. See *Festival of Freedom*, 21–24, 43–45, 131–34 (esp. 133 regarding *rahmonus*), and *Days of Deliverance*, 22–24.

A shared fate is simply the inability to rebel against fate; it is the tragic, Jonah-like incapacity to flee from before the God of the Hebrews . . . A shared destiny means the unconstrained ability of the will to strive toward a goal; it means the free decision to devote oneself to an ideal; it means yearning for God (71–72).

A life of destiny entails active efforts to transcend our given circumstances and to attain a more elevated form of existence. Within the covenant of destiny, Jews are no longer bound together only by a shared history or shared suffering, but also by shared values and ideals, and by joint striving to "be unto Me a kingdom of priests and a holy nation" (Ex. 19:6) and "to mend the world under the dominion of God" (from the *Aleinu* prayer). They are not only acted upon as a single entity, but also act together as a single entity.

Both covenants are necessary dimensions of Jewish existence. A convert joins both the Jewish people and the Jewish faith, both Jewish fate and Jewish destiny. Such, indeed, was the declaration of Ruth, the most famous convert to Judaism: "Your nation shall be my nation, and your God, my God" (Ruth 1:16). These two aspects of conversion are symbolized respectively by the acts of circumcision, an indelible physical sign of the Jew's distinctiveness, and immersion, a symbol of purification and elevation.

What is missing if a Jew accepts only one of the two components of Jewish identity? The Rav explains:

A Jew who participates in his people's suffering and fate but does not bind himself to its destiny, which expresses itself in a life of Torah and *mitzvot*, violates the fundamental principle of Judaism (*kotzetz bi-netiot*) and impairs his own singularity. Conversely, a Jew who does not grieve over the afflictions of his people, but seeks to separate himself from the Jewish fate, desecrates the holiness of Israel, even if he observes the commandments (61).[5]

One of the major questions of modern Jewish thought revolves around the nature of Jewish identity: is Jewishness defined as belonging to a religion, a people, or even – following the rise of Zionism – a nationality? A *religion* is defined by its beliefs and rituals, a *people* by its sense of kinship, history and

---

5 In the footnote to this statement (82, n. 22), the Rav cites Rambam's ruling that one who keeps *mitzvot* but separates himself from the Jewish people has no portion in the world-to-come (*Hilkhot Teshuvah* 3:11) – a very strong denunciation indeed. Note, however, that Rashi seems to disagree with Rambam's ruling. While Rambam's position is apparently based on the text of a *baraita* (*Rosh Hashanah* 17a) as it appears in the standard printings of the Talmud, Rashi has a different text of that *baraita* and consequently understands that the phrase "those who separate themselves from the ways of the community" refers to people who do not keep the *mitzvot*.

solidarity, and a *nation* by its territory and sovereignty. Non-religious Jews in the Diaspora have tended to see Jewish identity in terms of peoplehood, as an extended family, without religious or national dimensions. Secular Zionists tried to redefine Jewish identity in nationalist terms, emphasizing political and territorial elements while downplaying peoplehood and religion. Orthodox Jews, focusing on religious identity, have struggled to find a place within their world-view for Jews who do not keep the commandments – a group that two or three centuries ago was marginal and now constitutes the majority of the Jewish people. Following Rav Saadyah Gaon's famous assertion that "Our people, the Children of Israel, are a people only by virtue of our laws,"[6] some assert that the non-observant are Jews only in the most technical sense and tend to write them off, while others look upon them solely as observant Jews in potential.

These Orthodox approaches do not lend much dignity or legitimacy to non-observant Jews. With his idea of the two covenants, Rav Soloveitchik offers a religious theory of Jewish identity for non-observant Jews, one that sees them as having a dignified and legitimate (though not fully ideal) place within the Jewish world and within the halakhic world-view: they are partners in the covenant of fate but not in the covenant of destiny. Although they are not bound to other Jews in joint striving for the attainment of *kedushah* and in a shared vision of the Jewish mission, they are bound to all Jews in sharing a common fate, a common sense of identification with the Jewish people, and common participation in the *hesed*-community.

This distinction between the two covenants grants us new understanding of the Rav's policy, discussed in Chapter 18, of cooperation with non-Ortho-dox Jewish denominations on matters relating to Jewish welfare, antisemi-tism, defense of the State of Israel, etc. – in other words, the entire realm of Jewish fate. It is also one of the reasons the Rav parted ways with the Haredi anti-Zionist position in which he had been raised. The Rav believed that secu-lar Zionists were mistaken about both dimensions of Jewish existence: they rejected the destiny based on Torah and *mitzvot*, and they felt that the advent of a Jewish state would normalize Jewish fate and make Jews "like all the nations." Nevertheless, he felt bound to secular Zionists by the covenant of fate, and therefore advocated partnership with them (though not subservience to them) in the building of the State of Israel.

In fact, the Rav declared that the secular Jews who concern themselves with the welfare of the Jewish people have much to teach the observant community. Many observant Jews are lacking in their commitment to the

---

6 *Book of Doctrines and Beliefs* III:6 (III:7 in R. Kafih's Hebrew translation).

covenant of fate, as evidenced by their concern only for themselves or for those within their narrow circles. On the other hand, commitment to Jewish survival without concern for the *reason* for that survival is also insufficient. All members of the Jewish community, therefore, would benefit from greater attention to *both* covenants.

For Further Reference

1. **Two dimensions of Jewish peoplehood:** In an appendix to the Hebrew version of his article "On the Jewish People in the Writings of Rabbi Joseph B. Soloveitchik" (in Avi Sagi, ed., *Emunah bi-Zemanim Mishtanim* [Jerusalem, 1996], 168–71), Gerald Blidstein points to several thinkers who developed ideas somewhat parallel to fate and destiny, but shows how the Rav's concept, influenced especially by the Shoah, differed from earlier notions. He does not mention that the Aggadah section of the Rav's 1943 *yahrzeit* lecture for his father (published in a supplement to *Hapardes* 17:11 [Shevat 5704], 16–44, and reprinted in *Beit Yitzhak* 29 [5757], 145–97), delivered during the Shoah itself, contains an early usage of the concepts (if not the terms) of fate and destiny, referring to "*mahaneh*" and "*edah*," as well as to "the God of the Hebrews" and "the God of Israel." R. Zev Gotthold, *z"l*, in conversation with R. Yair Kahn, said that the Rav told him that he first developed the idea of two dimensions of Jewish community when he studied political science in Warsaw in the mid-1920s.

2. **Rav Soloveitchik and Religious Zionist thought:** In a series of books and articles, Prof. Dov Schwartz has proposed that there exists a theology common to all Religious Zionist thinkers and has mapped its varieties and fault lines; in English, see his *Faith at the Crossroads: A Theological Profile of Religious Zionism* (Leiden, 2002). He includes Rav Soloveitchik as a Religious Zionist thinker based, among other things, on his attitude towards cooperation with secular Zionists; see, e.g., his article on this subject in *Emunah bi-Zemanim Mishtanim* (*op. cit.*), 123–45. Gerald Blidstein cogently challenges this categorization of the Rav in his article, "*Ha-Rav Yosef Dov Halevi Soloveitchik ke-Hogeh Dati-Tzioni – Haumnam?*" in Yehoyada Amir, ed., *Derekh ha-Ruah: Sefer ha-Yovel le-Eliezer Schweid* (Jerusalem, 2005), 439–50. He argues that although Rav Soloveitchik was a Religious Zionist leader, Religious Zionism is not central to his thought: he did not devote much philosophical reflection to it, was not engaged by the problematics of national existence, and was not in dialogue with its thinkers or influenced by its ideas. Although the Rav's ideas are *relevant* to Religious Zionism, they do not draw their *sustenance* from it nor are they an organic *part* of it.

Chapter 27

The Significance of the State of Israel

The Two Covenants and the State of Israel

In 1935, on his only trip to *Eretz Yisrael*, Rav Soloveitchik submitted his candidacy for the chief rabbinate of Tel Aviv as the representative of Agudath Israel, a non-Zionist, perhaps even anti-Zionist, political-religious organization. By 1944, he was Chairman of the Central Committee of the Religious Zionists of America. He testifies that his move to Mizrachi was not an easy one, as it entailed a break with his family's position and rejection by his rabbinic peers:

> I was not born into a Zionist household. My parents' ancestors, my father's house, my teachers and colleagues were far from the Mizrachi religious Zionists . . . My links with the Mizrachi grew gradually; I had my doubts about the validity of the Mizrachi approach . . .
>
> I built an altar upon which I sacrificed sleepless nights, doubts and reservations. Regardless, the years of the Hitlerian Holocaust, the establishment of the State of Israel, and the accomplishments of the Mizrachi in the land of Israel, convinced me of the correctness of our movement's path. The altar still stands today, with smoke rising from the sacrifice upon it . . . Jews like me . . . are required to sacrifice on this altar their peace of mind as well as their social relationships and friendships (*Five Addresses*, 34, 36).[1]

---

1 Actually, the Rav's father had earlier associated himself with Mizrachi when, in 1920, he became head of religious studies at the Mizrachi-affiliated Takhkemoni Rabbinical Seminary in Warsaw. The question of the exact timing of the Rav's move from Agudah to Mizrachi has been raised by R. Shlomo Pick, "The Rav: Biography and Bibliography," *B.D.D.* 6 (1998), 31–37. However, what interests us here is the Rav's self-perception. The above-cited testimony was delivered in an address to the Religious Zionists of America in 1962.

A variety of factors – some related to fate and some to destiny – contributed to the Rav's support for Mizrachi and to his personal commitment to the State of Israel.

I. Fate: The last three of the six knocks described in Chapter 25 all deal with the State of Israel's contribution to Jewish survival. The State of Israel is a refuge for persecuted Jews; it establishes the principle of Jewish self-defense; and it serves as a bulwark against assimilation for Diaspora Jews, many of whom maintain their sense of Jewish identity through identification with Israel and concern for its welfare.

II. Destiny: The State of Israel aids in the attainment of Jewish spiritual goals in several ways. First, by settling the land and exercising sovereignty in it, the Jewish community fulfills one of the 613 biblical *mitzvot*, "You shall possess the land and dwell therein" (Num. 33:53).[2] Second, the Jewish state is a natural and congenial environment for Torah study, a land in which the Jewish people can transplant and rebuild the destroyed Torah centers of Europe.[3] By helping establish Jewish sovereignty in the Land of Israel and building Torah institutions there, the Mizrachi paved the way for Jewish spiritual continuity following the eclipse of traditional European Jewish society in the Enlightenment and its destruction in the Holocaust. In this, the Mizrachi followed the path of Joseph, who, foreseeing the winds of change that would challenge his father's traditional existence in the backwaters of an undeveloped country, prepared the way for Jewish spiritual continuity even in the sophisticated society of imperial Egypt. Like Joseph, the Mizrachi leaders were also shunned by their more short-sighted brothers for their convictions and actions. Third, the State of Israel can benefit not only the study of Torah but its application as well, for within the state it is possible to apply Halakhah to a broad range of issues, including modern technology and public life. Others, whether Reform or Haredi, may feel that the Torah cannot survive a confrontation with modern society, and therefore, it must either change in accordance with the times or retreat into isolation. The Rav strongly identified with the Mizrachi's position that Torah can and should engage the world, that it can meet any challenge and be applied in any circumstance.[4] Thus, ideally, the State of Israel can provide a framework within which to realize the covenant

---

2 *"Al Ahavat ha-Torah,"* 424–25; *Five Addresses*, 137–38. See also For Further Reference, #1.

3 *Five Addresses*, 31–33.

4 *Five Addresses*, 152–57, 174–75, and *"Mah Dodekh mi-Dod,"* 90–91 (the position that the Rav cites as "some say" seems to be his own, in contrast to that of his illustrious uncle R. Velvel).

of destiny by fostering Torah values and applying Halakhah to the full range of human endeavors.[5]

The Rav strongly felt the eternal connection of the Jew to the Land of Israel, and testified on many occasions that he had imbibed from his father and grandfather a love for the land and its sanctity.[6] Furthermore, he believed that divine providence had decreed that in the dispute between religious Zionists and anti-Zionists, the religious Zionists had been correct.[7] Yet when we ask ourselves which elements of Jewish destiny can be attained *only* in the Land of Israel, we see that it is just the first of them – the specific *mitzvah* of settlement. The Rav felt that the broader elements of destiny – building Torah institutions, striving for *kedushah*, applying Halakhah to modern society and engaging the world – were equally relevant to the Diaspora and could be achieved there as well. As we saw in Chapter 18, his identification with Mizrachi was based not only on its support for religious life in the State of Israel, but on broad philosophical principles with universal application: belief in anti-isolationism, human activism and creativity, and the Torah's ability to purify man and society.[8]

In *Kol Dodi Dofek* and elsewhere, the Rav expresses his strong belief that God's hand was manifest in the founding of the State of Israel.[9] Yet the fact of

---

5 *Kol Dodi Dofek*, 70–71.

6 See, for example, "*Al Ahavat ha-Torah*," 422–23; *Five Addresses*, 34–35; *Community, Covenant and Commitment*, 239.

7 *Five Addresses*, 31–36. This point is also apparent from the Rav's discussion of the six knocks.

8 See also *Community, Covenant and Commitment*, 201–02:

> I see two elements in the Mizrachi: (1) An Israeli political party that deserves credit for most of the achievements of the religious community in Israel . . . (2) A large movement committed to a specific ideology and worldview whose impact is significant both in Israel and in the Diaspora. This movement holds within its hand the answer to a serious dilemma: How can we insert our *eternal* [values] into the *splendor* of the modern world? How can we remain steadfast and strong in the very center of the modern society and sanctify the new and that which is occurring on a daily basis with utmost holiness? I cannot join up to any group or association that has emblazoned on its banner [the call]: "Separate from the vast world [and go] into dark caves and set yourselves apart from the world and the rest of the Jewish people." This retreat from the battle is the beginning of defeat and reflects a lack of faith in the eternity of Judaism and its ability to dominate the new world with its powerful currents and changing forms. According to the worldview of our movement, Judaism is immensely powerful and capable of achieving anything. The most developed society too, [even one] leaping and conquering new areas of the natural order, also requires our Torah, and only in it will it find satisfaction.

9 See, e.g., *Five Addresses*, 170–73. Regarding the question of whether to recite *Hallel* in

yad Hashem being present in Israel's creation does not necessarily mean that the State of Israel is "the first flowering of our redemption." Nor does the fact that the State is a gift from God mean that it is a value in itself. Rather, the Rav believes that it is an opportunity – an *important* opportunity but not the *only* one – for the Jewish people to protect its existence and pursue its destiny. The goal of combining the two covenants and thereby raising a people of fate to a holy nation of destiny is not limited to the Land of Israel. The State is an instrument that serves (or should serve) the larger values of the Jewish people and the Jewish faith.

The Third Way

In short, the Rav believed that the State of Israel is nothing less than a gift from God that plays an important role in safeguarding Jews' physical survival and identity, and that has the potential to serve as a basis for attaining their destiny. Yet it is also *no more* than that. In a letter written in 1957, the Rav stakes out his position against two other Orthodox approaches:

> I agree with you that there is a third halakhic approach which is neither parallel to the position of those "whose eyes are shut" and reject [the significance of the State] nor the belief of those dreamers who adopt a completely positive stance to the point where they identify the State with the [fulfillment] of the highest goal of our historical and meta-historical destiny. This third approach (which is the normative one in all areas), I would allow myself to guess, would be positively inclined toward the State, and would express gratitude for its establishment out of a sense of love and devotion, but would not attach [to it] excessive value to the point of its glorification and deification.[10]

Those "whose eyes are shut" are the Haredim, whom Rav Soloveitchik faults for refusing to acknowledge the miraculous nature of the State's founding, denying its historical significance, and showing no interest in taking part in its development. The "dreamers" are the followers of Rav Kook, who regard the State as possessing inherent spiritual value and assign it an overwhelmingly important role in the unfolding of Jewish destiny. Before pinpointing where Rav Soloveitchik parts ways with them, we must first understand Rav Kook's overall approach to the significance of the State of Israel – a state that in his day was yet to be born.

Rav Kook believes that Judaism comprises two "ideas," the national and

---

response to this miracle, see For Further Reference, #2.

10 *Community, Covenant and Commitment*, 163–64.

the spiritual.[11] These are not identical to fate and destiny. First, fate and destiny exist in a hierarchical relationship, while this is not so clear regarding the national and spiritual ideas. Second, the national idea means that the Jewish nation can express its inner essence only by exercising political sovereignty in the Land of Israel, while fate is a dimension of Jewish existence in all places and under all sovereignties. During the two thousand years of exile, Rav Kook believes, Judaism itself was deficient, for it lacked the national half of its identity. Secular Jewish nationalists, therefore, are to be regarded as "holy rebels," for although they reject the spiritual idea, they are helping foster a renaissance of Judaism itself through their restoration of the national idea. By re-establishing Jewish sovereignty in the Holy Land, they reconnect the Jewish nation to one of its two sources of vitality, hitherto missing, and thereby initiate an inexorable process of messianic redemption. Whether its founders are aware of it or not, the nascent State of Israel contains inherent spiritual value as "the foundation of God's seat in the world," and therefore it constitutes "man's ultimate happiness."[12]

All such talk of deterministic historical processes, inborn essences, and holy rebellions is foreign to Rav Soloveitchik. He does not perceive any *inherent* value in sovereignty, other than fulfilling the specific *mitzvah* of settlement, nor does he assign any *inherent* spiritual value to the State, seeing it rather as a base from which to attain *other* objectives.[13] These objectives, fate and destiny, are the same ones Jews pursued during their long exile, since they can be attained in the Diaspora as well. Prof. Gerald Blidstein points out that, unlike Rav Kook, Rav Soloveitchik does not accept the Zionist critique of Diaspora Jewish life. Therefore the Rav sees no need for a renaissance of Judaism, nor does he regard the secular Zionist rebellion against religion as a necessary stage in the dialectical unfolding of the Jewish essence.[14]

Furthermore, I would add, the Rav believes that if one can speak of a

---

11 For a succinct presentation of Rav Kook's views on this subject, see his essay, "*Le-Mahalakh ha-Ide'ot be-Yisrael*," in *Orot* (Jerusalem, 1985), 102–18.

12 *Orot Yisrael* 6:7, in *Orot*, 160.

13 In "*Yarhei Kallah*" lectures delivered in the summers of 1978 and 1981, Rav Soloveitchik suggested that the *mitzvot* of appointing judges in every city in *Eretz Yisrael* and eradicating idolatry in *Eretz Yisrael* are both fulfillments of the commandment of "possession and settlement" of the land. Based on these insights, R. Yair Kahn suggests that these two *mitzvot* are not merely additions to the literal fulfillment of "possession and settlement," but rather define its essence. In other words, mere sovereignty is not enough, but is instead a stepping-stone, or a *hekhsher mitzvah*, to the attainment of the larger goals of justice and divine worship. See his article, "*Leha'avir Gilulim min ha-Aretz*," *Alon Shevut* 145 (5755), 13–23.

14 "On the Jewish People in the Writings of Rabbi Joseph B. Soloveitchik," in *Exploring the Thought of Rabbi Joseph B. Soloveitchik*, ed. R. Marc Angel (Hoboken, 1997), 307–08.

Jewish national character, it is not one that is inborn and essential, but rather one shaped by the nation's historical experiences. Not only does the Rav not speak of the "essence" of the Jewish people, he does not even speak of the sanctity of *Eretz Yisrael* as an inherent metaphysical property. Prof. Blidstein reports that Rav Soloveitchik considered such thinking mythological: "I recall his developing the theme that the holiness of the land was not 'mythological' but a function of its providing the context for a holy society – again a fundamentally Maimonidean orientation."[15] In a striking passage, the Rav writes that the idea of inherent sanctity approaches fetishism, the belief in the supernatural powers of physical objects:

> For [R. Yehudah Halevi and the Ramban], the attribute of *kedushah*, holiness, ascribed to the Land of Israel is an objective metaphysical quality inherent in the land. With all my respect for the *Rishonim*, I must disagree with such an opinion. I do not believe that it is halakhically cogent. *Kedushah*, under a halakhic aspect, is man-made; more accurately, it is a historical category. A soil is sanctified by historical deeds performed by a sacred people, never by any primordial superiority. The halakhic term *kedushat ha-aretz*, the sanctity of the land, denotes the consequence of a human act, either conquest (heroic deeds) or the mere presence of the people in that land (intimacy of man and nature). *Kedushah* is identical with man's association with Mother Earth. Nothing should be attributed a priori to dead matter. Objective *kedushah* smacks of fetishism.[16]

Clearly, Rav Kook and Rav Soloveitchik are working with very different sets of assumptions. Yet even within Rav Soloveitchik's own school of thought, some have questioned the scant attention he paid to certain values that are consistent with and even congenial to his philosophy, and others have developed Rav Soloveitchik's line of thought further than he himself may have. For example, one of his preeminent disciples, Rav Aharon Lichtenstein, discerns in Israel the possibility of leading a more organic and integrated existence, as opposed to the fragmented nature of life in the Diaspora. Even the mundane aspects of one's life in Israel attain social and religious value by contributing to the stability and flourishing of the Jewish state, thereby lending one's life a greater sense of wholeness. Furthermore, without denying the validity or value of Diaspora Jewish life, Rav Lichtenstein views Israel as

---

15 Ibid., 309.

16 *The Emergence of Ethical Man* (Jersey City, 2005), 150. See also *Family Redeemed*, 64. For more on Rav Soloveitchik's understanding of holiness, see Chap. 28 below, For Further Reference, #3.

the epicenter of Jewish life and the locus of the Jewish future. Above all, the sanctity of the land, even when understood in halakhic and not mythological terms, lends a special quality to religious observance in *Eretz Yisrael* and fosters a sense of being nestled within the divine presence. Indeed, these dimensions of *Eretz Yisrael* and of Jewish national life within it exerted a powerful pull on Rav Lichtenstein, to which he responded by making *aliyah*.[17] These elements are not foreign to Rav Soloveitchik, but neither does he highlight them. Prof. Blidstein aptly comments:

> This image of the State of Israel as a potential embodiment of the broadest ethical and societal vocation of Judaism, a vocation based on a broad covenantal commitment, is perceived by many students of the Rav to be implicit in his teaching. Curiously (and regrettably?), this positive and challenging image does not recur frequently in the published texts available to us.[18]

Rabbi Joseph Soloveitchik saw himself in light of the biblical Joseph. The latter's constant preoccupation was to safeguard the continuity of Abraham's tradition when relocated into a different civilization. In the Rav's reading, Canaan and Egypt are not just locations but cultures – the simple and old vs. the sophisticated and new. In our day, the Rav felt, the tasks of perpetuating and applying the Torah within new environments would inevitably need to be pursued in both Israel and the Diaspora. He devoted his untiring efforts and creative energies to pursuing these tasks in the leading country of the West. At the same time, he involved himself and expended great concern in ensuring the Torah's continuity in the State of Israel and in shaping the character and future of the young state. It is now up to the next generation to carry forward his work in both centers of Jewish life.

---

17 See his "On *Aliya*: The Uniqueness of Living in *Eretz Yisrael*," *Alei Etzion* 12 (5764), 15–22, available online at www.haretzion.org/alei.htm. In an essay exemplifying the Rav's demand that his students think for themselves, that they be *talmidim* and not *hasidim*, R. Nathaniel Helfgot goes on to enumerate other components of Jewish national existence undeveloped by the Rav: Jewish autonomy as expressing *malkhut Yisrael*, the ability to apply Halakhah to national issues on all levels of governmental responsibility, the potential to develop a polity guided by Jewish values, and the consequent ability to serve as a "light to the nations." See his "On the Shoulders of a Giant: Looking Back, Yet Looking Forward," *Tradition* 39:3 (Fall 2006), 31–37.

18 Blidstein, *op cit.*

For Further Reference

1. **The *mitzvah* of settling the Land of Israel:** Rambam does not include this commandment in his *Sefer ha-Mitzvot*, but Ramban counts it as one of the *mitzvot* that should be added to Rambam's list (#4). While Rav Kook's followers make much of this Ramban, seeing it as a guiding factor for their socio-political activities and as a cornerstone of their worldview, Rav Yehuda Amital points out (in his book *Commitment and Complexity* [Jersey City, 2008], 106) that Rav Kook mentions it only once in his voluminous writings. It would seem that neither Rav Kook nor Rav Soloveitchik regards this as more than a *mitzvah* among *mitzvot*; therefore, Rav Kook bases his extraordinarily high evaluation of Jewish sovereignty upon other considerations, while Rav Soloveitchik does not assign sovereignty a privileged position among Jewish values. However, Rav Kook's disciples, with a narrower halakhic focus than their master, tethered their understanding of the overriding significance of Jewish sovereignty to this *mitzvah* (whose status is disputed among *Rishonim*) and thereby elevated "possession and settlement" to a preeminent place among *mitzvot*.

2. ***Hallel* on *Yom ha-Atzma'ut*:** There are various reports as to the Rav's position regarding the recitation of *Hallel* on *Yom ha-Atzma'ut*. However, even if we were to assume that Rav Soloveitchik opposed its recitation, Rav Aharon Lichtenstein cogently points out that one cannot derive from this ritual question any conclusions regarding the Rav's attitude towards Zionism or the State of Israel (see his "Rav Soloveitchik's Approach to Zionism," *Alei Etzion* 14 [5766], 21–24). He compares this to the opinion of the "eighty-five elders, among them several prophets," who regretfully felt that, for halakhic reasons, they could not acquiesce to Mordecai's and Esther's request to establish a new *mitzvah* of reading the *megillah* (*Yerushalmi, Megillah* 1:7). Does this mean that they denied that a miracle had taken place in Shushan, or that the great salvation of the Jews from Haman's plot had been unimportant? Analogously, Rav Lichtenstein suggests that Rav Soloveitchik recognized the magnitude of the miracle in his day, but did not necessarily feel that Halakhah warranted the creation of new rituals. Note also that Rav Soloveitchik felt that the true meaning and significance of events would become apparent only with the passage of time. Therefore, just as the Sages waited some time before declaring Hanukkah a holiday (*Shabbat* 21b), so too we should not be hasty in formulating new rituals after Israel's founding or after its astonishing victory

in the Six Day War (reported by R. David Hartman, *Conflicting Visions* [New York, 1990], 23, 158; and *Nefesh ha-Rav*, 94).

3. **Reading *Kol Dodi Dofek* in Israel:** In their contributions to the *Tradition* symposium on *Kol Dodi Dofek* (39:3, Fall 2006), R. Yuval Cherlow, Prof. Dov Schwartz and R. Avraham Walfish discuss its reception in Israel: its limited impact, its novel perspectives, and its potential to receive a hearing in the wake of recent religious and cultural shifts within the Religious Zionist community.

Section VI

HALAKHAH
AND THE RELIGIOUS QUEST

Chapter 28

The Dialectic of *Halakhic Man*

In his first major publication, Rav Soloveitchik sets himself a hugely ambitious task: to portray the personality and goals of halakhic man, "the master of talmudic dialectics." He proposes "to penetrate deep into the structure of halakhic man's consciousness and to determine the precise nature of this 'strange, singular' being" (4).[1] Such a task had never before been undertaken, and as an unfortunate result, says the Rav, halakhic man "is of a type that is unfamiliar to students of religion" (3).

The difficulty of the task is compounded by the fact that halakhic man is a complex personality: "Halakhic man reflects two opposing selves; two disparate images are embodied within his soul and spirit" (ibid.). Utilizing the typological method we have already encountered (most particularly in *The Lonely Man of Faith*), Rav Soloveitchik begins his depiction of halakhic man by first presenting portraits of two other ideal human types, *ish ha-da'at* and *ish ha-dat* – that is, cognitive man and *homo religiosus* (religious man).[2] Cognitive man is exemplified by the mathematical physicist, who concerns himself only with the world of physical reality and attempts to gain intellectual mastery over it. *Homo religiosus*, by contrast, is an otherworldly, mystical type, focusing on the mystery of nature and seeking to transcend the tangible world in favor of a pure spiritual realm. Halakhic man is both like and unlike these two types – and therein lies his uniqueness.

> On the one hand he is as far removed from *homo religiosus* as east is from
> west and is identical, in many respects, to prosaic, cognitive man; on the other
> hand he is a man of God, possessor of an ontological approach that is devoted

---

1 For bibliographical information, see For Further Reference, #1.
2 At the beginning of Chap. 2, we discussed what the Rav means by "ideal human types."

to God and of a world view saturated with the radiance of the Divine Presence. For this reason it is difficult to analyze halakhic man's religious consciousness by applying the terms and traits that descriptive psychology and modern philosophy of religion have used to characterize the religious personality. . . . In some respects he is a *homo religiosus*, in other respects a cognitive man. But taken as a whole he is uniquely different from both of them (3).

Halakhic Man is a sprawling, dense and riveting work. To get a handle on it, we first need to analyze the personalities of cognitive man and *homo religiosus*, and to discern in what respects halakhic man is like each and in what respects he differs from them. That will be our objective in this chapter. Then, in the next two chapters, we shall look at halakhic man's goals, try to identify on whom he is modeled, and attempt to discern the Rav's aims in writing this work.[3]

Before analyzing the "two opposing selves" of halakhic man, we should note that, contrary to the impression we gain from the programmatic statements above, *Halakhic Man* is not just a work of description and analysis, but also one of defense and advocacy. It both depicts *and* defends a certain type of religious personality, as well as a certain approach to religion and a certain understanding of Halakhah. To an outsider, the word "talmudist" conjures up images of a dry pedant squinting into the pages of a dusty tractate while remaining oblivious to both the world without and the spirit within. The force and originality of Rav Soloveitchik's vision sweeps away this false image, substituting for it one in which halakhic man – precisely through the rigorous study and practice of Halakhah – comes to embody what the Rav considers to be the best qualities of both cognitive and religious man.

Halakhic Man and *The Lonely Man of Faith*

Cognitive man, the theoretical scientist, is characterized by majestic and creative intellectualism. *Homo religiosus*, the God-intoxicated mystic, is characterized by burning religious passion. Halakhic man, the talmudic scholar, would seem to be far removed from both. How, then, can his personality be the product of a dialectic between them? We can gain insight into the dialectic that generates halakhic man by contrasting it with the dialectic between Adam I (majestic man) and Adam II (covenantal man) in *The Lonely Man of Faith*.

---

3 Since several studies cover *Halakhic Man* in depth, I will restrict my inquiry to the book's basic outlines. See For Further Reference, #2.

Though not identical, Adam I and cognitive man share a close affinity.[4] Both are active and innovative personalities; both have absolute faith in the power of the intellect; and both have limited interests, restricting their inquiry to the realm of the comprehensible and rational.

By contrast, Adam II and *homo religiosus* differ in crucial ways. Both Adam II and *homo religiosus* seek God; however, *homo religiosus* views the material world – in both its physical and social aspects – as an impediment to the spiritual, while Adam II displays no such dualism. Thus, Adam II seeks companionship; *homo religiosus* is solitary. Adam II desires a relationship with God; *homo religiosus* desires to lose himself within God. Adam II feels lonely in the world; *homo religiosus* feels trapped.

Adam II, covenantal man, tries to overcome his loneliness by forming relationships with God and with other people. *Homo religiosus*, a Romantic, attempts to escape the prison of physicality by exploring esoteric mysteries, leaping beyond objective reason into the realm of subjective intuitions. These bring *homo religiosus* to a dizzying vacillation between ecstasy and melancholy, often engendering asceticism, anxiety and psychic torment.[5]

Adam II is thus a much healthier sort than *homo religiosus*, and this fact impacts upon the nature of the dialectic in each book. For while *The Lonely Man of Faith* calls upon man to maintain the positions of both Adam I and Adam II in endless oscillation, the title character of *Halakhic Man* overcomes the duality of cognitive man and *homo religiosus* and thereafter does not return to the position of either. In terms we developed in Chapter 3, *The Lonely Man of Faith* presents a Kierkegaardian dialectic, wherein the thesis and antithesis remain in perpetual tension, while *Halakhic Man* presents a Hegelian dialectic, wherein the tension between two antithetical positions ultimately results in a third position, or synthesis. It would make little sense for Rav Soloveitchik to advocate a Kierkegaardian dialectic in *Halakhic Man* since he regards one side of the dialectic, *homo religiosus*, to be an exemplar of – or at least prone to be – what William James calls "the sick soul."[6]

There is yet a deeper reason for the different types of dialectic employed

---

4 Later we will examine the scientific activity of cognitive man, and it will become clear that he is more of a theoretical scientist, while Adam I is more of a technological scientist. However, this difference is not germane to the basic point I want to make at the outset of our analysis.

5 Though *homo religiosus* ascribes importance only to the spiritual world and not to the physical world, the Rav makes clear on pp. 15–16 that this does not *necessarily* lead *homo religiosus* to an extreme ascetic position – a point that has been overlooked in a number of articles that attribute to him such a position. Nevertheless, it is true that when the Rav takes issue with *homo religiosus* later in the book, he targets mainly the world-denying type.

6 *The Varieties of Religious Experience* (1902), lectures VI and VII.

in these two works. The fundamental dialectic in *The Lonely Man of Faith* is between conquest and sacrifice, while the fundamental dialectic in *Halakhic Man* is between this-worldliness and other-worldliness, or (to employ terms we will define in the following paragraph) between materialism and dualism. The Rav values both conquest and sacrifice, which is why he maintains both of them in an unending dialectic in *The Lonely Man of Faith*. However, he *rejects* both materialism and dualism, which is why in *Halakhic Man* he must find a third position that overcomes the deficiencies of both.

This-Worldly Spirituality

Cognitive man, a materialist, acknowledges only the physical universe. *Homo religiosus*, a dualist, recognizes both the material and spiritual worlds but sees them as standing in opposition to each other and wishes to flee the former to live in the latter. Halakhic man cannot accept either perspective:

> Halakhic man differs both from *homo religiosus*, who rebels against the rule of reality and seeks a refuge in a supernal world, and from cognitive man, who does not encounter any transcendence at all. Halakhic man apprehends transcendence. However, instead of rising up to it, he tries to bring it down to him. Rather than raising the lower realms to the higher world, halakhic man brings down the higher realms to the lower world (41–42).[7]

It is clear why, as a religious person, halakhic man cannot agree with cognitive man that the corporeal world is all that exists or all that should interest him. However, we confront the following question: If halakhic man agrees with *homo religiosus* that there is a transcendent realm and that it is desirable to encounter it, why doesn't he join *homo religiosus*' quest to "ascend to the heavens"? Why must he remain firmly rooted in *olam ha-zeh*, this world, while pursuing his quest for transcendence? Why would a religious person wish to stay in a world that is *not* transcendent?

Rav Soloveitchik offers three reasons (41–44).[8] First, he considers *homo religiosus*'s position unethical:

---

7 It is specifically through the study and practice of Halakhah that halakhic man brings the transcendent down into the physical world. This process will be explained below in the last three sections of this chapter. The active role of halakhic man is reflected in the Rav's understanding of *kedushah* (sanctity) as something that is not inherent in an object but rather created by human intervention. See For Further Reference, #3.

8 All these ideas are explained at greater length in Chap. 10 above. In addition to the above, there is also a philosophical reason: halakhic man must remain rooted in this world because the intellect has no direct access to metaphysical realm. See pp. 308 and 324–25 below.

Homo religiosus, his glance fixed upon the higher realms, forgets all too frequently the lower realms and becomes ensnared in the sins of ethical inconsistency and hypocrisy. See what many religions have done to this world on account of their yearning to break through the bounds of concrete reality and escape to the sphere of eternity. They have been so intoxicated by their dreams of an exalted supernal existence that they have failed to hear . . . the sighs of orphans, the groans of the destitute . . . . There is nothing so physically and spiritually destructive as diverting one's attention from this world (41).

Second, *homo religiosus*'s attempt to turn himself into pure spirit is unrealistic; man is unavoidably corporeal and must deal with this fact.[9] Third, the path of *homo religiosus* is undemocratic; it can be pursued only by a small elite, while Halakhah, in contrast, is meant to guide the entire community.

Rejecting cognitive man's materialism and *homo religiosus*'s dualism, halakhic man adopts a monistic stance that recognizes both the material and the transcendent and, rather than rejecting one in favor of the other, seeks to bring them together. In order to understand how he accomplishes this, we must now

---

9 Similarly, in n. 4 of *Halakhic Man* the Rav offers both moral and "realistic" reasons as to why the religious experience should not be regarded as something simple and tranquil. The "realistic" reason is that such a portrayal is simply false; the religious experience "is exceptionally complex, rigorous and tortuous . . . antinomic and antithetic" (141). The moral reason is that the desire for simplicity and serenity stems from a rebellion against knowledge and objective thought (which raise questions and thereby disturb one's peace of mind), and this rejection of reason – by sanctifying instinct, intuition and unrestrained emotion – ultimately leads to moral depravity. He concludes powerfully:

> And let the events of the present era [i.e., the Holocaust] be proof! The individual who frees himself from the rational principle and who casts off the yoke of objective thought will in the end turn destructive and lay waste the entire created order. Therefore, it is preferable that religion should ally itself with the forces of clear, logical cognition, as uniquely exemplified in the scientific method, even though at times the two might clash with one another, rather than pledge its troth to beclouded, mysterious ideologies that grope in the dark corners of existence, unaided by the shining light of objective knowledge, and believe that they have penetrated to the secret core of the world (ibid.).

See also *The Halakhic Mind*, 52–55, where the Rav, clearly declaring that "The ethical implications of any philosophical theory . . . should many a time decide the worth of the doctrine" (52), again assails the Romantic rejection of reason, noting that "When reason surrenders its supremacy to dark equivocal emotions, no dam is able to stem the rising tide of the affective stream" (53).

It should be noted, however, that the use of reason and cold logic can also lead to moral travesties, as in the case of Communism. Therefore, employing the moral criterion may not always privilege rational approaches over non-rational ones.

ask not how halakhic man differs from cognitive man and *homo religiosus*, but in what ways he is like them.

Like *homo religiosus*, "halakhic man reaches out to God" and "his soul ... thirsts for the living God" (40). He, too, experiences the affirmation and negation of a finite being standing before the Infinite (67–72), though, unlike *homo religiosus*, he overcomes this duality via the Halakhah.[10] Yet in almost every other aspect, he resembles cognitive man: in his rigorous intellectualism, his balanced temperament, his rational and objective approach to the world, his quantifying methodology, and his fundamentally this-worldly orientation. Like cognitive man, he "holds fast, with all his being, to the concrete reality of our empirical world" (40) and "occupies himself with intellectual constructions – experiencing all the while the joy of discovery and the thrill of creation – and then coordinating his ideal intelligibles [i.e., the creations of his thought] with the real world, as does the mathematician" (39–40).

How can a life devoted to the study and practice of Halakhah be compared to that of the mathematician? And how can such a life be said to bring transcendence into the world? To explain this, the Rav introduces two ideas: Halakhah as a cognitive system, and the doctrine of *tzimtzum*. These ideas define the nature of Halakhah and of the halakhist's activity, and highlight their uniqueness in the world of religion.

The Scientist and the Halakhist

The idea of "Halakhah as a cognitive system" must be understood by reference to the neo-Kantian view of science.[11] Generally, science is thought to be an empirical, a posteriori enterprise: this means that the scientist ponders reality with no apparent preconceptions, and when he finds some repeating patterns within it he begins to formulate laws to explain the observed phenomena.[12] The neo-Kantian view, by contrast, is that the scientist constructs

---

10 Halakhic man overcomes the crisis brought on by the question, "What is man when set against the vast universe?" (69), by realizing that "the Halakhah set man at the very center of its world" (70).

11 More precisely, this is the view of the founder of the Marburg school of neo-Kantianism, Hermann Cohen (whose thought the Rav studied intensively), as well as that of his students Paul Natorp and Ernst Cassirer.

12 The Rav attributes this view to "positivists" like David Hume and "pragmatists" like William James (146, n. 17). However, in light of Thomas Kuhn's insistence (in his *The Structure of Scientific Revolutions* [Chicago, 1970]) that all scientific research is conducted within a set of prevalent assumptions (what Kuhn calls a "paradigm"), it would be hard to maintain such a position today, although it remains the popularly-held conception of science.

an a priori, ideal system of laws and then views nature through it. It is "a priori" in that its categories do not proceed from experience but rather from pure thought; it is "ideal" in that it does not have to conform to reality, but merely must be internally consistent. After performing this supremely creative act, the scientist then looks at the world through the categories he has conceived and correlates physical reality with his constructions.[13]

Rav Soloveitchik sees the halakhist's activity as parallel to the scientist's. Halakhah, he maintains, is not just a normative system but a cognitive one as well. In other words, it is not just a system of laws that regulates the Jew's life, but also a system of concepts that mediates halakhic man's perception of the world, or a lens through which he views his surroundings. Halakhic man "orients himself to the world by means of fixed statutes and firm principles" of Halakhah (19). To take a celebrated example:

> When halakhic man comes across a spring bubbling quietly, he already possesses a fixed, a priori relationship with this real phenomenon: the complex laws regarding the halakhic construct of a spring. The spring is fit for the immersion of a *zav* (a man with a discharge); it may serve as *mei hatat* (waters of expiation); it purifies with flowing water; it does not require a fixed quantity of forty se'ahs; etc. When halakhic man approaches a real spring, he gazes at it and carefully examines its nature. He possesses, a priori, ideal principles and precepts which establish the character of the spring as a halakhic construct, and he uses the statutes for the purpose of determining normative law: does the real spring correspond to the requirements of the ideal Halakhah or not? (20).

These halakhic statutes and principles, though revealed by God, are subject to human interpretation and conceptualization. Therefore, they are the main arena in which halakhic man exercises his creativity. "Halakhic man received the Torah from Sinai not as a simple recipient but as a creator of worlds, as a partner with the Almighty in the act of creation" (81). Because of this dual aspect of Halakhah, halakhic man both *discovers* the principles divinely revealed at Sinai, and *creates* his own conceptualization of them.[14]

---

13 Though this conception of the scientific enterprise may seem counter-intuitive to the non-specialist, it was the view held by many of the leading scientists and philosophers of science at the time *Halakhic Man* was written. If we think in terms of mathematics instead of physics, this view becomes easier to comprehend. The mathematician creates abstract constructs and focuses his attention on them, without any reference to the concrete world of experience. Afterwards, he may investigate the world using these constructs and find physical phenomena that parallel his ideal constructions.

14 Rav Soloveitchik elaborates on the relationship between the divine component and the human component of Halakhah in both *"Mah Dodekh mi-Dod"* and *U-Vikkashtem mi-Sham*.

After creating this ideal halakhic world, halakhic man then "orients himself to the world" through his system of halakhic postulates. Since "There is no phenomenon, entity, or object in this concrete world which the a priori Halakhah does not approach with its ideal standard" (19), halakhic man must fix his attention upon all aspects of creation: nature, society, commerce, family, government, psychology, etc.

The Advantages of Halakhic Cognition

To summarize, the Rav presents halakhic cognition as having two stages: the creation of the ideal world, and its correlation with the real world.[15] Each stage addresses a distinct problem.

First, given that halakhic man combines cognitive man's creative intellectualism with *homo religiosus*'s concern with transcendence, the question arises: how can one apply human intellect to the transcendent realm? As a thinker well-trained in Kantian philosophy, Rav Soloveitchik tended to eschew metaphysics.[16] Therefore, in *Halakhic Man* as elsewhere, he shifts the application of intellect from metaphysics to Halakhah. Although man cannot penetrate the nature or essence of God, man can study Torah, which is a projection or manifestation of God's will and wisdom. Human intellect thereby gains access to the transcendent realm and, furthermore, is supremely creative within that realm.

The second stage of halakhic cognition addresses a different problem: If halakhic man is so interested in the ideal constructs of his mind, how can he stay grounded in this-worldly existence (something the Rav considers necessary for the reasons cited earlier)? The answer is that he uses these constructs as categories through which to perceive the world. This stage of cognition keeps halakhic man's focus on this world; furthermore, it brings God into the world by applying to it the categories of transcendence. As Rav Soloveitchik puts it elsewhere, "He is not concerned with interpreting God in terms of the world but the world under the aspect of God" (*The Halakhic Mind*, 45). The former enterprise ("interpreting God in terms of the world") was that of medieval metaphysics: applying the categories of the finite human intellect to understanding the Infinite. This, according to the Rav, is both an impossible and

---

See the discussion in Chap. 35 below.

15 See also the description of these two stages in *Community, Covenant and Commitment*, 273–74. After these two objectifying stages, one can practice the subjective stage of "reconstruction." See Chap. 31 below.

16 See Chap. 30, p. 327 below.

undesirable task. The latter enterprise ("interpreting . . . the world under the aspect of God") is that of halakhic man: applying the divine-human categories of Halakhah to cognize the world. This is both epistemologically possible and ethically-spiritually desirable.[17]

The Kabbalist and the Halakhist

One way of bringing God into the world is by means of halakhic cognition, or *talmud Torah*; the other is by means of halakhic action, or *shemirat ha-mitzvot*. To elaborate on these ideas, we must introduce the Rav's presentation of the doctrine of a Kabbalistic notion: *tzimtzum*, or divine contraction.

In Kabbalah – and note that the Kabbalist is a type of *homo religiosus* – *tzimtzum* is a tragedy. Before the creation of the universe, God filled all of existence, so to speak. Since nothing finite can exist within the Infinite, God had to "contract" His existence in order to make room for world. "The mystic sees the existence of the world as a type of 'affront,' heaven forbid, to God's glory; the cosmos, as it were, impinges upon the infinity of the Creator" (49). The world thus serves as a barrier between man and God; if the world were to disappear, all would be united within God. Since the Kabbalist's main desire is to unite with God, *tzimtzum* is a source of anguish to him.

Halakhic man understands *tzimtzum* differently. For him it is a source of joy and gives meaning to his existence. Harking back to a midrashic use of the term *tzimtzum*, Rav Soloveitchik takes it to mean not the contraction of God *away from* the world, but rather His contraction *into* the world.[18]

> When God said to Moses: "And let them make Me a sanctuary" (Ex. 25:8), Moses began to wonder, and he said: "The glory of the Holy One, blessed be He, fills the upper worlds and the lower worlds and yet He says: 'And let them make Me a sanctuary'" . . . God replied: "I am not of the same opinion as you. But twenty boards in the north and twenty in the south and eight in the west

---

17 *The Halakhic Mind* deals at length with the epistemological basis for the Rav's treatment of Halakhah as a cognitive system. Note that "*homo religiosus*" in *The Halakhic Mind* is not identical to "*ish ha-dat*" in *Halakhic Man*. In *The Halakhic Mind*, "*homo religiosus*" is a general term for any religious person, and would include even the figure of halakhic man.

18 Although Rav Soloveitchik does not say so explicitly, Lawrence Kaplan discerns a two-stage process of contraction: "In the first stage, performed by God Himself, God contracts Himself within the ideal complex of a priori halakhic concepts . . . In the second stage, performed by man, when a person actualizes within the concrete world this ideal Halakhah that he has studied, he thereby lowers the divine presence . . . to that world" ("Joseph Soloveitchik and Halakhic Man," in *The Cambridge Companion to Modern Jewish Philosophy*, eds. Michael L. Morgan and Peter E. Gordon [Cambridge, 2007], 217–18).

[will suffice]. And more than that, I will contract (*atzamtzem*) My divine presence [so that it may dwell] in one square cubit" (Ex. Rabbah 34:1).

Far from being an affront to God or a barrier between man and God, the world is the sole arena within which man can confront God. "God saw everything that He had created, and, behold, it was very good" (Gen. 1:31): God wants man to live in this world and to bring His presence into it. The means by which man concentrates God's infinite presence into the finite world is by realizing the Halakhah.[19]

To complicate matters, the "realization" or "actualization" of Halakhah (in Hebrew: "*hitgashmut ha-Halakhah*") seems to have two different meanings in *Halakhic Man*: the cognition of halakhic structures as they apply to the world,[20] which we have already examined, and the performance of halakhic norms, which bring the real world into closer correlation with the ideal.[21] This dual meaning, naturally, leads to the question of whether, for halakhic man, study or practice is paramount – a question we shall address in the next chapter.

---

19 *Tzimtzum* denotes not only the contraction of God's infinite presence into the finite world, but also, perhaps in emulation, "the act of objectification and quantification of that [human] religious subjectivity that flows from hidden sources" (108). This objectification is accomplished in two ways: through the performance of *mitzvot* and through the regulation of one's intention during this performance (59). See Chap. 10, pp. 113–15, and Chap. 30, pp. 327–28, for more on the need for objectification and quantification of religious subjectivity.

Interestingly, in both "The Community" (15) and "Majesty and Humility" (35–36), the Rav understands the human imitation of divine *tzimtzum* differently. In those essays, he explains that just as God withdraws His infinite presence to "make room" for the world, so must man limit the expression of his ego and desires. (See the discussions in Chaps. 2 and 3 above, pp. 45 and 59.) Although he cites the midrashic understanding of *tzimtzum* in "Majesty and Humility" (32), it is the kabbalistic understanding of *tzimtzum* that he develops in both essays as a model for human emulation.

20 See, for example, p. 38: "a life in accordance with the Halakhah means, first, the comprehension of the Halakhah per se and, second, comparing the ideal Halakhah and the real world – the act of realization of the Halakhah."

21 See, for example, p. 90: "Halakhic man implements the Torah without any compromises or concessions, for precisely such implementation, such actualization, is his ultimate desire, his fondest dream."

1. **Bibliography:** "*Ish ha-Halakhah*" was first published in 1944 in the journal *Talpiot*, vol. 1:3–4, 651–735, was reprinted in the volumes *Be-Sod ha-Yahid ve-ha-Yahad*, ed. Pinhas Peli (Jerusalem, 1976), 39–188, and *Ish ha-Halakhah: Galui ve-Nistar* (Jerusalem, 1979), 9–113, and was translated into English by Lawrence Kaplan as *Halakhic Man* (Philadelphia, 1983). Rav Soloveitchik reviewed this translation and suggested elaborations and clarifications; although the published translation ultimately adhered to the original and did not include these elaborations, the translator kept a record of them and described them in his article, "On Translating *Ish ha-Halakhah* with the Rav: Rabbi Joseph Soloveitchik's Supplementary Notes to *Halakhic Man*," in *Mentor of Generations: Reflections on Rabbi Joseph B. Soloveitchik*, ed. Zev Eleff (Jersey City, 2008), 334–45.

2. **Analyses of *Halakhic Man*:** In addition to a number of articles, some of which I reference in this chapter and the following ones, two lengthy studies have been devoted to an in-depth analysis of *Halakhic Man*: David Shatz, "A Framework for Reading *Ish ha-Halakhah*," in *Turim: Studies in Jewish History and Literature Presented to Dr. Bernard Lander*, vol. 2, ed. R. Michael A. Shmidman (New York, 2008), 171–231, and Dov Schwartz, *Religion or Halakha: The Philosophy of Rabbi Joseph B. Soloveitchik*, vol. 1 (Leiden, 2007).

3. **Defining *kedushah* (sanctity):** In his discussion of holiness in *Halakhic Man* (45–48), Rav Soloveitchik emphasizes two points.

   First, it is "the appearance of a mysterious transcendence in the midst of our concrete world" (46). By calling it "a mysterious transcendence," he takes issue with the understanding of Hermann Cohen, who defines holiness as an ethical category; by stating that it appears "in the midst of our concrete world," he takes issue with Rudolf Otto, who views holiness as something "wholly other" and removed from reality.

   Second, the Rav posits that "Holiness is created by man, by flesh and blood" (47). As we saw in the discussion of the sanctity of the Land of Israel in Chapter 27, the Rav believes that nothing becomes holy by itself; all sanctity requires human input. Man controls the calendar (upon which the festivals depend), sanctifies the temple, consecrates *kohanim*, dedicates sacrifices, and so on. Note, however, that the sanctity of the Sabbath seems to be independent of any human intervention, as expressed in the *Amidah* and the *Kiddush*: the blessing "who sanctifies Israel and the festive seasons" indicates that the Jewish people have a role in sanctifying the festivals, while the blessing "who sanctifies the Sabbath" indicates that God alone sanctifies *Shabbat*. In his *shiur* "*Kiddush ke-Mekaddesh ha-Shabbat*" (*Shiurim le-Zekher Abba Mari z"l*, vol. 2, 138–51), the Rav proposes that Shabbat contains two aspects, one dependent solely on God's sanctification and one on human sanctification. The first aspect, however, would still pose a problem for the Rav's definition of *kedushah* in *Halakhic Man*.

4. **Halakhah and science in Rav Soloveitchik's thought:** See Lawrence Kaplan, "Rabbi Joseph B. Soloveitchik's Philosophy of Halakhah," *The Jewish Law Annual* 7 (1988), 139–97, and David Shatz, "Science and Religious Consciousness in the Thought of Rabbi Joseph B. Soloveitchik," in his *Jewish Thought in Dialogue* (Brighton, MA, 2009), 138–76.

Chapter 29

Halakhic Man's Values and Character

In the previous chapter we explored the relationship between halakhic man and two other ideal types: scientific man and religious man. In this chapter we shall examine other facets of halakhic man – specifically, his commitments to study, practice and ethics, as well as the contours of his personality. This will lead us to explore the intriguing question of which real-life individuals most closely correspond to the ideal halakhic man.

Study and Practice

Halakhic man pursues two primary goals: the study of Halakhah and its practice. The study of Torah, as we have seen, means not just mastering texts, but grasping, via those texts, the a priori world of halakhic constructs: comprehending it, shaping it through one's own creative interpretation and conceptualization, and immersing oneself within it. By studying Torah in this fashion, halakhic man makes the Torah into his own possession, a part of himself. As Rashi explains the verse, "But his delight is in the Lord's Torah; and in His [or: his] Torah does he meditate day and night" (Ps. 1:2): "At the beginning it is called 'the Lord's Torah,' and when he studies and masters it, it is called 'his [own] Torah.'"[1]

Halakhic man's other goal, the practice of Halakhah, means implementing and actualizing these ideal constructs within the human world of action and experience. This has two ramifications. First, the performance of *mitzvot* concretizes, objectifies and, one might say, externalizes halakhic man's subjective, inner religiosity. Second, by applying halakhic constructs within the

---

1 *Kiddushin* 32b, s.v. *u-ve-torato.*

physical world, halakhic man brings reality into closer conjunction with the ideal halakhic realm, thereby drawing divinity down into the world.

Which is more important for halakhic man – study or practice? At some points in *Halakhic Man* study seems paramount, while at others it seems that the implementation of Halakhah (following upon its study, of course) is more significant.[2] Although Rav Lichtenstein observes that this antithesis is "ultimately . . . unresolved in the essay,"[3] it seems to me that, overall, study gains the upper hand over practice.[4] This is most striking when the Rav refers to the famous talmudic dispute on this very topic:

> Rabbi Tarfon and the elders were assembled in the upper story of Nitza's house in Lod. This question was posed to them: Which is greater, study (*talmud*) or practice (*ma'aseh*)? Rabbi Tarfon answered and said: Practice is greater. Rabbi Akiva answered: Study is greater. All [the elders] answered and said: Study is greater, for study leads to practice (*Kiddushin* 40b).[5]

Of course, the conclusion that "Study is greater, for study leads to practice" leaves open the question of which of these is more valuable *in itself*. However, halakhic man's interpretation of this passage makes the question almost moot. Noting that "*ma'aseh*" can refer either to "determining the . . . ideal norm" (a theoretical activity), or to "implementing the ideal norm in the real world" (a practical activity), Rav Soloveitchik writes, "Halakhic man stresses action ['*ma'aseh*'] in its first meaning." Thus, both *talmud* and *ma'aseh* (understood this way) become aspects of study.

In a sense, halakhic man is almost *forced* to give primacy to theoretical study, because even though every area of life is governed by Halakhah, many areas of Halakhah are not practically operative today (e.g., the laws of the Temple and of ritual purity). Consider the fact that Rambam, after enumerating the 248 positive biblical commandments in his *Sefer ha-Mitzvot*, lists only sixty (!) as "*mitzvot hekhrehiyot*," commandments that are in effect in all eras for all people. Were halakhic man to lay his primary emphasis upon practice, he would be left with far less motivation and justification for studying the vast

---

2 For sections where study seems primary, see, e.g., 23–29, 63–66, 85–86. For sections where practice seems primary, see, e.g., pp. 90–95, 99–109. In fact, the Rav uses the very same phrase, "*maset nafsho shel ish ha-Halakhah*" (translated variously as halakhic man's "longing" or "deepest desire"), to describe both the study (24 and probably 30) and practice (90, 94, 99, 105) of Halakhah.

3 "The Rav at Jubilee: An Appreciation," in *Leaves of Faith*, vol. 1 (Jersey City, 2003), 191.

4 See, for example, 23–24, 29, 38, 86.

5 This discussion also appears earlier in *Sifrei*, *Devarim*, 41, and *Midrash Tannaim*, Deut. 11:13.

areas of Halakhah that remain in the realm of the ideal – and this would be contrary to his very essence.

Although halakhic man of course keeps *mitzvot* scrupulously, his deep desire to realize Halakhah in its fullness within the concrete world is something of a messianic aspiration, and is not necessarily his prime motivation on a day-to-day basis. Note what halakhic man pursues actively and what he pursues passively in the Rav's summary of halakhic man's activities: "He *creates* an ideal world, *renews* his own being and *transforms* himself into a man of God, *dreams* about the complete realization of the Halakhah in the very core of the world, and *looks forward* to the kingdom of God 'contracting' itself and appearing in the midst of concrete and empirical reality" (137). In this summation, halakhic man is active regarding *study* and *self-creation* ("creates," "renews," "transforms"), and passive regarding the full *realization* of Halakhah ("dreams about," "looks forward to").

Halakhic Man's Ethical Commitment

In the previous chapter, we saw that halakhic man rejects the approach of *homo religiosus* because he finds it otherworldly and undemocratic. But if halakhic man indeed values study more than practice, can he himself really be considered this-worldly or democratic? In other words, if halakhic man lives within the realm of theoretical halakhic constructs that cannot all be actualized, in what sense is he this-worldly? And if he believes that Halakhah demands such a high level of abstract intellectual accomplishment, in what sense is he democratic?

Perhaps to combat the first charge, Rav Soloveitchik concludes Part One of *Halakhic Man* (which generally lays a heavier emphasis on study than on practice) in a manner reminiscent of the way the Rambam concludes his *Guide of the Perplexed*. Throughout the *Guide*, the Rambam presents a highly intellectualist version of human perfection. All human endeavors, it seems, should lead to the ultimate goal of intellectual perfection, or knowledge of God. Yet in the final chapter, the Rambam clarifies that this intellectual perfection is not purely contemplative, but rather entails concrete actions that proceed from knowledge. He explains this by means of an exegesis of a verse in Jeremiah: "But let him who glories glory in this, that he understands, and knows Me, that I am the Lord who exercises loving-kindness, justice and righteousness in the earth; for in these things I delight, says the Lord" (9:22–23):

> The prophet does not content himself with explaining that the knowledge of God is the highest kind of perfection; for if this only had been his intention,

he would have said, "But let him who glories glory in this, that he understands and knows Me," and would have stopped there . . . He says, however, that man can only glory in the knowledge of God and in the knowledge of His ways and attributes, which are His actions . . . We are thus told in this passage that the Divine acts which ought to be known, and ought to serve as a guide for our actions, are "loving-kindness, judgment, and righteousness." . . . The prophet thus, in conclusion, says, "For in these things I delight, says the Lord," i.e., My object [in saying this] is that you shall practice loving-kindness, judgment, and righteousness in the earth . . . The object of the above passage is therefore to declare that the perfection, in which man can truly glory, is attained by him when he has acquired – as far as this is possible for man – the knowledge of God . . . The way of life of such an individual, after he has achieved this knowledge, will always have in view loving-kindness, judgment, and righteousness, through assimilation to His actions (*Guide* III:54).

Similarly, after presenting throughout Part One halakhic man's pursuit of an intellectualist ideal, Rav Soloveitchik ends this section (90–95) by stressing halakhic man's ethical sensitivity and his commitment to ethical action.[6] These are a major part of his commitment to the realization of the Halakhah as a whole:

The standard notion of ritual prevalent among religious men – i.e., ritual as a non-rational religious act whose whole purpose is to lift man up from concrete reality to celestial realms – is totally foreign to Judaism. According to the outlook of Halakhah, the service of God (with the exception of the study of the Torah) can be carried out only through the implementation, the actualization of its principles in the real world. The ideal of righteousness is the guiding light of this world-view. Halakhic man's most fervent desire is the perfection of the world under the dominion of righteousness and loving-kindness – the realization of the a priori, ideal creation, whose name is Torah (or Halakhah), in the realm of concrete life (94).

Thus, for halakhic man, as for the Rambam, intellectual knowledge is both an end in itself and a spur to action. The Rav illustrates the seriousness of halakhic man's ethical commitment with a remarkable comment by his grandfather:

---

6 Although scholars and commentators have debated whether the Rambam believes that the action following intellectual perfection is ethical, political or halakhic, the structural similarity between the Rambam's discussion and the Rav's is striking. Regarding the debate surrounding the end of the *Guide*, see the sources cited in Chap. 3, For Further Reference, #2, and Chap. 34, For Further Reference, #3.

My uncle, R. Meir Berlin [Bar-Ilan], told me that once R. Hayyim of Brisk was asked what the function of a rabbi is. R. Hayyim replied: "To redress the grievances of those who are abandoned and alone, to protect the dignity of the poor, and to save the oppressed from the hands of his oppressor." Neither ritual decisions nor political leadership constitutes the main task of halakhic man. Far from it. The actualization of the ideals of justice and righteousness is the pillar of fire which halakhic man follows when he, as a rabbi and teacher in Israel, serves his community. More, through the implementation of the principles of righteousness, man fulfills the task of creation imposed upon him: the perfection of the world under the dominion of Halakhah and the renewal of the face of creation (91).

Although highlighting halakhic man's ethical commitment may mitigate the charge that he is not truly this-worldly, halakhic man still remains open to the charge that, with his strong emphasis on rigorous and creative Torah study, he is not truly democratic. Rav Soloveitchik returns to consider this theme in *U-Vikkashtem mi-Sham* when he explores the necessity of the exoteric and esoteric, or democratic and elitist, dimensions of Halakhah.[7]

The Structure of *Halakhic Man*

Let us pause to review the overall structure of *Halakhic Man*.

(a) Sections I–X of Part One (3–66) present the "ontological outlooks" (i.e., the perspectives upon the different domains of being) of cognitive man, *homo religiosus* and halakhic man – specifically, how each figure relates to both concrete reality and the transcendent realm. While the first two figures view this as an either/or choice, halakhic man chooses to relate to both realms and to bring them together. Namely, halakhic man draws down the ideal constructs of Halakhah from transcendence into the real world by creatively cognizing them, viewing the world through them, and actualizing them in practice.

(b) Sections XI–XV of Part One (66–95) explore how halakhic man's this-worldly spirituality, with its commitment to the ideal and attention to the real, shapes the contours of his personality, especially as contrasted with that of *homo religiosus* (who, indeed, serves as his major foil throughout the book).

---

7 See Chap. 33 below, pp. 358–59, and the references cited in the footnote there.

(c) Part Two focuses on halakhic man's creative capacity, as exercised in three domains: Torah, the world (sections I–II, 99–109), and especially the self (sections III–VI, 110–137).

We have explored (a) and the first part of (c) in this chapter and the preceding one, while we examined the topic of self-creation – the main focus of (c) – at length in our earlier chapters on prayer, repentance, and suffering.[8] Since so much attention was devoted to self-creation in these chapters, I will not examine the Rav's rich and evocative discussion of this theme in *Halakhic Man*. In brief, however, what (c) adds to our earlier treatments of self-creation is an analysis of providence and prophecy, not as articles of faith but as normative demands. Following upon the Maimonidean doctrine that God grants individual providence (as opposed to providence over species) and prophecy only to individuals who have earned them, halakhic man takes these beliefs as commands: one must strive to make oneself worthy of both individual providence and prophecy. One accomplishes this task of self-perfection by developing one's individuality and exercising one's creativity.[9] Indeed, it is quite striking that in Part Two, the Rav identifies *hiddush*, creativity, as the central characteristic of halakhic man, a figure whom outsiders might consider outdated and fossilized. In fact, the Rav exalts creativity to the point that it becomes the highest form of imitation of God (just as God is a Creator, so should man be a creator, 99–105) as well as the source of all sanctity (107–09).

What remains, then, is for us to consider (b), halakhic man's personality, which I would like to approach by asking: Who is a halakhic man?

Who is a Halakhic Man?

In a sense, the title of this section is unfair, for the Rav makes clear in the book's very first footnote that "the description of halakhic man given here refers to a pure ideal type . . . Real halakhic men, who are not simple but rather hybrid types, approximate, to a lesser or greater degree, the ideal halakhic man" (139, n. 1). Even so, however, we may ask which real figures correspond to the ideal halakhic man "to a greater degree." Let us start by considering one of Rav Soloveitchik's greatest heroes, the Rambam.

Many aspects of halakhic man's emotional profile correspond to traits the

---

8 See Chaps. 20, 22 and 23 above.

9 Note that the Rav contrasts halakhic notions of dynamism and individuality with Greek notions of stasis and universality (132–36). We will explore how Halakhah fosters individuality and creativity in Chap. 35 below.

Rambam prized, and indeed seem to match what we know about the Rambam himself from his books and letters. Halakhic man is motivated by deep piety and a passionate love for truth (79). His religious experience is powerful and penetrating; however, it is one that follows upon cognition, and it is modest, not flashy (84–85). He avoids melancholy (72) as well as exaggerated joy (76), possessing instead a festive dignity and solemnity (76), almost a stoic tranquility and extreme self-control (77–78). Halakhic man is confident (72), individualistic and autonomous (78), noble (78), bold and assertive (79). Supremely strong-minded (79), he hates intellectual flabbiness (79), does not seek anyone's approval (89), and is scornful of piety not based on knowledge (89).

Yet while emotionally similar, halakhic man and the Rambam diverge intellectually. Halakhic man approaches God solely through the medium of Halakhah, and is unconcerned with either metaphysical mysteries (49) or philosophical subtleties (58). In this sense, he could not be more different from the philosopher Rambam.[10] Halakhic man, indeed, regards the study of Halakhah in much the same way as Rambam regards the study of philosophy: it is the best way to know God, the peak of human knowledge, and the goal of our messianic aspirations. While the study of Halakhah has an important place in Rambam's system, the study of philosophy has no place in halakhic man's system.

There is another factor that distinguishes halakhic man not only from Rambam, but from almost all *gedolei Yisrael*: he avoids serving in rabbinic posts and is reluctant to render practical halakhic decisions (24). In light of this characteristic, the Vilna Gaon, who meets many of the above criteria and never held a rabbinic post, would seem to be a likely model for halakhic man. Since many of the anecdotes in *Halakhic Man* revolve around the Gaon,[11] it seems that in the Rav's mind he indeed is a model for this type.

However, this identification of the Vilna Gaon with halakhic man is problematic. The Gaon's worldview, which molded his entire "*mitnagged*" milieu, was not only suffused with Kabbalah (a subject that does not hold halakhic man's interest), but was, like that of *homo religiosus*, otherworldly and dualistic.[12] One scholar writes: "'Mithnagdic Man' is, very much unlike Halakhic

---

10 This also distinguishes halakhic man from another of the Rav's heroes, the kabbalist Ramban.

11 Pp. 30, 36, 57, 77, 87.

12 On *homo religiosus*'s dualism, see pp. 303–05 above. In their introduction to the Gaon's commentary on the *Shulhan Arukh*, the Gaon's sons provide astonishing first-hand testimony regarding his otherworldliness and asceticism: his only nourishment was a small amount of bread soaked in water, taken twice a day, and swallowed without tasting; he slept only two out

Man, starkly pessimistic, strictly dualistic, harshly ascetic and quite literally obsessed with death."[13] If we define *mitnaggedim* as the Vilna Gaon and his circle, it is, therefore, difficult to regard *Halakhic Man* as "a *mitnagged* phenomenology of awesome proportions."[14] As opposed to the early *mitnaggedim* who despaired of attaining religious perfection while still tethered to earthly existence, halakhic man "is completely suffused with an unqualified ontological optimism[15] and is totally immersed in the cosmos" (52). Far from viewing death as liberation from the shackles of physicality, halakhic man abhors death, for "It is this world that constitutes the stage for the Halakhah ... It is here that it can pass from potentiality to actuality. It is here, in this world, that halakhic man acquires eternal life!" (30).[16] Halakhic man, wholly focused on the mission and aspiration of studying and actualizing Halakhah, is entirely unconcerned with *olam ha-ba*:

> The world to come is a tranquil, quiet world that is wholly good, wholly everlasting, and wholly eternal, wherein a man will receive the reward for the commandments which he performed in this world. However, receiving of a reward is not a religious act; therefore, halakhic man prefers the real world to a transcendent existence because here, in this world, man is given the opportunity to create, act, accomplish, while there, in the world to come, he is powerless to change anything at all (32).

Could it be that halakhic man's scientific mode of thought, bold individualism, optimism and creativity indicate that the book is an autobiographical portrait? I think not, for the simple reason that halakhic man would have no interest in writing *Halakhic Man*, nor would he have the ability to write it.[17] The writer of the book *Halakhic Man* displays intimate knowledge of Jewish philosophy and mysticism, Christian thought, general philosophy and

---

of every twenty-four hours, in four half-hour stretches; he engaged in absolutely no small talk, even with his children; and he devoted all his considerable energy and fierce concentration to the study of Torah alone.

13 Allan Nadler, "Soloveitchik's Halakhic Man: Not a *Mithnagged*," *Modern Judaism* 13:2 (1993), 128. This article makes a convincing case that, despite the Rav's citations from the Vilna Gaon and his preeminent disciple R. Hayyim of Volozhin, the early *mitnaggedim* do not fit the typology of halakhic man.

14 Eugene Borowitz, "The Typological Theology of Rabbi Joseph B. Soloveitchik," *Judaism* 15:2 (Spring 1966), 209.

15 I.e., he is optimistic about the possibilities offered by life in this world.

16 Regarding Halakhah's and halakhic man's attitude towards death, see 30–37.

17 R. Jonathan Sacks ("Rabbi Joseph B. Soloveitchik's Early Epistemology," in *Exploring the Thought of Rabbi Joseph B. Soloveitchik*, 223, n. 10) and David Shatz ("A Framework," *op. cit.*, 197) have made similar observations.

literature; halakhic man himself, as described in this book, displays no curiosity about these subjects. Rather, halakhic man's entire mental world seems to be encompassed by the study of Halakhah. Furthermore, the person halakhic man and the book *Halakhic Man* employ entirely different methodologies in approaching their respective subjects of interest. The thought patterns that halakhic man (the person) uses to study Halakhah are akin to those employed in the natural sciences, which are suited to the analysis of abstract concepts and the formal interrelationships between them. However, the book *Halakhic Man*, as pointed out in its first footnote, depicts its protagonist by utilizing the phenomenological method of the human sciences, which describes states and structures of human consciousness.[18] With his "*lomdish*," science-patterned approach, halakhic man can write commentaries and novellae on the Talmud, but not a book like the one that describes him.

Once we have excluded all the above, as well as others whom the Rav contrasts with halakhic man (such as Kabbalists, the early figures of the *Musar* movement, and *Hasidut*, not to mention Reform Judaism), who, then, is halakhic man? All the stories brought to illustrate characteristics of halakhic man are drawn from the lives of Lithuanian *gedolim* of the 18th–20th centuries. The overwhelming majority of these anecdotes concern the Rav's grandfather, R. Hayyim of Brisk, and the Rav's father, R. Moshe Soloveitchik.[19] In fact, the Rav explicitly refers to each of them as a "halakhic man" (36, 38). In light of this, we can understand the book's epigraph, which is drawn from a talmudic *aggadah* concerning the Rav's namesake, the biblical Joseph: "At that moment, the image of his father came to him and appeared before him in the window" (*Sotah* 36b). When drawing his portrait of halakhic man, it seems, the Rav had before his eyes primarily Brisker man.

Although the specific contours of halakhic man's personality follow those of Brisker man, some of his traits and ideas have much broader application to all intellectual religious types, or all those whose *avodat Hashem* is filtered

---

18 For more on the distinction between the human and the natural sciences and their respective methodologies, see *The Halakhic Mind*, 30–36, and Lawrence Kaplan, "Rabbi Joseph B. Soloveitchik's Philosophy of Halakhah," *The Jewish Law Annual* 7 (1988), 186–87.

19 In *Halakhic Man* the Rav does not mention his uncle R. Yitzhak Ze'ev Soloveitchik (the Griz), but in his eulogy for his uncle the Rav clearly portrays him as a halakhic man, going so far as to call him "the singular halakhic man of his generation" and "the most authentic halakhic man" ("*Mah Dodekh mi-Dod*," 89). Aside from the Rav's father and grandfather, the largest number of stories in *Halakhic Man* concerns the Vilna Gaon, whom we have discussed above. There are also a small number of stories concerning the Rav's forebears: the Netziv, the Beit Halevi and R. Elijah Feinstein, his maternal grandfather. For details of where all these figures are mentioned, see R. Jeffrey Saks, "An Index to Rabbi Joseph B. Soloveitchik's *Halakhic Man*," *The Torah u-Madda Journal* 11 (2002–03), 107–22.

mainly through the medium of *talmud Torah*. Halakhic/Brisker man is an extreme version of this type in that he seems to derive his *entire* spiritual sustenance from the world of *lomdus*.[20] In *Halakhic Man*, then, Rav Soloveitchik portrays a type that he clearly considers beautiful and highly admirable. Yet, despite his great esteem for this type and even his identification with it, it describes only one facet of his own religious personality, which was open to a wider range of experience and feeling, and interested in broader areas and sources of knowledge, than those pursued by the pure exemplar of halakhic man he so powerfully describes.[21]

FOR FURTHER REFERENCE

1. **The early *mitnaggedim*:** See R. Norman Lamm, *Torah Lishmah: Torah for Torah's Sake in the Works of Rabbi Hayyim of Volozhin and his Contemporaries* (New York, 1989); Allan Nadler, *The Faith of Mithnagdim: Rabbinic Responses to Hasidic Rapture* (Baltimore, 1997); and Immanuel Etkes, *The Gaon of Vilna: The Man and his Image* (Berkeley, 2002).

2. **The self-sufficiency of halakhic study:** The question of whether the study of Halakhah needs to be supplemented by the study of "meta-halakhic" disciplines has a long and fascinating history. Interestingly, the primary chronicler in our day of the dialectic between "halakhic creativity and meta-halakhic concerns (e.g., philosophy, mysticism, pietism, or at a later period, hasidism, mussar)" was Rabbi Prof. Yitzhak (Isadore) Twersky, Rav Soloveitchik's son-in-law. Many relevant articles are collected in his *Studies in Jewish Law and Philosophy* (New York, 1982). A full bibliography can be found in Carmi Horowitz, "A Bibliography of the Works of Professor Isadore Twersky," in *Me'ah She'arim: Studies in Medieval Jewish Spiritual Life in Memory of Isadore Twersky*, eds. Ezra Fleischer, Gerald Blidstein, Carmi Horowitz and Bernard Septimus (Jerusalem, 2001), 1–10.

---

20 Regarding the self-sufficiency of halakhic study, see For Further Reference, #2.

21 I believe that it is for this reason that he felt compelled to write *U-Vikkashtem mi-Sham* as well. See Chap. 35 below.

Chapter 30

The Goals of *Halakhic Man*

Description and Defense

Given the date of *Halakhic Man*'s publication (1944), many have speculated that the Rav wrote it as a philosophical eulogy for his father, who had died unexpectedly three years earlier, and perhaps for the entire Lithuanian yeshivah world that was being annihilated in the Holocaust. While there may indeed be an element of eulogy in this work, I suggest that we look closely at the Rav's explicit programmatic statements on its first and last pages, and at the carefully-chosen terms he uses to characterize halakhic man throughout it. These will help us grasp – now that we have surveyed some of *Halakhic Man*'s major themes – what exactly the Rav was trying to accomplish in this work.

> ... [I]t is difficult *to analyze halakhic man's religious consciousness* by applying the terms and traits that *descriptive psychology and modern philosophy of religion* have used to characterize the religious personality ... He is of a type that is *unfamiliar to students of religion* ... Our aim in this essay is to penetrate deep into the structure of halakhic man's consciousness ... (3–4, emphasis added).[1]

> ... [M]y sole intention was to *defend the honor of the Halakhah and halakhic men*, for both it and they have oftentimes been attacked by those who have not penetrated into the essence of Halakhah and have failed to understand the halakhic personality (137, emphasis added).

---

1 Note a similar comment on p. 17: "All of the frames of reference constructed by the *philosophers and psychologists of religion* for explaining the varieties of religious experience cannot accommodate halakhic man as far as his reaction to empirical reality is concerned."

In these passages, the Rav articulates two goals: analysis (3–4) and defense (137); and he identifies two subjects that are to be analyzed and defended: halakhic man and the halakhic system. To be more precise, the Rav wishes to a) analyze halakhic man's religious consciousness, b) defend halakhic man, and c) defend the Halakhah.

The Rav does not define against whom he wants to defend halakhic man and the Halakhah. However, it seems to me that it is the inability of "descriptive psychology and modern philosophy of religion" and "students of religion" to understand Halakhah and halakhic men that leads the practitioners of these disciplines (and, more importantly, the broader circles influenced by them) to denigrate and even attack both of them.

Psychology and Philosophy of Religion

The American psychologist and philosopher William James (1842–1910) is widely acknowledged as the founder of the field that the Rav calls "descriptive psychology of religion."[2] In his survey of *The Varieties of Religious Experience* (1902), he describes numerous types of *homo religiosus*. Yet all of these types practice a religiosity based on emotion and tinged with mysticism. James cannot conceive of an intellect-centered religiosity like halakhic man's, in which experience only follows upon cognition, never preceding it. *Halakhic Man*, then, introduces an entirely new cognitive personality type to James's religious taxonomy.

The seminal figure in the "modern philosophy of religion" (as in many other areas in philosophy) is without a doubt the German philosopher Immanuel Kant (1724–1804). One of Kant's most basic distinctions is between noumena and phenomena, or things-in-themselves as opposed to things observed through our senses. Human intellect can be applied to the realm of phenomena, but it has no access to the realm of noumena, which includes the entire area of transcendent metaphysics (that which lies "beyond" the physical world). Thus, the metaphysical propositions of religion – God's existence, immortality of the soul, and free will – are not subject to either proof or disproof. They are not matters of *knowledge* but of *faith*.

---

2 Although some of James's contemporaries also worked in this field, it was James who "wrote the field's signature classic . . . [and] brought the field most prominently into view" (David Wulff, "Psychology of Religion," in *Encyclopedia of Psychology and Religion*, eds. David Leeming, Kathryn Madden and Stanton Marlan [New York, 2009], 732). James is the only psychologist of religion whom the Rav mentions by name in *Halakhic Man*.

Human intellect can be applied fruitfully, however, to a number of different areas, including:

(a) *Science*: This area was developed more by neo-Kantians such as Hermann Cohen than by Kant himself.[3]

(b) *The study of human consciousness*: Even if we cannot determine whether many of the things we think about are real, we do know that our thoughts themselves are real, and they can be studied. In fact, Kant's main project in his study of knowledge was to identify the structures by which the mind cognizes. By drawing attention away from the analysis of *things-in-themselves*, Kant opened the way for philosophers and psychologists to study the thought processes and subjective awareness of the *thinkers*. This turn to the self had a lasting effect on philosophy and led to the rise of the phenomenological method that the Rav employs in *Halakhic Man* and *U-Vikkashtem mi-Sham*, which (as we noted in Chapter 29) studies perceptions and consciousness rather than what lies behind them.

(c) *Ethics*: Man can and must formulate the universal ethical norm purely by using his own intellect. This is termed autonomy, i.e., self-legislation (*auto* = self, *nomos* = law). If one acts properly because one has been given an external command, and not because of the dictates of one's own conscience, one is acting not morally but rather slavishly. Kant terms such behavior heteronomous, meaning that it follows a law dictated from the outside (*hetero* = other, *nomos* = law).[4] For him, only autonomous acts have moral worth.

Although, according to Kant's theory of knowledge, we cannot assess the truth of religious propositions, religion plays an important practical role in supporting Kant's ethical theory. For in order to posit the existence of a moral order, it is necessary to assume that man has free will, that the soul is immortal, and that God exists.[5] However, this is no longer religion as commonly understood. God, the heteronomous commander, has no place in this system. For Kant, having true religion means following the moral imperative of one's conscience for its own sake, and not because it has been commanded from without. Man cannot have a personal relationship with God, nor does God

---

3 See "The Scientist and the Halakhist" in Chap. 28 above, pp. 306–08.

4 Following the dictates of desire instead of reason is also a form of heteronomy.

5 (i) If man lacked free will, he could not be a moral agent. (ii) The moral agent seeks to perfect himself, and it is impossible to attain this goal within the span of a life; hence, we must posit the immortality of the soul. (iii) A moral order entails that one's happiness should be proportionate to one's moral virtue. Yet only the existence of God can ensure that this will ultimately come about. For Kant, these are necessary postulates of his moral theory, but they are also factors that motivate moral behavior.

desire man's service or worship. Religious rituals and prayer, which constitute what he calls the "external cult," are meaningless. At best, religious worship has instrumental value in symbolizing and perhaps reinforcing man's commitment to the ethical ideal.

Kant and Halakhah

Based on Christian portrayals of Judaism stretching back to Christianity's very beginnings, as well as on the interpretation of Judaism offered by the apostate Jew and rationalist philosopher Baruch Spinoza (1632–1677), Kant views Judaism as nothing more than a collection of political laws and empty rituals designed to preserve group cohesion. For him, it lacks a moral core and any notion of autonomous duty; in fact, it makes no demands whatsoever on the inner self. Rather, Judaism demands the fulfillment of external observances, resulting in what he considered to be an ossified legalism. As the very epitome of heteronomy, Judaism creates a servile personality and thereby damages the causes of human dignity and morality. By Kant's definition, Judaism cannot be considered a religion at all.[6]

Most subsequent attacks on halakhic Judaism derived from Kant's critique in one way or another. This is not because the attackers were all sophisticated philosophers, but rather because the constellation of values that Kant or his successors espoused – autonomy, individuality, freedom, intellectual rigor, boldness and creativity – became regnant in modern western civilization. Whether due to Kant's direct or indirect influence, or because the "spirit of the age" dictated an approach like his, his ideas (even if watered down) became almost taken for granted.[7] And the values mentioned (autonomy, individuality and so forth) were invoked as a major indictment against Judaism, which seemed so lacking in these qualities. How was a religion devoted to the seemingly calcified study of ancient texts and the fulfillment of heteronomous laws to respond?

Whether Kant's approach to religion[8] is correct and whether his views

---

6 For a bibliography of Kant's relevant writings on this subject, see For Further Reference, #1.

7 As the eminent contemporary philosopher Alasdair MacIntyre notes, "For many who have never heard of philosophy, let alone of Kant, morality is roughly what Kant said it was" (*A Short History of Ethics* [New York, 1966], 190).

8 To recapitulate, Kant believed that true religion entails molding man's will in accordance with the moral duty dictated by his autonomous reason. (Interestingly, although Kant could not be considered a traditional Christian, his philosophical approach was influenced by his Pietist Protestant background, which stressed both duty and interiority.)

on the nature of Judaism are correct – those are two distinct issues. Many Jews thought that Kant was correct on both counts. Therefore, they concluded, Judaism either should be reformed and brought into closer accord with Kant's religion of reason by eliminating Halakhah's "ritual" laws and keeping only the "moral" laws (this was the approach of Liberal Judaism), or Judaism should be abandoned altogether (the approach of assimilationists). Others Jews, as different as R. Isaac Breuer and Hermann Cohen, felt that Kant's understanding of religion was essentially correct, but his understanding of Judaism was faulty – for Judaism in fact met Kant's criteria for true religion. A third group, though they wouldn't have said so in as many words, felt that, on the contrary, Kant's understanding of Judaism was correct but his understanding of religion was wrong: Judaism is indeed heteronomous and proud of it. (This approach may be attributed to ultra-Orthodoxy.) Finally, there were those who challenged both aspects of Kant's view: his approach to religion and his understanding of Judaism. Among this last group we can count Rav Soloveitchik.[9]

Critique and Response

On the one hand, Rav Soloveitchik accepts Kant's delimitation of the intellect to the realm of phenomena (things as they appear to us), and the consequent impossibility of pursuing metaphysics. Instead of studying the metaphysical claims of religion, Rav Soloveitchik, like others, turns to the self and studies the religious *personality*.[10] He of course does not assert that religion is a purely human creation, but he does study it from the human, not divine, point of view, analyzing its influence upon man, man's role within it, and man's task in shaping it in partnership with God.

Many Romantic thinkers took the "turn to the self" to an extreme, coming to regard religion as purely subjective and emotional. Rav Soloveitchik's focus on human consciousness and the inner self does not lead him in this direction. On the contrary, halakhic man, as we have seen, is far closer to cognitive man than to *homo religiosus*. Halakhic man's religiosity is based on the intellect, and his primary goal is to bring objectivity to religion. He

---

9 To be more precise, Rav Soloveitchik, as we shall see, challenged some aspects of Kant's approach to religion while he accepted others, but he completely rejected Kant's understanding of Judaism.

10 At various points in his career, Rav Soloveitchik studied the religious personality through phenomenological lenses, focusing on states and structures of consciousness, and through existential lenses, focusing on the concrete dilemmas of the individual, his ability to communicate and form communities, etc.

does this both by objectifying halakhic concepts in his rigorous and precise Torah study and by actualizing them in his observance of *mitzvot*. Both of these commitments prevent him from being swept away by the tide of subjectivity and unrestrained emotion that characterizes many contemporary forms of religion.[11]

Nevertheless, I believe that Rav Soloveitchik displays sensitivity to Kant's critiques even when he does not explicitly indicate that he is engaging in polemic or defense.[12] For example, Kant and others viewed the *mitzvot* as empty and soulless rituals. However, as we saw at length in Chapters 6–9 above, the Rav demonstrates in many of his writings – both halakhic and philosophical – that Halakhah addresses not just external observance but also the inner realm of emotion and experience. Furthermore, in *The Halakhic Mind* the Rav asserts that there are values embedded within halakhic norms, and these can be identified after rigorous conceptual study of those norms.[13]

As for Kant's indictment of Judaism as being heteronomous, Rav Soloveitchik responds in two ways. First, he shows that there is broad autonomy within Judaism (at least for the master of halakhic study).[14] Second, he shows that heteronomy is also important and has its place. As Moshe Sokol notes, more than the Rav addresses the technical philosophical issue of autonomy, he fosters an *ethic* of autonomy, a positive evaluation of halakhic man's sense of freedom, individuality and self-worth.[15] In *Halakhic Man* especially, Rav Soloveitchik is far more concerned with the consequences of heteronomy for the religious personality than he is with the question of the heteronomy of the halakhic system per se. While the heteronomous personality is passive,

---

11 See also David Shatz, "A Framework," 207–11. R. Jonathan Sacks pithily notes that both *Halakhic Man* and *The Halakhic Mind* share the sense "that romantic religion and philosophical subjectivism have failed, and that the need is for a presentation of religion as a form of cognitive, disciplined perception" (*Tradition in an Untraditional Age*, 294).

12 Whether the Rav confronted these critiques in the writings of figures from the Haskalah (Jewish Enlightenment), Liberal Judaism, Protestant theology, philosophy, the social sciences or elsewhere, they all derive secondarily from Kant and from the Enlightenment *zeitgeist* that produced him. Therefore, I will not treat each critic separately, but instead will address Kant himself, the source of the critique.

13 In *The Halakhic Mind*, R. Soloveitchik analyzes at length these two stages: (a) cognition and construction of objective forms; (b) reconstruction of subjective values and experiences out of these objective data. See Chap. 31 below.

14 See the section on "The Rule of the Intellect" in Chap. 35 below.

15 See R. Moshe Sokol, "Master or Slave? Rabbi Joseph B. Soloveitchik on Human Autonomy in the Presence of God," in *Turim: Studies in Jewish History and Literature Presented to Dr. Bernard Lander*, vol. 1, ed. R. Michael A. Shmidman (New York, 2007), 275–330, and For Further Reference, #2.

uncreative and servile, halakhic man is active, creative and majestic. Halakhic man achieves this sense of autonomy by the complete identification of his will with God's will (i.e., the Halakhah), attained through his creative partnership with God in determining and realizing the law.

The Rav's use of the term "autonomous" to describe halakhic man, even if not in the exact sense Kant used it,[16] leads us to a crucial point regarding *Halakhic Man*. In describing Halakhah and halakhic man, the Rav consistently employs loaded Kantian and neo-Kantian terms: autonomous, a priori, creative, scientific, etc. By doing so, he is making two statements: first, he values many of the same characteristics as do the Kantian and other modernist critics of halakhic Judaism; moreover, these very traits and values can be attained precisely through the study and practice of Halakhah. As he states in a succinct and striking formulation, "The goal of [halakhic man's] self-creation is individuality, autonomy, uniqueness, and freedom" (135).

We can infer from here and elsewhere that the Rav is responding to critics of Halakhah who asserted that "a life devoted to Torah study stifles the mind and stunts the spirit; the halakhic way of life deprives an individual of his freedom and intellectual creativity, and robs him of individuality."[17] As one who had grown up among the giants of Brisk, the exemplars par excellence of halakhic man, Rav Soloveitchik saw these accusations as being patently absurd. It is reasonable to assume that he realized that if serious Torah study and halakhic commitment were to flourish in the modern world, it was necessary to elaborate the ideological underpinnings of conceptual *talmud Torah* and to portray the *talmid hakham* in a manner that would be both comprehensible and attractive to modern man. Halakhah, he explains, is a cognitive discipline; it demands the scholar's creative input; and it fosters a majestic and fully-realized personality while avoiding the excesses of *homo religiosus*. Thus, as David Shatz concludes,

> The very values which modern critics felt could be realized only by leaving the *dalet amot shel Halakhah*, the four ells of Halakhah, could, in fact, be achieved by remaining squarely within them. *It is as if modernity is being turned against itself; its value system is revealed not to oppose tradition, but to support and vindicate it.* And we are not dealing here with . . . an argument that uses the premises of the modern critic only to convince the critic of the validity of Rabbi Soloveitchik's praise of halakhic man, without Rabbi Soloveitchik endorsing those premises. On the contrary, Rabbi Soloveitchik

---

16 Regarding Kantian autonomy and halakhic autonomy, see For Further Reference, #3.
17 Shatz, "A Framework," 193.

seems genuinely to accept the values of freedom, creativity and individuality because they are affirmed in Jewish sources . . . [18]

Conclusion

In sum, *Halakhic Man* aims to accomplish several goals. First, it depicts a type of intellect-based religiosity and religious personality that is unfamiliar to modern psychology and philosophy of religion. Second, it defends Halakhah against charges that it is heteronomous, non-cognitive, non-moral and slavish. Third, it defends the halakhic personality against charges that he is otherworldly, passive and uncreative. In the course of accomplishing these goals, *Halakhic Man* provides a justification for *talmud Torah*, explaining its meaning and significance in terms comprehensible to modern individuals; it argues for the superiority of halakhic man's religiosity which, through the use of reason and the maintenance of boundaries, overcomes *homo religiosus*'s subjectivity and extremism; and it establishes the centrality of creativity in halakhic life: creativity in the realm of Torah study, creativity within the world (by realizing halakhic ideals), and creation of the self.

In *U-Vikkashtem mi-Sham* (8 ff.), Rav Soloveitchik writes that people naturally seek to anchor their existence in something stable and transcendent. This is doubly true of modern man, who is perplexed and conflicted. Such a reader – and not only one already immersed in the world of conceptual *lomdus* – can find *Halakhic Man* quite compelling, despite the "strange, singular" (4) nature of its title character. The book begins by acknowledging that conflict is a creative force, a point with which many would agree but would be hard-pressed to find in earlier Jewish sources. The book then proceeds to build a stable and objective, yet dynamic and creative, religiosity. This religiosity avoids the pitfalls that many associate with contemporary religion – be they passivity and otherworldliness, vapid ceremonialism and sentimentality, or technical ritualism and intellectual laziness. Halakhic man lives a life of high seriousness and heroism, of drama and engagement, as he immerses himself in the demanding and meaningful struggle to grasp and formulate halakhic concepts, to actualize divine ideals within the concrete world, and to craft an individualistic personality that is intellectual and ethical, creative and majestic.

It is hard to do justice in three short chapters to the rich range of ideas overflowing from the pages of *Halakhic Man*. I can close only by paraphrasing the book's conclusion: "These are but some of the traits of *Halakhic Man*.

---

18 Ibid., 196.

Much more than I have written here is imprinted in this book. These essays are but an incomplete sketch of a few of *Halakhic Man*'s features. But it is revealed and known before Him who created the world that my sole intention was to explicate the book's basic themes and goals, for they have often been misunderstood. And if I have erred, may God, in His goodness, forgive me."

FOR FURTHER REFERENCE

1. **Kant's critique of Judaism:** Kant formulates his theory of knowledge in his *Critique of Pure Reason* (1781; 2nd ed. 1787); his ethical theory in *Groundwork of the Metaphysics of Morals* (1785) and *Critique of Practical Reason* (1788); and his criticism of Judaism in *Religion within the Limits of Reason Alone* (1793), Book Three, beginning of Division Two. Regarding Kant's negative assessment of Judaism, see Jacob Katz, "*Kant ve-ha-Yahadut: ha-Heksher ha-Histori*," *Tarbiz* 41:2 (1972), 219–37.

2. **Submissiveness and self-assertion:** Moshe Sokol ("Master or Slave," 300–02) suggests that *Halakhic Man* presents the majestic side of the *talmid hakham* not only to counter the view of the moderns that he is passive and otherworldly, but also to counter the "ethic of submissiveness" prevalent in many circles of traditionalist Orthodoxy. David Shatz ("A Framework," 201–03), distinguishing between what Rav Soloveitchik intends in *Halakhic Man* and what readers can derive from the work, notes that "There is no direct internal evidence" that the Rav intended *Halakhic Man* as a polemic against the Haredi posture of worldly and religious submissiveness. Nevertheless, if readers wish to contrast *Halakhic Man* with Haredi positions, Shatz suggests that *Halakhic Man* can also be read as a defense of creative and conceptual Brisker *lomdus*, which exalts the innovative thinker, against the strictures of Haredi critics like the Hazon Ish, Rav Avraham Yeshaya Karelitz (1878–1953). The latter's approach to learning, as opposed to Brisk, is tightly bound to the text, searches for the straightforward non-abstract meaning, and values diligence and humility over self-expression and intellectual autonomy. (In characterizing the Hazon Ish, Shatz references Lawrence Kaplan's article, "The Hazon Ish: Haredi Critic of Traditional Orthodoxy," in *The Uses of Tradition*, ed. Jack Wertheimer [New York, 1992], 145–73.)

   It is interesting to note that charges similar to those leveled by the Hazon Ish against the Briskers were leveled more than seven centuries earlier by *Sefer Hasidim* against the Tosafists, who had pioneered a new analytic method of study that fostered an ethic of self-assertion and innovation. This critique was analyzed in articles by Profs. Haym Soloveitchik and Israel Ta-Shma and is summarized by the latter in his *Ha-Sifrut ha-Parshanit la-Talmud*, vol. 1 (2nd ed., Jerusalem, 2000), 81–84 (see there for further references).

3. **Kantian and halakhic autonomy:** Kenneth Seeskin ("Ethics, Authority, and Autonomy" in *The Cambridge Companion to Modern Jewish Philosophy*, *op. cit.*, 195–96) notes that, for Kant, autonomy does not mean doing whatever I want. Kant believes that norms are universal, and not based on individual desires. Autonomy is achieved when, and only when, human reason establishes that how I act is right – and it can tell me that only if my prescription for myself applies to everyone and is not predicated on my personal desires. In other words, my reason does not so much *innovate* the norm as *endorse* or *appropriate* the universal norm.

If we understand Kantian autonomy in this way, perhaps Rav Soloveitchik concedes too much when he writes: "The freedom of the pure will in Kant's teaching refers essentially to the creation of the ethical norm. The freedom of halakhic man refers not to the creation of the law itself, for it was given to him by the Almighty, but to the realization of the norm in the concrete world" (*Halakhic Man*, 153, n. 80). Even according to Kant, the individual is not really creating the law; he is assenting to it and identifying with it.

Of course, Kant also says that external revelation has no binding power, and the source of moral authority is the self. Rav Soloveitchik cannot agree with this. However, Rav Soloveitchik could respond that once revelation *has* occurred, the self can give authority to that which has been revealed, which is precisely what halakhic man accomplishes with the unity of wills. Rav Soloveitchik emphasizes the centrality of *berit*, covenant, which demonstrates that man is a free agent and assents of his own will. Man is not the source of the law, but he freely adopts it as his own. Furthermore, through his freedom of conceptualization, halakhic man participates in the unfolding and elaboration of the revealed law.

Thus, the gap between Kant and the Rav shrinks when we take into account two factors: a) norms do not depend upon one's personal desires even according to Kant; b) even a revealed norm can be endorsed autonomously by appropriating it after it is revealed. Note Hermann Cohen's observation: "God's law does not contradict the autonomy of the moral will. There is a difference only in the method of formulating the concept, which is the difference between ethics and religion" (*Religion of Reason out of the Sources of Judaism*, trans. Simon Kaplan [New York, 1972], 339). See also *The Emergence of Ethical Man*, 154 ff.

Chapter 31

Subjectivity and Objectivity in Halakhah

Objectification and Reconstruction

We have seen throughout this book that Rav Soloveitchik takes issue with advocates of two extreme schools of thought: on the one hand, those who claim that religion is purely subjective and does not require objective and normative manifestations, and on the other hand, those who claim that Judaism consists only of objective forms and that it ignores subjectivity. In many of his writings, such as *Halakhic Man* and *The Halakhic Mind*, the Rav establishes that both the subjective and the objective dimensions are central to Judaism.[1] In *The Halakhic Mind*, the Rav adds an important methodological principle regarding the study of religious subjectivity: the only legitimate way to access the subjective dimension is through its objective manifestations. The method of gaining access to the subjective elements of a given religious system was developed by the Marburg Neo-Kantian philosopher Paul Natorp (1854–1924) and is called "reconstruction."

What are the objective elements of a religion by means of which we can reconstruct the subjective elements? Rav Soloveitchik believes that religion is objectified not only in the form of rituals and scriptures, but also, indeed more fundamentally, as a system of concepts that constitutes an autonomous cognitive domain.[2] Isolating religion's objective elements is therefore a two-step

---

1 This is true of all manifestations of the spirit, but for the purpose of our discussion I will focus on its application to Judaism.

2 See the discussion of Halakhah as a cognitive system in Chap. 28, as well as the discussion of epistemological pluralism and *The Halakhic Mind* in Chap. 16 (esp. in For Further Reference, #1 there).

process. First, the inquirer must gather all the crystallized, objectified forms of religious consciousness, such as texts, norms, rituals, doctrines and prayers; second, the inquirer must subject these to rigorous, creative analysis so as to draw out and define their conceptual principles. This is especially true when studying Halakhah, which, as we saw in *Halakhic Man*, is not just an assemblage of laws but an a priori system of ideas. Texts and norms are manifestations of Halakhah; its essence, however, is a system of formal concepts. These concepts were given at Sinai but are then abstracted and elaborated by human reason, employing methods of thought and analysis that are singular to Halakhah. Only once these concepts have been postulated and their formal interdependencies defined do we have objectified and quantified data upon which we can practice reconstruction.

In reconstruction, we do not ask "why" these objectified concepts are as they are, nor do we seek their antecedent causes. Since religion is an autonomous domain, to find a "cause" would be to subordinate the religious concept to some other, foreign domain. Moreover, we cannot retrace the original subjectivity that gave rise to objective religious concepts and phenomena. Instead, reconstruction accepts the objective data as they are, asking "what" they entail and what ideas emerge from them: "[B]y exploring the norm retrospectively through vectorial hints which point towards subjectivity, the religious act with its unique structure retains its full autonomy" (*The Halakhic Mind*, 95). The importance of asking "what" instead of "why" is, of course, a recurring theme in the Rav's writings.[3]

To translate all this into more familiar terms, the technique of objectification that the Rav advocates is *Brisker lomdus*, but reconstruction is his favored method for pursuing Jewish *philosophy* – a philosophy that, as we have seen repeatedly, must derive from Halakhah.[4] In attempting to formulate a philosophy of Judaism, it is crucial not to skip either step in this process.[5] To try to engage in Jewish philosophy without reference to the objective forms

---

3 The "what, not why" approach, which Rav Soloveitchik ascribes to both the scientist and the halakhist, characterizes cognitive man in *Halakhic Man*, Adam I in *The Lonely Man of Faith*, the topical Halakhah in *Out of the Whirlwind*, and the man of destiny in *Kol Dodi Dofek*.

4 Regarding *Brisker lomdus*, see For Further Reference, #1. Regarding the role of Aggadah in the formulation of Jewish philosophy, see For Further Reference, #2.

5 The stage of conceptualization, of *lomdus*, is not only a necessary precursor to reconstruction, but is of supreme value in itself, as we saw in *Halakhic Man*. And in studying the Rav's philosophical thought, it is important for us to recall that he devoted the vast bulk of his time and energy over the course of his career to *lomdus* and not to reconstruction. For more on the relationship between *lomdus* and reconstruction, see For Further Reference, #3.

of Halakhah, or without properly conceptualizing them first, would be a futile undertaking.

Case Studies

By starting with the objective forms of Halakhah already referred to, we may reconstruct three types of subjectivity:
(1) philosophical concepts, or components of a world perspective;
(2) halakhic values;
(3) elements of the religious experience, and particularly the inner experience of *mitzvot*.
To clarify, let us bring examples of each.

(1)   *Philosophical concepts*

In *The Halakhic Mind*, the Rav lists a large number of philosophical and cognitive concepts that can be reconstructed out of objective data: causality, space, quantity, quality, necessity (50); time, substance, ego (99); freedom, God-man relationship, creation and nihility (101). Although the Rav set an ambitious agenda here, he followed through explicitly only on a number of these areas, as in his multiple examinations of the halakhic conception of time (e.g., *Halakhic Man*, 117–23; *The Halakhic Mind*, 46–50; *Out of the Whirlwind*, 14–17).[6]

(2)   *Halakhic values*

A number of elements can be included in the category of halakhic values. First, the derivation of halakhic values refers to the ability to start with the letter of the law and to extrapolate the spirit of the law, extending principles to situations not covered by the law as well as to seemingly neutral areas (*devar ha-reshut*). We saw this method employed in a number of the Rav's halakhic rulings and public policy decisions discussed in Chapter 18, such as his objection, based on the halakhic philosophy of prayer, to having the prayer leader face the congregation. Even in a case like mixed seating in the synagogue, where the Rav believed there was a technical halakhic prohibition involved, the ability to understand and articulate halakhic values allowed him to present a compelling case to an audience not versed in halakhic study or observance.

The category of halakhic values also includes general *mitzvot* that by their nature cannot be circumscribed and whose application requires extrapolation

---

6 See the discussion of time in Chap. 22 above, and R. Mayer Twersky, "Towards a Philosophy of Halachah," *Jewish Action* 64:1 (Fall 2003), 49–62.

from other norms. Examples of such *mitzvot* are "You shall be holy" (Lev. 19:2) and "You shall do that which is right and good in the eyes of the Lord" (Deut. 6:18). The Ramban's approach to these *mitzvot* exerted a powerful influence on the Rav. Note, for example, the Ramban's comments on the "right and good":

> The previous verse stated that you should obey "His decrees and testimonies that He commanded you" (Deut. 6:17). Now this verse adds that even regarding matters in which you have not been commanded, take heed to do what is good and right in His eyes, because He loves the good and the right.
>
> This is a great principle, for it would be impossible for the Torah to mention all aspects of one's conduct with neighbors and friends, and all of one's transactions, and the ordinances of all societies and countries. But since He mentioned many of them, such as "You shall not be a talebearer" (Lev. 19:16), "Do not take revenge nor bear a grudge" (ibid. 19:18), "Do not stand idly by your fellow's blood" (ibid. 19:16), "Do not curse a deaf person" (ibid. 19:14), "Rise before the elderly" (ibid. 19:32), and so on, He returned to state in a general way that, in every matter, one should do what is good and right . . . until one is called perfect and upright in all matters (Ramban, Deut. 6:18).

The Rav took the Ramban to mean not merely that the Torah had to state general *mitzvot* because it was impossible for the Torah to address every possible contingency. Rather, the fact that the Torah commands these general *mitzvot* teaches how important it is to be able to extrapolate values from specific halakhic cases and norms.

In addition to reconstructing the values of specific and general *mitzvot*, the Rav also develops philosophies of entire halakhic institutions. A good example of this is his discussion in *Family Redeemed* of the axiology of marriage (that is, the system of values expressed by the Jewish approach to marriage).

Finally, in some writings the Rav takes the atypical step of suggesting a teleology of Halakhah in general.[7] In *Halakhic Man*, for example, he portrays Halakhah as centering around creativity, while in *The Lonely Man of Faith* he sees its general tendency as the attainment of catharsis. This does not mean that the "goal" of Halakhah is to attain these ends. Rather, it means that these are overarching patterns the Rav finds in Halakhah, with subjective meaning and significance for one's service of God.

---

7 See the discussion of the teleology of Halakhah in Chap. 14 above. "Teleology" is the study of causes.

(3) *Religious experiences*

This category, consisting of the experiential components of *mitzvot*, is very familiar from our study of prayer, repentance, mourning, festival rejoicing, honoring parents, etc. The Rav devoted a great deal of attention to it in works such as *On Repentance, Family Redeemed, Out of the Whirlwind* and *Worship of the Heart*, and even in the halakhic essays contained in *Shiurim le-Zekher Abba Mari z"l*.[8]

In some of these places, grasping the emotional element of a *mitzvah* opened wider vistas. For example, an examination of the laws of *avelut* (mourning) revealed that this *mitzvah* mandates an interior dimension beyond its external observances. By exploring the conflict between the inner experiences of festive joy and mournful sadness, the Rav linked the former with the sense of God's presence and the latter with the sense of His absence. Furthermore, by juxtaposing *avelut* with the norms of the *metzora* (leper) and *menudeh* (excommunicate), the Rav posited a broader structural pattern. The *avelut* of an individual is canceled by a festival because he remains part of the community; the forms of *avelut* practiced by the leper and the excommunicate are not canceled by a festival because these individuals have been excluded from the community and therefore cannot share in the joy of the festival. One's experience of divine nearness on a festival, we see, is mediated by God's connection with the community.

It is important to note that all the *mitzvot* just mentioned – mourning, festival joy, prayer, repentance, etc. – are examples of a category of *mitzvot* that is particularly congenial to an investigation of subjectivity, since the formal, objective Halakhah itself mandates inwardness in the implementation of these laws. The Rav refers to this category as *mitzvot* with an external action and an inner fulfillment (*ma'aseh hitzoni ve-kiyyum penimi*, or *ma'aseh ba-evarim ve-kiyyum ba-lev*). In his discussion of one of the *mitzvot* in this category (namely, the recitation of *Shema*), the Rav admits that it is easier to reconstruct subjectivity in these cases than in other *mitzvot*:

> I have always maintained that the halakhic elements constitute the most appropriate and reliable material out of which a philosophical understanding might emerge. If this approach is cogent in regard to other themes, it is certainly true of the recitation of *Shema*, which is . . . a subjective norm [i.e., it is performed through speech but fulfilled in the heart]. The Halakhah has never left this [experiential] motif out of sight. Therefore, the halakhic rules are very revealing as to the inner essence of the experience. *Because the subjective elements are*

---

8 See the appendix to Chap. 6 above.

salient, the objectification process here has not gone through a multitude of phases and the objective element is closely correlated to the subjective correlate (Worship of the Heart, 103–04, emphasis added).

But what of the experience of other areas of Halakhah, such as purity, oaths, agricultural laws, *kashrut*, civil law, the various types of Temple service, etc.? Does their subjective content exhaust itself in philosophic concepts and value statements, as in categories 1 and 2 above? Or do they possess an inner emotional correlate, yet one harder to access because it is not mandated by formal Halakhah and therefore has gone through "a multitude of phases" of "the objectification process?" The Rav does not address this question, but his approach to *ta'amei ha-mitzvot* (rationalization of commandments) might point us in the direction of an answer.

"There is a Hint in It"

In *The Halakhic Mind* (91–99), the Rav takes up the vexed problem of *ta'amei ha-mitzvot*. He cites approvingly the Rambam's statements in *Mishneh Torah* that even though the *mitzvot* of *shofar* and *mikveh* purification are *gezerot*, divine decrees, they nevertheless contain *remazim*, hints or allusions. For example, the Rambam writes:

> Although the blowing of the *shofar* on Rosh Hashanah is a decree of the Holy Writ, nevertheless there is a hint in it, as if saying, "Ye that sleep, bestir yourselves from your sleep, and ye that slumber, emerge from your slumber. Examine your conduct, return in repentance and remember your Creator" (*Hilkhot Teshuvah* 3:4).[9]

Here, Rav Soloveitchik explains, the Rambam is not searching for "the objective causation of the commandment," which is something we cannot know, but rather "attempts to reconstruct the subjective correlative" (94). The Rav defines this subjective correlative as "the general tendencies and trends latent in the religious consciousness" and "the structure of the most basic religious cognitive concepts" (99). In *The Halakhic Mind*, the "subjective correlatives" the Rav seeks are to be found in two related areas: philosophical-cognitive concepts and phenomenological structures of consciousness.

However, taking up the same problem of the meaningfulness of a *gezerah* thirty years later (1974, in the context of a discourse on *parah adumah*, the red heifer), the Rav seeks the subjective correlative in a somewhat different

---

9 Regarding the two specific *remazim* cited by the Rambam, see For Further Reference, #4.

domain, asking what the *mitzvah* means to the person who observes it, how it impacts upon him and how it fits into his service of God. What spiritual message does it convey and what is its central motif? He even seems to go so far as to suggest that all *mitzvot* ultimately possess an experiential or emotional correlative:

> However, even though it is forbidden to ask for motivation and reasoning pertaining to God's imperatives and norms, we may inquire as to the meaningfulness of the *hok*, the unintelligible law, for ourselves. It is perfectly legitimate to search for the spiritual message of the *hok*. Nahmanides as well as Maimonides emphasized time and again that the element of *avodah she-ba-lev* – worship of the heart – must be present in every religious act. (See Nahmanides, e.g., comments to *Sefer ha-Mitzvot*, positive commandment no. 5; Maimonides, *Guide* III:51.) The ritual as well as moral actions must be endowed with emotional warmth, love and joy, and the mechanical act converted into a living experience. Of course, all this is unattainable if there is no message to deliver, no idea to suggest, no enriching meaning. In order to offer God my heart and soul, in order to serve Him inwardly, one thing is indispensable – understanding, the involvement of the logos.
>
> Of course, I must never say that the message I detected in the *mitzvah* explains the *mitzvah* and answers the illegitimate question of why the Almighty commanded us to act in such an unintelligible way. However, I am permitted to raise the question of what this *mitzvah* means to me. How am I to understand, not the reason for the *mitzvah*, but the essence of the latter as an integral part of my service of God? Let us therefore see what the *parah adumah* tells us. How do we experience this *hukkat ha-Torah*? What is the central motif of the whole institution? In a word, I am asking not "why *parah adumah*?" but "what is *parah adumah*?" (*Out of the Whirlwind*, 43–44).

Throughout his career, the Rav maintained his striking and original position that the best source for deriving a philosophy of Judaism is the Halakhah. He also consistently maintained the corollary of this doctrine – namely, that despite its basis in the objective data of Halakhah, the endeavor of deriving philosophy from Halakhah is inherently subjective. Although the focus of the Rav's search for the subjectivity of *mitzvot* may have shifted over the years from cognitive-philosophical concepts to halakhic values and experiences, his call to action at the conclusion of *The Halakhic Mind* continues to retain its cogency and power: "Out of the sources of Halakhah, a new world view awaits formulation" (102).

FOR FURTHER REFERENCE

1. **Brisker lomdus**: Everyone agrees that the Rav did not innovate the methodology of *Brisker lomdus*; that distinction belongs to his grandfather, R. Hayyim of Brisk. However, the Rav was the first to articulate the religious and philosophical assumptions and consequences of *Brisker lomdus*, as we saw in this chapter and in those concerning *Halakhic Man*. He characterizes the nature of Brisker *lomdus* in many other works as well, sometimes referring to it by name ("*Mah Dodekh mi-Dod*") and sometimes simply calling it "Torah study" (e.g., *U-Vikkashtem mi-Sham*, chapter 15).

   Within the field of *Brisker lomdus* proper, the Rav of course made very many innovative contributions. These included not only *hiddushim* on individual *sugyot*, but also the extension of the Brisker technique to new areas (such as *Orah Hayyim*) and the formulation of new *hakirot* (such as the external *ma'aseh* and inner *kiyyum*).

   Regarding the state of *Brisker lomdus* today and its prospects for the future, see *Lomdus: The Conceptual Approach to Jewish Learning*, ed. R. Yosef Blau (New York, 2006), and the literature cited there. This volume contains articles that display great methodological self-awareness, written by some of the leading practitioners of *lomdus* among two generations of the Rav's students, such as R. Aharon Lichtenstein, R. Michael Rosensweig and R. Mosheh Lichtenstein. Of special interest is the debate between R. Elyakim Krumbein and R. Dr. Avraham Walfish regarding the extent to which the Rav's approach to learning (*derekh ha-limmud*) differed from that of his grandfather R. Hayyim of Brisk.

2. **Aggadah**: Among the objective data of Judaism are religious texts such as the Aggadah, i.e., the non-legal writings of the Sages. The Aggadah would seem, at first glance, to be an excellent source for deriving Jewish philosophy. Nevertheless, the Rav considers Halakhah to be the primary source for a philosophy of Judaism and Aggadah only secondary. He explains his methodological hesitation about utilizing aggadic material in *Worship of the Heart*:

   > [Regarding Aggadah,] I must, of course, emphasize the need for great caution in order not to fall prey to one's own imagination and read into the texts alien ideas. Particularly those of us who are rabbis are prone to the homiletical approach. The tendency is to utilize the Aggadah as merely a point of departure or as a decorative motif, without full commitment to the cogency of our interpretation. We therefore must be especially careful not to substitute our own thought for that of the Aggadah. However, the undertaking is

not a hopeless one, as long as we allow ourselves to remain on our guard and not drift on the tide of our own fantasy. *From time to time it is good to check aggadic interpretations against halakhic ideas in order to ascertain the adequacy of our approach* (104, emphasis added).

3. *Lomdus* **and reconstruction:** In a fascinating 1952 letter on the nature of Halakhah (*Community, Covenant and Commitment*, 273–77), which deserves close study, the Rav contrasts two methods of approaching Halakhah: the "eidetic normative" and the "teleological." I believe that these refer to the two methods discussed above: objectification (*lomdus*) and reconstruction, respectively. Note his closing remarks:

> As to the teleological method, I employ it in interpreting the Halakhah against its philosophico-metaphysical background. However, I doubt whether such a method would be workable in the field of pure Halakhah. Like the scientist who studies his object on its own merits without referring to any ends which lie beyond its area, the halakhic scholar must separate halakhic logical essences from halakhic metaphysics. *Since abstract halakhic thinking must precede all philosophical interpretations, the eidetic normative method is to be considered as primary* (277, emphasis added).

For the circumstances surrounding the writing of this letter, see Lawrence Kaplan, "From Cooperation to Conflict: Rabbi Professor Emanuel Rackman, Rav Joseph B. Soloveitchik, and the Evolution of American Modern Orthodoxy," *Modern Judaism* 30:1 (Feb. 2010), 46–68.

4. **The "hints" in** *shofar* **and** *mikveh*: While Rav Soloveitchik expresses appreciation of the Rambam's *methodology* of *remez*, this does not necessarily mean that he finds the Rambam's specific *remazim* fully compelling. Although he voices no criticism in *The Halakhic Mind* of the Rambam's idea of *shofar* as hinting at repentance, he offers a more compelling and halakhically-based reading in his *shiurim* and in the essay *"Be-Sod Si'ah ha-Shofar"* (*Yemei Zikkaron*, 137–52): *shofar* as a form of non-verbal prayer.

Taking the Rav's argument a step further, I would say that since in *tekiot di-me'umad* the blowing of *shofar* is integrated into the very structure of the Rosh Hashanah *Musaf* prayer, it stands to reason that *shofar* hints at the themes expressed in that prayer: coronation (*Malkhuyot*), remembrance (*Zikhronot*), and revelation and salvation (*Shofarot*). If Rambam's *remez* is applicable, it is more likely to be with reference to *tekiot di-meyushav*. *Tekiot di-me'umad* would seem to be directed – like the prayers with which they are intertwined – towards God, while *tekiot di-meyushav*, which are blown independently of any prayer, may well be directed at man.

Regarding purification in a *mikveh* (*Hilkhot Mikva'ot* 11:12), the Rav apparently found Rambam's *remez* so unconvincing that he ended his quotation with the words, "Nevertheless, a hint is contained in this . . .", and did not bother to quote the *remez* itself. The *remez*, which concerns purification of the soul, is indeed distant from the *mitzvah*'s objective content. Perhaps a more likely subjective correlative would link impurity to death (as expressed in many laws of *tum'ah*) and the waters of *mikveh* to rebirth.

5. **Intuition and individuality in *lomdus*:** Although the Rav presents Brisker analysis as an objectifying and objective discipline, he admits in both "On the Nature of Halakhah" and "*Mah Dodekh mi-Dod*" that in *lomdus* – as in science – the great scholar develops an intuition that guides his conceptualization. Furthermore, in Halakhah, perhaps unlike science, this intuition is linked not only with formal thought structures but with values as well. See, for example, the following dense but resonant passage in "On the Nature of Halakhah":

> Halakhah-noesis is a great experience replete with all the peculiarities of the ineffable personality. Of course, there is objectivity and stability in the Halakhah. Yet these do not preclude diversity and heterogeneity as to methods and objectives. The same idea might be formulated differently by two scholars; the identical word accented differently by two speakers; the same letter written differently by two scribes; and Halakhah, regardless of its identic content, could also be expressed in a variety of ways. Halakhah mirrors personalities, it reflects individuated *modi existensiae* and it conveys a message otherwise inexpressible.
>
> Since the halakhic gesture is not to be abstracted from the person engaged in it, I cannot see how it is possible to divorce halakhic cognition from axiological premises or from an ethical motif. If halakhic research were limited to its interpretive phase – deciphering some obscure texts – such a discrepancy between the logical and axiological judgments would be warranted. Since, however, halakhic thought is creative, original, flowing from the inner recesses and mysterious spring-wells of the personality where logical-cognitive and ethico-axiological motives are interwoven, any attempt at separation would result in crippling human creativity. From my own experience I know that in any halakhic investigation I have always been guided by a dim intuitive feeling which pointed out to me the true path, and this intuition has never been stripped of an ethical intention (*Community, Covenant and Commitment*, 276).

Chapter 32

U-Vikkashtem mi-Sham (1):
The Natural Search for God

U-Vikkashtem mi-Sham is perhaps Rav Soloveitchik's most profound and heartfelt work. Writing it in a surge of inspiration after completing *Halakhic Man*, he later concluded, "In my opinion it surpasses [*Halakhic Man*], in content and form."[1] His son-in-law and disciple, Rav Aharon Lichtenstein, describes the circumstances of its writing:

> His essay "*U-Vikkashtem Mi- Sham*," published only [in 1978], was written at the end of the Second World War; originally entitled "*Ish Ha-Elokim*," it was intended as a counterpart to "*Ish Ha-Halakhah*." He wrote it as one possessed. At times he sat down to write in the evening, and he would continue without stop till dawn. [His wife] *z"l*, concerned for his health, would object, "Why? Can't it wait until tomorrow?" But he, deep in spiritual and emotional struggle, remained adamant.[2]

Indeed, the echoes of the Rav's "spiritual and emotional struggle," of his deep personal engagement with the issues raised in the book, of his creative and powerful grappling with core issues of religious and halakhic life, are apparent to anyone who reads *U-Vikkashtem mi-Sham*. At the end of Chapter 35, we shall discuss the book's history and explore its relation to *Halakhic Man*. First, however, we shall analyze its major ideas and their significance.

---

1 From a 1963 letter to Rabbi Dr. Samuel K. Mirsky, published in *Community, Covenant and Commitment*, 322. R. Shalom Carmy, a close student of Rav Soloveitchik, reports that the Rav regarded *U-Vikkashtem mi-Sham* as "his most important theological contribution" ("The Beginning of Wisdom," *First Things* 195, Aug/Sept 2009, 39).

2 "The Rav in Retrospect: *Divrei Hesped*," in *Leaves of Faith*, vol. 1 (Jersey City, 2003), 221.

The Central Metaphor

The book's title is drawn from Deuteronomy 4:29, where the Jewish people are told that in the future they will go into exile due to their sins but, nonetheless, "And from there you shall seek (*u-vikkashtem mi-sham*) the Lord your God, and you will find Him if only you seek Him with all your heart and all your soul." The words of this verse provide a crisp, pointed formulation of the book's main theme: the quest for God. But despite the title's derivation from Deuteronomy, the book's central metaphor comes from a different biblical work, the Song of Songs.

The latter work presents us with a narrative concerning two lovers, and was interpreted by Jewish tradition as an allegory for either the relationship between God and the people of Israel, or the relationship between God and the individual.[3] Rav Soloveitchik stresses a strange element within the Song of Songs. The lovers pine for each other, yet repeatedly they fail to take advantage of opportunities to meet. At the very moment he can meet his beloved, the lad retreats and hides among the rocks. Why does he flee? Strange, too, is the behavior of the Shulammite maiden. She searches for her beloved with her whole being and depicts herself as "faint with love" (Song 2:5). Yet when her lover finally arrives and knocks at her door, she is slow to rise and let him in. Then, by the time she leaps off her bed and opens the door – her love raging, her heart expanding – he has left: "my beloved has turned and gone" (Song 5:6).

What is the significance of a lover who yearns yet hides, and a beloved who longs but conceals herself? The Rav understands this strange "game" in terms of his own allegorical interpretation: God does not reveal Himself fully, and man retreats from God just at the moment of a potential encounter. The book seeks to depict how man experiences this dialectical to-and-fro, and how he can overcome it.

Reason and Revelation as Religious Experiences

There are two main avenues for man to encounter God. The first, where man takes the initiative, is accomplished through examining the created world (both natural and human) using reason and other human capacities. The second, where God takes the initiative, is through divine revelation, which comes

---

3 The Midrash, the Targum, Rashi and R. Yehudah Halevi offer the first interpretation, while R. Bahya and Rambam offer the second. See the discussion in n. 1 of *U-Vikkashtem mi-Sham*, 151–53.

from beyond the created world and beyond the realm of human understanding. Although medieval religious philosophy revolved around the tension between reason and revelation, Rav Soloveitchik "deals with this issue in a characteristically modern way. Reason and revelation are viewed not so much as two distinct sources of knowledge or two bodies of teaching but rather as two different modes of experience, as two different ways of relating to God, as two different personal stances the individual assumes."[4]

Since, according to modern philosophy, the categories of human reason are applicable only within the realm of nature (and not within that of metaphysics), Rav Soloveitchik refers to the experience of God within the natural realm as the "rational religious experience," the "creation (*Bereishit*) experience," the "cosmic experience," the "natural consciousness," and the "ontological consciousness." On the other hand, he refers to the experience of God granted by revelation simply as the "revelational consciousness," the "prophetic consciousness," or the "Sinai experience." One of the book's central and most important themes is that both forms of religious awareness, the natural and the revelational, are crucial to religious (and indeed human) life.

U-Vikkashtem mi-Sham depicts a three-stage development in the religious consciousness, which we can map out in a short diagram:

	Bereishit	**Sinai**
(I)	Trust	Fear
(II)	Love	Awe
(III)	Cleaving	

I shall present this development now in the briefest terms, and shall explain each stage later in greater depth. In Stage I, man seeks to encounter God within the realm bounded by nature and reason, yet ultimately finds this encounter inadequate, at which point God's revelation takes him by surprise. There ensues a dialectic between the trust or security engendered by the "natural consciousness" of God and the fear brought on by the "revelational consciousness." In Stage II, the dialectic of contradictory experiences (trust and fear) deepens into a dialectic of complementary experiences, love and awe. At the ultimate level, Stage III, the dichotomy of the rational experience and the revelatory experience is overcome by the singular experience of *devekut*, or cleaving to God.

---

4 Lawrence Kaplan, "Joseph Soloveitchik and Halakhic Man," in *The Cambridge Companion to Modern Jewish Philosophy,* eds. Michael L. Morgan and Peter E. Gordon (Cambridge, 2007), 221.

We can now see that the book's chapters fit into a neat structure:

(a) Chapter 1 is a lyrical introduction to the book.

(b) Chapters 2–7 depict Stage I.

(c) Chapters 8–10 depict Stage II.

(d) Chapters 11–19 depict Stage III.

(e) Chapter 20 is a summary of the three stages.

This structure also divides the book into two major sections: the last ten chapters essentially break down the dichotomies of the first ten chapters.

The Searching Heart

The best way to summarize the book is to scan its chapter titles; they chart the odyssey of the individual questing for God. The repeated appearance in the chapter titles of the word "heart," understood as the seat of the emotions or awareness, emphasizes that this is a work of religious phenomenology, not religious philosophy. This means that the book deals with types of religious consciousness and experience, and not with intellectual problems of logic, proof or evidence.[5] As such, it is fitting that the imagery in the chapter titles and epigraphs derives mainly from the Song of Songs, the Bible's sublime poem of love.

1. **Overt Halakhah and Covert Love** – This title captures the book's essential theme, namely, finding love within the seemingly oppressive Halakhah: love on the part of both the divine Giver and the human fulfiller.
2. **The Yearning Heart** – man's free, joyful search for God within the realm of nature and human creations (the *Bereishit* experience), encapsulated by the epigraph, *"Draw me after you, let us run!"* (Song 1:4).
3. **The Disappointed Heart** – the failure of purely rational religious experience, as expressed in the verse (that appears as the epigraph of chapter 3, section B), *"My beloved had turned and gone"* (Song 5:6).
4. **The Surprised Heart** – God's sudden revelation (the Sinai experience); *"I am asleep, but my heart is wakeful. Hark, my beloved knocks!"* (Song 5:2).

---

5 This is especially striking in chapter 2.B (11–15) and n. 3 (157–58), where the Rav reinterprets logical proofs of God's existence in experiential terms. This subject has come up already in our discussion of *The Lonely Man of Faith* and we will come across it again at the end of Chap. 34.

5. **The Yearning Yet Fearful Heart** – a comparison of the *Bereishit* and Sinai experiences and the dialectic between them; the desire to draw close to God and the fear of doing so are symbolized by the verse, *"'But,' He said, 'you cannot see My face, for man may not see Me and live'"* (Ex. 33:20).

6. **The Divided Heart** – same as the above: the dialectic of the *Bereishit* and Sinai experiences; *"Thy heart shall fear, and be enlarged"* (Isa. 60:5).

7. **The Heart which Runs and Flees** – same dialectic as above; *"And when the people saw it, they retreated and stood at a distance"* (Ex. 20:15).

8. **The Comforted Heart** – Stage II: the contradictory and tense dialectic of trust and fear is replaced by the complementary experiences of love and awe.

9. *No title* – examples of the centrality of the dialectic of love and awe to the service of God.

10. **"This is My God and I Will Imitate Him; the God of My Father, and I Will Exalt Him"** (Ex. 15:2) – imitation of God (*imitatio Dei*) as the expression of the complementary dialectic of love and awe.

11. **From *Imitatio* to *Devekut*** – examples of Stage III, *devekut*; from here on, the titles attain increasing intensity of passion.

12. **The Heart that Cleaves to God** – differences between mystical "union with God" and halakhic *devekut*, or "cleaving to God."

13. **"His Left Hand Was Under My Head, and His Right Arm Embraced Me"** (Song 8:3) – the philosophical basis of *devekut*.

14. *No title* – more on the philosophical basis of *devekut*.

15. *No title* – two techniques or expressions of *devekut*: supremacy of the intellect and elevation of the body.

16. *No title* – Halakhah and the world.

17. **The Prophesying Heart** – the peak of *devekut*; man finds in the Sinai experience what he sought in the *Bereishit* experience.

18. *No title* – creation and continuous revelation.

19. **The Heart that Runs without Returning** – *masorah* as continuous revelation: *"Let me be a seal upon your heart, like the seal upon your arm"* (Song 8:6).

20. **Summary**

Now let us take a closer look at each of the three stages of the development of the religious consciousness.[6]

---

6 In the "Summary" section of Chap. 35 below, we shall see that these can be viewed not only as three stages of the development of the religious consciousness, but as three ways of

Stage I (a): The Natural-Rational Search for God

Stage I commences with man freely and hopefully undertaking the search for God within the natural, rational realm. In conducting this search, he is not always aware that it is God he seeks; rather, he is looking for the absolute, for truth, for a stable anchor within the universe, for something that can ground his life and give it meaning. These goals can be attained only by discovering reflections of the transcendent in the world, for example, the sublime in art, the lawfulness of nature, the purity of philosophical concepts, or the deep yearnings of the human soul. Traces of the transcendent, or of God, can be found within the natural and human worlds as well as beyond them:

> There is no hidden corner of the natural or spiritual world which man's consciousness, pining for its divine beloved, does not peer into and scrutinize. Human consciousness carefully investigates the buds of transcendence that appear every so often in the spiritual desert . . . Flesh-and-blood man longs to escape from the straits of the limited, bounded and contingent world and go out into the limitless, independent, wide-open spaces. This search is an act of self-transcendence, which is truly the essence of man's cultural ascent (8).[7]

For Rav Soloveitchik, then, the search for the transcendent, or for God, is basic to human nature, and is in fact the engine driving many of man's cultural endeavors.[8] In his immediate experience of the glory of the cosmos, in the constructs of his intellect, in the depths of his psyche, and in his metaphysical yearnings, man experiences intimations of the Creator.

When confronting nature, man can apply his intellect to master the created order, and he can also sense God by means of his unmediated and direct experience of the cosmos. Both of these abilities are implanted within man by God – "God made man a scientific creature, able to understand the truth, and at the same time an individual who longs for God and is capable of transcending the shackles of science" (44) – and hence both are sanctioned by Judaism. The divine command to "fill the earth and the subdue it" (Gen. 1:28) mandates scientific inquiry and progress (see 43–44), while the halakhic institution of *berakhot*, blessings, attests to the Jew's wonder and amazement upon finding God within the dynamics of the cosmos:

---

relating to Halakhah. For a detailed presentation of the three stages, see also the introduction (by David Shatz and myself) to *And from There You Shall Seek*, trans. Naomi Goldblum (Jersey City, 2008), xi–xxxix. Parts of this chapter and the next three draw on that introduction.

7 All page references are to the English translation of *U-Vikkashtem mi-Sham*.

8 For the Rav, "culture" refers not just to art or literature, but to any product of human creativity, including technology, government, etc.

We are commanded by the Halakhah to utter a benediction over every cosmic phenomenon: over the afterglow of the fiery sunset and the purple of the sunrise trickling along the mountaintops; over the rising moon sprinkling its pale light; over the stars in their courses and the comets leaping from clear space; over the sight of the rainbow in the clouds; over the thunder and lightning arising from mist; over the budding trees and the sweet-smelling exquisite flowers; over the murmur of the ocean and the rushing of the surf; upon eating water and bread, the fruits of the trees and the crops of the fields; over the healthy body, created with wisdom, with its muscles and nerves; over the ability to move and to stand erect. In short, we utter a benediction over everything man encounters that demonstrates the power of creation. What is a benediction – whether *birkat ha-nehenin*, a blessing over something we imbibe, or *birkat re'iyah*, a blessing over something we behold – if not praise and thanksgiving to God for the nature of the world, a nature that changes, in the instant that the benediction is uttered, into a supernatural, miraculous universe; if not the redemption of nature from its muteness, deprivation, and solitude; if not the identification of the cosmic dynamics with the primordial will of the Creator, which is hidden and acts from within its hiding place on organic and inorganic matter, on animal, vegetable, and mineral! What does the benediction attest to if not the strange fact that – in spite of the psychological law that habit and custom dull the subtleties of feeling, dim the alertness of the intellect, and extinguish the flame of ecstasy – the Jew is enthusiastic about each and every phenomenon? (21–22).

Yet, although Judaism approves of this intellectual and experiential encounter with God within the cosmic-rational realm, and acknowledges "its importance, greatness, and force" (22), it ultimately finds it insufficient. Let us now explore the reasons for this.

Stage I (b): Failure of the *Bereishit* Experience

We stated above that there are two powerful and significant avenues for discovering God via the created world: experiential encounter and intellectual examination. However, both of these are problematic. The experiential encounter is insufficient because, although one can gain intimations of God's presence through one's experience of the cosmos, the divine presence nevertheless proves to be both revealed and hidden. God eludes His creation; this, partly, because sin precludes man from seeing God everywhere.[9] God

---

9 What the Rav means by this (26) is not entirely clear. One possible understanding is that, due to man's primordial sin, or to man's inherent sinfulness, God has hidden His presence and

is everywhere, yet His presence cannot always be seen or experienced. He is enveloped, as the Bible says, by a thick cloud.

The intellectual avenue to God via the created world is likewise inadequate, and this is true for several reasons.

First, our rational grasp of the universe is necessarily incomplete. Science itself, the Rav asserts, has become aware of its limitations.[10]

Furthermore, when human reason attempts to prove God's existence, it bases its proofs on the orderly nature of existence. But this willfully ignores another side of existence:

> From the lawful, the regulated, the good, and the beautiful [in the world], the general theologian ascends to the absolute, the perfect, and the One. But philosophical theology is perplexed and confused when it encounters impermanence, disorder, evil, negativity, privation, and formlessness (31).

Moreover, like many other modern philosophers, Rav Soloveitchik submits that all rational proofs of God must fail, "for we have no right to use these categories [formulated by the human intellect], which result from our finite, contingent, temporal existence, to prove the truth of an infinite, absolute, eternal reality" (12). That is, one cannot prove God's existence, but neither can one disprove it; it is not within the realm of proof and disproof.

Finally, even if these proofs were valid, they would lead at best to a cold, abstract, impersonal idea of God. This abstract view of God can lead to dire consequences:

> Essentially, rational cosmic religiosity devolves into pantheism[11] . . . [which is] but a single step away from atheism. In a word, if religiosity derives its substance only from the intellect and cultural consciousness, it leads to denial of God (24).

This is an important point, and should not be overlooked. Many religious thinkers view denial of God as the result of stupidity, mental disease, igno-

---

is no longer obvious within the world. Alternatively, the Rav may mean that the attempt to perceive God only through the intellect and the cosmic experience does not take into account sin, impurity and the need for redemption. The natural religious approach may, to some extent, reveal the cosmic God who is the Source of the universe, but it will not reveal the redeeming God who grants man salvation.

10 The Rav explains that while modern physics can set up mathematical models that parallel the quantifiable workings of nature, it cannot explain the human "qualitative reality" – the realm of immediate sensory experience.

11 Pantheism is the doctrine that God and nature are identical.

rance, spite or malevolence.[12] For Rav Soloveitchik, however, denial of God can stem not just from "the pride and madness of the mind" (25) that imagines that it can account for all of reality, but also from the basic characteristics of the human experience of the world:

> However, the world itself, with its strange qualities, is also to blame for the human confusion that leads people to dissidence and rebellion. Scientists see the world as enveloped in an abundance of formal lawfulness; positivists see it as full of dim, thick sensuousness.[13] Both of these conceal the secret of creation [i.e., God within nature]. The [scientific] symbolic husk and the [positivist's] perceptible husk form a barrier between man and the Creator. Sometimes the construction created by the mind is perceived as an absolute entity and is maintained as a total solution to the eternal problem. Man's pride and impudence drive him to deify himself as the solution to the mystery. Then the scientist goes mad and denies God. At other times, it is the sensuous quality, in its powerful primitivity, that seizes the center of man's consciousness and blocks his path toward God. Then the hedonist goes mad and denies God (25).

Thus, it is not necessarily ignorance or malice that leads to confusion or denial regarding God. Rather, the cause of confusion or denial is the very attempt to find God within nature, which is doomed by the limits of human understanding:

> Seeking God only within existence is a daring and risky adventure, which sometimes meets up with threatened failure . . . There is a powerful experience of God here, but it is manifested within the limitations and restrictions of human cognitive ability and through its clash with the mystery. A bold attempt of this sort – revealing the *Shekhinah* within nature, with all nature's glory and greatness, but without going outside nature – does not bring man closer to God. The end result of the effort at revealing God in the realm of being, using cognitive stratagems, is spiritual weariness and bankruptcy (25).

Nevertheless, it is important to bear in mind that denial of God is not a *necessary* result of the search for God in the natural-intellectual realm, but only a *possible* one:

> [M]an's search for God expresses itself in intellectual activity . . . but when the seekers reach the ultimate boundary of reality they become alarmed and retreat. When they confront eternity, with its terrifying spaces that both attract

---

12 See For Further Reference, #1.

13 Positivism is a philosophy that relies only on actual sense experience instead of using the scientist's symbolic abstractions.

and repel, both encourage and mock – they all cease their journey. Many of them are confused; many are frightened and uproot their faith. Only a few remain steadfast in the face of the mystery and expect salvation from the God they seek (29).

Yet all seekers – those who "are confused," those who "uproot their faith," as well as those who "remain steadfast" – experience a sense of crisis when they "reach the ultimate boundary of reality." It is precisely because of this crisis that man needs revelation, and it is precisely out of this crisis that revelation arises. But we shall see that when man first encounters revelation, he does not experience it as the answer to his needs.

FOR FURTHER REFERENCE

1. **Orthodox attitudes to nonbelief and nonobservance:** *See Jewish Tradition and the Non-Traditional Jew*, ed. R. Jacob J. Schacter (Northvale, NJ, 1992), and Adam S. Ferziger, *Exclusion and Hierarchy: Orthodoxy, Nonobservance, and the Emergence of Modern Jewish Identity* (Philadelphia, 2005).

Chapter 33

U-Vikkashtem mi-Sham (2):
The Dialectic of Reason and Revelation

Let us continue charting the stages of the religious odyssey depicted by Rav Soloveitchik.

Stage I (c): Revelation as an Event and Experience

When man finds himself in the midst of crisis and confusion, God sometimes reveals Himself, even though man is unprepared and does not expect it. Yet when God does so, it is not for the sake of granting man an intellectual grasp of the absolute and eternal, nor is it in order to help man find peace and security in some other fashion. Rather, God reveals Himself so that He may express His will and impose His commands upon man.

> When man seeks God, he is seeking an intellect that is beyond him. He wants this intellect to take note of him and to enlighten him about the universe, about the essence and fate of man, but instead of finding the Hidden Intellect, he encounters the Inscrutable Will. This Will reveals itself to man, and instead of telling him the secrets of creation, it demands unlimited discipline and absolute submission (35).

This revelation of Will is not just a one-time experience, nor does it belong only to the special few whom God has chosen as prophets. Instead, it becomes a lasting part of man's religious consciousness, just as the "natural search for God"[1] constitutes a permanent component of the human religious consciousness:

---

1 By "the natural search for God," the Rav means the search for God through nature (which includes both the natural world and the human realm). This subject was covered in Chap. 32.

God's revelation to man ... became for posterity a perpetual experience, a unique awareness. In all generations, man lives and feels this revelation the way he lives and feels a natural longing for God (39).

Thus, while in chapter 4 (29–37) the reader might receive the impression that revelation supplants the natural search for God, subsequent chapters explain that, as perpetual experiences, both co-exist in man's consciousness (albeit in constant tension). Judaism demands both forms of religious awareness, the natural and the revelational:

> [*First, the natural religious consciousness:*] Man is commanded not only to believe in God, but also to know God, as Maimonides formulated the first commandment: "to know that there is a First Existent who brought every existing thing into being" (Laws of the Foundations of the Torah 1:1). The meaning of "knowledge" is knowing God by knowing His works – the works of creation. [*Next, the revelational religious consciousness:*] Yet, on the other hand, our sages insisted that knowing God through nature is insufficient. The paramount principle is faith in His revelation to man, and readiness to fulfill His will unconditionally. [*Finally, the coexistence of both:*] Man seeks God [*i.e., the natural consciousness*] and is also a captive of God [*i.e., the revelational consciousness*]. This duality gives a special, original content to the religious experience advocated by our Torah. Thus it was the primordial will of the Creator to plant two sorts of consciousness in man – a dual-faceted approach (41).

Stage I (d): The Dialectic of Trust and Fear

Chapters 5 and 6 (39–50) highlight the tension between these two religious approaches, the natural and the revelational, by presenting a series of contrasts between them, while chapter 7 (51–60) shows why each approach by itself is insufficient and why both therefore are necessary. First, let us briefly list the characteristics of each type of religious consciousness so that the contrasts between them will become apparent.

In the "natural" mode of religious consciousness, man searches for God out of a desire for liberation from nature's tyranny, out of a thirst for freedom and expansion. He yearns for a shelter of grace and for the redemption of reality. The feeling of God's nearness grants him increased freedom and joy. The "natural" search for God grounds man in this-worldly existence, encouraging his participation in the improvement of the world and society. The natural pursuit is open to many forms of expression and tolerates many approaches; it is a cognitive, ethical and aesthetic enterprise. In fact, it is, as we have mentioned, the peak of cultural attainment. Since this consciousness is intimately related to human culture, it is dynamic and progresses along with man's general progress.

Revelation, on the other hand, emerges from a realm closed to human understanding and seemingly unconcerned with human desires. The revelatory religious approach is unrelated to freedom and creativity, uninterested in culture, closed up within its own autonomous realm. Demanding exclusivity, it shows no tolerance for multiple approaches or competing enterprises. Man experiences coercion and enslavement, sensing that nothing less than total commitment is demanded of him. God seems remote and frightening, the distance between Him and man bridged only by His absolute commands. Whereas the natural consciousness perceives God as hidden within creation, the revelational consciousness sees God beyond creation and standing apart from it. Since they derive from a separate and eternal realm, the contents of the revelatory religious consciousness are static and unchanging.

With regard to both the natural and the revelational approaches, the Rav says, "the yearning is natural and instinctive, while its fulfillment is spiritual" (49). This means that, in Stage I, both the rational and the revelational approaches aim to perpetuate human existence, and as such they are born of the biological instinct for survival. Yet, in order to fulfill this natural, pragmatic urge, man finds that he must adopt spiritual means. In the "natural" dimension of religion, lonely and restless man, seeking tranquility, wishing to defeat death, and seeking purpose, finds that he can approach these goals by means of self-transcendence, by seeking the absolute, by drawing near to God. However, he is unaware of any demands this may entail. In the "revelational" dimension of religion, man encounters God as a fearsome judge and commander; since man, who is sinful and lacks wholeness, cannot possibly justify himself in the face of God, he finds that his survival instinct impels him not to draw near to God, but rather to maintain his distance. Yet, precisely in this experience of fear he serves God, for fear gives rise to the decision to obey God's absolute will and turns into an ongoing revelational awareness.

Although the fear emanating from the revelatory experience stands in contradiction to the security and trust emanating from the natural experience, the Rav portrays these feelings as co-existing in dialectical tension, for both are necessary components of man's religious consciousness. It is acceptable to look to God for reward and to flee from Him to evade punishment. Such experiences are valuable and significant; Judaism accepts natural man and his simple desire for continued existence.[2]

---

2 In an important aside (52–53; see also 65), the Rav adds that even at the highest levels of religious development (to be detailed later), man retains this simple desire for reward and,

The fact that the antithetical experience of love and fear – of the desire to run toward God and the desire to run away from Him – is rooted deep in our biological nature and in the situation of man as a psychosomatic[3] creature does not make this experience any the less valuable or significant. Halakhah has always dealt with real human existence, restraining it with the awareness of reward and punishment, without seeing any defect in man's will to exist in the biological sense, to enjoy his existence to the fullest, and to be free of physical or psychological pain. For this reason, Halakhah restrains man with the promise of reward and punishment and gives him the choice between the blessing and the curse. The blessing is the good in the natural life, and the curse is the dominion of evil in it. In order to subjugate him to the supernatural revelational command, the Halakhah both frightens and reassures natural man (52).

Stage I (e): The Necessity of Both Approaches

Judaism, we have seen, approves of both the "natural" religious awareness and the "revelational" religious awareness. Neither one, however, is sufficient by itself. Let us turn initially to the problems of a natural religiosity when it is not balanced by revelational religiosity. First, lacking the imperative element of revelation, it can turn into something purely contemplative and spiritual, not behavioral. Second, absent the objective element of revelation, it leads to subjective religiosity, which cannot long endure.[4] Third, lacking the absolute foundation of religion, it makes religion subservient to culture and subordinates God to human desires.[5] Religion thereby loses its autonomy and primordial force, leading man, who sees himself as the source of the norm, to moral anarchy. Love not balanced by fear, subjectivity unrestrained by the absolute, and spirituality devoid of commands, bring chaos upon the world.

Now let us turn to the problems of revelational religiosity when it is not balanced by natural religiosity. Since the revelatory experience is imposed from without, man perceives it as being unrelated to his cultural consciousness and unresponsive to his desires and needs. It becomes for him a coercive system characterized mainly by fear of punishment. Yet, God wants man to worship Him not only out of sadness and dread, but also out of spontaneous and joyful yearning: "Serve the Lord out of joy" (Ps. 100:2).

---

especially, avoidance of punishment. One cannot simply discard the lower levels of religiosity when ascending to the higher levels, for one is unavoidably human, and to imagine otherwise guarantees failure in attaining one's spiritual goals.

3 "Psychosomatic" here means composed of both spirit and body.

4 Regarding these two issues, see the discussion in sec. 3 of Chap. 9 above.

5 This, of course, is a major theme of *The Lonely Man of Faith*. See esp. Chaps. 15 and 16 above.

When man does not see God and sense His presence at every turn; when he thinks of God only out of fear of punishment, with a cool intellect, without ecstasy, joy, or enthusiasm; when his actions lack soul, inwardness, and vitality, then his religious life is flawed (56).

Moreover, an exclusive focus on obeying commands, while shutting one's eyes to the splendor and challenge of the world, leads to asceticism, to withdrawal from the task of improving and settling the world and of tending to man's physical and psychological needs. This, too, is unacceptable, for man was placed in the world to live in it and perfect it. Man's partnership in creation is reflected not just by his actions but also by his attitudes:

> The natural consciousness that was given to him by God is the source of man's longing for infinity and eternity. It is the wellspring of human feelings of joy and wonder, it gives rise to the stream of happiness and sweetness in life . . . it tells man to progress, to elevate and improve himself (56).

In a later chapter, the Rav gives striking expression to the problems of fear untempered by love by presenting the psychological and religious distortions that it fosters. First, such excessive fear "is the ultimate source of all neuroses and psychic anomalies in man" (67). Additionally, "Religiosity that remains too long in the realm of this terrible fear . . . deteriorates into magic" (ibid.). By this he means that instead of viewing God as a moral being, a person engulfed by fear will see God as an implacable and irrational force that can be propitiated and manipulated by ritual actions and offerings.

The Rav sums up the need for both kinds of religious consciousness – natural and revelational – thus:

> If all of a person's consciousness and experience is natural, inner, rooted in his personality, then he is like a secular individual who stands outside the authority of religion. On the other hand, if he lacks natural consciousness and experience, and does not entwine them in his revelational experience within his comprehensive spiritual experience, then he is liable to abandon practical action and the real world. Unless there is a mutual relationship between the two types of consciousness and experience, the religious ideal cannot be realized (56–57).

Rounding out his discussion, Rav Soloveitchik notes (57–60) that whereas the natural-intellectual religious experience is an esoteric phenomenon – that is, something limited to an elite few who can undertake deep inquiry and experience the sublime – revelational faith is exoteric,[6] for the revelation is

---

6 Exoteric means "outer" and readily accessible to the many.

addressed to all, and its commands can be fulfilled by all, regardless of intellectual capacity and spiritual ability. Again, he explains why both approaches are necessary. On the one hand, religion belongs to everyone, to the whole community. On the other hand, it must provide the opportunity for the exceptional individual to deepen and broaden his experience and perception of divinity. Korah was right in declaring that "All of the community are holy," but wrong in complaining "so why do you raise yourselves above the Lord's congregation?" (Num. 16:3). The exoteric holiness of the community (*kedushat Yisrael*) does not distinguish between great and small, but esoteric holiness depends on the greatness and depth of the individual.[7]

Stage I: Summary

Before moving on to Stage II, let us briefly summarize the complex development of Stage I. Man, seeking meaning and security, initiates the search for God, using all his powers of intellect, spirit, creativity and freedom. He meets with some success in this enterprise, finding traces of the absolute within science, philosophy, art and the human psyche, especially within the cosmic experience (that is, the direct encounter with nature that gives man a sense of the infinite). This success fosters within man a sense of security and confidence, as he finds order in the universe and hints of something that transcends him. He is drawn to God's attribute of mercy, which offers comfort and support.

However, though man searches, he can't quite grasp God – in the metaphor of the Song of Songs, the maiden catches glimpses of her Beloved, but cannot meet Him. The seeker realizes that his intellect, cultural creativity and cosmic experience take him only so far. The categories of the human mind break down when they encounter the infinite; more than God is revealed by nature, He remains hidden within it; man's very partial and unclear perception of God remains abstract and impersonal; and man still cannot account for the existence of chaos and evil. Confounded and despairing, man gives up his search.

Therefore, man is unprepared for God's sudden revelation – all the more so because God reveals Himself not as the creator and sustainer of all that exists, but as a lawgiver who takes away man's freedom and demands absolute commitment. Instead of being attracted and comforted by God's attribute of mercy, man is now filled with dread and anxiety by God's attribute of justice. He experiences the antithesis of his earlier state, where he had deployed his freedom and creativity in a yearning quest for the divine.

---

7 For further discussion of the esoteric and exoteric aspects of religion, see Chap. 10 above (sec. 5 and For Further Reference, #2).

Yet this consciousness of fear should not cancel out his earlier conscious-ness of trust. There must follow a dual awareness of trust and fear, of natural and revelational religiosity. Both are necessary, for a life based only on natu-ral consciousness evades the authority of religion, lacks restraint and becomes essentially secular; conversely, a life based only on revelational conscious-ness forsakes practical action and improvement of the world. However, at this stage of religious development, both types of consciousness are self-centered, focusing only on how God will affect one's personal existence. The individual seeks God in order to anchor and affirm his own existence, and obeys the revelatory commands only in order to attain reward and avoid punishment.

Stage II: Love and Awe

After the stage of self-interested worship, man may rise to a higher level of religious consciousness, which focuses less on his own personal existence and more on God Himself. At this level, one worships God not to fulfill one's own needs, but rather out of an appreciation of God's greatness.

> Judaism says that the dichotomy between the quest for God and the revelation of God is only the surface layer of our awareness of Him. When we go deeper into the complexities of this awareness, we find an entirely different layer. Both approach and flight are raised in spiritual grandeur and ascend from the depths of nature to the heights of ontological and metaphysical conception. The utilitarian desire for reward and fear of punishment are transformed into love and awe, transcendent mysterious experiences (61).

The Rav calls the lower level of worship "utilitarian" or "eudaemonic," both terms meaning that it seeks happiness and well-being. He terms the higher level "ontological," meaning that it stems from the nature of being. While on the lower level one worships God out of ulterior motives, on the higher level one's worship is *lishmah*, for its own sake.

What aspect of God's greatness motivates the higher form of worship? God relates to the world in a dual manner. On the one hand, God creates and sustains all being: "All existing things . . . exist only through His true exis-tence" (Rambam, *Hilkhot Yesodei ha-Torah* 1:1). On the other hand, God's infinite and singular existence negates all else: "Everything is considered as nothing before Him" (*Zohar* I, 11b). At the higher level of religious aware-ness, man has a dual reaction upon grasping these truths. He desires to come close to God, not in order to gain something by this, but simply out of an overwhelming attraction to the Source of all being, wisdom and goodness. This is no longer a utilitarian longing for security, but rather spiritual love.

And yet, when he approaches God, man grasps how paltry he is by comparison, and therefore is filled not with instinctive fear but with spiritual awe. Unlike fear (*pahad*), which expressed man's desire to flee from God, awe (*yirah*) expresses a longing for God that man knows cannot be fully actualized because of his own inadequacy and God's unfathomable greatness. The closer he comes to God, the more he realizes that he cannot truly cling to the Infinite.

The Rambam beautifully characterizes the duality of love and awe of God. Far from presenting love and awe as contradictory emotions, he shows that they are, in fact, two sides of the same coin. Both stem from the recognition of God's greatness and from the pure desire to come close to Him:

> And what is the way to [achieve] love and awe of Him? When a person contemplates His great and wondrous works and creatures, and from them obtains a glimpse of His wisdom, which is incomparable and infinite, he will straightaway love Him, praise Him, glorify Him, and long with an exceeding longing to know His great Name; even as David said, "My soul thirsts for God, for the living God" (Ps. 42:3). And when he ponders these very matters, he will recoil frightened, and realize that he is but a small creature, lowly and obscure, endowed with slight and slender intelligence, standing in the presence of Him who is perfect in knowledge. And so David said, "When I consider Your heavens, the work of Your fingers – what is man that You are mindful of him?" (Ps. 8:4–5) (*Hilkhot Yesodei ha-Torah* 2:2).

For the Rav, these complementary movements of attraction and recoil are the essence of the religious experience:

> Man's running toward and fleeing from his Creator, as he is hurled back and forth by the two colossal forces of love and awe, embodies the most magnificent worship of God. The Kabbalists called this mysterious pendulum-like movement of the man of God *ratzo va-shov*, "dashing back and forth" (69).

Moreover, he continues, "Together they constitute the foundations of halakhic religious consciousness" (70); hence, they are reflected in several halakhic institutions. For example, blessings begin by referring to God in the second person ("Blessed are *You*") and end by referring to Him in the third person (e.g., "that everything was created by *His* word," not "by *Your* word"). The second-person address expresses a loving aspiration to enter into direct conversation with God, but this is overbold, and the third-person reference reflects a realization of God's concealment and our distance from Him. Similarly, in the *Kedushah* prayer, the Jew feels God's nearness and declares, "His presence fills the entire world" (Isa. 6:3), but then he senses God's distance and pronounces, "Blessed is the Lord's presence from His place" (Ez. 3:12), referring to God's transcendent and hidden abode. The framers of the *Kedushah* added a question to the recitation of these verses: "His servants ask one another: Where is the place of His presence?" Even though God is present everywhere, everyone asks where He is, for He dwells in seclusion.

Stage II: *Imitatio Dei*

This dialectical experience assumes the form of *imitatio Dei*, imitation of God, which is a central principle of Judaism.[8] In *imitatio Dei*, man finds a solution to the dichotomy between his desire for moral freedom (the *Bereishit* experience) and his enslavement to divine command (the Sinai experience).

Imitatio Dei contains an admission of failure: man despairs of the possibility of cleaving to God, so he decides, as a more realistic and attainable goal, to imitate God. Practically this means that he imitates God's goodness as expressed in His will – namely, in His revealed law, the Halakhah. He sees that the law, though indeed imposed by God, is the meaningful product of God's wisdom and not just the arbitrary product of His will. Therefore, he not only feels *forced* to obey it, but *chooses* and *desires* to obey it. By doing so, he overcomes the tension he had felt in Stage I, when he had perceived the divine command as negating human freedom. By shifting his focus from himself to God, and by changing his perception of the revealed law, man comes to realize that there is no longer a stark contradiction between the natural consciousness and the revelatory consciousness.

To be more precise, *imitatio Dei* reconciles freedom and coercion, or natural yearning and revelatory command, in three ways. First, when experiencing awe of God, man recognizes that he is indeed a slave to God's revealed command, but he no longer feels oppressed by this fact. Rather, man senses that God is a great, wise and benevolent master, and he derives joy from serving such a master.

Second, when experiencing love of God, man does not just obey happily, but freely *chooses* to imitate God, because he recognizes God's greatness. He is not just a happy slave – sometimes, he does not even feel like a slave at all. Man no longer sees revelation as an imposition or threat that arouses in him feelings of fear and duress. While earlier he saw revelation as proceeding from God's attribute of justice, he now understands that it proceeds from God's attribute of mercy as well. It is not impenetrable and frightening,

---

8 See Chap. 3 above for more on *imitatio Dei*.

but meaningful and enriching. Of course, given the *ratzo va-shov* nature of love and awe, he will swing back to the consciousness of compulsion. Nevertheless, he will obey the divine command not only out of coercion but also out of desire, "out of the continual aspiration for ascent" (76).

Third, man realizes that he can find in the Halakhah the absolute point of reference he sought at the beginning of Stage I; the revealed law, far from being a threat to his existence, is a transcendental entity that can anchor his turbulent existence. To recall, in Stage I.a ("trust"), man freely, creatively and joyfully searches for a refuge in the absolute; in Stage I.b, he fails to find this; and in Stage I.c ("fear"), he encounters its frightening antithesis. It now becomes apparent that, even though he didn't know it at the time, he actually found in Stage I.c that for which he had quested in Stage I.a. Only when, in Stage II, he overcomes the initial feeling of terror caused by revelation, can he see that the absolute point of reference and the affirmation of his existence that he had sought are in fact provided by the revelatory law itself.

The reconciliation in Stage II of freedom and coercion, of the two forms of religious consciousness, solves the problems we encountered in Stage I when trying to yoke together two antithetical modes of religiosity. In Stage II, man recognizes the existence of an external and imposed command, but he chooses to follow it. He yearns for God's closeness, but this yearning guides his behavior and is no longer purely contemplative. Religion has the power necessary to restrain man's chaotic urges, but without paralyzing man with terror. The desire for freedom no longer leads to moral anarchy, while, conversely, revelation no longer crushes him, denies his individuality, or extinguishes his yearning. Religion is no longer subservient to culture, but neither is it static and unchanging. The revealed law becomes part of, perhaps the essence of, man's natural religiosity.

Imitatio Dei would seem to be the highest level man can reach. Man alternates between attraction to God's greatness and shrinking before His majesty. Out of this fluctuation arise both acceptance and resolve: acceptance of the fact that he must remain at a distance from God, and resolve that, from that distance, he will imitate God's moral attributes as they are expressed in the Halakhah. "In this situation, the unexplained revelational decree is blended with creative normative consciousness, turning into purpose-filled moral commandments" (76). Were he able to cling to God, to be God's full partner, he would thereby "attain metaphysical and moral freedom and . . . deepen and broaden his existence" (78); but this goal seems unattainable, for how can man overcome the distance between his finite self and the infinite Creator?

Logically, the book should end here. But to our great surprise, we find that God has in fact provided the means to bridge the seemingly unbridge-able, to allow man to close the abyss between himself and God, to overcome completely the dichotomy between the natural and the revelational awareness. Man may cling to God in love, without recoiling. How this occurs will be the subject of our next chapter.

Chapter 34

U-Vikkashtem mi-Sham (3):
Cleaving to God

Stage III: *Devekut*

At the highest level – the ultimate stage of religious consciousness – the human being attains *devekut*, cleaving to God. In *devekut*, man experiences pure love without fear:

> At first, the yearning of love is joined with the repulsion of fear, but in the end a wave of pure love, ablaze with the fire of longing, surfaces and expels the anxiety and dread. The man of God begins with duality and ends with unity, starts with love mixed with terror and ends with love that transforms the repulsive power into attractive power and the deterrence into yearning. The individual who is fleeing suddenly senses the hand of the *Shekhinah* caressing him like a gentle, compassionate mother. He turns around, trembling and dumbstruck, covers himself with his cloak, and then uncovers a little of his face. He looks with amazed eyes, full of fear and astonishment, until his gaze encounters the smile of the *Shekhinah*, who is revealing Herself and running after him. Then the runaway who is being pursued immediately falls in love with his Pursuer, who loves him with an endless love (91–92).

The experience just described expresses an important idea. Revelation does not desire to enslave or frighten man, but rather to redeem him. The main motif of divine revelation is the infinite love of the Creator for His creation, and His approval of "man's complete existence" (92). That is, God wishes not to restrict man's existence but to expand it. He reveals Himself to searching, storm-tossed man in order to inform him of the meaning of temporal existence and the possibilities inherent in it. It is the suddenness of the revelation, not its contents, which terrifies man. In the end, however, revelation produces "joy born of love, and permanent friendship between God and man" (ibid.).[1]

Realizing that the purpose of revelation is to enhance his life, man – through a process to be detailed shortly – comes to internalize the revelatory law and thereby becomes, so to speak, God's partner.[2] He finds that the law actually demands his freedom and creativity, rather than denying them. The revelatory law affirms and sanctifies his existence as a concrete individual, as opposed to denigrating him as an anonymous slave or a speck of finitude.

> [M]an cleaves to God through the full realization of his personality, by uncovering all the possibilities latent in the depths of his being. It is the broadening rather than the narrowing of the spirit that provides the opening to cleave to God metaphysically. In this sense, Judaism has given a measure of approval to the ethical view that fulfilling the ideal of coming close to God is the result of man's fulfilling his own essence through activities directed at both the self and the other (89).

The Difference between Cleaving and Uniting

The significance of the point that the revelatory law requires – rather than extinguishes – human individuality becomes clear when we contrast *devekut* with the idea of *unio mystica*, mystical union with God. Seekers of *unio mystica* desire to lose their finite selves within the absolute unity of the Infinite. To that end, they negate the variegated and complex nature of man, emptying his life of color and freezing him at a point of eternity that is devoid of dimension and content.

Because these mystics deny any significance to individuality and to concrete life, they do not grasp the value of a specific lifestyle that fulfills God's will, nor do they understand the moral, activist nature of religion. All that matters to them is their internal ecstatic experience. Since *unio mystica* is possible only in a state of seclusion, they extol solitude and dismiss social life. Furthermore, out of their negation of society and their focus on that which is eternal, they also come to negate the living historical process, which both shapes society and is shaped by it.

---

1 The use of the term "friendship" (*yedidut*) to describe the God-man relationship is quite striking because, especially in his discussions of prayer, the Rav displays acute sensitivity to the dangers of being overly familiar with God, a state that the Gemara criticizes as "*havruta kelappei shemayya*" (*Berakhot* 34a, *Bava Batra* 16a).

2 Recall that in Chap. 28 above, man partnered with God in conceptualizing the Halakhah. In Chap. 35, we shall see further expressions of man's partnership with God.

The doctrine of *devekut* disagrees with every one of these points. First, it does not speak of *unity with* God, but rather of *clinging to* God. Uniting with God extinguishes man's separate and unique essence; clinging to God, however, requires that man remain man, that he preserve his human individuality:

> [M]an does not cleave to God by denying his actual essence, but, on the contrary, by affirming his own essence. The actual, multicolored human personality becomes closer to God when the individual lives his own variegated, original life, filled with goals, initiative, and activity, [but] without imagining some prideful, insolent independence. Then and only then does the personality begin to have a divine existence. Judaism insists that destroying man's uniqueness and originality does not bring man closer to God, as the mystics imagined (87–88).

Devekut proclaims that contemplation lacking action does not redeem man; rather, man fulfills his religious destiny by both studying *and realizing* the revelatory halakhic command. Since Halakhah relates to the individual and to the community, its realization can be attained only via attachment to a larger social group. Therefore the rabbis formulated the *mitzvah* of cleaving to God in terms of social *devekut*:

> "And to cleave to Him" (Deut. 11:22) – How is it possible for a person to ascend to Heaven and cleave to the fire? For it is written, "For the Lord your God is a consuming fire" (Deut. 4:24), and it is written, "His throne was fiery flames" (Dan. 7:9)! Rather, cleave to sages and their students . . . (*Sifrei*, Deut., 49).[3]

Not only is *devekut* unattainable in solitude, but "God joins with the individual only in the merit of the community which is loyal to Him and seeks Him" (89). Halakhah thus recognizes the importance and influence of one's social environment. Since society is so central, history too is obviously significant, for society formulates its character only within historical progression. Summarizing many of the differences between *devekut* and *unio mystica*, the Rav concludes, "The morality of the practical life, which is actualized within

---

3 Rambam offers the following explanation in his *Sefer ha-Mitzvot* (*aseh* 6): "He has commanded us to cleave to the scholars, to commune with them, to be in their company frequently and to participate in all manner of social contact with them – such as eating, drinking, and business – so that we may thereby come to imitate their actions and to accept true beliefs on the basis of their words." Of course, this begs the question of how the scholars themselves come to know God and cleave to Him. The Rav offers two answers: first, through their own direct connection to Torah (as we shall explain shortly); second, through their connection to their teachers and to the entire chain of tradition until Sinai (as we shall see in the next chapter).

time, is on a higher level than abstract aspirations and experiences that are focused on eternity" (90).

The Philosophical Basis of *Devekut*

Having established that, according to the Halakhah, one cleaves to God by cleaving to "those who know Him,"[4] we invite the question: how do "those who know Him" cleave to God? "The simple answer is: through their knowledge" (93). In the course of explaining this "simple answer," however, the Rav employs a somewhat arcane and decidedly un-simple Maimonidean doctrine[5] – the unity of the knower and the known – to which he adds two twists of his own, as we shall see.

Briefly stated, the Rav argues that there is a form of knowledge where, in the act of knowing, the knower becomes one with the known.[6] God perpetually "knows" the world in this manner, and man is also capable of such knowledge. It follows that if both God and man have the same object of knowledge (namely, the world), and each unites with that object of knowledge, then God and man are united with each other via this knowledge. In other words, if A unites with B, and C unites with B, then A unites with C.

To the claim that man unites with God via mutual knowledge of the world – which the Rav infers from his understanding of the Rambam – the Rav adds two further claims of his own.

(1) This "knowledge" is not purely contemplative but rather knowledge that unites thought, will and action.

(2) That which God and man both "know" is not only the world but also Halakhah; in fact, the latter is of greater relevance to the Rav's articulation of *devekut*.

In other words, the Rav's reading of the Rambam can be summarized as:

---

4 The Rav derives the formula of "cleaving to *those who know Him*" (*lehidabbek be-yod'av*) from the heading to Rambam's *Hilkhot De'ot*; the body of *Hilkhot De'ot* (6:2), like the *Sifrei*, refers to "cleaving to *sages*" (*lehidabbek be-hakhamim*).

5 This doctrine, which has its roots in Aristotle, was adopted by many subsequent philosophers. The Rav, unsurprisingly, focuses on its articulation by the Rambam.

6 To be more precise, the knower's intellect unites with that which is intelligible about the object. "When one grasps the intelligible essence of an entity, one penetrates it and unites with it. Instead of cognition as an act of imaging external objects which retain their stability and independent existence even after they are apprehended (as asserted by the ancient realism of images), there is an active, creative cognition; it penetrates the realm of the object, conquers its otherness, takes it captive, and conjoins with it" (97). For a fuller exposition of this argument, see For Further Reference, #2.

$$\text{God} \rightarrow \text{world} \leftarrow \text{man}$$

with the arrows representing knowledge or cognition; the Rav revises this into:

$$\text{God} \rightarrow \text{Halakhah} \leftarrow \text{man}$$

with the arrows now representing not cognition but "Thought = Will = Action" (103).

The basis for the Rav's first modification (labeled 1 above) is fairly straightforward. In man, thought, will and action are often disjunct: for example, a person can *know* that smoking is unhealthy, but he still *wants* to smoke; or he can *want* to quit smoking, but *in practice* he continues to smoke. In God, however, such a thing is inconceivable. His thought-will-action is a single unity, and man, in his own life, must try to emulate this consistency.[7] Pure knowledge, which has no effect on one's will or one's actions, is insufficient to bring about a state of cleaving to God.[8]

But what is a suitable object for this kind of multifaceted yet integrated "knowledge" that allows for *devekut*? This question brings about the Rav's second modification of Rambam's theory. Both the cosmos and the Halakhah reflect God's wisdom and will, and both can be the subject of man's intellectual inquiry; but man can identify his will with, and pattern his actions after, only the Halakhah.[9] Hence, all the techniques of *devekut* that the Rav describes from chapter 15 and onward relate to man's cleaving to God via the Halakhah, and not via the world.[10]

Rescuing Rambam

Before we move on to examine the techniques of *devekut* (in the coming chapter), a few observations are in order regarding the Rav's enlistment of the

---

7 Rav Soloveitchik (104) connects this doctrine with *Guide* III:54, which links thought with action. God's unity of will and action is implicit in *Guide* I:65–67, which immediately precedes the discussion of the unity of knower, known and knowledge within God (*Guide* I:68).

8 Of course, the necessity of incorporating thought, feeling and action in religious life, and the interplay between them, are central themes in the Rav's thought. Therefore, Sec. II of this book (Chaps. 4–10) was devoted entirely to these topics.

9 Rambam himself would disagree with this assessment. He believed that by studying the created world (both physical and metaphysical), one could discern God's "attributes of action," and one could try to apply these in one's own life (*Guide* I:54). A modern person, however, who views nature in mechanical and not teleological (purposeful) terms, would have difficulty adopting Rambam's position. See For Further Reference, #3.

10 Regarding the shift from the world to Halakhah as the medium of *devekut*, see For Further Reference, #4.

Rambam in our context and others. Anyone who – like the Rav – relates to the Rambam with the utmost respect and seriousness must confront the question of his philosophical datedness. The Rambam's philosophy incorporates many Aristotelian assumptions and doctrines that have largely been superseded, indeed rendered obsolete, by later philosophical and scientific developments. If we remove the Aristotelian scaffolding or foundations (and there is a crucial difference between these two metaphors), can the Rambam's philosophical edifice remain standing?

Our discussion of the philosophical basis of *devekut* exemplifies the Rav's response to this challenge. He frequently recruits Maimonidean doctrines that might be perceived as archaic or obsolete and tries to give them new life by reinterpreting them, recasting them in light of modern philosophical assumptions, or trying to show their relevance to contemporary religious issues.[11] Just as Rav Soloveitchik's father appears as the Rambam's champion (in the halakhic realm) in the famous story at the end of *U-Vikkashtem mi-Sham*, Rav Soloveitchik himself appears as the Rambam's champion (in the philosophical realm) here and elsewhere.[12]

Both champions are open to the charge that, while the ideas they attribute to the Rambam are compelling, they may not always capture the Rambam's original intent.[13] Sometimes, the Rav himself would accept this claim. In these cases, he self-consciously sets out to reinterpret medieval doctrines, such as in his fascinating discussion of how medieval proofs of God are still valuable today as reflections of experiences rather than as rational demonstrations.[14] At other times, it is not clear whether the Rav feels that his interpretation accords with the Rambam's intent or whether he is proposing a modern adaptation of it. Either way, animated by the conviction that the words of the great master

---

11 See, for example, our brief discussion in Chap. 29 above regarding the Rav's utilization of the Rambam's theories of providence and prophecy in *Halakhic Man*.

12 This does not mean that he is never critical of the Rambam's philosophical positions. See, for example, his harsh critique in *The Halakhic Mind* (91–99) of the Rambam's doctrine of *ta'amei ha-mitzvot* (reasons for the commandments) as presented in the *Guide*.

13 Of course, the Briskers champion the view that Torah study is not merely an antiquarian pursuit, and that creative interpretation is a legitimate part of the processes of *talmud Torah* and *masorah*. See, for example, Rav Aharon Lichtenstein, "*Torat Hesed* and *Torat Emet*: Methodological Reflections," in his *Leaves of Faith*, vol. 1 (Jersey City, 2003), 61–87.

14 For example, instead of the cosmological *proof*, which deduces from the existence of the world that there must be a Creator, we have the cosmological *experience*, which refers "to the immediate awareness that overcomes man who sees God in the innermost essence of the world as well as in its surroundings" (13). See the extended discussion in *U-Vikkashtem mi-Sham*, 11–15, and For Further Reference, #5.

are perpetually relevant, the Rav always strives to read them in a way that maintains their abiding significance.

FOR FURTHER REFERENCE

1. *Unio mystica* **in Judaism:** Though the Rav attributes the doctrine of *unio mystica* to the third-century philosopher Plotinus, it is conceivable that he also has in mind some kabbalistic and Hasidic masters who seem to advocate a similar doctrine. The question of whether one can find advocates of true *unio mystica* within Judaism has been debated by scholars: see Gershom Scholem, *The Messianic Idea in Judaism* (New York, 1971), 203–27; and Moshe Idel, *Kabbalah: New Perspectives* (New Haven, 1988), 59–73.

2. **Unity of the knower and the known:**
   (a) For the philosophical background of the Rav's theory of knowledge, see Aviezer Ravitzky, "Rabbi J. B. Soloveitchik on Human Knowledge: Between Maimonidean and neo-Kantian Philosophy," *Modern Judaism* 6:2 (1986), 157–88.
   (b) To explain the Rav's argument in greater detail, I will cite the introduction to *And from There You Will Seek*, xxv:

   > In many instances of human knowledge – for example, "I know that the table is solid" – there is a differentiation between the knower, the subject, and the known, the object. Even in a statement like "I know that I exist," I split my personality, as it were, between the knowing subject and the known object. For God, however, as explained by Maimonides in the *Mishneh Torah*, there is a perfect unity – the knower is one with the known and with the knowledge. Further, God's knowledge of the world is one with knowledge of Himself, for the world cannot exist separately from God. The world is not an independent object.
   >
   > The thesis that the knower is one with what is known is expounded by Maimonides in *Hilkhot Yesodei ha-Torah* (2:10) with reference to God, and in *Guide of the Perplexed* (I:68) with reference to man. There is, to be sure, a certain type of knowledge in which one merely "photographs" what is known, with no active, creative input. But in other cases, the sort the Rav is interested in, cases of active, creative knowledge, the knower unites with the known. "When one grasps the intelligible essence of an entity, one penetrates it and unites with it . . ." (97). Despite the parallel between divine knowledge and human knowledge,

a difference must be noted. Divine cognition has no end, since if God were to stop thinking about the world, all would revert to chaos, but human beings do not cognize continuously. At times, they know only potentially, and the dualism of subject and object is reinstated. Still, when man knows, his cognition blends and unites with the universe; He "conquers" it and conjoins with it.

The critical point now is this: when the individual unites with the world, he also unites with his Creator. For the world, the creation of God's thought, is the object of both God's knowledge and human knowledge. "By knowing the world the individual knows his Creator and cleaves to Him" (102), for "man and God are united in knowledge of the world" (103). God is united with the world, man is united with the world, and man is thus united with God.

3. **Rambam on the study of creation:** Rambam, as mentioned in footnote 9 above, believed that the study of physics and metaphysics could yield an understanding of God's "attributes of action," which man could then apply in his own life. Some, most famously Hermann Cohen, understand this application in terms of ethics; see his *Ethics of Maimonides*, trans. Almut Sh. Bruckstein (Madison, 2003). Others understand man's imitation or assimilation of God's attributes of action in terms of political leadership and legislative activity; among more recent writers, see, for example, Warren Zev Harvey, "Political Philosophy and Halakhah in Maimonides" (Heb.), *Iyyun* 29:3 (1980), 198–212 (abridged translation in Joseph Dan, ed., *Binah: Studies in Jewish History, Thought, and Culture*, vol. 3 [Westport, 1994], 47–64), and Howard Kreisel, *Maimonides' Political Thought* (Albany, 1999).

4. *Devekut* **via the world and via Halakhah:** It seems as if throughout chapters 13 and 14 Rav Soloveitchik sets up the model of *devekut* via joint cognition of the world only in order to undermine it at the end of chapter 14 by substituting cognition of Halakhah for cognition of the world. There are several ways to account for this shift.
   a. Above, I suggested that for the Rav, the unity of thought-will-action can be attained only with reference to Halakhah.
   b. David Shatz ("Science and Religious Consciousness in the Thought of Rabbi Soloveitchik," in his *Jewish Thought in Dialogue* [Boston, 2009], 152) concurs and adds another suggestion: only the study of Halakhah, not the study of nature, fuses the natural consciousness and the revelatory consciousness, and therefore only Halakhah can help man overcome the central dialectic of *U-Vikkashtem mi-Sham*.

372

c. Aviezer Ravitzky (*op. cit.*, 169) suggests a further reason: "Since medieval thought created a barrier between human knowledge and the essence of God, to which modern thought [i.e., Kant] added the barrier between human knowledge and the essence of the world [i.e., man cannot know the 'thing-in-itself,' but only his own perception of it] – was there any remaining realm to which man's intellect could really penetrate . . . into the realm of the absolute? Is there some sphere which is 'idealistic' by its very nature? This is the root of the transition from the cosmos to Halakhah, from Creation to Sinai." (David Shatz [*op. cit.*, 151–52] and Moshe Sokol ["Master or Slave," 321–22] take issue with Ravitzky's suggestion.)

d. I would add a final consideration: the shift in chapter 14 is not so stark if we consider that in chapters 17 and 18 the Rav asserts a sort of unity between the cosmos and Halakhah (or, as the Rav puts it, between the ontological law and the revelational moral law).

An additional question now demands to be addressed: If *devekut* is fully attainable via Halakhah, what role is left for the cosmic approach to God? This will be addressed in Chapter 35, For Further Reference, #1, after we finish examining the end of *U-Vikkashtem mi-Sham*.

5. **Reinterpreting Rambam:** Interestingly, while in the text of *U-Vikkashtem mi-Sham* (11–15) Rav Soloveitchik indicates that he is consciously transmuting medieval proofs of God into experiences of God, and admits that this is not what the medievals intended, in footnote 4 (158–59) he presents an experiential reading of the opening passage of *Mishneh Torah* as representing the Rambam's original intent! The Rambam writes: "The basic principle of all basic principles and the pillar of all sciences is to know (*leida*) that there is a First Existent who brought every existing thing into being" (*Hilkhot Yesodei Ha-Torah* 1:1). Referring to the key term "*leida*," the Rav explains that "This knowledge is not based on logical inference, but is, rather, immediate: the knowledge of reality as divine reality . . ." (158). See also *On Repentance*, 144–50.

It is noteworthy that Prof. Simon Rawidowicz (1896–1957), the Rav's friend from the University of Berlin, had also proposed that "*leida*" does not refer to rational knowledge (but rather to firm belief): see his "On Maimonides' *Sefer ha-Madda*," in *Essays in Honour of the Very Rev. Dr. J. H. Hertz*, eds. I. Epstein et al. (London, 1942), 331–39; reprinted in his *Studies in Jewish Thought* (Philadelphia, 1974), 317–23. However, in two 1954 letters to Prof. Rawidowicz (printed in *Community, Covenant, and Commitment*, 283–87), the Rav takes a more rationalist view of the

Rambam than does Rawidowicz, noting that for the Rambam, "the commandment to affirm God's existence and unity contains both an obligation of complete faith [as Rawidowicz would claim] as well as maximal intellectual effort which translates this faith into rational concepts" (284).

Thus, contrary to his reading of the Rambam in footnote 4 of *U-Vikkashtem*, in his letter to Rawidowicz the Rav seems to understand *leida* as signifying rational cognition. Strikingly, in his letter the Rav contrasts the Rambam's rationalist conception with R. Yehudah Halevi's experiential one, expressing preference for the latter:

> It is not important at this moment to examine if his [i.e., Rambam's] position is correct from the perspective of the religious reality that we encounter. I am inclined to accept the perspective of Rabbi Yehudah ha-Levi regarding the [issue] of the intellectual religious experience [advocated by Rambam] in contrast to the "concrete" transcendental religious experience [advocated by Halevi]. However, our great teacher [Rambam] was dedicated to his [rationalist] perspective with all his heart and soul, though it cannot be maintained in day-to-day religious life (286–87).

Chapter 35

U-Vikkashtem mi-Sham (4): *Devekut* via Halakhah

The goal of *devekut*, we said, is to overcome the dichotomy between man's free, natural religious consciousness and his compelled, revelational religious consciousness – put in other terms, to overcome the *Bereishit*-Sinai dichotomy. The Rav now details three techniques for attaining *devekut*, or, we might say, three ways in which *devekut* is expressed:

(1) the rule of the intellect;
(2) the elevation of the body;
(3) the perpetuity of God's word (p. 107).

Note that the basis for *devekut* (as explained in Chapter 34) is the linking of God and man via their mutual connection to Halakhah, and that this connection to Halakhah entails thought, action and will. Given this, I would assert that the three means (or expressions) of *devekut* just mentioned relate to the three modes of connection:

Thought = rule of the intellect (Torah study);
Action = elevation of the body (*mitzvah* observance);
Will = perpetuation of God's word (prophecy, *masorah* and identity of wills).

None of these familiar elements – *talmud Torah, shemirat ha-mitzvot* and *masorah* – is a simple matter of performance or obedience. Rather, each is a creative enterprise into which man pours his individuality, thereby making the concepts and dictates of Halakhah his own and in that way cleaving to their Giver. Let us now examine each of the three elements.

The Rule of the Intellect

Halakhah is the product of divine revelation. But once Halakhah was given at Sinai, it was not closed to the human intellect; on the contrary, human reason is its final arbiter. This is true both on the level of study (*lomdus*) and application (*pesak*). Regarding the latter, the Rav cites the well-known Judaic doctrine that, following the Sinaitic revelation, halakhic decisions are to be determined not by prophecy or oracles, but by human argumentation and persuasive reasoning:

> The only authority [in Halakhah] is reason. The Halakhah expels from its realm all mysterious obscurity, whispers of intuition that are beyond rational cognition, and even supernatural revelations. A prophet who expresses his opinion on matters of Torah law in the form of a prophecy is punishable by death. . . . Human thought, which is subject to the principles of logic, has "dared" to penetrate into and occupy a realm that does not belong to it (107–08).

In the realm of *pesak*, the free activity of the halakhist is bound by precedent, by majority decision, and by the need to erect safeguards around the Halakhah; but in the realm of *lomdus*, his creative intellect is given free rein.[1] Here, the halakhist's exercise of intellect involves the construction of *hiddushim*, novel concepts, interpretations and ideas. These novellae must arise from within the bounds of certain fixed, a priori postulates presented by revelation; but the freedom of creative interpretation and conceptualization granted to halakhic personalities within these limits gives the lie to the allegation that Halakhah is ossified. *Rishonim* and *aharonim*, medieval and modern commentators, "created new worlds that are breathtaking in their beauty and sublimity" (108).[2]

The use of reason in halakhic thought not only creates new ideas, but even infuses the fixed axioms of Halakhah with life and freshness. While the axioms are revealed and cannot be rejected, there is a "marvelous freedom" in the creative conceptual activity of the halakhist (p. 109). The halakhist organizes the data and postulates of the Halakhah into new conceptual frameworks that uncover their inner logic and coherence:

---

1 Despite the constraints placed upon the halakhist in his legislative-judicial role, his activity is still firmly within the human domain; "It is not in heaven" (Deut. 30:12). The above-mentioned constraints upon his freedom of decision – legal precedent, majority decision, and the need to erect safeguards around the Halakhah – are themselves products of the human intellect. Moreover, his freedom of conceptualization (*lomdus*) impacts upon any *pesak* he may render.

2 Regarding the nature of halakhic creativity, and specifically of the conceptual revolution wrought by R Hayyim of Brisk, see "*Mah Dodekh mi-Dod*," 74–82.

In every generation man must deeply investigate the foundations of the Halakhah, the definitions of its concepts, its epistemic principles, and the ordering
of its achievements. The goal of halakhic inquiry is to hew out new ideas and
fresh, surprising conceptions (ibid.).

Thus, the freedom and creativity that characterize the "natural" consciousness are now infused into the revelational consciousness. "The Holy One,
Blessed Be He, gave the Torah to Israel and commanded us to innovate and
create [within it]" (110). In turn, by demanding the participation of the human
intellect in the halakhic process – even more, by granting it the power "to
innovate and create" within Halakhah – the revelational consciousness shows
its esteem for the natural consciousness, even as it sanctifies it.

Elevation of the Body

In depicting the "rule of intellect," we focused on how the human element
penetrates the revelatory realm. As we now turn to examine the concept of
"elevation of the body," our focus is on the reverse: how the revelatory element penetrates the human realm.

Judaism does not view the natural, biological aspect of the human being
with disdain or despair. Therefore, the revelatory commands do not come to
deny and repress man's physical existence. Judaism instead declares that the
body's instinctual biological drives must be refined, redeemed and sanctified,
but not extirpated. Through the imposition of *mitzvot* that make demands of
the body, those drives are stamped with "direction and purposefulness" (111).
The Torah thus allows man to experience pleasure, even as it prevents him
from being enslaved to desire and from indulging in pleasure to excess.[3]

Revelation, Rav Soloveitchik concludes, does not negate worldly existence but rather validates it: "Revelational faith does not clash with what
exists or deny its importance. On the contrary, its teaching is a reality-based
doctrine, a doctrine of what exists, whose purpose is the sanctification of
biological existence [i.e., elevation of the body], and whose strategies are inherent in logical thought [i.e., the rule of the intellect]" (119). In other words,
revelation directs man to a full natural existence; it affirms the significance of
reality and links it to the attainment of transcendent values.

Furthermore, the Rav continues, revelation does not distract man from reality but rather focuses his attention on the world. In order to apply Halakhah,
man requires an intimate knowledge and deep understanding of the world.

---

3 We need expand no more on the topic of elevation of the body, since it was the subject of
Chap. 5 above.

The Halakhah "is enclosed within the realm of the actual. Its object is the world that encompasses us completely" (120). Halakhah takes account of all scientific and technological innovations, and its articulation and application depend upon understanding concepts like space, causation, intention and compulsion, and disciplines such as physiology, anatomy, astronomy and politics. Adapting Galileo's maxim that the book of Nature is written in the language of mathematics, Rav Soloveitchik states: "Halakhah writes in the language of orderly scientific reality" (121).

Summarizing the first two components of *devekut* – which are, essentially, deeper understandings of the activities of *talmud Torah* and *shemirat ha-mitzvot* – the Rav writes that "Judaism placed the rule of reason and the sanctification of the body at the center of its world" (119). By so doing, "it eliminated the dualism that encases man's consciousness of God," namely, the dualism between the natural-cosmic religious consciousness and the revelatory-prophetic religious consciousness. How so? With reference to "elevation of the body," he explains, "When the revelational content is directed at real, natural existence, with all its colors and tones, the abyss in religious experience [i.e., the abyss between the natural and the revelational experiences] is closed up." And with reference to "rule of the intellect," he continues, "The halakhic ideal is embodied in its striving for joint revelational and intellectual activity. Halakhic man grasps supra-rational topics and discusses them in an objective, rational manner." Thus, by means of these two types of *devekut*, "Transcendence descends into limited, contingent being; the reality outside the limits of human understanding is absorbed by a reality that is accessible to human understanding" (119–20).

Perpetuation of God's Word (I): Prophecy

The third component of *devekut*, "perpetuation of God's word," refers both to prophecy (123ff.) and to prophecy's contemporary counterpart: the *masorah*, that is, the ongoing process of transmitting the Torah (135ff. and 139ff.). Let us begin with prophecy.

At the onset of prophecy, God reveals Himself to man and thus transports the prophet into a supra-rational world. But the prophet does not remain in that world exclusively; he is commanded "to return to the actual world, to repair it and purify it" (123). Prophecy thereby reflects – like the rule of the intellect and the elevation of the body – the blending of revelation and this-worldly reality, the merging of the revelatory consciousness with the natural-rational consciousness.

Even though God reveals Himself to human beings, He expects the individual to seek Him and to prepare for the prophetic encounter. Preparation requires a concentration on "penetrating 'the secrets of the world' (*Hagigah* 13a), living a pure and holy life, perfecting one's halakhic ethical personality, and rising to the peak of cleaving to God" (123–24). This demand is encapsulated in the *mitzvah* of "*Kedoshim tihyu*, You shall be holy" (Lev. 19:2), which aims at the creation of "a personality worthy of prophecy" (124).

The obligation to prepare for prophecy is not just a *mitzvah*, but a crucial medium of *devekut*. It effects a significant attitudinal, experiential shift with regard to revelation. When divine revelation *precedes* human preparation and self-perfection, the natural consciousness and revelational consciousness are discontinuous with each other. As a result, man feels frightened by revelation, even threatened by it.

> Judaism says to one [who is given an unexpected revelation], "You have felt a great fear, you retreated when God appeared to you because you did not expect Him and you did not pray for Him to come, and so His coming terrified you. But this fear, which stems from your lack of anticipation and the suddenness of the revelation, does not occur with a revelation that you are hoping for with all your heart and soul. If you seek God[4] and He answers your prayer and appears to you, then you will not be afraid of Him. You will be happy with Him, and you will find rest and repose in His bosom" (126).[5]

When, in contrast to the case of unexpected revelation, the individual encounters God after seeking Him and *after* preparing himself for the encounter with the divine, then he welcomes the revelatory experience, for he grasps its inner meaning.[6] We have seen that, at the outset of his journey, man utilizes his "free creative consciousness" to seek an answer to the riddle of existence. If he prepares himself for prophecy, he will discern that "the 'compelled' revelational consciousness" provides the riddle's solution. Thus, via preparation for prophecy, "reason unites with faith, the free creative consciousness unites with the 'compelled' revelational consciousness, and a relationship *of*

---

4 In Hebrew: "*Im tevakkeshu et ha-E-lohim*" – note the echo of the book's title. The title verse appears only once in the book, on p. 20.

5 If revelation were a one-time occurrence, this argument would be circular. How can one prepare oneself for revelation by fulfilling the dictates of that revelation? Since, as we shall see, revelation is an ongoing process and awareness, we may understand that while the initial revelation at Sinai was indeed frightening (see Ex. 20:14–15), the continuing experience of revelation (via *masorah*) need not be.

6 This is not to say that the revelation is brought about entirely by human effort. Nevertheless, "God attends to man who seeks Him and longs for the revelational encounter" (126).

question and answer, of longing and fulfillment, bursts forth" (126, emphasis added).

This section of *U-Vikkashtem mi-Sham* is significant but somewhat obscure. Therefore, it is important to explain what the Rav means when he says that the "longing" of the natural consciousness is "fulfilled" by revelational consciousness, and that revelation "answers" the "question" posed by reason.

Without the benefit of revelation, reality perplexes man and confounds him. He seeks order and meaning in the universe, but encounters elements that frustrate this search:

> Modern man's entire cultural outlook is full of contradictions and oppositions. It encounters non-rational elements that cannot be grasped by the mind. Physico-mathematical science encounters the living, qualitative reality; metaphysics encounters the blind and impenetrable substance, mechanical nature; morality encounters sin and evil; art encounters the ugly and the repulsive, and so on. The weight of the irrationality and inconsistency in the perceived world lies heavily on the cultural *Weltanschauung* (worldview). In spite of man's many human technological achievements and his conquest, to an extent, of matter, the eternal riddle continues to emerge from all the realms of the creation, especially those illuminated by reason (127).

Creation, thus, is a mystery. Man, with his "natural consciousness," tries to discover his place within creation, or to make an enduring place for himself within creation. Yet his success in this endeavor is, at best, only partial and limited, and is ultimately unsatisfying.

Sinai heralds the solution for which man "longs." Via revelation, man finds what he had sought, for the all-encompassing system of Halakhah imparts meaning and significance to *all* aspects of existence (even those impenetrable to reason). Man finds within it his existential anchor. Even more significantly, since man plays an indispensable role in the formulation and realization of Halakhah, it is precisely from within revelation that his personal uniqueness and freedom are affirmed.

The very compulsion felt by man, a compulsion that binds him to the authority of the revelation, becomes his "savior." Revelation "frees him from the chains of the natural world" – chains that frustrate his efforts at self-transcendence – "and raises him to the level of freedom of the man of God" (128). By fully appreciating the meaning of revelation, and therefore desiring revelation instead of fearing it, "The heavy weight of [revelatory] laws and regulations is transformed into an intensely attractive force that raises the individual from the mire of impenetrable reality to an existence full of purpose and yearning" (ibid.).

Thus, the individual begins with a free search for meaning and significance, the search being a product of his natural consciousness. He later encounters revelatory compulsion. But by virtue of revelation he ends with the experience of freedom – freedom from the confines of nature, freedom to connect to the source of true being, freedom to transcend himself. "There is no one as free as one who is engaged in the study of Torah" (*Avot* 6:2). The experience of the commandments is one of joy, happiness and total freedom, as if the divine commandments were identical with the demands of the creative rational mind. The individual fulfills the commandments not out of compulsion, nor out of emulation, but out of identification and partnership. Man does not necessarily find within himself the details of the Halakhah, but rather the need for a cognitive-normative system of absolute validity that desires his input, affirms his value, and elevates his existence. The revelational law thereby answers his deepest desires.

Earlier we saw that the rule of intellect signifies the *devekut* of thought, while elevation of the body signifies *devekut* of action. Now, we see that prophecy (and *masorah*, which we will discuss shortly), by bringing reason and revelation into a relationship "of longing and fulfillment," signifies *devekut* of the will, or *devekut* of emotion and experience. How so?

All three forms of *devekut* are achieved through man's merging with Halakhah, his intertwining of the natural consciousness with the revelational consciousness. Via the "perpetuation of God's word," man achieves union with Halakhah not just in the realms of thought and action, but in the realm of emotional identification. By seeking prophecy, man grants a dimension of freedom to the revelatory experience. By grasping the true meaning of revelation (as the answer to his question, the fulfillment of his longing), he gains the total freedom attained through the unity of his will with God's. At the level of *devekut*, then, revelation takes on a new meaning: it represents freedom, not compulsion; affirmation of man's natural life, not its denial; and it infuses his entire existence with meaning.

Perpetuation of God's Word (II): *Masorah*

Although, technically speaking, the age of prophecy ceased long ago, in truth God's revelation is not confined to ancient biblical figures like Isaiah, Ezekiel and Amos, but carries on all through the generations. "The historical revelation that occurred at a particular time remains a living and continuous awareness of the divine revelation" (134). Earlier, the Rav asserted that all Jews should *prepare* for prophecy; now he claims that they can actually *participate* in the prophetic tradition, for God's revelation is "an eternal vision that sails in the stream of time and the flow of the generations" (135).

The proposition that the revelation does not end is reflected in the *maso-rah*, the transmission and reception of the Torah, which joins together generations and eras. Just as joint cognition of the Halakhah unites the human being with God, it also unites human with human, both contemporaneously (in the relationship between student and teacher)[7] and throughout the ages.

When biblical prophets communicated to people, they bestowed their personal glory and shared some of their essence. For example, the Bible relates that Moses shared some of his glory with his disciple Joshua (Num. 27:20) and with the seventy elders (ibid. 11:17). Likewise, when a teacher transmits his teaching, he is not only conveying information; he is sharing of himself. This is especially true of the study of the Oral Torah, "a Torah which by its nature and application can never be objectified, even after it has been written down. 'Oral Torah' means a Torah that blends with the individual's personal uniqueness and becomes an inseparable part of man. When the person then transmits it to someone else, his personal essence is transmitted along with it" (142).[8] Torah in not a static object passed from teacher to disciple. Everyone who receives it impresses upon it his own individual stamp and then conveys that renewed and refreshed Torah, in turn, to the next generation.

Teaching and transmitting Torah is an act of *hesed*, loving-kindness. Prophets and sages are "guardians for the distribution of spiritual wealth" (146). By sharing their Torah with the community, they thereby merge existentially with the community.

This community extends not just to one's contemporaries, but to those who come before and after. It is by "an act of historical identification with the past and future, the fate and destiny, of the Jewish people" (ibid.) that individual and community come together. *Knesset Yisrael*, the community of Israel, refers to "the coupling of the first and last generations of prophet and listener" (ibid.).

Rav Soloveitchik vividly illustrates the living nature of *masorah* by recounting the tale of his childhood "friendship" with the Rambam.[9] Reflecting on this childhood experience, the Rav writes of its impact in later years:

> When I sit down to study the Torah, I find myself immediately in the company of the sages of the *masorah*. The relations between us are personal. The Ram-

---

7 It is noteworthy that the Rav, like the Rambam, never discusses the relationship between student and student – the *havruta*.

8 For more on this understanding of the Oral Law, and on the teacher-disciple relationship, see the end of Chap. 2 above.

9 I will not summarize the story, so as not to spoil it. See *U-Vikkashtem*, 143–45.

bam is at my right, Rabbenu Tam at my left, Rashi sits up front and interprets, Rabbenu Tam disputes him; the Rambam issues a ruling, and the Rabad objects. They are all in my little room, sitting around my table . . . Torah study is not solely an educational activity. It is not a merely formal, technical matter embodied in the discovery and exchange of facts. It is a powerful experience of becoming friends with many generations of Torah scholars, the joining of one spirit with another, the union of souls. Those who transmitted the Torah and those who received it come together in one historical way-station (145).

The "perpetuation of God's word" thus accomplishes several things. First, by uniting the longing of the natural consciousness with its fulfillment in the revelational consciousness, it brings man's will into conjunction with God's. This, in turn, highlights the emotional and experiential dimensions of the other two components of *devekut*, namely, the study[10] and practice[11] of Halakhah. Finally, while the other components of *devekut* sometimes can be construed as largely solitary and a-historical pursuits, the perpetuation of God's word brings both of them into the social realm and the flow of history through the creation of the *masorah* community.[12]

Summary

From the point of view of man's inner experience, *U-Vikkashtem mi-Sham* depicts a movement from freedom to compulsion to freedom (128). From the point of view of his relationship to revelation (Halakhah), man moves from seeing it as a threatening imposition upon him, to something imposed but welcome, to an internalized element of his being that has merged with his natural awareness. While Halakhah initially appears indifferent (at best) to man's aspirations, it turns out to be exquisitely attuned to the deepest needs of man's being. It seeks out man's active partnership, thereby validating and sanctifying man's intellectual creativity, his physical existence, his social and cultural life.[13]

---

10 "The transmission and reception of the Oral Torah . . . are embodied in the infusion of the revelational consciousness, in the transmission of the vision of the living God, through an *experience* that rages from one generation to the next" (139).

11 "Does not the fulfillment of the commandments constitute an *experience* that sweetens the bitterness in man's life, purifies the individual, and redeems him from his distress, loneliness, and grief?" (129).

12 Regarding this final point, see R. Shalom Carmy, "On Cleaving as Identification: R. Soloveitchik's Account of *Devekut* in *U-Vikkashtem Mi-Sham*," *Tradition* 41:2 (Summer 2008), 100–12.

13 Lawrence Kaplan eloquently traces the trajectory of *U-Vikkashtem mi-Sham*: "The

Rav Soloveitchik himself helpfully ends *U-Vikkashtem mi-Sham* with a summary of its basic argument, which I will quote in full:

Active participation in the work of reconstructing the content of revelation is the goal of Judaism as it wends its way through the three layers of transcendent consciousness. From a state of trust alternating with fear, it evolves into a state of love combined with awe, and from there it climbs up to a state of love characterized by desire and cleaving.

At first, human questioning brings man to the revelational encounter. Through his striving for the absolute, for the non-contingent and the eternal, he encounters the divine command and the supranatural authority that demand of him to follow a particular way of life. The revelational experience on this level denies and contradicts man's intellectual values and aspires to replace the free activity of man's spirit with the passivity of compulsion and anxiety.

In the second stage, man begins to befriend the revelational experience and to feel trust in it; he tries to link it to his experience of God within the system of lawful and orderly nature; he identifies with the consciousness of the God of the world, which expresses the wonder of loving-kindness, compassion, and blessings, as well as with the consciousness of a God above and beyond the world, which demands absolute subjugation and commitment from the individual. This stage includes aspects of imperative subjugation and revelation, with all the weight of the supra-rational authority that oppresses man's consciousness; but it also includes the serenity of complete trust and the expectation of absolute reward. Man performs God's commandments against his will; but as a side effect of the compulsion, he feels the complete tranquility of the slave who does his master's bidding, and the revelation thereby provides support for the wanderer in the paths of the creation. The goal is to imitate God. It includes aspects of necessity as well as aspects of joy and security.[14]

The imperative nature of man's behavior gradually palls at the dawn of the

---

Halakhah, despite its revealed quality, sheds its 'otherness,' its threatening nature. The initial impact of revelation constrains man. But the content and purpose of that revelation, both in terms of study and practice, give rise to the sense of freedom, self-affirmation, affirmation of society, culture and civilization, and above all, affirmation of man's creative spirit that had initially characterized the creative-rational religious consciousness. But the dialectical switch can take place only if man accomplishes it, if man in the practice and study of the Halakhah himself transforms the experience of necessity into one of freedom" ("Joseph Soloveitchik and Halakhic Man," 226–27).

14 It is interesting that the summary gives so much attention to Stage II, even though the book itself devotes far less attention to Stage II than to either of the other two stages. The latter fact is itself even more noteworthy: *U-Vikkashtem mi-Sham* as a whole pays relatively little attention to Stage II, even though it would seem to be the highest level the average Jew can reach.

third stage, the stage combining love with awe, when the soul longs for its Creator out of the aspiration for total attachment and strives to achieve this in a running movement without any retreat. While the goal in the second stage is to imitate God, the end of the third stage is to cleave to Him. What is the difference between the two aims? Imitating God includes aspects of total freedom and total subjugation. Cleaving is entirely free activity. Man lives according to the Torah and the commandments in great joy. He desires to do the will of God as if the will of the Infinite were also the will of the finite individual. In the third stage we see the wonder of the identification of wills (149–50).

Ish ha-Halakhah and *U-Vikkashtem mi-Sham*

Rav Soloveitchik drafted *U-Vikkashtem mi-Sham* in the 1940s, shortly after completing *Ish ha-Halakhah* (*Halakhic Man*). Despite the work's importance – or perhaps because of it – it did not appear in print until 1978, when the Rav published it in the rabbinic journal *Hadarom*.

In the three decades he took to publish the essay, the Rav experimented with various titles. In its early stage it was called "*Ish ha-Elokim*," "The Man of God"; in a 1963 letter to the rabbinic scholar Dr. Samuel K. Mirsky (1899–1967),[15] the Rav refers to it as "*Halakhah Geluyah ve-Ahavah Mesuteret*," "Overt Halakhah and Covert Love," the same title as the final version's first chapter; then, in the published version, he opted for the name "*U-Vikkashtem mi-Sham*," "And from There You Shall Seek," a title that, as noted in Chapter 32 above, derives from a biblical verse: "And from there you shall seek the Lord your God, and you will find Him if only you seek Him with all your heart and all your soul" (Deut. 4:29).

The mid-1940s were a time of immense creativity for the Rav, during which he wrote three major works – *Ish ha-Halakhah*, *The Halakhic Mind* (written in 1944, published in 1986), and *Ish ha-Elokim*, the ancestor of *U-Vikkashtem mi-Sham*. It is difficult to know why he published *Ish ha-Halakhah* soon after its composition (in 1944 in the rabbinic journal *Talpiyot*) but waited so long before publishing the other two. Perhaps he felt impelled to publish *Ish ha-Halakhah* because it contained an element of eulogy for his father, Rav Moshe Soloveitchik, who had died in 1941. But the postponement of the other works is curious, and Rav Soloveitchik left no indication of its cause. What can be noted, though, is that when *The Halakhic Mind* finally appeared, it was in its 1944 incarnation, without any changes except the title and the omission of several technical footnotes, whereas *U-Vikkashtem*

---

15 *Community, Covenant and Commitment*, 321–22.

mi-Sham (then *Ish ha-Elokim*) underwent rewriting prior to its publication – rewriting that apparently involved more than merely reorganizing or putting fine touches on sentences. The first revision we know of was done during the 1960s, when the Rav prepared the essay for publication in *Talpiyot*, the journal that had published *Ish ha-Halakhah* two decades earlier. This revised manuscript was lost, but a photocopy of the original, unrevised manuscript eventually was located, and Rav Soloveitchik once again revised and expanded the essay in the 1970s. The work we have certainly differs from the original essay of the 1940s.

There can be little doubt that the three works from the 1940s – *Ish ha-Halakhah*, *The Halakhic Mind*, and *Ish ha-Elokim* – are parts of an ambitious intellectual program and are related to one another in various ways, involving both comparisons and contrasts. In the aforementioned 1963 letter to Dr. Mirsky, Rav Soloveitchik characterizes the unpublished essay that was to become *U-Vikkashtem mi-Sham* as "a continuation of my first essay on the halakhic man." The aim of the unpublished essay, he continues, is "to trace out the portrait of the character of the halakhic man in terms of his inner world, his experience and his desire to run toward the Holy One, Blessed Be He."

The Rav's declaration to Dr. Mirsky that the essay he had "hidden away" was a continuation of *Ish ha-Halakhah* suggests a particular relationship between the two works: namely, that *U-Vikkashtem mi-Sham* fills out the portrait of halakhic man by exploring his inner world and religious experience, perhaps even exposing facets of his personality and development omitted in the earlier essay. Of interest also is that the Rav himself proposed the title of the book that contains both *Ish ha-Halakhah* and *U-Vikkashtem mi-Sham*, namely *Ish ha-Halakhah: Galui ve-Nistar* (*Halakhic Man: Revealed and Hidden* [Jerusalem, 1979]). The implication of the subtitle is that *Ish ha-Halakhah* portrays the "external" aspect of halakhic man, while *U-Vikkashtem mi-Sham* captures the hidden, inner core. On such a reading, the "cleaving" personality depicted as the apex of the three-stage process in *U-Vikkashtem mi-Sham* presumably would be identical to halakhic man. Since *U-Vikkashtem mi-Sham* focuses more on the development of "cleaving man" rather than simply on his phenomenology, another way of stating the relationship between the two works would be that whereas *Ish ha-Halakhah* presents halakhic man analytically – breaking down the whole into parts – *U-Vikkashtem mi-Sham* is synthetic, showing how a halakhic personality may be built.[16]

Yet, while there are clearly points of contact between halakhic man and

---

16 This is the formulation of Aviezer Ravitzky, "Rabbi J. B. Soloveitchik on Human Knowledge: Between Maimonidean and Neo-Kantian Philosophy," *op. cit.*, 160.

the "cleaving" personality described in the final section of *U-Vikkashtem mi-Sham* – most prominently, halakhic creativity and the "identity of wills" – the two typological individuals appear to differ in several ways. For example, "cleaving man" is receptive to mystical themes, while halakhic man is not. Another point of divergence is that when confronted by reality, halakhic man – like the scientist – tends to quantify and classify, while "cleaving man" is attracted as well by those qualitative aspects of reality that cannot be quantified. Finally, the process of development undergone by "cleaving man," which involves broad cultural engagement and a diverse range of experiences, does not sit easily with the more narrowly focused outlook and austere nature of halakhic man. In both his personality and his religious approach, "cleaving man" displays a multidimensionality that, *prima facie*, is lacking in halakhic man.

A case can be made that these divergences are only apparent. But a case can also be made that these divergences cannot be explained away. And if one indeed chooses to acknowledge them, several explanations for the differences present themselves. It is conceivable that, whatever the author's intentions, "halakhic man" and "cleaving man" present two different models of Jewish religiosity; it is also possible that "cleaving man" encompasses "halakhic man" and goes beyond him; or perhaps Rav Soloveitchik's view of "halakhic man" evolved between the publication of the two works.

This much we can say with confidence: regardless of whether one should read *Ish ha-Halakhah* and *U-Vikkashtem mi-Sham* in conjunction to understand the respective *works*, one must certainly read them in conjunction in order to understand their *author*. It is precisely the breadth, depth and originality of his vision that make these works so compelling – and assure them a permanent place in the canon of Jewish and general religious thought.

1. **Paths to *devekut*:** If, according to the conclusion of *U-Vikkashtem mi-Sham*, *devekut* is fully attainable via Halakhah, what role is left for the cosmic approach to God? Recall that *U-Vikkashtem mi-Sham* began with man searching for God within the natural realm: through science, through the experience of God in nature and in the human psyche, etc. In the end, is there any value to attempting to attain *devekut* via the world?

   It is plausible to read the Rav as saying that, ultimately, the cosmic approach has been superseded and is essentially useless, since everything man seeks is available via Halakhah alone. This reading gains strength if one strongly binds *U-Vikkashtem mi-Sham* to *Ish ha-Halakhah* and assumes that "cleaving man" in the former is equivalent to the title character of the latter.

   However, it is also possible that the Rav believes that the cosmic search for God is not rejected, but rather is incorporated into Halakhah. As we saw in Chapter 32, the halakhic mandate to recite blessings over natural phenomena requires the perception of God within nature. Additionally, the divine directives to "subdue the earth" and to "cultivate and guard" it (which, though given in Eden and not at Sinai, the Rav nevertheless views as binding) grant religious value to scientific and cultural endeavors. When the Rav writes, "Indeed, contemplating the acts of creation, *when not accompanied by subjugation to the divine halakhic moral law*, does not lead to love of God, or to cleaving to God, or to the unification of the knower and the known" (104, emphasis added), this leaves open the possibility that when accompanied by acceptance of Halakhah, contemplating acts of creation can lead to *devekut*. Indeed, the "natural-cosmic" endeavor of phenomenological inquiry into the human psyche and the religious experience, as exemplified by the Rav's own book, can bring one to love God and cleave to Him.

2. **The relationship between *Ish ha-Halakhah* and *U-Vikkashtem mi-Sham*:**
   a. Some scholars view the two works as describing the same figure from two perspectives, whether objective and subjective, analytic and synthetic, or destination and journey. See, for example, Aviezer Ravitzky and Lawrence Kaplan.[17]

---

17 Ravitzky: *op. cit.*, 160; Kaplan: "Joseph Soloveitchik and Halakhic Man," in *The Cambridge Companion to Modern Jewish Philosophy*, eds. Michael L. Morgan and Peter E. Gordon (Cambridge, 2007), 227.

b. Others view them as describing different figures. David Shatz writes: "*U-Vikkashtem mi-Sham* paints a religious personality whose pursuits, experiences and orientation go beyond those attributed to halakhic man in *Ish ha-Halakhah*."[18] R. Walter Wurzburger sees "halakhic man" as leaning more in the direction of cognitive man, while "cleaving man" leans more in the direction of *homo religiosus*.[19] Michael Berger, in claiming that *Ish ha-Halakhah* demonstrates the importance of Halakhah for the cognitive personality while *U-Vikkashtem mi-Sham* demonstrates its importance for the religious personality, draws a conclusion similar to that of R. Wurzburger.[20] Dov Schwartz sees an even stronger disjuncture between the two figures, with *Halakhic Man* representing the Rav's Brisker antecedents and *U-Vikkashtem mi-Sham* portraying the Rav himself.[21]

c. Moshe Sokol suggests that both works describe the figure of halakhic man, but Rav Soloveitchik's view of this figure has evolved between writing the two works, and therefore the figure of halakhic man includes more aspects of *homo religiosus* in the later work.[22]

d. Among the views presented in the chapter above is one towards which I lean: Rav Soloveitchik wanted to believe that halakhic man and "cleaving man" are the same person presented in two different dimensions – external and internal. (This is similar to the dichotomy of the inner and outer personalities that he develops in "*Be-Seter u-ve-Galui*.") However, we, the readers, sense that these two personalities – despite their many overlapping elements – cannot forcibly be yoked together. They represent differing pulls on the author, or different aspects of his capacious and inharmonious inner self.

---

18 "A Framework for Reading *Ish ha-Halakhah*," in *Turim: Studies in Jewish History and Literature Presented to Dr. Bernard Lander*, vol. 2, ed. R. Michael A. Shmidman (New York, 2008), 173 n. 3.

19 "The Centrality of Creativity in the Thought of Rabbi Joseph B. Soloveitchik," in his *Covenantal Imperatives*, 157.

20 "*U-Vikkashtem mi-Sham*: Rabbi Joseph B. Soloveitchik's Response to Martin Buber's Religious Existentialism," *Modern Judaism* 18 (1998), 108.

21 *Haguto ha-Pilosophit shel ha-Rav Soloveitchik*, vol. 2 (Ramat Gan, 2008), 9.

22 "Master or Slave? Rabbi Joseph B. Soloveitchik on Human Autonomy in the Presence of God," in *Turim: Studies in Jewish History and Literature Presented to Dr. Bernard Lander*, vol. 1, ed. R. Michael A. Shmidman (New York, 2007), 312–14. Sokol also writes that although *Halakhic Man* and *U-Vikkashtem mi-Sham* place greater stress on human autonomy than do his later writings, there is nevertheless great unity between his early and late works, since there is a tension inherent in the issue of human autonomy even in the early works, and fideistic submission finds a place within them as well.

Section VII

SUMMATION

Chapter 36

Review

At the end of Chapter 1, I wrote that in setting out to explore the Rav's thought, we were embarking on a journey as exciting and dramatic as the Rav's own impassioned spirit. Now that we near the conclusion of that journey, I hope that it has been not only exciting and dramatic, but also enlightening and inspiring. Having surveyed many of Rav Soloveitchik's philosophical writings in the previous chapters, let us review in this chapter some of the topics we have covered and then address in the next chapter some of the broader issues that emerge from this survey.

Elevation of the Personality (Chapters 1–10)

After presenting a brief biography and situating him in his historical context, we commenced our investigation of the Rav's thought by studying two introductory essays that broached themes explored in greater depth later in the book. In reading "The Community," we examined the Rav's views on the necessity of experiencing both aloneness and togetherness in order to attain human fulfillment, on different ways of forming that "togetherness" in the context of a community (developed further in *The Lonely Man of Faith*), and on the nature of Jewish peoplehood (elaborated in *Kol Dodi Dofek*). When analyzing "Majesty and Humility," we explored the Rav's dual view of man, as well as the idea of *imitatio Dei* and the centrality of dialectic in his thought. (In the next chapter we will take up the question of why dialectic is so important.) The Rav's discussion of the ethic of victory and the ethic of defeat set the stage not only for "Catharsis," but also for the duality at the heart of *The Lonely Man of Faith*.

The next chapters used the essay "Catharsis" as a springboard to discuss the concept of halakhic heroism (also called withdrawal or catharsis) and its manifestation in four realms: the physical-hedonic, emotional, intellectual and religious. We reviewed how Halakhah affirms the value of human engagement in all four realms, but also demands the acceptance of limitations in order to purify, channel and elevate this engagement. Halakhah wants man to enjoy life, but not in a selfish or base fashion. It also wants man to feel deeply the gamut of worthy emotions, while always keeping emotion within his control. It of course advocates intellectual and religious engagement – but the intellectual gesture, when unaccompanied by an awareness of its limits, is arrogant, and the religious gesture, when made without acknowledgement of human imperfection and frailty, is self-righteous and unredeemed. In these chapters, we also explored the tension in the Rav's writings between two-stage and three-stage catharsis. In other words, does one humbly retreat only to purify one's bold advance, or is retreat a goal in itself?

This discussion led in the following chapters to a more general examination of the respective roles of intellect, experience and action in religious life, and of the necessary interaction between them. When not balanced and complemented by the others, each element will produce detrimental results. Conversely, when these three elements act in concert, one can live a meaningful and worthy religious life and rise to great heights. All of one's abilities should be harnessed in the service of God: mind, heart and limbs. Everyone knows that Judaism demands Torah study and performance of *mitzvot*, but inwardness is no less important. One's religious experience should derive from both knowledge and observance, and, conversely, learning and *mitzvot* should give rise to experience. Thought directs feeling and action; feeling animates thought and action; and action concretizes thought and feeling.

Religion and Modernity (Chapters 11–18)

While some may believe that secularism demands advance and religion demands retreat, Rav Soloveitchik posits that Judaism demands both. This duality lies at the heart of *The Lonely Man of Faith*, the Rav's classic meditation on the place of religion in the modern world. In his reading of the two accounts of the creation of man in Genesis, Rav Soloveitchik discovers two human types: Adam I, the creative and majestic personality, and Adam II, the humble, covenantal personality. While Adam I wishes to attain dignity through mastery of the world, Adam II, who is plagued by a sense of incompleteness, wishes to attain redemption through self-mastery and through the fostering of deep relationships with others, and especially with God. Though these two positions may seem irreconcilable, God bids us to adopt both of them, to oscillate between two modes of existence in a perpetual dialectic.

This analysis of the two basic tasks of man leads to a number of important conclusions. First, Adam I's existence is willed by God and therefore his majestic and creative actions have religious value. Rav Soloveitchik, accordingly, had a positive attitude towards the extension of human dominion through general scientific and technological progress, the spreading of culture and the development of civilization. However, we must also give Adam II his due, which leads to the second conclusion: Adam II and his quest for redemption have independent value, regardless of whether they aid Adam I's quest for majesty. Faith (the realm of Adam II) is not subservient to culture (the creation of Adam I); it is a primordial force that has no need to legitimize itself in other terms.

While living with the perpetual dialectic between Adam I and Adam II is never an easy experience, since before man strikes roots in either position he is summoned by the other, it is nevertheless a constructive and positive engagement for those who are sensitive to the dual call. The contemporary man of faith, however, finds himself in a predicament that leads to an entirely negative and destructive form of loneliness: he is misunderstood and marginalized by modern society, which recognizes only the Adam I side of existence. Even the religious realm itself has been commandeered by Adam I, for modern man expects religion to serve his own need for dignity and majesty, and does not admit that religious faith has its own autonomous and sacrificial demands.

In *The Lonely Man of Faith*'s conclusion, we encounter a phenomenon we noted in a number of the Rav's writings – namely, a dual ending that presents us with two alternatives. According to the first, the man of faith may have to withdraw from the realm of Adam I (both in surrounding society and in himself) in order to preserve the autonomy of his faith commitment. According to the second, after a temporary withdrawal for the sake of strengthening himself, Adam II will reintegrate with Adam I and together they will pursue the goal of "perfecting the world under the rule of God." In this dual ending, we again encounter the tension between the two-part catharsis and the three-part catharsis.

The autonomy of faith, a central theme in *The Lonely Man of Faith* and in the Rav's thought in general, occupied our attention throughout Chapters 16–18. We explored its theoretical basis as well as its consequences in the intellectual and practical realms. In the intellectual realm, positing both the methodological autonomy of Halakhah and the irreducibility of the faith experience allows one to approach challenges to faith more confidently and effectively. In his practical halakhic decision-making, Rav Soloveitchik insisted that Halakhah maintain its systemic integrity and internal logic, instead of tailoring itself to fit the fashions of the times. The autonomy of faith also served as a guiding principle for the Rav in his capacity as a communal leader. While ever cognizant of the value of communal unity, when it came to matters of faith he asserted rabbinic autonomy within the Orthodox world, Orthodox autonomy within the Jewish world, and Jewish autonomy within the interfaith world.

Fate, Destiny and the Human Condition (Chapters 19–27)

After elaborating on the duality of majestic and covenantal man in *The Lonely Man of Faith*, we explored other aspects of the Rav's doctrine of man in his teachings on family, prayer, repentance and suffering. In *Family Redeemed*, the Rav demonstrates that family relationships are not only important in themselves but are also crucial in the God-man relationship, serving as a "reflection of and prologue to" the latter. Relations with parents, spouses and children contain both actional commitments and emotional connections, and only by fulfilling these properly can one learn how to love, revere and serve God. Indeed, these family relationships themselves can become part of one's service of God and help redeem the human personality.

In his many writings on prayer, Rav Soloveitchik does not inquire into its effect upon God, but rather, in keeping with his general approach, on its function for man. Through an examination of the laws and texts of Jewish prayer, he identifies three functions. First, it is an encounter with God, a dialogue continuing that of the prophets, and it must be integrated into a broader life of service. Second, prayer is a means for man to refine his own need-awareness by separating genuine needs from false ones, and thereby to create a better and more authentic self. Third, in prayer one offers oneself up to God, for "The very gesture of falling before God and acknowledging His unlimited sovereignty and man's utter impotence, constitutes an act of sacrifice" (*Worship of the Heart*, 175). The order of the last two components – namely, whether self-sacrifice comes before or after self-acquisition – is presented differently in the Rav's various writings, and this again harks back to the dialectic between two-stage and three-stage catharsis.

Prayer arises from a sense of crisis, an awareness of want, which exists both on the surface level of physical and social needs and on the deeper level of man's consciousness of his inadequacy, sinfulness, vulnerability, limitations and mortality. Yet, even as prayer demands an admission of man's humility and insufficiency, the fact that Halakhah permits man to engage the Almighty in dialogue and enumerate his requests before God indicates that his life has significance, purpose and value. Repentance entails the same dual recognition of human majesty and humility. In *teshuvah* man gazes upon his failures; yet the very fact that God has granted him free will and the ability to remake himself validates his worth and signifies that his service is desired.

In Chapters 22 and 23, we explored two major aspects of the Rav's doctrine of *teshuvah*. First, we saw that he regards *teshuvah* as the ultimate expression of human creativity – namely, creation of the self. This approach to *teshuvah* was then contrasted on a number of levels with Rav Kook's view of *teshuvah* as return to the self. Second, we examined the Rav's view of *teshuvah* as the halakhic response to suffering. When one encounters distress, one should not ask the metaphysical question of why this has happened, for this question reflects a conception of oneself as merely the passive victim of external forces. Rather, one should ask the active halakhic question of how to respond to the distressing circumstances. The answer to the latter question is that one must utilize the traumatic event, which has disrupted one's settled patterns and habitual routines, as an opportunity for change and growth – in other words, for *teshuvah*. In this way, the sufferer moves from being an object buffeted by external forces to a subject who charts his own course through the storm. Rav Soloveitchik elaborates three lessons that he learned from his own encounter with mortality, and we explored how they are relevant in less extreme circumstances as well. This led us to consider the role of crisis in his thought, the dialectical experience of life, and how these come to expression in the laws of *aninut* and *avelut*. Finally, we noted that the Rav's very writings on death and suffering are sterling examples of responding to adversity in a constructive and redemptive fashion.

The consideration of the categories of fate and destiny in the life of the individual led to a consideration of these categories as applied to the national existence of the Jewish people. In responding to the Holocaust, as in responding to evil in general, we should ask not the unanswerable question of why, but rather what actions we are to take in its wake. However, while the individual can transcend fate, the community cannot avoid it. The Jewish people are bound together by a covenant of fate, expressed in shared suffering and mutual responsibility, as well as by a covenant of destiny, expressed in the shared values and goals of being "a kingdom of priests and a holy nation" (Ex. 19:6) and of "mending the world under the dominion of God" (*Aleinu*). Therefore, a proper response to the miracle of the State of Israel is to dedicate ourselves to strengthening both covenants – to extend support to the Jewish state and to imbue it with the values of Torah. We ended our consideration of *Kol Dodi Dofek* by contrasting the Rav's approaches to the Holocaust and the State of Israel with those of other thinkers, and by expanding on the implications of the Rav's theory of the two covenants for the question of Jewish identity today.

Halakhah and the Religious Quest (Chapters 28–35)

Halakhic man embodies what the Rav considers the best qualities of both cognitive and religious man, or, loosely translated, of the scientist and the mystic. Cognitive man, a materialist, acknowledges only the physical universe, and approaches it with creative, conceptual, rigorous intellectual tools. *Homo religiosus*, a dualist, acknowledges both the material and spiritual worlds, but sees them as mutually negating and therefore wishes to flee the former to live in the latter. Halakhic man uses the methods of cognitive man to attain the sanctity sought by *homo religiosus*. Instead of fleeing to the supernal realm, as does *homo religiosus*, halakhic man brings transcendence into the human world, resulting in a this-worldly spirituality.

Halakhic man rejects religious man's otherworldly and subjective approach because he regards it as being unethical, unrealistic and undemocratic. His goal is to bring objectivity to religion, both by objectifying halakhic concepts in his rigorous and precise Torah study and by actualizing them in his observance of *mitzvot*. Halakhah, the Rav explains, is a cognitive discipline; it demands the scholar's creative input and fosters a majestic and fully-realized personality that, through the use of reason and the maintenance of boundaries, avoids the excesses of *homo religiosus*.

After situating halakhic man between the extremes of cognitive man and religious man, we traced how halakhic man succeeds in infusing transcendence into this world and how this enterprise shapes his personality and his activities. We then examined a number of possible models for halakhic man and concluded that, even though he is a theoretical, ideal type, he is clearly based on the models of the great scholars of Brisk (though they would not necessarily have framed their enterprise in the same terms as did the Rav). The Rav's stated goal in writing *Halakhic Man*, however, is not merely to pay tribute to his forebears. It is to depict an intellect-based religiosity and religious personality that is unfamiliar to modern psychologists and philosophers of religion; to defend Halakhah against charges that it is heteronomous, non-cognitive, non-moral and slavish; and to defend the halakhic personality against charges that he is otherworldly, passive and uncreative. In the course of accomplishing these goals, *Halakhic Man* explains the supreme value of *talmud Torah*; argues for the superiority of halakhic man's stable and objective, yet dynamic and innovative, religiosity over that of *homo religiosus*; and establishes the centrality of creativity in halakhic life: creativity in Torah study, creativity in the world (by realizing halakhic ideals), and creativity in self-construction. Halakhic man lives a life of high seriousness and heroism, of drama and engagement, as he immerses himself in the demanding and meaningful struggle to grasp and formulate halakhic concepts, to actualize divine ideals within the concrete world, and to craft an individualistic personality that is intellectual and ethical, creative and majestic.

While in *Halakhic Man* the Rav takes issue with the position that religion is purely subjective and does not require objective and normative manifestations, in other writings he counters those who claim that Judaism consists only of objective forms and that it ignores subjectivity. In *The Halakhic Mind*, the Rav establishes the principle that the only legitimate way to access the subjective dimension of Judaism is through its objective manifestations. This is accomplished through the method of reconstruction, as explained in Chapter 31. Reconstruction allows us to derive from the objective forms of Judaism a number of subjective elements: philosophical components of a world perspective, halakhic values, and the inner experience of *mitzvot*. We then proceeded to exemplify these with several case studies.

U-Vikkashtem mi-Sham is a counterpoint or counterpart to *Halakhic Man*; we discussed the precise nature of the relationship between these two works at the end of Chapter 35. In this work, the Rav discusses reason and revelation not as two methods of accessing the truth but rather as two modes of experiencing God. The book describes a three-stage development in which the relationship between the rational religious experience and the revelatory religious experience progresses from contradiction, to complementarity, to unification.

In Stage I, man, seeking meaning and security, initiates the search for God, using all his powers of intellect, spirit, creativity and freedom. He meets with some success, finding traces of the absolute within science, philosophy, art and the human psyche; he finds order in the universe and hints of something that transcends him. However, the seeker realizes that his intellect, cultural creativity and cosmic experience take him only so far. God generally remains hidden; when man does catch a glimpse of God, it is abstract and impersonal; and man cannot account for chaos and evil. At the point that man is ready to give up the search in despair, God reveals Himself; but instead of offering succor, God appears as a lawgiver who denies man's freedom and demands absolute commitment. There follows a tense duality of trust and fear, of natural and revelational religiosity. Both are necessary, for trust not balanced by fear, subjectivity unrestrained by the absolute, and spirituality devoid of commands, bring chaos upon the world. Conversely, fear without trust leads to asceticism, world-denial, and abandonment of practical action.

Both the trust and the fear of Stage I are self-centered: the individual seeks God in order to anchor his own existence, and obeys the revelatory commands in order to attain reward and avoid punishment. However, in Stage II, these mature into love and awe, both of which stem from an appreciation of God's greatness. Freedom and coercion are reconciled, because man now *chooses* to follow the law. Through the law, man emulates God, the object of his veneration.

In Stage III, man fulfills the commandments out of neither compulsion nor emulation, but rather out of identification and partnership. Halakhah answers man's deepest desires by providing him with a cognitive-normative system of absolute validity that desires his input, affirms his value, and elevates his existence. He finds that the law actually *demands* his freedom and creativity, rather than denying them. "[M]an cleaves to God through the full realization of his personality, by uncovering all the possibilities latent in the depths of his being" (89). At this level, termed *devekut*, the familiar concepts of *talmud Torah*, *shemirat ha-mitzvot* and *masorah* are revealed to be creative enterprises into which man pours his individuality, thereby making the concepts and dictates of Halakhah his own and, in that way, cleaving to their Giver. By seeking out man's active partnership, Halakhah validates and sanctifies man's intellectual creativity, physical existence, and his social and cultural life. And by bringing one into dialogue with one's contemporaries as well as with preceding and succeeding generations, the halakhic enterprise of *masorah* strengthens one's bonds to the communities of past, present and future.

Having completed a brief survey of this book, we may now consider some of the broader themes that emerge from the Rav's writings, and offer some concluding reflections about the Rav and his work.

Chapter 37

Major Themes and Concluding Reflections

The Centrality of Halakhah

In 1963, when Rav Soloveitchik had published only a handful of essays, Rav Aharon Lichtenstein characterized the main concerns of the Rav's thought in these words: "What is [Halakhah's] meaning in everyday life? How does it meet man's basic spiritual needs? What do its laws reveal of God's purposes for Israel? How is it related to the conditions of modern life?"[1] Despite the shelves of books and essays by the Rav that have been published in the decades since then, this description still holds true.

Halakhah, in the Rav's view, is extraordinarily multifaceted. It is a body of knowledge, a method of thought, a lens for perceiving and interpreting reality, a blueprint for shaping the world, and a guide to human development and self-transcendence. Halakhah facilitates and mediates man's encounter with God, offering insight into God's will and wisdom and shaping the religious experience. It sanctifies man's natural existence, filling all areas of his life with meaning and direction. In this way, Halakhah provides a means of coping creatively and constructively with the human condition, of negotiating irreconcilable dialectics and of dealing with unanswerable questions without presuming to solve them. Though its demands are many, they are not meant to crush man but rather to affirm his value, to expose him to new dimensions of existence and to elevate his being.

However, the Rav does not hide the fact that, in guiding man towards a theocentric existence, the discipline of Halakhah will often be experienced as

---

1 "R. Joseph Soloveitchik," in *Great Jewish Thinkers of the Twentieth Century*, ed. Simon Noveck (New York, 1963), 281.

difficult and demanding. Sacrifice is a major category in his thought, and he offers no guarantees that sacrifice will be repaid with success in one's endeavors. Moreover, Halakhah engages all human faculties – intellect, will, emotion, activity – and recognizes no domain of life as neutral. Every talent and every endeavor must be harnessed towards the goal of serving God. Whereas many forms of religion in the modern world promise much and demand little, Rav Soloveitchik espouses a religion for adults: one that is honest, complex and demanding.

Of particular importance to Rav Soloveitchik is the interplay between the subjective and the objective in Halakhah. On the one hand, religious inwardness and feeling are of crucial importance; indeed, there are certain central halakhic precepts, such as repentance and prayer, that a person cannot fulfill in their absence. On the other hand, religious subjectivity is often fleeting and ethereal. If it is not expressed in objective and externalized forms, it will lack the power to endure over time, overcome potent drives and exercise a lasting impact. Halakhah therefore addresses these concerns by objectifying the subjective religious impulse, while at the same time suffusing the objective religious act with subjective content.

No less important than religious action and religious feeling is religious intellection, that is, Torah study. *Talmud Torah* is, of course, both a guide to halakhic performance and a central religious experience. Primarily, however, it is a supremely important endeavor in itself. Man cannot fathom God's essence, but Torah study allows him to penetrate God's revealed will. *Talmud Torah* brings man's highest faculty, reason, into the realm of divine service, and thereby helps actualize his *tzelem Elokim*. Moreover, through his creative interpretation and conceptualization, man becomes God's collaborator in the development of Halakhah itself.

Throughout the ages, the interplay between law and spirituality has commanded the attention of Jewish thinkers. Medieval philosophers and kabbalists often regarded Halakhah as dry and technical, and they sought to spiritualize it by imposing upon its study and performance a layer of symbolic and mystical meaning. In the Rav's thought, however, there is no need to turn to the esoteric disciplines of philosophy and Kabbalah to infuse the Jew's life with religious meaning. This is attained, instead, through the exoteric study of Halakhah. The Rav says about Halakhah what medieval thinkers said about their favored extra-halakhic pursuits: it is the supreme knowledge – indeed the supreme good – to be sought by man, and it is the best avenue to connect to God. Thus, for Rav Soloveitchik, the study and practice of Halakhah are the very sources of Jewish spirituality.

Moreover, for the Rav, any attempt to elaborate a philosophy of Judaism must begin by taking the dictates and concepts of Halakhah as the objective data on which this philosophy must be built. Whereas many earlier thinkers had attempted to explain Halakhah in light of external philosophical systems, or had attempted to harmonize Torah with the regnant philosophies of the day, Rav Soloveitchik asserts that Halakhah requires no harmonization because it itself is the crystallization and most authentic expression of Jewish thought. Therefore, a genuine Jewish worldview will have to be extracted from the sources of Halakhah and not from some extra-halakhic system. Since the Halakhah expresses a value system and is to be explained in its own terms, the Rav repeatedly insists on maintaining the autonomy of Halakhah in both theory and practice. In other words, Halakhah is to be understood and applied according to the tenets of its own inner logic.

Doctrine of Man

The relationship between God and man stands at the heart of Judaism. A proper grasp of Judaism, then, requires an understanding of both parties to the covenant. This accounts for two central characteristics of the Rav's thought: his halakhocentricity and his sustained efforts to elaborate a religious anthropology. How so? As mentioned earlier, we cannot understand God's essence. However, we can try to understand His revealed will, and this is accomplished precisely through the activity discussed above – the study of Halakhah. On the other hand, while we cannot fathom God's nature, it is feasible and proper to inquire into the nature of man; and the Rav, believing this task to have great religious value, mines the sources of Judaism in order to construct a doctrine of man. If, as the Rav says, "the human personality is the true sanctuary of the Holy One" (*On Repentance*, 225–26), then we must understand the human personality in order to build a proper sanctuary for God. Because of this duality, the Rav characterizes Judaism as "theo-centric but anthropo-oriented" – it revolves around God, who is the source and goal of all existence, but pays close attention to and lavishes great care on man, who is God's covenantal partner.

The human personality, as perceived by the Rav, is complex and multi-layered. This complexity and the variety of situations a human being faces in life call forth different responses: majesty and humility, *gadlut ha-mohin* and *katnut ha-mohin*, etc. In developing a doctrine of man, the Rav addresses a very wide variety of human experiences and psychological subjects: pleasure and the sublimation of natural urges; marriage and sexuality; parent-child relationships; suffering, bereavement and death; individual and community; sin, repentance and upheavals of the personality; intellect and will; boredom and loneliness; moral freedom and coercion; autonomy and heteronomy; emotional breadth and wholeness of personality. All of these, of course, are framed within the context of religious existence, for that is the lens through which the Rav views life.

Among all of God's creations, man is unique by virtue of his ability to make of himself more than he is by nature. He is capable of active, conscious self-fashioning – indeed, of self-transcendence. Man is not only pragmatic and pleasure-seeking, but also possessed of a deep-seated yearning for that which is great, meaningful and redeeming. He possesses both the ability and the desire to strive for something higher than himself; he naturally tends to seek God, even if he calls God by a different name, such as the absolute or the sublime. However, the elevated form of existence to which man aspires is not granted to him as a divine gift, nor is it a plateau that one can reach and remain on thereafter. Rather, an elevated existence is an endless summit, a life-long struggle accompanied by the pain of overcoming desire and by the pangs of giving birth to a new self. And yet, the struggle per se is purifying. Man himself must decide to undertake this active struggle for self-creation and self-transcendence; otherwise, he will remain a hylic being. Only he can transform himself from a passive object into an active subject.

Even while rising to ever-higher planes of existence, however, man can never leave behind his natural self and become pure spirit. He is inevitably situated within the natural world and cannot deny his needs for bodily sustenance, social companionship, and so on. Therefore, Halakhah directs man to attain sanctity within and through the natural world, a world that God Himself has evaluated as "very good."

The highest human aspiration is not to attain union with God, in which the individual melts away into divine infinity, but rather to attain *devekut*, which is the fullest development of one's capacities and individuality through creative partnership with God. Yet this quest for self-development and for a relationship with God should not lead one to lose focus on one's fellow: "The supreme human purpose is to live a complete, perfected experience, as well as to take part in elevating the existence of the other" (*U-Vikkashtem mi-Sham*, 131). One must cultivate individuality while remaining committed to the community; in fact, one's connection to the community is not merely incidental to one's self-development but rather is an integral part of it. Within the community of one's contemporaries, one can practice *hesed* and mutual responsibility; and by joining the community of past and future via receiving and conveying the *masorah*, one transcends mortality and attains a higher form of *devekut*.

Although self-creation remains a constant theme in the Rav's thought, in his later writings he directs attention to an inherent problem in attaining human self-actualization: self-creation hones one's uniqueness, and this in turn heightens one's loneliness. "'To be' means to be the only one, singular and different, and consequently lonely" (*The Lonely Man of Faith*, 39). Joining others in a community of commitment can help partially in overcoming loneliness. Nevertheless, there remains something irreducibly unique and incommunicable in the human personality, something that can be shared only with God, thereby bringing the individual into a closer relationship with the divine.

This closeness to God helps ameliorate another cause of loneliness, namely, the individual's sense of incompleteness. Two factors account for this incompleteness: humans are finite in relation to God, and male and female need each other in order to attain wholeness. Inevitably, however, the individual remains finite, mortal and imperfect, never fully overcoming the feelings of incompleteness and loneliness. This engenders an existential crisis. Realizing that ultimate fulfillment can be found only in God, one can harness this crisis awareness in the service of complete dedication to God. Since subordination to God frees man of other enslavements, this sacrificial commitment is ultimately cathartic and redemptive. The burden of commitment does not provide ease or comfort, but rather dignity and greatness.

Just as there is an irreducible duality in the Rav's view of man as both majestic and humble, there is an essential duality in his view of human fulfillment. The ultimate human goal is, on the one hand, development of one's uniqueness and individuality (self-acquisition) and, on the other hand, consecration and sacrifice. Halakhah directs man, accordingly, both to be creative and to attain catharsis. It is through the interplay between these goals that the individual can rise to greater heights and realize his or her own unique role and mission in the world.

Approach to Reality

Rav Soloveitchik's thought is grounded in reality, and therefore avoids both speculative metaphysical theorizing and ascetic world-rejection. He treats only phenomena he knows from experience, and affirms the value of man's talents and pursuits by finding their place within the service of God. He does not regard man's physical existence, emotional life and intellectual ability as trials to be overcome in the service of God, nor as burdens to be extirpated. Rather, they are necessary means to human development, which can and must be harnessed toward higher ends. The world is not meant to be denied but to be elevated and redeemed.

Since the world is not a barrier to seeking God, but rather the very arena within which the meeting between God and man takes place, an understanding of the world is necessary for the religious endeavor. Hence, Halakhah requires knowledge of physiology, botany, astronomy, geometry, psychology, political science, sociology, and many other disciplines. Furthermore, the Rav assigns religious value not only to *mitzvot* narrowly defined, but also to man's creative scientific and cultural endeavors, as long as these are framed within the broader context of serving God and not just serving oneself. "Revelational faith does not clash with what exists or deny its importance. On the contrary, its teaching is a reality-based doctrine, a doctrine of what exists, whose purpose is the sanctification of biological existence, and whose strategies are inherent in logical thought" (*U-Vikkashtem mi-Sham*, 119).

Since Rav Soloveitchik deals with the world as it is, he does not deny the existence or legitimacy of conflicting impulses within the self, as we saw above, nor does he advocate constriction of one's interests or of one's emotional range. He does require, however, that we use halakhic and ethical criteria to judge which emotions and aspects of the personality we wish to cultivate and in which situations we deem them appropriate. Moreover, he acknowledges that sometimes man lives in harmony and sometimes in tension and dichotomy. Forced harmonizations and metaphysical reconciliations of opposites are not part of his repertoire. He prefers frank acknowledgement of inconvenient facts, such as the reality of human suffering, and of unanswerable questions, such as why God allows evil to exist. Instead of passive inquiry into these dilemmas, his approach dictates an active and creative response.

In confronting reality, Rav Soloveitchik arrives armed with full confidence in the Torah's ability to withstand any assaults and in its capacity to redeem mankind. A religious Jew need not retreat into a corner and seal himself off from the surrounding world. "It is our belief that Judaism has the means to give meaning and significance, value and refinement, to the multi-faceted existence of modern life. We do not fear progress in any area of life, since it is our firm conviction that we have the ability to cope with and redeem it" (*Community, Covenant and Commitment*, 203–04). The proper attitude towards surrounding society is that of a "*ger ve-toshav*, stranger and resident" (Gen. 23:4), one who participates in promoting the general welfare of society while retaining a value system that is unique and separate from that of general society.

Dialectic

Clearly, the concept of dialectic is central to the Rav's thought. His writings are filled with dialectical pairs: cognitive man and religious man, the natural religious experience and the revelatory religious experience, Adam I and Adam II, intellect and emotion, individual and community, majesty and humility, and many more. According to the Rav, Judaism disagrees with Aristotle's law of the excluded middle, which states that if two propositions are contradictory, only one of them can be true. Rather, Judaism believes that both can be true.

This is the case in many realms. For example, in the area of values, we are bidden to adopt both the majestic approach of Adam I and the humble approach of Adam II. With regard to the religious consciousness, we are to regard God as both distant and near, and to relate to Him with both fear and love. "That religious consciousness in man's experience which is most profound and most elevated, which penetrates to the very depths and ascends to the very heights, is not that simple and comfortable . . . Where you find its complexity, there you find its greatness" (*Halakhic Man*, 141, n. 4).

Although this approach is "exceptionally complex, rigorous and tortuous" (ibid.), it is necessary because it accurately reflects a complex reality. Moreover, a dialectical approach is actually important for mental health, for only an approach that acknowledges multiple values and demands can save one from the neuroses stemming from excessive and unbalanced commitment to a single value. The dialectical experience of life, which finds room for the totality of one's emotional range and which merges opposite experiences into a coherent whole, gives rise to a broad perspective on life that fosters both dignity and *hesed*.

The centrality of dialectic in modern religious thought was established by Søren Kierkegaard, Rudolf Otto and Karl Barth, whose writings the Rav studied carefully. However, no less important are the Jewish antecedents to his dialectical approach to religion, such as Rambam's view of *ahavah* and *yirah*, the kabbalists' attitude toward diametrically opposed attributes such as *hesed* and *gevurah*, and especially the Brisker method of conceptual Torah study that encompasses conflicting approaches without diluting the uniqueness and validity of each.

In Rav Soloveitchik's writing we encounter both Hegelian dialectic, wherein the clash between thesis and antithesis results in a synthesis, and Kierkegaardian dialectic, wherein the thesis and antithesis remain in perpetual tension. *Halakhic Man* is an example of the former, and *The Lonely Man of Faith* of the latter. In a related fashion, the conflicting notions of two-stage

407

and three-stage catharsis arise repeatedly in the Rav's writings without resolution. We can say that, overall, his writings contain a Kierkegaardian dialectic between the two forms of dialectic themselves.

Human Perspective

Rav Soloveitchik accepts the limits Kant placed on the reach of human knowledge. Hence, as we said earlier, he avoids metaphysics and instead focuses on the human and especially the religious personality. He uses a variety of techniques to approach this subject. His earlier writings utilize the tools of phenomenology, which analyze states and structures of consciousness. His later writings place heavier emphasis on the existential perspective, which focuses on the individual's concrete dilemmas, crises and vulnerabilities. In both early and late writings, the Rav makes heavy use of the technique of typology, which constructs theoretical personality types who embody certain ideas or guiding principles. By understanding the internal coherence of each personality type, we can better understand the functioning of complex human beings, who may combine two or more of these types.

In his writings, then, the Rav is not trying to *prove* truth claims, as did medieval rationalist philosophers. Rather, he attempts to *describe* religious positions and states of consciousness. He does not try to show *how* or *why* to be a halakhic man or a lonely man of faith, but only *what it is like* to be these figures. And by understanding these figures, we gain insight into important aspects of religious existence.

In addition to his philosophical reasons for avoiding the metaphysical viewpoint, Rav Soloveitchik recognizes that this perspective is ill-suited to the temperament of modern man, who is grounded in this-worldly reality. Therefore, the Rav addresses all issues from the human perspective: for example, not how God relates to prayer, but what prayer accomplishes for man; not why God allows evil, but how man is to respond to suffering.

Rav Soloveitchik encompasses the breadth of the human perspective, emphasizing both its intellectual and its emotional components. Surprisingly, he also integrates elements of his personal experience, which gives his thought "its particular power: its ability to move from highly individualized experiences to ideal types, and then to discover those types in biblical narrative, rabbinic homily and halakhic detail."[2] Indeed, within a single essay we can often find an extraordinary range of expression: abstract philosophy, techni-

---

2 R. Jonathan Sacks, *Tradition in an Untraditional Age* (London, 1990), 40.

cal Halakhah, textual exegesis, psychological observation, religious insight, poetic flights and personal confession.

Despite the fact that he values not only the analytic but also the experiential, and despite the fact the he views the faith commitment as ultimately non-rational (but not irrational), the Rav nevertheless is unwavering in his commitment to rational and objective thought. Halakhah demands the use of our reason, he points out, and there is ethical peril in being swept away by the tide of subjectivity.

Rav Soloveitchik's thought is solidly rooted in Jewish tradition, but always sensitive to the general human condition. Therefore, like the Rambam, he uses Jewish sources to confront universal issues. Furthermore, because of his sensitivity to the human condition, he is not content to engage in abstract philosophy alone; he always relates theory to practice.

Since he adopts a human perspective that is necessarily limited, the Rav, unlike philosophers of an earlier age, does not propose a "grand unified theory of everything." Rather, he addresses issues topic by topic as they capture his interest, and always leaves his ideas open to reexamination and reformulation. Furthermore, he generally explores a number of perspectives on any given matter because "consciousness is infinitely layered, and no one ought to be so presumptuous as to claim that he or she has defined *the* religious consciousness with any degree of finality or exhaustiveness."[3] This tendency, which reflects intellectual humility, is salient, for example, in *Halakhic Man* and *The Lonely Man of Faith*. For all these reasons, although overarching themes emerge from the Rav's thought, as detailed above, it is important not to read his philosophy as being more systematic than it really is.

As one situated in the modern era and adopting a human perspective, the Rav displays keen awareness of the modern world and addresses the issues that arise within it. He deals with social trends such as secularization and assimilation, events such as the Holocaust and the birth of Israel, and attitudes such as pragmatism and romanticism. Moreover, he scrutinizes the emotions characterizing modern man, such as loneliness, alienation and crisis on the one hand, and the joy of knowledge and excitement of creativity on the other. Sensitive to the opportunities, challenges and pitfalls of modernity, while passionately committed to perpetuating the timeless tradition of Judaism, he formulates a modern Orthodox approach as an ideal and not as a mere compromise.

---

3 David Shatz, "A Framework for Reading *Ish ha-Halakhah*," in *Turim*, vol. 2, ed. R. Michael A. Shmidman (New York, 2008), 183–84.

Continuity in the Rav's Thought

We noted above that the Rav employs different kinds of dialectic in his various writings. The type of dialectic he utilizes reflects the nature of the personality he is depicting: halakhic man and *U-Vikkashtem mi-Sham*'s "man of God" are harmonious personalities, while the lonely man of faith and the majestic-humble personality are torn and conflicted. These contrasting personalities originate in different periods of the Rav's writing: his earlier works portray harmonious personalities, and his later works portray conflicted ones. We also noted a shift from a phenomenological approach to an existentialist one, as well as the fact that in general the Rav strove to consider matters afresh each time he addressed them, leaving contrast and even inconsistency a possibility. These discontinuities might lead one to posit a rupture and disconnect between earlier and later periods in the Rav's thought, along the lines of thinkers like Wittgenstein and Heidegger, who famously repudiated their earlier systems in their later philosophy.

I do not think such a conclusion is warranted; the continuity in the Rav's thought far outweighs the change. There are many constants in the Rav's thought, such as his belief that faith is a foundational awareness and not a reasoned conclusion; that man is both a natural and a spiritual being; and that Halakhah brings together the natural and the spiritual in man. Note also his ongoing interest in uncovering both the deeper meanings and the drama of *talmud Torah* and *shemirat ha-mitzvot*. Further, even when his emphasis or focus shifts, it is generally the case that both poles of the dialectic in question – such as subjectivity and objectivity, or freedom and submission – are present in both early and late works. As to the natural question of why the changes in emphasis and focus occur, the basic answer is that we should expect no less from a dynamic, creative and dialectical thinker who is sensitive to the changing human condition.

Let us examine two instances of the Rav's shifts in focus. We noted above that halakhic man and the "man of God" are ultimately harmonious figures, while the lonely man of faith is torn. This is part of a larger shift from descriptions in the early writings of personalities who, having attained full identification with God's will, are at a pinnacle of human development, to depictions in the later writings of the deeply-felt struggles of incomplete and imperfect individuals. Furthermore, the earlier treatments tend to be more abstract and ideal, and the later ones more concrete and personal.

A second shift of focus relates to the Rav's depiction of man as both natural and spiritual. Early in his career, he took issue with those who saw man only as a spiritual being; later in his career, he took issue with those who saw man solely as a natural being. Thus, in *Halakhic Man* the Rav's main dispute is with the otherworldliness of *homo religiosus*, while in *The Lonely Man of Faith* his major dispute is with Adam I's despiritualization of man.

These shifts in emphasis – from peak figures to more grounded figures, from ideal states of consciousness to concrete dilemmas, from highlighting the cognitive-objective to stressing the emotional-subjective – could be attributed to many different factors. During the early stage of his career, the Rav was not yet a leader and teacher of the masses. His early works were written in the privacy of his study and not meant for a broad audience. Hence, they could focus on peak figures and abstract ideas, and be written in an elevated idiom. His later essays were all composed in the context of an extraordinary teaching load and were meant to be presented orally before diverse audiences. Therefore, they had to address broader concerns and be formulated in a more accessible style (even if one that still placed demands upon the reader or listener). Of course, other factors are also relevant: the shifting perspective that comes with age and adversity; the absorption into consciousness of historical watersheds like the Holocaust and the State of Israel; changes in American society and in American Jewry; and so on.

Regardless of the specific causes of the Rav's shifts in focus, what is most critical for us to realize is that when one espouses a dialectical philosophy, changing circumstances demand a changing emphasis, but nevertheless it is always imperative to view the dialectic in its fullness. In other words, we must bear in mind *both* sides of the assorted dialectics the Rav propounded – *both* values, concepts or approaches – and not just the side the Rav wished to emphasize in a particular essay. This sets a model for us in applying the Rav's thought: we must reassess which side of the various dialectics he posits requires strengthening today, even if it is not the same element the Rav felt the need to highlight in his time and place. Furthermore, we should learn from the Rav the importance of developing our own creative Torah thought, making sure that it rests on the foundations of a firm grasp of Halakhah and of the human spirit.

Legacy

Historians will determine the extent of the Rav's contribution to the revitalization of Orthodoxy in America and beyond, and *talmidei hakhamim* will assess his contribution to the exposition and creative enhancement of Brisker *lomdus*. What is clear is that his public impact was amplified by the fact that he was a consummate master of both Halakhah and *mahshavah*, and of both Torah and general knowledge. He defended Jewish tradition and yet

411

confidently embraced science, technology and philosophy, thereby allowing Orthodox Judaism to flourish among those who engage the modern world instead of closing themselves off from it. In the assessment of R. Yitzhak Twersky, the Rav demonstrated that "one towering scholar – whose grasp of the *masorah* is majestic and magisterial, whose teaching is original and insightful, whose influence is profound and pervasive – is indeed able to change the entire landscape . . . His teachings suffused *masorah* with new charm and fascination, revealed its profundities and thereby buoyed the confidence of many."[1]

The Rav's contributions to Jewish thought are legion; it will suffice here to mention but a few. He introduced the figure of halakhic man, who now has a permanent place in Jewish thought. Before the Rav, few would have viewed the talmudic scholar as combining the rigor and creative majesty of the scientist with the scope and passion of the religious visionary. Regarding Jewish identity, his distinction between fate and destiny has become a staple of Jewish discourse. As a theoretician of the Halakhah, the Rav was the first to articulate the religious and philosophical assumptions of the conceptual Brisker approach, as well as its consequences for Jewish thought and life. By so doing, he restored in-depth Talmud study to a place of preeminence even for those living fully modern lives.

Rav Soloveitchik proposed a new agenda for Jewish thought by demonstrating how Halakhah is not merely explained by Jewish philosophy but rather is the very source of Jewish philosophy. In attempting to derive philosophy from Halakhah, he insisted, one must first understand Halakhah properly. This means that one must first engage in rigorous conceptual analysis of Halakhah in its own terms (*lomdus*), and only then explore its philosophical implications. The Rav only partially realized this agenda of "reconstructing" Jewish thought out of the objective manifestations of Halakhah, leaving to succeeding generations the task of mining his extensive *lomdus* (and that of others) to extract the values, experiences and philosophical concepts contained within Halakhah.

Apart from introducing *lomdus* as the raw material out of which to reconstruct the subjective aspects of Judaism, the Rav employed a number of methods, such as typology, phenomenology and religious anthropology, that were not commonly used in Jewish philosophy. His contributions range widely in other directions as well. He propounded a non-messianic religious Zionist perspective that is increasingly seen in Israel as a counterbalance to

---

1 "The Rov," in *Rabbi Joseph B. Soloveitchik: Man of Halacha, Man of Faith*, ed. R. Menachem Genack (Hoboken, 1998), 40.

voices emerging from the school of Rav Kook. On another front, his writings "allowed certain personality types and mental frameworks to take their place in Judaism"; especially in his later writings, he "has given a home to the previously unhoused: to the Jew in the modern world who experiences conflict, loneliness and the sharp unease of faith."[2]

The main question in his writings is how Halakhah helps one relate to the world, to God, and to oneself. He conveys the depth and drama of halakhic existence without diluting its disciplined demands. His thought ranges over vast territories, revealing the capaciousness and profundity of his intellect and his spirit. In a succinct evaluation of the Rav's contribution to Jewish thought, R. Aharon Lichtenstein concludes:

> The areas of experience explored, the mode and level of inquiry, the resources employed, the problems formulated, above all, the ideas and emotions expressed – these indeed constitute, conjunctively, a new departure . . . The Rav's was an authoritative voice, elucidating the substance of Halakhah in all its ramifications, and relating it to general axiological and human concerns, whether personal or collective. In so doing, he broke fresh ground and put us all very much in his debt.[3]

---

2 R. Jonathan Sacks, *Tradition in an Untraditional Age* (London, 1990), 282.
3 *Leaves of Faith*, vol. 1 (Jersey City, 2003), 193, 195.

Acknowledgements

This book is the product of many years of studying, teaching and editing the Rav's writings. I was first exposed to the Rav's writings as a high school sophomore, when my father handed me a copy of *The Lonely Man of Faith* and told me he thought I would find it interesting. That was an understatement; I was captivated. The Rav's writings spoke to me personally in a manner unlike anything I had read before, and I devoured everything that had been written by him or in his name (which, in those days, amounted to only a small number of books and essays).

It was only natural that I would want to share with others my engagement with and passion for the Rav's thought; and so, when I studied in Yeshivat Har Etzion's *kollel* years later, I offered a course on the Rav to second-year students in the yeshivah. This course, which I taught for a number of years, served as the basis for a distance-learning class on the Rav's philosophy that I wrote for Yeshivat Har Etzion's Israel Koschitzky Virtual Beit Midrash (www.vbm-torah.org) in 1997–1999. That, in turn, served as the basis for the first half of this book. The questions and comments of the students in these courses – both actual and virtual – helped hone the presentation and analysis of the ideas contained in this book. I thank Yeshivat Har Etzion for having given me the opportunity to teach this course both in the yeshivah and on the Internet. And I am especially grateful to my revered teachers, Rav Yehuda Amital *zt"l* and *yibbadel le-hayyim* Rav Aharon Lichtenstein, not only for their roles in my personal development but also for building a true *akhsanya shel Torah* in whose shadow I am proud to make my home. Although I never had the privilege of knowing Rav Soloveitchik personally, I am fortunate to have been exposed to true greatness by studying under Rav Lichtenstein and Rav Amital.

At the time I was teaching these courses, I had the privilege of being appointed Director of Archives and Research for the Toras HoRav Foundation, headed by Rav Soloveitchik's daughters, Dr. Atarah Twersky and Dr. Tovah Lichtenstein. As a result, I came to have access to hundreds of Rav Soloveitchik's unpublished manuscripts, along with thousands of tapes. My job has been, among other things, to identify and piece together manuscripts, oversee transcription, divide the essays into volumes, co-edit a number of volumes in English and Hebrew, and see the books through to publication. The work has been profoundly rewarding. It has afforded me the thrill of reading manuscripts that until then had been viewed only by the Rav himself; the excitement of discovering and disseminating ideas of the Rav that were new to me and to the public; the privilege of working closely with my fellow members of the editorial board, Dr. David Shatz and Dr. Joel Wolowelsky; and the gratification of seeing others benefit from my efforts. Not everyone is placed, as I was, in circumstances that allow him to turn an avocation into a vocation. I extend deep gratitude to the Toras HoRav Foundation, and especially to Dr. Tovah Lichtenstein, for the privilege it has granted me and for the faith it has placed in me.

Several years after taking on these responsibilities, I was likewise very fortunate to have this book commissioned by the Rabbi Joseph B. Soloveitchik Institute, a Boston-based organization devoted to perpetuating the legacy of the Rav through publication, teacher training, leadership development and community education. For this, my profound thanks go to the then Dean of the Rabbi Soloveitchik Institute, Rabbi Dr. Jacob J. Schacter, and to the institute's board of directors. Rabbi Schacter, demonstrating both a sharp eye and a generous spirit, shepherded this book from beginning to end, reading a number of drafts and commenting extensively on both content and style. Without his encouragement and meticulous editing, this book would not have been produced, and for this I am truly indebted to him. I am likewise grateful to Harvey Gertel, a leader of the Maimonides School in Brookline, MA, for his commitment to spreading the Rav's teachings and his dedication to producing this volume as a fitting memorial to his father-in-law, Abraham Levovitz z"l. Finally, I extend my thanks to Joshua Wolff, former executive director of the Maimonides School, for his untiring efforts to see the book through to completion.

This book also benefited from the careful attention of a number of additional readers.

With typical generosity, analytic acuity and stylistic felicity, Prof. David Shatz provided detailed comments on the entire manuscript of this book, and, over the years, has discussed with me many relevant issues in our extensive correspondence. His contribution immeasurably improved this work, and any expression of thanks on my part, though surely heartfelt, is inadequate.

I also greatly appreciate the contributions of two other discerning readers, Rabbi Yair Kahn and Aliza Israel, who graciously agreed to read the entire manuscript and provided valuable comments. Dr. Joel Wolowelsky, thoughtful and collegial as always, continually expressed interest in the progress of the book and offered sage advice. Over the years, I have benefited immensely from discussing the Rav's philosophy (and many other subjects) with *mori ve-rabbi* Rabbi Michael Rosensweig and with Rabbi Shalom Carmy. Rabbi Elyakim Krumbein and Rabbi Yakov Nagen reviewed Chapter 22 and shared their expertise on Rav Kook. The experience of bringing the book to print was a pleasure due to the professionalism of Tzvi Mauer and his staff at Urim Publications. I also thank Rabbi Menachem Genack and the OU Press for copublishing this volume, Rabbi Aryeh Lieberman for helping date the Rav's works, and Rabbi Dov Karoll for preparing the indexes.

Writing this book has been a privilege in many ways, not least because the book itself constitutes an expression of thanks to Rav Soloveitchik *zt"l* for all I have learned from him. By sharing the wealth of his teachings with others, I have been able to give him something in return for all he has given me.

As in everything I do, my deepest thanks go to my family. It is impossible to express adequately my appreciation, admiration and love for my parents, Rabbi Zvi and Sandra Ziegler. *Sheli shelahem* – everything I am is due to them, and to say more would only detract. My grandparents *z"l*, who exemplified modesty and strength of character, continue to inspire me many years after their passing. My sister Sharon has always provided encouragement and support, and it is a pleasure to see our close relationship continuing into the next generation.

Although my children Tehilla, Yisrael, Ariel, Yehoshua and Noam express genuine interest in my work and are unfailingly enthusiastic whenever it culminates in publication, it is actually they who are my truest labor of love, and it is they who give me the greatest pride and joy. It is a privilege and a pleasure to be their father.

Aharonah havivah. Without using superlatives, I could not express my gratitude to my wife Yael nor my feelings for her. Since she would not want me to do so in public, I will simply pray that God grant us many more years together, that He help us build a home of *hesed ve-emet* and of *ahavat Torah ve-yirat Shamayim*, and that He spread His protection over our family.

Beyond all thanks and praise, my greatest debt is to the *Ribbono shel Olam*, who has graced me with innumerable blessings.

Events in the Life
of Rabbi Joseph B. Soloveitchik

1903   Born in Pruzhan, Poland

1910   Moves to Raseyn, Lithuania

1913   Moves to Khoslavitch, Belorussia; leaves *heder* and begins studying full-time with his father

1921   Moves to Warsaw, Poland

1924   Enrolls in Free Polish University

1926   Enters University of Berlin

1931   Marries Dr. Tonya Lewit during a year spent in Vilna, Lithuania

1932   Emigrates to the United States; hired as rabbi of *Va'ad ha-Ir* of Boston; receives doctorate

1935   Travels to *Eretz Yisrael* to seek rabbinate of Tel Aviv

1937   Founds Maimonides School in Boston

1939   Founds a yeshivah, Heikhal Rabbenu Hayyim Halevi, in Boston

1941   Succeeds his late father as *rosh yeshivah* at Yeshivat Rabbenu Yitzchak Elchanan (RIETS), Yeshiva University; teaches there until 1985, commuting weekly from Boston to New York

1942   Begins tradition of annual *yahrzeit shiurim* for his father, to last until 1981

1943   Joins Mizrachi, later becoming its honorary president

1944   Publishes "*Ish ha-Halakhah*"; works on "*U-Vikkashtem mi-Sham*" and *The Halakhic Mind*

1952   Appointed head of the Rabbinical Council of America Halakhah Commission

1956   Delivers the address later published as "*Kol Dodi Dofek*"

1959   Undergoes cancer surgery

1964   Publishes "Confrontation"

1965   Publishes *The Lonely Man of Faith*

1967   Death of his mother, brother and wife

1978   Publishes "*U-Vikkashtem mi-Sham*" and "*Ra'ayonot al ha-Tefillah*" in *Hadarom*, and five English essays in *Tradition*

1983   Publishes vol. 1 of *Shiurim le-Zekher Abba Mari z"l* (vol. 2 in 1985)

1985   Retires from public activity due to illness

1986   Publishes *The Halakhic Mind*

1993   Passes away in Boston

Bibliography

Although Rav Soloveitchik published relatively little during his lifetime, many of his manuscript writings have been published posthumously, and his students have also published many volumes of adaptations of his oral discourses. A full and frequently updated bibliography of writings by and about Rav Soloveitchik can be found on Prof. Eli Turkel's website: http://www.math.tau.ac.il/~turkel/engsol.html. What follows is a list of the editions of Rav Soloveitchik's works cited in this book.

I. Works published by Rav Soloveitchik

"*Al Ahavat ha-Torah u-Ge'ulat Nefesh ha-Dor.*" In *Be-Sod ha-Yahid ve-ha-Yahad*, ed. Pinhas Peli. Jerusalem: Orot, 1976. 403–32.

"*Be-Seter u-ve-Galui.*" In *Divrei Hagut ve-Ha'arakhah*. Jerusalem: World Zionist Organization, 1982. 163–86.

"Catharsis." *Tradition* 17:2 (Spring 1978): 38–54.

"The Community." *Tradition* 17:2 (Spring 1978): 7–24.

"Confrontation." *Tradition* 6:2 (Spring 1964): 5–29.

Halakhic Man. Trans. Lawrence Kaplan. Philadelphia: JPS, 1983.

The Halakhic Mind. New York: Free Press, 1986.

Kol Dodi Dofek = Fate and Destiny. Trans. Lawrence Kaplan. Hoboken: Ktav, 2000.

Kovetz Hiddushei Torah. Jerusalem: Makhon Yerushalayim, 5744.

The Lonely Man of Faith. New York: Doubleday, 1992.

"*Mah Dodekh mi-Dod.*" In *Divrei Hagut ve-Ha'arakhah*. Jerusalem: World Zionist Organization, 1982. 57–98.

"Majesty and Humility." *Tradition* 17:2 (Spring 1978): 25–37.

"*Peleitat Sofreihem.*" In *Divrei Hagut ve-Ha'arakhah*. Jerusalem: World Zionist Organization, 1982. 137–62. Abridged translation: "A Eulogy for R. Hayyim

Heller." Trans. Shalom Carmy. In *Shiurei Harav*, ed. J. Epstein. Hoboken: Ktav, 1994. 46–65.

"*Ra'ayonot al ha-Tefillah*" = "Reflections on the *Amidah*" in *Worship of the Heart: Essays on Jewish Prayer*. Ed. Shalom Carmy. Jersey City: Ktav, 2003. 144–82.

"Redemption, Prayer, Talmud Torah." *Tradition* 17:2 (Spring 1978): 55–72.

"Sacred and Profane." In *Shiurei Harav*, ed. Joseph Epstein. Hoboken: Ktav, 1994. 4–32.

Shiurim le-Zekher Abba Mari z"l. 2 vols. Jerusalem: Makhon Yerushalayim, 5743 and 5745.

"A Tribute to the Rebbitzen of Talne." *Tradition* 17:2 (Spring 1978): 73–83.

U-Vikkashtem mi-Sham = And from There You Shall Seek. Trans. Naomi Goldblum. Jersey City: Ktav, 2008.

II. Adaptations that appeared during Rav Soloveitchik's lifetime

Divrei Hashkafah. Ed. Moshe Krone. Jerusalem: World Zionist Organization, 1992.

Five Addresses (*The Rav Speaks*). Ed. David Telsner. Jerusalem: Tal Orot, 1983.

On Repentance. Ed. Pinhas Peli. Jerusalem: Orot, 1980.

Reflections of the Rav. 2 vols. Ed. Abraham Besdin. Jerusalem: World Zionist Organization, 1979 and 1989.

Shiurei Harav. Ed. Joseph Epstein. Hoboken, NJ: Ktav, 1994 (orig. 1974).

Yemei Zikkaron. Ed. Moshe Krone. Jerusalem: World Zionist Organization, 1986.

III. Posthumous works from Rav Soloveitchik's archives

Abraham's Journey: Reflections on the Life of the Founding Patriarch. Eds. David Shatz, Joel B. Wolowelsky and Reuven Ziegler. Jersey City: Ktav, 2008.

Community, Covenant, and Commitment: Selected Letters and Communications. Ed. Nathaniel Helfgot. Jersey City: Ktav, 2005.

Days of Deliverance: Essays on Purim and Hanukkah. Eds. Eli D. Clark, Joel B. Wolowelsky and Reuven Ziegler. Jersey City: Ktav, 2007.

The Emergence of Ethical Man. Ed. Michael Berger. Jersey City: Ktav, 2005.

Family Redeemed: Essays on Family Relationships. Eds. David Shatz and Joel B. Wolowelsky. New York: Toras HoRav Foundation, 2000.

Festival of Freedom: Essays on Pesah and the Haggadah. Eds. Joel B. Wolowelsky and Reuven Ziegler. Jersey City: Ktav, 2006.

Iggerot ha-Grid Halevi. Jerusalem: Morasha Foundation, 5761.

The Lord Is Righteous in All His Ways: Reflections on the Tish'ah be-Av Kinot. Ed. Jacob J. Schacter. Jersey City: Ktav, 2006.

Out of the Whirlwind: Essays on Mourning, Suffering, and the Human Condition. Eds. David Shatz, Joel B. Wolowelsky and Reuven Ziegler. Jersey City: Ktav, 2003.

Worship of the Heart: Essays on Jewish Prayer. Ed. Shalom Carmy. Jersey City: Ktav, 2003.

General Index

Aaron, 82
Abraham, 44, 62, 283n1, 296;
    see also Patriarchs
R. Abraham, son of the Rambam,
    52
action, see *mitzvah* observance
Adam the first (Adam I, majestic
    man), 121-23, 125, 129,
    132-34, 138-39, 141, 143,
    144, 147-49, 153, 154-56,
    159-66, 167, 171, 184, 192,
    195-96, 302-03, 335n3,
    394-95, 407; *see also* natural
    work community; philosophic
    anthropology
Adam the second (Adam II,
    covenantal man), 121-23, 125,
    129, 132-33, 135-36, 139-44,
    147-49, 153, 154-56, 159-65,
    167-71, 184, 192, 195-96, 216,
    302-03, 394-95, 407; *see also*
    covenantal faith community;
    philosophic anthropology
Aggadah, 341
Agudath Israel, 35, 290
akedah (binding of Isaac), 60
R. Akiva, 314
Albo, R. Yosef (*Sefer
    ha-Ikkarim*), 219n18
Amaru, R. Joshua, 117n6, 222,
    226
America, attitude toward, 188
Amital, R. Yehuda, 282, 297
Anselm of Canterbury, 175
apologetics, refraining from, 178
Aristotle, 59, 69, 179, 182,
    368n5, 407
Aristotelian science and logic,
    171, 172
Arnold, Matthew, 178
asceticism, rejection of,
    73, 76-78, 150, 303,
    319-20, 358, 405; *see also*
    world-acceptance
atheism, 351-52
autonomy, human, 70, 155,
    156n14, 325-29, 333, 389n22;
    see also faith, autonomy of;
    Halakhah, autonomy of

Bahag: see R. Shimon Kayyara
Bar-Ilan, R. Meir: see R. Meir
    Berlin
Barth, Karl, 30n21, 407
Biblical criticism, 174, 177,
    179-180

Ben-Gurion, David, 190n12
Bereishit experience (or creation
    experience, cosmic experi-
    ence, natural consciousness,
    ontological consciousness or
    rational religious experience),
    346-62, 375, 377, 380-81, 383,
    399; *see also* dialectic of trust
    and fear; Sinai experience
Berger, Peter L., 166
Bergson, Henri, 30n21, 247
Berkovits, R. Eliezer, 277n4
Berlin (Bar-Ilan), R. Meir, 317
Berlin, R. Naftali Zvi Yehudah:
    see Netziv
Bernstein, R. Louis, 185, 188
Bick, R. Ezra, 233
Blau, R. Yitzchak, 216n9, 247
Blidstein, Gerald (Yaakov), 50,
    190n12, 233, 289, 294-96
blessings (*berakhot*,
    benedictions)
    over food, 350
    over natural phenomena, 90,
        350
    transition from second to third
        person, 157, 361
Benor, Ehud, 233
Borowitz, Eugene, 320n14
Breuer, R. Isaac, 327
Brisker method of study
    (*lomdus*), 26-28, 131, 170, 177,
    335, 341-43, 407
    affect on the personality,
        321-22
    intuition and individuality
        in, 343
    and philosophy, 335, 342, 412
    the Rav's contribution to, 341
    response to critique of
        excessive intellectualism,
        25n5, 108
    see also Halakhah;
        halakhic man; R. Hayyim
        Soloveitchik; Torah study
Brunner, Emil, 248
Buber, Martin, 108

Carmy, R. Shalom, 39n2, 95,
    102-03, 105, 219, 177, 223,
    235-36, 344n1, 383n12
Cassirer, Ernst, 306n11
catharsis, 151, 152, 393-94
    definition of the term, 69
    in aesthetic-hedonic realm,
        72-77, 377-78

in emotional realm, 79-85
in intellectual realm, 88-90
in religious realm, 92-94
in Torah study, 109
    see also heroism
charity, 47-48, 76, 87, 140, 266,
    285; *see also*: hesed
Cherlow, R. Yuval, 298
Chief Rabbinate of Israel, 35-36,
    189-190
Christianity, 198, 264, 279; *see
    also* interfaith dialogue
cleaving to God: see *devekut*
cognitive man (*ish ha-da'at*),
    301-09, 317, 335n3, 398; *see
    also* philosophic anthropology
Cohen, Hermann, 247, 306n11,
    311, 325, 327, 333, 372
commandments: see *mitzvah*
    observance
commitment
    between husband and wife, 73,
        205-11, 396
    to fellow man, 46-47, 139-41,
        404-05
    to God, religion (study, prayer,
        ethics), covenant, 69, 94,
        139-43, 168-69, 181, 184,
        190, 192, 194, 205-11, 215,
        217, 224, 231, 246, 255,
        259-60, 296, 313-17, 356,
        359, 384, 395, 399, 405
    to Israel, 281, 291
communion (Catholic rite), 75
Communism, 305n9
community, 39-50, 76, 82n8,
    100, 115-17, 215-16, 237n9,
    338, 393, 404-05, 407
    God, as member (and leader)
        of, 142-43
    masorah community, 34, 383
    see also covenantal faith
        community; family relation-
        ships; fate and destiny;
        Knesset Yisrael; natural
        work community
Community of Israel: see
    Knesset Yisrael
concern for others: see *hesed*;
    responsibility between fellow
    Jews
confession: see *viddui*
contemporary religious life,
    97-98, 105, 159
"continuity of emotional experi-
    ence," 264-65, 268

423

Index prepared by Dov Karoll

Index of Rabbi Soloveitchik's Writings

431

Index prepared by Dov Karoll

About the Author

Rabbi Reuven Ziegler is Director of Research and Archives of the Toras HoRav Foundation and has edited numerous volumes of Rabbi Soloveitchik's writings. He is also a founder of Yeshivat Har Etzion's Israel Koschitzky Virtual Beit Midrash and serves as its Editor-in-Chief.

About the Series Editor

Rabbi Dr. Jacob J. Schacter is University Professor of Jewish History and Jewish Thought at Yeshiva University and Senior Scholar at its Center for the Jewish Future.